ORANGE COUNTY

A Literary Field Guide

Edited by Lisa Alvarez and Andrew Tonkovich

Foreword by Gustavo Arellano

Heyday, Berkeley, California

Library of Congress Cataloging-in-Publication Data is available.

Cover Art: Photo by dave_dubyuh, licensed under CC BY 2.0,
    https://www.flickr.com/photos/brokenhachi6
Cover Design: Rebecca LeGates
Interior Design and Typesetting: Leigh McLellan Design
Printing and Binding: Printed in East Peoria, IL, by Versa Press, Inc.

Orders, inquiries, and correspondence should be addressed to:
    Heyday
    P.O. Box 9145, Berkeley, CA 94709
    (510) 549-3564, Fax (510) 549-1889
    www.heydaybooks.com

10 9 8 7 6 5 4 3 2 1

MIX
Paper from
responsible sources
FSC® C005010

FSC
www.fsc.org

CONTENTS

The Santa Ana Mountains and the Canyons

Santa Ana and Orange

The Flatlands

Irvine

Anaheim

Gustavo Arellano

BETWEEN PARADISE AND HELL, WE MUST WRITE

MY TWO FAVORITE quotes about Orange County, California—my homeland of thirty-four cities and more than three million souls living in 989 square miles of beaches, mountains, antebellum-esque gated communities, and some of the worst poverty in America—come from those peas in a pod, Ronald Reagan and R. Crumb. It was the Gipper who emblazoned "the OC" (don't call it that) into the American consciousness as the area "where all the good Republicans go to die," uttering that line to a delighted national press corps just before he launched his 1984 reelection campaign here (although he had been throwing that catnip to us since 1981).

Crumb, on the other hand, wasn't as magnanimous. "Orange County is a vortex of evil. I really believe that—the place is an evil place," he said back in 1996 to a reporter with *OC Weekly*, the newspaper I now edit. "If this is the future of the planet, oh, man. How depressing."

The truth, of course, is somewhere in between. But both Crumb's and Reagan's thoughts share one overriding trait that no one can contest: Orange County is *something*. Something horrible. Something beautiful. Something that deserves praise. Something that deserves a nuke. But, more than anything, something irresistible that demands and eventually earns everyone's attention. OC has drawn tourists and settlers, holy men and serial killers, the rich and the poor and the middle class and everyone in between for nearly two hundred years, all heeding the siren call of... *something*.

And all along the way, chroniclers have documented this strange, bizarre, overachieving vortex of paradise. I know this well. As someone who has lived in OC my entire life, covered it for fifteen years, and even written a book about this infernal land, I've read hundreds of books and thousands of articles on the subject. And so believe me when I say that the anthology you're holding is the finest attempt to ever try to lasso together the Orange County that sits between Reagan's heaven and Crumb's hell.

Orange County: A Literary Field Guide is a fantastic book, one that collects the OC observations and experiences of everyone from literary legends to local cranks, Pulitzer Prize winners to alt-weekly hacks, poets to novelists to essayists, both homegrown and not. It's the best creative distillation of the Orange County story this side of a No Doubt or Social Distortion song. And it's not just the writing that sings, although you've already got an operetta whenever you put Didion, Chabon, Isherwood, Philip K. Dick, and M. F. K. Fisher together in the same volume. And it's not even in the diversity of voices—Mexicans, Vietnamese, African Americans, Persians, surfers, mountaineers, suburbanites, and gang members, all finding common ground in marveling at this weirdness we call home. No, this book excels by paying attention to all the quirks that define this place—including Disneyland, toll roads, endangered gnatcatchers, bikinied goddesses, killer cops, acid-loving hippies, and everything in between and beyond—and finding the best writing to give each of our flaws and virtues its proper justice or evisceration.

One of the overriding themes within the book, though, goes back to Crumb and Reagan: Orange County as Paradise Lost or Found. Whether the subject is nineteenth-century Belle Époque Polish artists looking to establish a utopia in canyon country, the killing of the last grizzly bear in California, the eradication of orange groves by bulldozer or by disease (aptly called *la tristeza*—the sadness), or actor Steve Martin wistfully recalling his days moonlighting at Disneyland and Knott's Berry Farm, the authors here draw attention to Orange County as a special place. Whatever that allure is, it stays with us and deserves a romp on the written page.

Is this a perfect collection? Of course not. It would've, for instance, been great to include a voice that had experienced one of Orange County's many Christian megachurches; the *Baffler* trashing the infamous Crystal Cathedral, even if just for a few paragraphs, is literary perfection. (While the building still exists, it's now called Christ Cathedral and serves as the headquarters of the Catholic Diocese of Orange; the former tenant, the Rev. Robert Schuller, led his ministry into bankruptcy and died loathed and estranged from family members. Paradise Lost). Also underrepresented is the vibrant music subcultures—the rockabillies and skankers, punks and *rockeros*—that make OC an ever-replenishing source of youth culture for the rest of the country.

While our notorious conservatism and avarice is ever present throughout this anthology (and masterfully destroyed in Jon Wiener's account of a visit to the Nixon Library shortly after its opening), it would've been great to read a bit more about the contemporary scene. (Nixon, after all, was a state and national figure, only falling back on OC for refuge—Paradise Found.) And, really, the best serialized treatment about Orange County remains the original run of *Arrested Development*, the cult FOX comedy that captured our classes, ethnicities, races, and geographic divisions with the eye of Edith Wharton and the anarchic glee of *Mad* magazine.

But I digress. Anthologies are meant to be incomplete, meant to pique the readers' interest about the stories omitted, the authors to come. So view this "literary field guide" as your starter pack to learning more about Orange County, California. And just remember, *cabrones*: don't call it "the OC." No one does that.

Gustavo Arellano is the editor of the *OC Weekly* and the author of the syndicated column "¡Ask a Mexican!" and the book *Orange County: A Personal History*. His family has drifted back and forth between Anaheim and their ancestral villages in Zacatecas, Mexico, for nearly a century—between paradise and hell.

INTRODUCTION

FIELD GUIDES TYPICALLY focus on flora and fauna of the natural world, assisting readers in identifying animals and flowers, suggesting how and where to find them, and elaborating on what exactly to look for once they are located. As helpful handbooks they may be read in advance of a visit, on-site in real time, or even later, just for the pleasure (and perhaps self-congratulation) of knowing, finally, some fact about a glimpsed plant, tree, bird, or butterfly—this new information contributing to the feeling of being in the know, grounded in idiom, confident and connected.

This literary field guide attempts something similar, locating readers in both the natural and unnatural worlds of Orange County, California, USA, a much-constructed and -contrived locale, a pestered and paved landscape built and borne upon stories of human development both factual and apocryphal, and of destruction as well as, happily, of enduring wild places. Our strategy in these pages has been to arrange the assembled selections—short stories, essays, chapters from novels and memoirs, and poems—in correspondence with the vivid geography of the county, itself historically much arranged and rearranged. Thus it is a field guide to, if you will, a territory of words and images paralleling, sometimes idiosyncratically, the physical world, both as it once was and as it is today: mountains to sea, with an iconic river running right down the middle.

In this collection, we have attempted to map the topography of the real and the imagined Orange County, from the Santa Ana range across the wide basin, over the coastal foothills and down to the sea, with special focus on a handful of undeniably important landmark locales.

A reader may open this book anywhere and be immediately immersed in a specific place. Diverse in character, these locations come together as a cohesive region, defined by their general proximity to the Santa Ana River, a reliable point of reference and one that so many before us have used to situate, remind, and affirm this territory. Celebrated in ancient Tongva stories as well as by the area's early explorers, pioneers, and boosters, the river, now sometimes paved and channeled, still flows through canyons and fields and below overpasses to a jetty, still as recognizable and even comforting a feature of our landscape as are the famous Saddleback, the "island" of upscale stores in Newport Beach, the string of picture-perfect public piers, the City of Santa Ana's quintessentially hometown water tower, the artificial Alpine peak visible from the interstate, and the geometric street grids and the massive concrete overlay of the freeways themselves.

For the most part we've selected for this anthology work already in print, settling on terrific writing that not only stands on its own literary merit but that also authoritatively or uniquely tells the story of a place. This process involved making difficult choices, although we were pleased to have so much from which to choose. Indeed, our challenge was something like that faced by the totemic and perpetually curious and ambitious coyote, who, in the instructive Tongva tale, attempts to outrun, yes, the river.

Readers may find some satisfaction, as did we, in the work of writers who are referenced here although their work is not included in these pages (primarily because their contributions to the larger project of telling our county's story are already justifiably well known). This partial list of essential scribes of the Orange County experience includes early chronicler Richard Henry Dana Jr., socialite travel writer Emma Adams, Polish actress and memoirist Madame Helena Modjeska, novelist Susan Sontag (who wrote a novel based on the life of Modjeska), journalist and social reformer Carey McWilliams, Zorro originator Johnston McCulley, and the sincere and charmingly folksy local historian and scholar Jim Sleeper, whose books and almanacs are classics. Read them, too!

We're proud to share the diverse work assembled here, some of it previously familiar to us, much discovered as a result of reading, researching, and listening. Some pieces were found in regional magazines and small literary journals, such as Irvine Valley College's *The Ear* (formerly *The Elephant Ear*) and Santa Monica College's *Santa Monica Review*, publications sponsored by taxpayer-supported public education institutions committed to promoting community through the arts. Other selections were chosen from once revered but perhaps now overlooked books, today out of print or at least under-read. More than a few came from graduates and faculty of UC Irvine's MFA programs in fiction and poetry, which have nurtured writers for half a century. Many pieces are from new voices just making their way.

Wherever and however you have acquired this book—as a resident eager to hear a story again, as a writer searching for artful interpretations of place, as a student assigned it for a course on the region, as a new resident given this book as a welcome gift, or as a tourist who purchased this collection after a visit (perhaps in an attempt to make sense of the place!)—we hope that you find usefulness in it. You might use it as a foundation upon which to expand your reading on the subject, perhaps let it inspire you to plan an excursion to a site referenced by a favorite writer, or possibly find fresh motivation to learn or relearn the basics of Orange County history. Or maybe you'll keep it in your car's glove compartment as you might a more traditional field guide, always available in the event that you require a literary correlative to a place name, urban myth, intersection, scenic overlook, or historical marker.

Our fondest wish is that our literary field guide helps you find where you are, where we are, where others have been, and also perhaps where we might go from here.

—*Lisa Alvarez and Andrew Tonkovich*

THE COAST AND
THE BEACH TOWNS

A Coyote, which, like all the rest of his kin, considered
himself as the most austere animal on the face of the
earth, not even excepting man himself, came one day
to the margin of a small river. Looking over the bank, on
seeing the water run so slow, he addressed it in a cunning
manner, "What say you to a race?" "Agreed to," answered
the water very calmly. The Coyote ran at full speed along the
bank until he could hardly stand from fatigue and on looking over the bank saw the water running smoothly on.

He walked off with his tail between his legs and had
something to reflect upon for many a day afterwards.

—GABRIELEÑO/TONGVA STORY COLLECTED
BY HUGO REID, LOS ANGELES, 1851

M. F. K. Fisher

PACIFIC VILLAGE

M. F. K. Fisher was born in Michigan in 1908 and moved at an early age to California. Fisher became an acclaimed prose stylist who transformed both food and memoir writing in a career lasting half a century, much of it spent chronicling her life in Southern California, including childhood weekends and summers spent in Laguna Beach. She is the author of the classics *Serve It Forth*, *How to Cook a Wolf*, and *The Gastronomical Me*.

This short story, originally published in 1934 in *Westways*, the iconic magazine of the Automobile Club of Southern California, was the first for which the young Mary Francis Kennedy Fisher was paid for her writing. Her portrayal of crosstown political rivalries in an only slightly fictionalized Laguna Beach considers the divide between residents of the coastal arts village, pitting artists and old-timers against developers and civic improvers. That divide endures to this day and is part of what defines the town, and makes it both beloved and bedeviled.

OLAS IS A coast village, beautifully located. Artists and pseudo-artists flock to it, and people in hurrying autos go more slowly along the smooth state highway past its hills sloped up behind and the coves and curving beaches along its edge. And Olas itself, the village, is far from ugly—if you know where to look. It has many most desirable qualities, social, political, commercial—if you know how to choose.

And Olas is on the spot, for those who have long known it as a quiet, lovely place and want it to remain so, and those who feel in its present restless state a promise of prosperity and prominence as a booming beach resort, are lined up grim and hateful on either side of a wall of bitter prejudice.

Santa Catalina lies west from Olas on the sea-line, with San Clemente its shadow southward. A hard, broad road, as neat and empty of character as a dairy lunchroom, strings the village. Out of Olas to the north it hurries toward Los Angeles, and south, down the coast, curves less straightly to San Diego and the dimming pleasures of Mexican border freedom. Inland, roads lead from Olas through the endless tawny rollings of round hills, through orange-valleys to the mountains.

Near Olas, the coastline is erratically lovely. It is the kind that inspires nine out of ten visitors interviewed by the weekly news sheet to reminisce of the Riviera, Italian or French. They usually speak of the blue sky, the yellow sand, and the foam-sprayed cliffs of any correct postcard, comparing them more or less hazily with the sky, the sand, and the cliffs of Olas. And they are more or less right.

There are people, though, who feel that if a place is a place, with a personality strong and clear, comparisons are as unnecessary as they are annoying. There are people, many of them, who feel that Olas is such a place.

Some of them, artists, old settlers, young enthusiasts for life in the raw with no hate and no golf clubs, want to keep it just as it is—or, even more desirable, as it used to be: quiet, so unknown that Saturday and Sunday were like Tuesday, beaches empty, rocks and cliffs free for uninterrupted sketching of any kind.

Olas' other lovers, just as sincerely, want to exploit to the bursting point its strong and attractive character. They want to develop it, to lure more people to it, so that all the houses may be full. Then more roads will be built into the silent hills, more houses sown on more lots, and more businesses will flourish on the bustling streets of what will soon change from village to town.

Olas itself is very sensitive to this inner struggle. There is restlessness in the air, and a kind of bewilderment. Change bubbles and fumes like yeast in a warm beer crock. Overnight the face of the village changes.

Streets are being smoothed and straightened. Old eucalyptus trees are uprooted to make way for curbings. "Desecration!" the artists shriek. "Necessity," soothe the progressives, and they plant more trees in much more orderly rows.

Hills are chopped and scarred into level roads, and the old guard moans in pain. "Ah, but we must take out dangerous curves," the developers explain, and as a palliative, "See how we are planting groups of ornamental shrubs, and neat rows of ice plant on the banks."

In the meantime, the outlines of the village are intact. Hills behind and around, sea before, it lies small and pleasant in a little hollow, with houses clustered north and south along the coast. The streets are not quite straight. Fine trees shade some of them. The buildings are small and for the most part extremely ugly, possessing the one architectural virtue of unadornment.

The upper end of the village proper, with the housing and amusement of impecunious weekenders its main excuse, is plainly hideous. It is Olas' more interesting half. A tent city, many umbrella and hot-dog concessions, a movie house, and a squat dance hall make patterns vivid and noisy.

Strange here are the two municipal halls to Beauty and Science, the art gallery and a California college's marine laboratory. One, knowingly built like an electric power plant, houses monthly collections of bilge and occasional greatness. The other, strangely suggestive of a ratty old Louisiana mansion, fills every summer with earnest biology majors and peculiar smells.

Toward the south, the other half of the village pulls discreetly away. Its tent city is a bulky hotel or two. Its hash houses become restaurants whose food, if no better, is served with less clatter and more pomp. Its shops of abalone shell souvenirs and leather pillows stamped X *the Beach Beautiful* suddenly change to "antique" shops. They are equally cluttered, but here the prices are higher, the variety is infinite, and the wares range from raffia beach sandals to jade—real jade—opium pipes. There are Chinese, Mexican, Florentine, and Persian stores. And there are a myriad "Gifte Shoppes." Most of them, like their humbler competitors at the other end of Olas, are promisingly crowded on weekends, and quite deserted in between.

The weekly visitors are, of course, divided like the village topography into two main camps. To the first belongs the usual army of clerks from banks and stores, college professors, movie extras, and various types of professional weekenders. They are in Olas to get away from noise and business, or to make noise, or to do business. They live inexpensively in a part of the village that makes enough money from their two days' occupancy to send its proprietors to Palm Springs or Lake Arrowhead for the other five.

The other army that swarms into Olas on Fridays and Saturdays heads straight for the synthetic luxury of the hotels and restaurants to the south. It comes in bigger cars. It has fatter paunches and purses. It is made up of bank presidents and college trustees, movie magnates of the first and second rank in white turtleneck sweaters, fussy old ladies in conservative town cars. And, as in the other army, there are many professional weekenders. And business flourishes.

For two days the beaches teem with people. Back roads have their full share of puffing bicyclists, and the dusty bridle paths more than theirs of riders trying to make tired rented nags prance like polo ponies. The dance hall sags and shudders and every hole-in-the-wall sends up a cheery reek of popcorn and hamburger. Drugstores outdo their own versatility. Motorcycle officers herd people handsomely across the car-lined streets.

Monday morning is like dawn on another planet. The hordes have fled. Six or seven cars are parked sheepishly in the quiet streets. A few people walk about. At eleven, after the morning mail is distributed at the post office, the villagers do their marketing. There is a mild stir. A few go to the sand in the afternoon. At five, mail again collects small gossiping crowds. At night, a quiet shuffling about sends various groups to rehearsals, the movie, the chamber of commerce, the bridge clubs. Olas is normal again, living that life so completely unsuspected by the people who come and go each weekend.

Socially this seven-days-a-week Olas is very complex. Two main divisions separate it roughly into the artistic and the progressive elements, but that is a crude simplification. Each element has its interweaving intricacies, with all the bad and most of the good qualities of a small-town society long and firmly established.

Old settlers, in Olas since its cow-pathian days, take quite for granted their positions as social and political arbiters. They would be politely incredulous if by some shock they were made conscious of the affectionate mockery which surrounds them. They live smugly, simply. Reminiscence flows in mild flood from them, monotonously interesting.

They speak of the old road, the true Camino Real that wound like snail-silver along the cliffs. Indians once camped by it, and gave fish to the ambling padres. There are gardens now whose grey soil prickles with the thin bones of their bass and corbina—gardens and gas stations.

Then there were the old ranches, five or six of them back in the hills. The cowboys would sweep down the canyons in the fall of the year, and gather on the beach at Olas for three-day drunks. They sang wildly. Their children still race seaward, still sing, but oftener.

Then the days of the old post office with its high steps easy for sitting—ah me!—and the little newspaper! Didn't that old Dutchman write it, set it up, print it, sell it all himself? And the artists! Real ones they were, not pretty boys who just love color! Well, those were the days, the good days.

And the old settlers shake their heads, lonesomely. All about them is bustle and confusion. They hear nothing but wind in the groves of tall trees long leveled to the earth.

Theatre groups breed plays like maggots. They inter-hate ferociously. Two and three shows open on one night, ethics and economics are swept aside, clandestine throat-cutting springs gleefully into the light. Whole casts are shanghaied. The result is amusing and valuable. Directors of unusual ability, in their burning hope and hate, drag powers of beautiful, almost great acting from local lifeguards and waitresses and unemployed professors. Butchers and service-station flunkys design fine sets and do most artful lightings.

There are writers in Olas—too many to count. Some have made a steady sum for years from pulp magazines; a few have sold to publishers novels that people wouldn't buy, or have seen lone stories starred in minor anthologies. One or two have written best-sellers. But most of Olas' "authors" rank among the permanently unpublished. Their publics are small: wives, friends, awed offspring. They write for the chosen few, quite happy. They gossip glibly among themselves of agents and markets and pulps and slickies. And sometimes they discuss Letters.

Somewhere between this group and the theatre enthusiasts lies a strange band of stragglers from both: the Talkers. Where do they sleep, where eat? With an uncanny knowledge of when to appear, they crop up from nowhere at picnics and parties and informal meetings. At the first lull in sound, they pounce. And the evening is theirs. Art, politics, abalone fishing, sex, Tahiti, California wines: information fills the air, like a rushing of winds. The Talkers are pests. Oddly enough, they are for the most part charming pests.

And it is these muse-fed villagers and these old settlers who lead the artist faction in Olas. It is they who cry "Down with billboards! Away with publicity! Out with subdividers and go-getters!" And they are very bitter. "Olas has been ruined, prostituted," they howl. "Her trees are felled, her hills pitted—give us back our old Olas!" And they stay in Olas and bring their friends, who usually stay too.

And all, artists and old settlers and the indeterminate stragglers of many professions, are equally unaware of the amused tolerance with which they are treated by the other half of the village. Misunderstanding is mutual, perhaps, but where the artists dismiss with scornful ravings the dull bourgeois of Olas, the latter view with a kind of embarrassed enjoyment the incomprehensible antics of their enemies.

They live the ordered existence of good citizens of any small town on the earth. Their pleasures are cautiously licentious, their business dealings honestly corrupt. They support, with some prodding, a Red Cross branch and a municipal church.

Clubs thrive in their circles. There are several different varieties of women's organizations: junior, senior, garden, parent-teacher, sewing. The men have rival luncheon clubs with all the usual backslappings and buttons and good ostentatious charities. The children of the club-goers go to clubs: puppy clubs, doll clubs. And bridge clubs knit the whole faction into a nightly knot of systems and four-sided animosities.

Frequent elections exercise all the political muscles of the various groups, and real estate salesmen, garagists, and chain-store managers stalk past each other on the street with an axes-at-twenty-paces look which changes at the next primaries and then shifts again.

And all these people, these reactionary progressives, these bank employees and owners of drugstores and gifte shoppes and eating places—why do they want Olas to thrive and grow fat? It is very natural. They want to grow fat with her, to thrive that their children may thrive.

Real estate dealers need water in distant subdivisions. They cut holes in the hills for pipes. Then they sell lots and make money and build more houses to rent to more people. And those people buy food and bathing caps and Chinese lanterns. And billboards bring people, and so does publicity in the city papers and on the air.

To the progressives it is a natural, a logical thing to want Olas to be bigger and noisier and more popular. They are patient enough with the grumbling, sneering artists, and, most ironically, use them as part of their publicity program. *Olas, Famous Artists' Colony*, the billboards blurb, and *Visit Olas, Artist Haunt*. At the New Year's parade in a near neighbor, a great palette of roses represents the village, with hired Hollywood beauties dressed in transparent smocks and berets to represent Art. And at the annual fiesta, the aesthetic high note is reached when all the storekeepers and mechanics and beer-drawers don orange-and-green tam-o'-shanters and flowing ties. They too represent Art.

So the two sides live together in the little village. One could not well exist without the other. Each fights with the tactics of righteous sincerity: each fights dirty.

And while shouts and sneers and low groans gather like warring birds in the air, Olas lies still in the creases of the ocean-slipping hills, one bead strung with many like it on the long coast road. It is rather uncomfortable. It aches at times. Rheumatism or growing pains?

P.S. Meanwhile—meanwhile the real artists, those men and women whose pictures of Olas will perhaps still be looked at in a hundred years, continue to paint. They are few—as always. They are unconscious of any village strife. All the high talk of Art, all the politics and scandal, all the hullabaloo of growth and change, is to them as unimportant and as natural as a sea gull's dropping on a clean canvas. They paint as they did those years gone, trees and rocks and an old mission in a garden. And three hundred years from now—

Oakley Hall

---

from *REPORT FROM BEAU HARBOR*

Born in San Diego in 1920, Oakley Hall studied at UC Berkeley and served in the marines during World War II. He earned his MFA from the Iowa Writers' Workshop and wrote more than twenty-five novels, many with a focus on the West and Mexico, including *Warlock,* a finalist for the Pulitzer Prize in 1958. Hall cofounded the graduate creative writing program at UC Irvine, nurturing hundreds of writers (including many represented in this volume) over his thirty-year teaching career. Among his honors were lifetime achievement awards from the PEN American Center and the Cowboy Hall of Fame. He also cofounded the Community of Writers at Squaw Valley, one of the country's longest-running summer writing conferences.

In these excerpts from 1971's *Report from Beau Harbor*, Hall revisits the protagonist of his first major novel, *Corpus of Joe Bailey.* Joe is now a middle-aged businessman in Newport Beach married to Polly, and we find him in the following selections running on the beach with his dog and unable to shake the unease of knowing what is inevitably in store for the beautiful landscape around him: fire, flood, mudslides, and earthquakes—Southern California's ecological disaster menu for as long as anyone can remember. It strikes Joe as the worst kind of pathetic fallacy, and one that corresponds to the social tumult of youth and drug culture, the Vietnam War, protest, and especially his own family's parallel turmoil.

I N A SWEATSHIRT and old blue swimming trunks, accompanied by the lead-gray Weimaraner Butch, he ran on the stretch of sand between the black rock jetty and Balboa Pier, spidery-legged in the morning distance. The beach in its entirety extended from the channel to the mouth of the Santa Ana River along the Balboa Peninsula, a three-mile sand-spit narrow as a beetle leg, half beach and half crowded residential streets, terminating in the clenched fist of Peninsula Point. The Peninsula enclosed Balboa Bay and Newport Harbor, in which were two large islands, a number of smaller ones, and over eight thousand pleasure craft. Older residents of the area complained that they now paid yearly in taxes as much as their property had originally cost.

As he jogged along the damp sand, Butch splashed through the shallow water, compensating for his master's slower gait by continual joyous switchbacks. The pier loomed. He tagged the damp, creosoted wood and reversed his course.

Now he could see the boats spilling out of the channel mouth, sails blossoming beyond the jetty. Soon surfers would appear with short belly-boards, and languid bikinied girlfriends would spend the day reclining on the sand as spectators to the wave riding. Families would come with blankets and lunches; fishermen, skindivers, couples with transistor radios. Frequent helicopters would pass over the beach with abrasive rips of sound, marine corps training gunships from the nearby El Toro airbase, lifeguard and sheriff patrols. At night aerial police would harass young lovers with a floodlight and bullhorn.

Thirty miles offshore Santa Catalina was fading behind the smog draining out of the Los Angeles Basin. He could remember when the island had floated magically close, with its buff cliffs and green icing. Still, once in a while after a rain it would reappear briefly in that remembered clarity, Catalina and the northern mountains standing close in the washed air.

He ran more and more mechanically, panting, sweat dripping from his chin. Occasionally he mopped his forehead with the sleeve of his sweatshirt. Once he had to break his stride when the racing dog cut in front of him to sniff a dead fish at the high water line. Polly was worried about the fish, some of which had been found lately to have unhealthy skin growths. She worried about ecology, and blacks, and poverty, and young people, and the draft. He was worried about the state of the nation.

The war continued, but a number of the county's aerospace plants had been forced to cut back, and unemployment was becoming a serious problem in Southern California. The stock market was down, interest rates were up. Rioting students who might have been his own sons had been shot by terrified National Guardsmen and infuriated police. A generation was growing up to hate the police, a hatred from which he thought it might never recover, as his generation had never recovered from the Depression. And yet it seemed to him that drugs, and contention, and violence, were everywhere increasing.

With his daily stint finished and Butch trotting beside him, he trudged off the beach end of Channel Road where the white police cruiser the kids called Moby Dick was parked, red turret flasher on the roof and reinforced bumper against the barrier. The officer leaned out the window, his cap pushed back on his forehead: he had a sharp, acne-scarred chin. "Been running?" he asked.

With a grip on Butch's collar he answered that he had. He was uneasy, not having brought the dog's leash. His son Rich claimed the Balboa cops hassled him because of the length of his hair. His wife said times had changed when your daughter's beach picnics were not threatened by rough kids, but by the law.

"I like running in the afternoons better," the cop said, grinning. "More girls around." There was no trace of a southern accent. Polly Bailey had a fine ear for outlander speech, offended as a fourth-generation Californian by the swarming immigration from the South and Middle West. He asked where the cop was from.

"Just on up Old Coast Highway a ways—I went to Huntington Beach High. How long've you lived down here on the Point?"

"Ten years," he said, and, when the cop's flat-lipped mouth tilted with the superiority of longer California residence, he added that he had been born and raised in San Diego. They exchanged names and parted as fellow Californians and beach runners, but as he moved away, still awkwardly gripping Butch's collar, he felt guilty of a disloyalty to his son.

Rich's little MG was not parked in the driveway as he had hoped to find it when he returned from his run. At his gate he stooped to pick up the folded bulk of the Los Angeles *Times,* familiar acceleration of his heartbeat as he opened it to glance over the headlines.

But day by day nothing seemed to change. The market remained under seven hundred, the cost-of-living index was up again. There was no news concerning an easing of tight money, an end of the draft, peace prospects. He separated the sports section from the rest of the paper as he went on inside the house, where his wife would now be in a hurry to get to the airport and fly north to her father.

Outside again with his daughter and departing wife, cup of coffee in his hand, the May air as soft as though it had substance, he was proud of the handsome sleek surface the Joseph Bailey family presented, very proud of his slim, forty-five-year-old wife clad and coiffed with expensive taste, standing beside her sports car glancing toward Balboa Boulevard—proud of his pretty daughter in tight white levis and loose fair hair, and astonishing breasts in a sweatshirt imprinted: WAR IS NOT HEALTHY FOR CHILDREN AND OTHER LIVING THINGS.

Count your blessings, Polly would say when he was worried or depressed. And they were manifest. He had more than fulfilled his youthful ambitions. He owned and operated a grading-and-paving company, a hot-asphalt plant, a rock crusher, heavy equipment and trucks, and a lucrative concrete-block franchise. He owned 321 acres of prime Orange County subdivision land and a fine home on a valuable Channel-front lot. He drove a Cadillac, his wife a Porsche, one son an MG and the other a VW. They owned a small catamaran and a sailing dinghy, and for some time he had had his eye on a larger boat. His statement of net worth showed something over a million-five, although he recognized, along with his accountant, his attorney, and his banker, that this was a paper figure. However, he was also a millionaire by that cynical method of computation that sets a man's worth at three times his debts.

His oldest son was a senior at Long Beach State College, a handsome, graceful, very popular boy who could have been a tennis champion. Unfortunately he was on probation for a year for possession of marijuana —but so were a number of other kids from well-to-do Peninsula Point homes, the result of a police raid last Christmas. His second son was an honor student with an IQ of 154, now a sophomore at the university. His daughter was just coming out of her baby fat into Southern California bloom. He was proud of them all, and grateful for his life, but more and more everything had begun to seem to him very perishable. Last year's earthquake terror, which had come to nothing, had made him realize that the unease was widespread; this year, except for Rich's probation and an overdue mortgage payment, the fear was more abstract.

He was careful not to spill his coffee as he kissed Polly good-bye. Her fingers patted his cheek, her eyes were invisible behind curved dark lenses. She slipped into the expensive little car, adjusted the seatbelt and stared down Channel Road toward the boulevard with a set mouth.

"I'm sorry I'll miss the mixed-doubles thing," she said. "Who'll you play with?"

"Probably with Irene."

An ancient station wagon appeared, dark-tinted windows and jacked-up rear end, surfboards on the roof with colored sharkfin skegs. Inside were two tan, blondined, hairy boys. The wagon slowed and they hailed Sary.

"Oh, hi, Ken! Oh, hi, Boyd!"

He smiled uneasily at these exotics. Once he had been a boy driving to the beach on a weekend morning with surfboards on the roof. What had happened to him in thirty years passing that these creatures seemed wild and strange as saucerites? The wagon passed on by, dark-windowed. More and more these wagons and vans with painted or curtained windows were being declared outlaw in Orange County communities.

Polly raced her engine, glancing at her wristwatch. "Maybe I can get the late plane back Monday night," she said. "But it'll probably be Tuesday."

"Right," he said.

Sary put her face in the window to kiss her mother. "Have a good trip, Mom! Love to Grandad and Gladney and everybody. And Dave!"

"Good-bye!"

"Joe, phone me when Richie turns up."

"Sure," he said.

"Good-bye!"

"Good-bye!"

The grilled tan rear of the Porsche sped away up Channel Road, diminishing, and disappeared into the boulevard headed for the airport.

Moving back through the gate with his half-empty cup, he laid an arm across his daughter's sweatshirted warmly alive shoulders. "What're you going to do today, honey?"

"I guess Suzy and I'll go to the beach."

What did Sary and her friend Suzy Dixon do at the beach all day? Surely their tiny bikinis would not hold together in the surf. At Sary's age he had spent long days at the beach too. They had ridden their boards, they had bodysurfed, jumped skimboards along the water's edge, played touch football, horsed around. What did girls do nowadays? Probably boys like Ken and Boyd came to pay court, and they listened to the top forty on someone's transistor. Did they ride up and down Balboa Boulevard in cars? Did they go to someone's house? Did they smoke pot?

"Are you going in to the office today, Daddy?"

He said he had to go in to look at the mail.

Now on the Friday morning before Labor Day weekend, he ran along the beach with the gray Weimaraner sailing on ahead. The combers that had been crashing in throughout August had been flattened by the Santa Ana, the hot wind that dried out the sinuses and chapped the skin and spread brushfires through the mountains. The sky to the north was black from the fires on the Angeles Crest and in the San Bernardinos, and there was a kind of electric irritability in the atmosphere. It was the worst season for fires in many years, and winter in consequence would bring disastrous floods and mudslides.

Butch reversed his field and sprinted toward him with ears laid back and teeth bared with the joy of his passage. When he feinted a step toward the dog, Butch yelped and splashed into deeper water to pass.

He had extended his morning run to three miles. A physical examination had shown him to be in good shape, except for his tennis elbow, which had required cortisone shots for the Newport Harbor Tennis Tournament, in which he and Jack Frye had reached the quarter finals in the senior vets doubles.

Ahead of him a fisherman with a long pole was picking his way out along the rocks of the jetty. Higher on the beach a leathery old man in a bill-cap was scouring the sand with a metal detector, looking for coins dropped by the beach people. In his own search for funds he had located money at eleven point two percent, interest to be paid quarterly instead of monthly; so that pressure was off for the moment.

When he reached the jetty he swung around and started on his third lap back to the pier. He would have breakfast at the little café near it, with Butch tied to a parking meter outside. Polly and Sary had flown to Tahoe for the George Davis Birthday–Labor Day Weekend, probably the last for that fast-failing old man. Polly was spending much more time in attendance on her father, with Gladney gone, though the new general manager seemed to be working out. Tonight she would call at eight, or else he would phone her at nine.

At sea Catalina was obscured by the low-lying bank of smoke drifting south from the Los Angeles Basin. Only a few miles inland ashes accumulated on sills and blew into windward corners. Sunsets, in this smoky air, were beautiful. He panted through chapped lips as he ran, his feet splatted on the sand, Santa Ana sweat dripped from his chin. Ahead Butch was sitting, waiting for him. It pleased him that the dog slowed down in the third mile.

Sary was at Beau Harbor with her mother, Rich in Vancouver with Gladney and Ronnie, and Dave was backpacking with a friend in one of the Grand Canyon tributaries, which was soon to be flooded by the completion of a dam. He was returning for fall quarter at Cal. They were watching the mails for his induction notice.

Several times now he had gone out to work with Shorty Fitzgerald, the loquacious little welder at the Pardo Canyon yard, who had helped him mount a worn-out dozer sprocket on a stand, where he burned and shaped its teeth into something he had no final clear image of yet. At the same time he was spending longer hours at CAP, bidding on more jobs than he was accustomed to; needing more money. He had retained a Los Angeles law firm in Dave's behalf; a bearded abrasive young Jewish attorney was very interested in what Dave proposed to do. He also sent Rich a remittance every month. Gladney had written that it seemed possible that Rich could get on the ski patrol at Grouse Mountain, near Vancouver, when ski season began.

The war continued, and the economy staggered—maybe toward recovery; at least money seemed to have loosened. To the north the mountains smoked, and more and more threats seemed to appear daily, in the air, the water, the food. A helicopter flapped eccentrically along the beach and over him, gazing down with its swollen plastic eye.

A diminishing figure, he jogged toward the pier that seemed suspended in space and time beyond him, aimed over the opaque water toward the shrouded island. Radiating out from this beach, in the thickening atmosphere, lay tract on tract, subdivision on subdivision, congealing into one vast and centerless suburb that merged along clotting freeways into the enormous sprawl of Los Angeles, above which the mountains blazed, and smoke rose to fill the sky.

Nick Schou

---

from *ORANGE SUNSHINE*

Born in 1970, Nick Schou is the managing editor of *OC Weekly* and an award-winning investigative journalist whose articles have led to the release from prison of wrongly convicted individuals as well as the federal indictment, conviction, and imprisonment of a Huntington Beach mayor. In addition to *Orange Sunshine: The Brotherhood of Eternal Love and Its Quest to Spread Peace, Love, and Acid to the World*, his history of OC drug culture, he is the author of *Kill the Messenger: How the CIA's Crack-Cocaine Controversy Destroyed Journalist Gary Webb*; *The Weed Runners: Travels with the Outlaw Capitalists of America's Medical Marijuana Trade*; and, most recently, *Spooked: How the CIA Manipulates the Media and Hoodwinks Hollywood*. His work has been featured in *The Best American Crime Reporting*.

In *Orange Sunshine,* Schou takes apart popular lore surrounding the legendary counterculture drug syndicate that fueled the hippie scene, as embodied most famously in Laguna Beach's Mystic Arts World gallery and head shop. In this excerpt he recounts the story of a notorious 1970 Laguna Canyon rock concert, exploring both its documented and apocryphal elements.

AS THE END of 1970 approached in Laguna Beach, the Brotherhood of Eternal Love prepared to unleash another surprise on the local establishment: a three-day free music festival to take place over the Christmas holidays. Although the Brotherhood played a major role in the event—commonly known as the "Christmas Happening" or simply, "the Happening"—the concert was originally the brainchild of Curtis Reed, manager of Thing, a local hippie boutique, and Ted "Star Rainbow" Shields, the former *LA Oracle* art director who had moved down to Laguna Beach after dropping Orange Sunshine [acid] at Altamont. Along with two friends of Shields's, Venus Rainbow and Nebula Rainbow, he moved in to a Laguna Canyon shack called the Rainbow House and began experimenting with what eventually would become a worldwide art fad: airbrushing faces and bodies. For the past few years, Reed had been a big part of Laguna Beach's hippie scene. With funding from Brotherhood member and Orange Sunshine superpromoter Johnny Gale, Reed held "Feed-Ins" on the beach each summer, distributing free ham and cheese sandwiches, watermelon, and other fruits and vegetables to the local flower children, many of whom were homeless and camping either on the beach or in the Living Caves near the Top of the World.

With help from the Brotherhood, Reed also opened a couple of soup kitchens, including Love Animals, Don't Eat Them, a vegetarian restaurant that health workers closed for health code violations involving a camel that wandered from table to table. (Reed promptly reopened Love Animals, Don't Eat Them as a religious temple, thus avoiding the need for a food permit.) At some point in late 1970, Reed had a vision that he could convert the world to vegetarianism by holding a massive rock concert in Laguna Beach. "Reed asked me to help him put together this big festival," Shields recalls. "He had this place, Millabee's Treats, a vegetarian natural food restaurant on Thalia Street. That became our headquarters for the concert."

Reed and Shields set about spreading rumors that artists like Bob Dylan, the Beatles, and the Grateful Dead were going to play a Christmas concert in Laguna Beach, inviting everyone who was anyone in America's countercultural movement to come along. "We had an office and a telephone, and because we were working with the Brotherhood we had a connection with the phone company, the local operators, and they gave us an open line to call anybody in the world we wanted," Shields says. "We just told people to come. We wanted to get a big crowd, a mob. We even called the Pope. It was crazy."

Dion Wright designed a poster for the event, depicting a bearded hippie very similar in appearance to Jesus Christ. The poster declared that 144,000 people would be attending the show. It was Wright who came up with the notion of giving the concert a spiritual significance.

"My idea was to transform the event from a political one that could turn violent into a spiritual one that would probably end up okay," he says. "If this concert was going to happen on Christmas, why not call it a birthday party for Jesus?"

A fellow Laguna Beach artist named Bill Ogden drew a separate poster depicting a nude woman with wings. "All Wise Beings Who Perceive the Inner Light Shining Brightly on This Village Arc Requested to Bring Their Presence to Laguna Beach, California, Spiritual Center of the World," it declared. "Be a Witness to the Birth of a New Age." Countercultural newspapers like the L.A. *Free Press* ran free advertisements for the show. But perhaps the most effective advertising for the concert were handmade invitations—mailed and hand delivered to every hippie commune along the coast of California and beyond—that depicted a butterfly and the slogan "Let Sunshine Do." Attached to each card was a single tablet of Orange Sunshine, courtesy of the Brotherhood of Eternal Love.

When Neil Purcell became aware of the concert, he sent two informants to infiltrate the group that was organizing it. "They worked undercover," Purcell says. "It was going to be on the beach. I credit my two guys with finally convincing the folks that the beach was not the best place and to have it in the canyon." Shields, however, denies that there was ever any plan to hold the concert on the beach. "There wasn't enough room there," he says. "We wanted to have another Woodstock, a massive love-in, and the only place to do that was Laguna Canyon."

The concert ended up taking place in a grassy area near the top of Laguna Canyon called Sycamore Flats. From the beginning, it was clear that none of the bands that had supposedly been invited to the concert were going to be playing. Most of them probably hadn't even been contacted, and had no idea the concert even existed. The one band that did consider playing, the Grateful Dead, sent a team of roadies to investigate. What they found was some twenty-five thousand hippies crowding into Laguna Canyon, most of them high on acid, and a series of police roadblocks blocking off the city from all directions. "The Grateful Dead couldn't get in," Shields says. "They had to turn back.

The police had sealed off the entrance to the canyon and both ends of Pacific Coast Highway."

"It was mayhem," Purcell recalls. "We closed down the city." John Saporito, the undercover narcotics investigator who helped Purcell bust countless hippies in Dodge City and along the beach, donned a uniform for the first time in years. "We had this Toyota jeep with police decals and a red light," he says. "We went through with cameras and videotaped everything. We spent a lot of time videotaping all the naked girls and people having sex. I don't think they were used as evidence, because there was no court action brought." Saporito also helped man one of the barricades near the concert. He says he and other Laguna Beach police officers set up trash cans near the entrance to Sycamore Flats and told the hippies marching in to toss their drugs in, no questions asked. "We'd say, 'You can go in, but we'll search you: Throw your dope in the barrels,'" he says. "We were burning them and you wouldn't believe what went in there: kilos of marijuana and LSD by the tons, and underage kids with wines we were pouring in the gutter. Dogs coming by were drinking the wine and LSD. It was pretty funny."

Purcell also recalls seeing tables full of marijuana, mushrooms, and LSD set up at the checkpoints. "It was just ridiculous," he says. "We were absolutely outnumbered. We couldn't take the organizers down. We'd be stomped and killed, that's for sure. It was one of those things you had to bear and grin." Danelle Adams, who decades later went on to replace Neil Purcell as chief of the Laguna Beach Police Department, was a teenager at the time and walked up the canyon to see the show with her boyfriend. "I saw a nude woman on a white horse, people making love in a ditch in a haze of marijuana," she says. "My boyfriend and I were frightened by it."

The concert began when Eiler Larsen, the town's legendary "Greeter," welcomed the crowd to "celebrate the birth of Jesus Christ." Fred Lewis, who owned a countercultural clothing store in Los Angeles called London Britches, had helped fund the event and thus got a backstage ticket to the show. "At one point in the afternoon I was asked to step on the stage, which I did," he recalls. "Looking out at all the people who were in attendance, it became apparent these were all my brothers and sisters and I had a primal experience. I started to cry and felt a great deal of love in my heart, and oneness for everyone."

The fact that none of the big rock bands that had been advertised actually showed up didn't seem to matter to the crowd, which gleefully cheered a procession of local musicians, even as rumors of crowd sightings and supposedly imminent performances of Bob Dylan and George Harrison circulated. As it happened, the only rock star who actually took the stage was Buddy Miles, Jimi Hendrix's drummer, who played guitar and mesmerized the audience with his impersonation of Hendrix. In the midst of one of the performances that afternoon, a man parachuted from the sky, landing in the middle of the crowd, which roared with excitement, thinking it was Leary himself. It wasn't Leary, and nobody ever found out who he was.

The mysterious skydiver wasn't the only surprise to drop from the heavens. Later on Christmas Day, a propeller airplane flew low over the crowd. As people scanned the heavens, thousands of pieces of paper floated down toward them: the remainder of the Brotherhood of Eternal Love's Orange Sunshine invitation cards, air-dropped party favors for the already-tripped-out audience. "It was a single-engine plane," Purcell says. "All of a sudden, out of the plane came thousands of little gray cards, and each had a tab of Orange Sunshine, compliments of the Brotherhood. Supposedly, Johnny Gale used to take credit for it. Fat Bobby took credit for it, too. I think it was both of them. The plane had its numbers blocked off." Saporito says he saw the plane, too. "It was a big-ass plane that threw a ton of dope out the back," he says. "These cards had some Native American saying on them and a piece of tape and a tab of LSD. The cards said something like, 'As long as the grass grows and the river flows: Eternal peace.'" Shields claims the airdrop was definitely Gale's doing. "John Gale was behind it," he says. "He put the cards in the plane. He did that."

The extra dose of Sunshine made a weird situation even weirder. At least three women gave birth during the show, which had no sanitary facilities. Naked people were everywhere, many of them making love in the mud or on blankets spread out in the bushes—a somewhat more energetic, frenzied version of the famous hippie love scene in the Michelangelo Antonioni film *Zabriskie Point,* which was released to bewildered audiences earlier in the year. At one point a Black Panther spokesman took the stage and began chanting "Get the pigs!" and cursing President Nixon, at which point Shields grabbed the microphone and shouted down the angry Panther. "Neil Purcell probably put that guy up there," he theorizes. "It's not about hate, man," Shields exclaimed. "It's about love! Love, love, love!"

So many people had converged on Laguna Canyon that by the end of the first day there was no food left. Shields tried to hire a helicopter to deliver food at the concert, but after calling every airport in Southern California, he concluded that the Federal Aviation Administration had declared Laguna Beach a no-fly zone. "They probably did that because of the plane that dropped all the acid," he says. "We needed food, so I drove up to L.A. and bought a bunch of veggie burgers and avocados and tomatoes and fruit. With Fred Lewis's help, Shields spoke with the National Guard, loaded up two or three trucks and drove around the blockades. As his friends began distributing the vegetarian food, Shields walked onstage and declared a moratorium on carnivorism. "We are going to have a funeral now," he announced. "We brought veggie burgers! It's a new world! Try veggie food! Bring up your hot dogs and hamburgers. We are going to bury them right now. If you love animals, don't eat them!"

Although the concert was supposed to last three days, by December 28, there were still thousands of hippies marooned at Sycamore Flats who were too high to walk. Lewis tried to negotiate with Purcell to find a peaceful solution that would allow everyone to leave peacefully, but the police were under pressure to immediately clean out the canyon. "It was freezing cold," Purcell says. "We had fifteen cases of frostbite. We had babies born up there. Two people died from overdose. We had our little jail filled up with people freaking out on PCP, bleeding from the nose, and people having sex in front of God and everyone watching them. It was an unruly mess, and our intelligence was that they were going to stay there."

As the sun rose that morning, the cops lined up in riot gear and threatened to teargas anyone who wouldn't comply with their orders. The police herded everyone onto school buses that would drive them to the city limits. But about fifteen hundred people refused to budge. "They decided it was the new mecca," Purcell says. "We had four hundred fifty police officers and we just routed them out." Saporito helped with the mop-up operation. "We marched up early in the morning from the ridge above the stage and swept through there and sent them down Laguna Canyon Road," he recalls. "They were forced on buses and we made sure they didn't come back. We had police everywhere. We had some cops that were just tired of taking shit from these guys. They were going along these buses with a giant spray can of Mace and just spraying the windows."

The event marked the nadir of the rocky relationship between Laguna Beach's hippie culture and the city's conservative political establishment. Even the concert's organizers agree that, in some respects, it was a disaster. "We were all jacked up on this utopian view of the world where we actually thought everyone would tune into what we were doing," Shields concludes. "It wasn't that drugs were the main focus but having fun and dancing and doing arts."

Today, decades later, many veterans of Laguna Beach's hippie scene fondly recall the concert as the last great happening of their generation, but at the time, it must have seemed more like a death knell. The fact that the concert's organizers never obtained permits to stage the show at Sycamore Flats provided the cops with all the pretext they needed to shut it down with military force. After the last of the hippies had been cleared out of town, city bulldozers buried a mountain of discarded clothing and drugs beneath the ground. "If anyone ever dug up that area," Purcell concludes, "there'd be quite an archeological find."

Wright recalls the bulldozers well nearly forty years later. At the time they struck him as a metaphor for the death of the utopian idealism that he and his friends in the Brotherhood had tried to create. As he watched the machines bury the detritus of the great gathering of tribes—the last big spectacle spawned by the Brotherhood of Eternal Love in Laguna Beach—he marveled at the significance of it all. "The birthday party for Jesus was the last gasp of hippiedom," Wright says. "People tried to keep it moving forward, but as a sociological phenomenon, the hippie movement was over."

T. H. Watkins

from ***ON THE SHORE OF
THE SUNDOWN SEA***

T. H. Watkins was born in Loma Linda in 1936 and grew up in San Bernardino. After graduating from the University of Redlands, he moved to San Francisco, where he worked with Wallace Stegner at *American West* magazine. He went on to edit *American Heritage* magazine and *Wilderness* before accepting the Stegner Chair in Western American Studies at Montana State University, in Bozeman. Perhaps best known for his National Book Award finalist *Righteous Pilgrim,* a 1990 biography of New Deal administrator Harold L. Ickes, Watkins wrote more than twenty other books and hundreds of articles that celebrated his passion for the West and conservation.

In this selection from a book about California's coast, published in 1973 by the Sierra Club, Watkins returns with his wife, Joan, to Dana Point, fondly recalling his childhood sojourns there with his family.

ALL THE PEDDLERS of a lost, bittersweet nostalgia had been telling me for years that you can't go home again. I should have believed them, I suppose, but a stubborn little kernel of yearning would not let me. Besides, I was with someone I loved, and when you are stricken with that "first, fine, careless rapture," it seems profoundly important to explain yourself, unstitch the layers that cover secret dreams in an effort to blot out the fearful possibility that you are not much different from anyone else. And so I launched our vague pilgrimage, she willing and tolerant in her own affection, gently amused at my intensity, perhaps suspecting the truth I had chosen to ignore.

The homeland to which I was taking her had nothing to do with my home town, which had long since succumbed to progress, the landmarks which guide memory either destroyed or altered beyond recognition. No, this homeland was the most precious part of the geography of my youth, a stretch of Southern California coast that lay between Salt Creek Beach in the north and San Clemente in the south—little more than ten miles in length, but once a whole continent to a child's eye, a landscape which had given me my first and last taste of what freedom might be. And it was here, like a snake shedding winter skins, I had passed from one image of myself to another in the journey from boy to man.

We set out from Culver City southwest of Los Angeles, where we had been covering the 1970 auction of MGM's forty-year collection of props and costumes (a genuine wake in the land of celluloid dreams; perhaps it should have told me something). Near Long Beach, we abandoned the freeway and took to Highway 1, the old coast highway, which was what I would have had to do in the age before freeways; if you're going to revisit your past, you might as well do it up right. Most of the trip was a dismal experience, as it always had been, for there are parts of Highway 1 in this region that are as ugly as any stretch of highway in the United States, an attenuated wilderness of neon, cheapjack used-car lots, dreary bars, drive-in restaurants made of weathered plastic, service stations greasy with age, "mission-style" motels with missing roof tiles and peeling plaster, and on the ocean side black pumps that dipped and rose, dipped and rose in long lines, busily sucking oil from beneath the sand. Over it all, as if a brush fire were raging somewhere out of sight, lay a reddish-gray pall of smog. Joan quickly developed a pained look between the eyes.

The smog thinned gradually as we traveled south past Seal Beach and Huntington Beach, catching occasional glimpses of surf between convalescent hospitals and oil pumps. By the time we reached Newport Beach, the smog had nearly disappeared. So had Newport Beach, as I remembered it. It was once an aging, quietly charming place that had been half–fishing village and half–tourist town, with a rickety old pier from which I had fished for mackerel more than once. Now I could hardly find it, what with a freeway interchange, motels, shopping centers, and what appeared to be a high-rise department store. The hills were alive with condominiums.

"Jesus," I muttered. "Where did all this come from?"

"How long has it been since you were here?"

I had to think. "Twenty-two, twenty-three years, maybe." In Southern California, that was more than enough time for a life-style to vanish. Two or three life-styles.

South of Newport Beach the highway began to hug the land much closer to the sea, rising with the coast as it alternately swelled to hills and bluffs, then sank, roller-coaster fashion, into hollows with crescent-shaped beaches. Much of the rolling grassland was crowded with spanking new housing developments that clustered like immobile lemmings at the very edge of the sea, but in the late morning sun the ocean flashed with the brassy sheen I remembered. If you looked at it too long, your eyes would begin to ache from the glare and the heat of it.

Laguna Beach had not changed appreciably. Even in my childhood it had been an artsy-craftsy place, and the tradition lingered—even flourished, to all appearances. It was still a town that took its manufactured Mediterranean heritage seriously, with much tropical vegetation punctuated by little white-washed houses with red tile roofs. There were parking meters now in the short downtown section through which the highway ran, strung with block-after-block of pottery shops, galleries, bookstores, leather emporiums, sliver-sized restaurants, and bungalow-like motels almost hidden by bougainvillea and palm trees. Two noticeable differences were the presence of long-haired young people, the men with hairy faces, the women in worn, artfully patched Levis, and the absence of the red-bearded old man who had once stood on the street corners in raggle-taggle clothing bellowing welcome to passing motorists as the town's unofficial greeter. I supposed he had died, his memory shoveled into the dustbin of yesterdays like the ramshackle fishing village of Newport. At least the town had not replaced him with a Disney-like, walking, talking replica—or even a hand-hewn granite statue along carefully modern lines, which would have been much more its style.

Next stop: Salt Creek Beach, about five miles south of Laguna. Here was the base of my memoried youth, for it was here that I had spent at least half of my summers by the sundown sea. It had been a gentle little scoop out of the coast with a good line of surf, a beach littered here-and-there with clumps of dead kelp, and under its one rocky point, a collection of tidepools harboring a miniature submarine world. Just to the south of the curving beach a little dirt road had crawled between the bluffs and the sea, dotted with occasional outhouses and communal water faucets, and it had been along this stretch that most of our camps had been made.

When we reached the site of the beach, I pulled to the shoulder of the road and stopped, glaring balefully at another outraged memory. The little terraced bluff overlooking the beach had once harbored a collection of summer tents; now it harbored a collection of summer homes for the rich folks. The little road that led down to the beach—asphalt now—was chained off. Private Road. No Trespassing. Gone was the two-bit general store near the highway. Gone was the withering kelp on the beach, which glistened now as if it had been laundered. Gone was anything I could fix my memory on, except the sea itself.

"Well, hell," I said. "It ain't fair."

"*Life* is not fair," she reminded me.

My expectations lay tattered, but I have always been a stubborn type. I pulled back to the road for yet another guidepost: Dana Point, a thrust of land that had been the most awesome Presence in this childhood landscape, an Olympus whose mute bulk I had had the temerity to challenge once and only once. They couldn't have destroyed Dana Point, I reasoned—it was just too damned big.

They hadn't. As we topped the slope above Salt Creek Beach, the point came into view about two miles south of us, probing into the sea like an inquisitive finger. In some lights and times of day, I knew, it would at this distance appear gray-blue against the darker ocean, as vague and transient to the eye as the wisps of a dream. This day, in this light, it was etched clearly, crowned by a tonsure of iceplant and sea grass; below that, it tumbled toward the sea in a great rush of tan-and-white sandstone. At the foot of the plunging cliff, a single great block of stone stood isolated, collared by breaking waves—testament to where the point had once ended, in some dim epoch.

The point was not as large as I remembered it, but I had expected that. The giants of youth lose stature in middle age. At a height less than 150 feet above the sea, this little mass of land was no match for the looming, primordial slopes of the Big Sur Coast, or parts of the North Coast. Still, it was the largest chunk of anything along this stretch of the South Coast, quite respectable even when robbed of the dimensions of memory. And I knew something now that I had not known in my youth: Dana Point was one of California's earliest and most enduring literary landmarks, for it was on its rim that Richard Henry Dana had stood in the spring of 1834 and tossed dried cowhides to the beach below. Stripped from the backs of tough black Mexican cattle, the hides were as stiff and heavy as sheets of plywood, yet they fluttered and swooped and tumbled in the wind like the autumn leaves of Dana's native New England (where the hides were destined to be made into shoes and boots for the Great Unwashed). On the beach, men retrieved the hides from the sand, put them on their heads, and waded through the surf to waiting longboats, which delivered great stacks of them to the brig *Pilgrim,* bobbing a hundred yards offshore in the uncertain anchorage of Dana Cove. In a brief and eloquent passage, the whole scene had been limned by Dana in *Two Years Before the Mast,* one of the greatest books ever written about the sea.

A few minutes after sighting the point, we pulled into the little parking lot on its top, placed there for the convenience of tourists who wished to gaze out from what had since become a State Historic Landmark. To their further convenience, a little wooden observation tower, complete with ten-cent telescopes, had been erected on the curving rim of the cliff above the cove, perhaps very near to where Dana himself had once stood. I took Joan's hand as we stepped into the observation tower and walked toward its farthest railing; what the hell—a man isn't privileged to present a moment of high drama every day.

The drama was high enough, but someone had been mucking about with the screenplay. There was no cove of curling surf, white sand, and rocks below us. What there was below us was a huge marina under construction. Where the sand and surf had once danced their primeval saraband, a broad expanse of well-packed earth spread over the beach, covering rocks, water, and sand alike with engineered fill. From this massive foundation, large finger piers extended a hundred yards or so out into the water. There was nothing makeshift or impermanent about them; they appeared to be made of concrete, probably poured right down to the floor of the cove. Farther out, beyond the fill and the piers, a long rock-fill breakwater was tacked on to the tip of the point. Behind this breakwater the cove was as still and peaceful as a pond in a meadow. On the big fill itself, scabrous yellow earth-moving equipment —bulldozers, graders, and the like—scuttled over the ground like beetles, their gutteral grunts and roars washing up the slope of the cliff and obliterating the sound of wind and water.

I expressed myself in one four-letter word as eloquent as it was inadequate. Joan took my arm without saying anything. We did not yet know each other too well, but she knew that time had pierced me. I knew her well enough to know that she was saying she understood, but of course she did not. How could she? I was not sure myself why I felt suddenly hollow, stripped of certitudes. I suppose it may have been that all those things in which I had expressed belief for a long period of time had finally touched me personally and made me feel, as well as know, what I believed. Imagine a man believing in miracles all his life and finally being privileged to witness one; or a man knowing that death could be ugly, then watching his best friend ripped up the middle by a land mine in a moist Vietnam jungle.

For years, I had written about man and his assault on the land, about the threat to the fragility of life—all life. I had written about the cutover stands of redwood trees, dead and dying fish, deserts guttered by motorcycles and fourwheel drive vehicles, overdeveloped coastal regions, dammed rivers, poisoned bays, disappearing wilderness areas, mismanaged national forests, overcrowded national parks, potential urban parks bargained away to the speculator's itch. First-rate polemic, all of it, I liked to think, well-reasoned, to the point, and written out of conviction.

Yet much of it was done in the style a good reporter brings to his work: just enough involvement to make the writing interesting, the rest a matter of figures, interviews, balanced speculations, and information organized to a logical conclusion. Nothing had raked across my personal nerve ends enough to abandon the detachment necessary to a good job of work. My mind had been geared to the inarguable intellectual precept that time was running out for man and the land he called home. But my heart had not found a home for anger, or even understanding. Now it had, for I had been robbed—me, personally—of my memories. Those blind and possibly uncontrollable forces against which I had pitted my skills with such detached energy had *gotten* me.

When a man says he was stricken with the inspiration for a book in a single moment, or out of a single experience, he is probably lying; books are neither conceived nor made that easily. Yet I think I knew, standing on the rim above concretized Dana Cove, that someday, somehow there would have to be a book. Not a book of polemics or lamentations, but a book that honored what the coast had given me when it was the homeland of my youth, and what those parts of it that remained still gave to me.

But the book was tomorrow. I still had today to deal with. We returned to the car and sped off down the Coast Highway, past Doheny Beach State Park, past Capistrano Beach, and on into San Clemente, which as a kind of mild antidote to Dana Point had neither disappeared nor been entirely remodeled. With the exception of two or three additional motels, a little more neon, a shopping center, and the San Diego Freeway, which sliced through the eastern fringe of the town,

San Clemente had not succumbed to the fever of growth as near as I could tell. The same four-story hotel was still the tallest building in town; the same theatre still advertised the same kind of fifth-run movie; the same hamburger stand, I was sure, still served the same cardboard hamburgers and chalky malts (with an inflated price, of course). Not even the vague presence of the President in his western White House had apparently been enough to shake the town out of its seaside torpor.

Between the southern edge of the town and San Clemente Beach State Park, a few miles down the road, the freeway was the dominant presence. The state park was the last card in my inadequate deck, and as we turned off the freeway onto the little road that led down a deep gully to the beach, I was relieved to see that it was not even as crowded as it sometimes had been in my youth. Nor had it changed appreciably. The parking area was still gravelled dirt, the little rest rooms still reeked of stale urine and a generation of wet bathing suits, and you still had to tiptoe gingerly across the tracks of the Santa Fe Railroad to make your way down to the beach, which edged some of the finest swimming surf in the world.

I turned to the waves, then, my first love, and waded through the troughs and the boiling surf of dying combers. Then I reached the cresting point, and reaching back into the experience of childhood, like a man jumping onto a bicycle after an absence of twenty years, I timed a large curling wave and dove under it, hearing the tumbling roar of its breaking just as I sliced into its fat base.

Coming up from that first wave was like a rebirth, a tiny triumph in a day of defeats. The joy and the release were not gone, nor was the challenge of knowing I was dealing with an element that could kill me. These were waves to be reckoned with—five, six, as much as eight feet from base to crest, with the power to stun the senses with awe, and sometimes honest terror. Yet, with the calculated abandon, if not the stamina, of my boyhood, I let the surf batter me mindless for God only knows how long, straining, diving, letting the waves carry my arched body like a pudgy surfboard, returning to do it again, miscalculating and being slammed into the sand with the force of a Mack truck. When I finally stepped out of the surf, spent, the sun had dipped several degrees and the northward-moving currents, which I had forgotten, had carried me more than a half a mile from where I had started. One shoulder was scraped raw by sand, and I could feel the sun stinging my back as I trudged down the beach. I knew I would be sore and miserable all night, and cursed myself for a middle-aged idiot. But for all my exhaustion and pain, my walk back to where Joan sat, one hand shading her eyes in search of me, was a parade of celebration. For a while, for a brief while, I had been privileged to experience again the outlines of my life. For an hour or so, I had indeed been home.

Peter Carr

---

from **ANTHEM: ALISO CREEK**

Peter Carr was born in Pasadena in 1925. He received his PhD at USC
and went on to teach at CSU Long Beach, where he helped establish the
comparative literature department. A poet, painter, teacher, and activist,
Carr lived above Aliso Creek, which flows into the Pacific from the Santa Ana
Mountains. A cofounder of the grassroots antinuclear Alliance for Survival,
he died in 1981 after completing a project of collecting oral histories from
American peace and disarmament activists from across the country.

What follows is a self-published prose poem, an "anthem" of love and
despair for the region and its diminished ecology, and an homage to its
indigenous pre-Columbian residents written from alternating perspectives:
a contemporary viewer, teenage lovers, and a sailor voyaging with explorer
Juan Cabrillo. The original 1974 chapbook was part of a series he called
"The Discovery of California," and it includes Carr's pen-and-ink drawings,
which are stylistically and politically suggestive of the tradition of poet-
illustrators Kenneth Patchen and Lawrence Ferlinghetti.

EVERYBODY KNOWS THAT nobody wants peace. Everybody knows
that everybody wants excitement and glory. Even everybody down
here by the beach wants to get out of a stupid dull existence. And
everybody knows that the best way to do any of all this is with a lot of
money. The American system is about this.

Everybody says thoughts to people; people talk to people now that
the rains have come again. They are scared of the government and runoff. High tides are dangerous. Death could happen. In the absence of
official doctrine, in the light of liberty and justice for all, in the orange

glare of color TV, everybody clings to scraps of paper in pants pockets, well-creased ends of torn envelopes with the words of the President written on them, "Everything is going to be OK."

The big brown slime wipes across L.A.

Everybody watches on the tube as the planet slides into the galaxy bearing too-brief lives and much death where all this is needed by God for His Big Plan which sounds Groovy and about as Big a Thing as anyone has ever thought of.

There will come too much rain. I know it. All the hills about L.A. and even now where Salt Creek used to be that they chop and carve and burn will sink and slide slowly into the ocean. All the beautiful land will go down the rivers with all the wrecked cars, boards, plumbing fixtures, styrofoam cups, cigarette ends, and the poisonous wastes of pill-supported lives.

The fumes rise every day to greet the sun. The people do too. They say how are yuh? Maybe I won't have to go to work today. Maybe school will be closed.

Before I came up this coast looking for money like all the other white Christian Europeans, I had devoted my life to money and enjoyment like all other white European Christians back in holy Spain. I hoped to strike it rich and moral like Henry Ford or T.A. Edison. As we were sailing along I said to Juan, Juan Cabrillo that is, look Juan, when we get there God will be on our side as usual, but in case something goes wrong we had better take some priests along. He did what I told him and we all got rich. My brother-in-law got a land-grant and they named a town, a lot of streets and a university after him. He was good and he was rich and he owned everything after the Indians were killed off. His name was Irvine.

Mission San Juan Capistrano is no longer a cattle ranch and a jail. They sell weddings there instead of pigeon food, and they charge you fifty cents to get in.

The two main features of once-holy Aliso Canyon are a golf course and a sewage disposal plant.

The rock off the coast where the spirits spoke to men is now private, of course, and is the main feature of a trailer park called Treasure Island. Across the highway is another feature—Alpha Beta Market and shopping center.

Shall I tell the truth? Am I safe enough to say it? That violence washes down the streets of the L.A. basin and finally ends up here at the sea, banging on their fancy houses by the beach where they keep everybody out who is inferior—everybody who is less than white, sun-browned, dangerous to other humans and the planet.

Can I say it in public? Can I say what happened to the cliffs where the Spaniards threw hides to the first white predators on my coastline here—where sea-otters and seals and whales and abalones lived and the men and women worshipped and played and fucked and died to the whistle of cold winds over sun-bleached sands—where the popeyed flounders groped for sea-bugs and the crayfish died their countless numberless deaths and birth into piles of seashell and skeleton?

What happened?

Jack-in-the-Box.

A boy and girl squeeze each other on the beach where the ocean breaks and slides to a stop on the sand. He is wearing a red sweater and cords. He's got his hand on her ass (in her back pocket where the sun is). Her face pushes and rubs him on the mouth while the foam, while the salty ocean ride swells up and fragments, runs, and pours up over the black mussel shoals, wakes up all the barnacles, erects their little tongues—the stones are hard and shiny and her face is chapped. She squeals and chases gulls, knowing he stalks her, that he'll make it soon back on the blanket, in the car, over in heaven, while the sea does its work, endlessly. Do it now. Do it now. Don't wait. The winter sea will take the sand away or they will walk upon the beach and see you; someone will watch and disapprove and you'll be gone, gone wherever girls and boys go, endlessly.

The orange peel will dissolve. The salt water will rub it against the rocks and sand and make it smooth out into nothing. I won't be able to see it happen, but all the cells it's made of that are so small will feed all the bellies of all the unseen individual animals that live in the sea and become food for the fishes. That small boy over there by the rocks (he's cute and blond and is fiercely loved by his father) doesn't know about all this, and so he gouges the life out of a sea-anemone with a sharp stick.

Several miles down the shore the Edison Co., with the inevitability of the sun, moves toward more power.

Firoozeh Dumas

BIENVENIDOS A NEWPORT BEACH

Firoozeh Dumas was born in 1965 in Abadan, Iran. In 1972 her family moved to Southern California, and they eventually settled in Newport Beach, where her parents still live. She attended UC Berkeley and has published two best-selling memoirs, *Funny in Farsi,* a 2004 finalist for the PEN Center USA Literary Award, and *Laughing Without an Accent* (2008). Her work has appeared in the *New York Times*, the *Los Angeles Times*, and the *Wall Street Journal,* among other publications. Her novel for middle-grade children, *It Ain't So Awful, Falafel*, was published in 2016.

In *"Bienvenidos a* Newport Beach," which first appeared in *My California: Journeys by Great Writers* (2004), Dumas recounts with characteristic humor her family's transition from working-class Whittier to the upper-class enclave of Newport Beach.

W HEN I WAS eleven years old, my father came home and announced that we would soon be moving to Newport Beach. I had never heard of the place but when I told the news to the kids at school, they all said, "Ooooh! You must be rich!"

Our rental in Whittier had a view of the busy main street that I was never allowed to cross by myself, not that I ever wanted to. From our living room window, we could see the big Kentucky Fried Chicken bucket that was always lit up at night. We could also see the Taco Bell and Wienerschnitzel signs. My mom and I had tried a taco once at Taco Bell and really liked it but we had never tried anything at Wienerschnitzel. We never even learned how to pronounce the name. My parents just called it "The Dog Place." We knew there were no dogs in their food but it just seemed like a risk we weren't willing to take.

Our move to Newport Beach would be our eighth. I had started out in Abadan, Iran, where for six blissful years I lived in the same house. That was the last time I lived in one place for that long.

I was sick of moving and always being the new kid but I really wasn't very fond of our home in Whittier. The neighbors had two dogs that always pooped on our front lawn and when we had asked them to please not let their dogs do that, they had used some four-letter words. My dad didn't know what the words meant exactly, but sometimes you don't need to know the meaning of words to understand the message.

Our other neighbors had a couple of junk cars on their front lawns that were really ugly. Of course, you can do whatever you want with your lawn but putting rusty junkers with no tires on them is just wrong. I don't know why they even kept them. It's not like they were plants that could one day sprout back to life.

Our new rental in Newport Beach was in a "planned community." All the houses looked alike and were maintained by an "Association." This meant that if you wanted to paint your front door fuchsia, you were out of luck. The exterior of your house and all the lawns belonged to the Association. You could do whatever you wanted with the inside, but the outside had to look like everyone else's. When it was time to repaint the exterior of the homes, the Association would have many meetings and then the members would vote. Would it be painted egg-shell, off-white, fawn, or ecru? The Association decided.

There were also rules pertaining to trash. Only standard trashcans with lids were allowed. You could not put out your trash more than twenty-four hours in advance, nor could you leave the empty cans out there once the trash had been emptied. You also had to keep your garage door closed. And no cars were allowed to park overnight on the street and it goes without saying that none were allowed on the lawn. But, then again, there were no junkers in Newport Beach, only Cadillacs and other expensive-looking cars. It's funny how people with expensive cars, those cars you wouldn't mind looking at if the owners actually did park them on your front lawn, those owners always put their cars away at night. The uglier the car, the more the owner is willing to share it with the rest of the world.

There were lots of rules for dog owners. They were asked to clean up after their dogs, and most did, thank goodness! Nothing like having to clean someone's doggie souvenirs to make you want to kiss the hand of responsible dog owners.

We felt like we had landed in heaven. Every day when he came home, my dad said he felt like he was on vacation.

What made it seem like a vacation was the pool. For every dozen streets or so, there was a pool. It came with so many rules that there was a whole pamphlet just about the pool rules. Our landlady had mentioned it to us several times, each time TALKING VERY LOUDLY AND S-L-O-W-L-Y.

We had two pool keys and they cost one hundred dollars each to replace. We never lost ours. Lord knows there was more of a chance of my parents losing me in Fashion Island shopping center than them ever losing those pool keys. My mother kept one key hidden at all times. We attached a Universal Studios key chain to the other one and we always kept it in the top drawer in the kitchen. One time two of my cousin's wife's relatives, Touraj and Jamshid, came over and forgot to put the key back in the drawer. I hated having visitors all the time but that's what happens when you move to Newport Beach. Turns out one of them had left the key in the pocket of his terry cloth bathing suit cover. Hadn't they noticed that no one wore those kinds of cover-ups in Newport Beach? It was bad enough that they wore Speedos, which absolutely no one wore. If you asked a man in Newport Beach, "Would you rather die or wear a Speedo?" the answer was obvious. My cousins wondered why none of the cute Kahleefornia girls paid any attention to them.

The pool hours were 7 A.M. to 10 P.M. No loud music. No glass. No unaccompanied guests. We let Touraj and Jamshid go by themselves since frankly, I would not be caught dead with them. They had so much body hair. It was like the Missing Link and his twin were visiting us and using our pool. No way did I want to claim any relationship to those two. Keep the neighbors guessing, I figured.

Of course, if you wanted to have a party, you had to tell the Association, but we never had a party. Iranians don't have pool parties. We have indoor parties where women wear a lot of jewelry and make-up and the men wear suits and talk to other men. Even if we had a pool party, people would still dress the same. We don't do casual pool attire.

I used that pool more than anybody else did in that entire neighborhood. Sometimes you have to live in a house facing the Kentucky Fried Chicken bucket before you can appreciate a clean pool. Every so often, the neighborhood kids threw the pool furniture into the pool at night and ruined it, and then the Association had to take money from the budget to replace the furniture. My father said this is what happens when a person has never been hungry. I had never been hungry but I had never wanted to throw patio furniture into a pool.

All the streets in our planned community had Spanish names starting with "Vista" meaning "view of" in Spanish. This was really wishful thinking since the homes mainly had views of the other houses that looked just like them. There was Vista Suerte, which means View of Luck. I guess you were lucky to have that view instead of a clunker on the neighbor's lawn. There was Vista del Oro, view of gold. I think that referred to real estate prices. My favorite was Vista Roma, view of Rome. That street overlooked the elementary school parking lot. I don't know how you say "elementary school parking lot" in Spanish but I'm sure Roma sounds nicer.

You'd think with all the Spanish names there would be a few people speaking Spanish here and there. Twice a week, the Spanish-speaking gardeners came riding in the back of pickup trucks. They'd mow and blow, trim the hedges, cut overgrown branches and look in the houses whenever they could. Who could blame them? I'd be curious, too. Heck, if I were one of the gardeners, I'd bring binoculars.

A couple times a year, the Mexican gardeners would replant the flowers. Corner houses always had a semi-circle of flowers in front of their lawns. The Association decided what to plant. You never saw old flowers in Newport Beach; they were always replaced before they got old. The old people in Newport Beach didn't look so old either. They were always exercising. You'd go to the grocery store and see everyone in tennis clothes. "They're always half-naked," my parents used to say.

We didn't look like anybody in our neighborhood. We looked like the gardeners. I think the gardeners knew that too because they always looked at me kind of funny. It was like they wanted to know how I got in the house.

Every once in a while, one of the neighbors would ask me to please tell that gardener over there that he forgot to trim the hedge on this side. When I'd say I didn't speak Spanish, they were so shocked!

My parents still live in the same house they bought when I was in seventh grade. They have never lost their pool key. The exterior of their house was recently painted Navajo white.

Yusef Komunyakaa

NEWPORT BEACH, 1979

Yusef Komunyakaa was born in Bogalusa, Louisiana, in 1947. He served in the US Army in Vietnam and worked on the army newspaper *Southern Cross* there. Upon his return, he began writing poetry. He studied at the University of Colorado at Colorado Springs, at Colorado State University, and at UC Irvine, earning a BA, MA, and MFA, respectively. He has published more than a dozen books, including *Neon Vernacular*, for which he was awarded the Pulitzer Prize and the Kingsley Tufts Poetry Award in 1994. He teaches at New York University.

Komunyakaa wrote "Newport Beach, 1979" while a student at UC Irvine. The poem is taken from *Copacetic*, the 1984 collection that first garnered the poet wide attention.

> To them I'm just a crazy nigger
> out watching the ocean
> drag in silvery nets of sunfish,
> dancing against God's spine—
> if He's earth, if He's a hunk of celestial bone,
> if He's real as Superman
> holding up the San Andreas Fault.
>
> Now look, Miss Baby Blue Bikini,
> don't get me wrong.
> I'm not the Redlight Bandit,
> not Mack the Knife, or Legs Diamond
> risen from the dead

in a speak-easy of magenta sunsets perpetually
overshadowing nervous breakdowns.

I'm just here where first-degree eyes
look at me like loaded dice,
as each day hangs open
in hurting light like my sex
cut away & tied to stalks
of lilies, with nothing else
left to do for fun.

Garrett Hongo

THE PIER

Garrett Hongo was born in Volcano, Hawai`i, in 1951 and grew up on the North Shore of O`ahu and in Los Angeles. He was educated at Pomona College, the University of Michigan, and UC Irvine, where he received an MFA in poetry. His work includes two books of poetry, three anthologies, and his latest collection, *Coral Road*. He is the editor of *The Open Boat: Poems from Asian America*. He currently teaches as a Distinguished Professor of Arts and Sciences at the University of Oregon.

He told us that his poem "The Pier" was written in the aftermath of his father's unexpected death in 1984, while Hongo lived in a small rental on the Balboa Peninsula of Newport Beach and taught at UC Irvine. On his way to the university, he sometimes passed workers gathered in the shade under a tree on the bluff in Costa Mesa, queuing up for the daily stream of pickups, panel trucks, and vans looking for day and hourly laborers. He recalled to us "a matron driving a pearlescent white luxury sedan, likely a Lexus, passing them slowly by one morning, then speeding away, as she must have changed her mind, disappointment on the faces of all the workers."

In winter, those first mornings after my father died,
I'd get out of the apartment and take walks
along the boardwalk while the wind scuffed
over low dunes on the deserted beach
and skipped trash through alleyways
I walked through on my way to the pier.
Coastal fog would sometimes shroud everything—
the few motels, small cottages miscellaneous in design,
the Bauhaus beachshack absurd with its concrete stilts

and assortment of cutout windows and color panels
like a make-up tray styled by Mondrian—
as if some gray ghost of a manta or skate
had, overnight, chosen this beachtown as its bottom
and settled, wraithlike, over all its weather and dilapidation.
Or, it would have stormed for days,
or a storm would be on its way, the pioneer
or remnant clouds like huge purple swans
gliding across the channel from Catalina
over the choppy aquamarine to the inland plains,
trailing their small skirts of rain and glory
past buzzing power lines flexing in the strong, on-shore wind.
Up on the pier, by the glassed-in lifeguard station,
I'd see couples in ski parkas and peacoats clenched against
                                        each other
while a few gulls hovered overhead, hoarding the wind,
screeching their mild complaints. I'd see fishermen
waddle by burdened with plastic buckets filled with bait
or their poor catch of leopard sharks and Spanish mackerel,
the black, swordlike bracts and blossoms of their tails
drooping like loose bunches of glutinous flowers over the rims.
I had no heart, I felt nothing, could think
only that I didn't believe he'd died
so close to making it through—retirement
just around the two-year corner like a beacon
cutting through the gray present, the best moments
of our friendship, silent as the burst of yellow light
like a brushfire catching in all the windows
up the far, west-facing shore at sunset,
still ahead for us, loomings riding under cloud-cover
a rosy blaze reaching out to small crafts at sea.
I'd see Vietnamese in small, family groups,
or they were Cambodians—Asians as foreign to me
as my grandfathers might have been

to the Yank seaman who stared, stopped
in his climb up the worn rigging of his tall ship,
as they tramped in wooden clogs off the *City of Tokio*
and down the "China Bridge," a long, wooden plank,
over marshy land to the Immigration Station
at Honolulu Bay. They'd be mothering handlines over the railing,
jigging a "Christmas tree" of small, feathered hooks
to catch the baitfish they'd need for the mackerel,
bonito, and flounder cruising the musseled pilings
in the green waters frothing under the pier.
For splendor, for his cheap fun, my father
would go to the track, lose himself in the crowd
milling around the paddock, weighing the odds
against the look of the horse, handicapping,
exchanging tips, rushing the window just before post-time
and rising to his feet for the stretch run,
beating cadence and whipping a gabardine pants leg
in rhythm and chant to the jockey's ride.
I think splendor must be something of what we all want
somehow, respite from privation and a world
of diminishment, a small drama so strange
it exiles the common yet thrills us with our own stories:
the mother, having lost her child, who sees,
through reeds on the riverbank, a glimpse
of the boy her child might have become,
and then herself is swept away in the river's next flooding;
the drunk who constructs, in a series of baroque fantasies,
the fabulous mansion with its Moroccan pool
surrounded by wrought-iron gates and fences, magnificently Byzantine,
while he lives out his life on the edge of a junkyard
by the drive-in, in the hulk of an abandoned automobile;
or, the poor painter who steps out from behind a woodpile
after chapel one day to denounce his younger brother,
himself a master of religious painting,

accusing him of pride and falsity, destroying his brother's faith,
gaining a small advantage and the impermanent rise of his own
                                                        reputation;
or, my favorite, the young voluptuary, frigid in her marriage bed,
who flees on a winter's night through barren woods,
escaping her peasant husband, the village, and this life,
stripping nude at riverside and plunging in,
beginning an alabaster, fetal crawl through the roiling
                                         green waters
collapsing in mock pleasure around her as she drowns,
engulfed by the image of a rising moon
breaking up and coming together again
on the slick, mutable surface of the water.
My father believed in what he could imagine for himself—
a set of numbers written like calligraphy on a handicap sheet
that translated into his occasional but regular movements
through a world made beautiful by his own need
for that beauty and its sequence of splendid events,
desire that metamorphosed into scenario after scenario
and their ritual demarcations—swans gliding
on the infield pond while a trumpet blared its call—
while that other world went on with its load of pain,
its twelvescore of humiliations and ridicule.
These immigrants, on workdays, line a certain street
up in Costa Mesa on the bluff, stationing themselves
like whores at a bus stop, while cars cruise by,
suburban wagons and Euro-sedans, housewives at the wheel,
picking and choosing their day-domestics
from the lineup of illegals and boat people
begging for work, grinning at each electric window
as cars drive up, stop, and a matron leans out,
negotiates a price, opening a back door
and waving them in, or else demurs, passing all of them by,
gliding along in her polished, nearly perfect world.

Robert Peters

_____

HOWARD WARNER
(HUNTINGTON BEACH ARTIST)

Born and raised in Wisconsin, Robert Peters was a poet, memoirist, performance artist, scholar, and professor of English at UC Irvine. His life as a
creative writer began with the death of his young son and coincided with
Southern California's regional poetry renaissance in the 1970s, which he
added to as a participant and also documented as editor of the landmark
anthology series *The Great American Poetry Bake-Off*. His memoir *Crunch-
ing Gravel* tells the remarkable story of his harsh childhood on a farm in the
years before his military service, education in Victorian literature, marriage,
and experience as a father.

In this poem, Peters, who lived until age eighty-nine, considers the final
days of acclaimed Huntington Beach photographer and longtime Golden
West College fine arts professor Howard Warner, who shot thousands of
photographs from the city's iconic pier.

> with one good eye
> reading is problematic
> and since the other bed is empty
> there is no one there until we visit him
>
> his arms are shriveled
> he must be guided to the shower
> he can't comb his hair
>
> nurses reposition him
> punctuating the hours

when we say goodbye
he's comatose
he won't shake hands

the lifeguards and surfers he photographed should
assist his transition

but we see no footprints
only the gull moans on the beach

Kem Nunn

---

from *TAPPING THE SOURCE*

A third-generation Californian, Kem Nunn was born in 1948 and grew up in Pomona. He received an MFA in creative writing from UC Irvine and is the author of the novels *Unassigned Territory, Pomona Queen, The Dogs of Winter, Tijuana Straits,* and *Chance,* as well as *Tapping the Source*, his first book, excerpted here. A surfer and magazine and television writer, he collaborated with producer David Milch on the HBO western series *Deadwood*. Milch and Nunn also cocreated the HBO series *John from Cincinnati*, set in Imperial Beach in San Diego County.

Nunn is responsible for that distinctly Southern Californian literary innovation known as the surf noir novel. Published in 1984, *Tapping the Source* takes place in the then seedy downtown of 1970s Huntington Beach, a fitting backdrop for a gritty story featuring a biker gang and a young man searching for his missing sister. In this modern mystery classic, the reader and Nunn's hero, Ike, are introduced to the protocol-heavy world of the Orange County surf scene.

THE BEACH WAS crowded, the sun bright, but the breeze at his back was cool, and as he stood in the wet sand and felt the Pacific Ocean touch his feet for the first time, sending ribbons of coldness up his legs, he began to see why many of the surfers wore wet suits. Still, he did not hesitate. He had this feeling that every person on the beach was watching. He waded into the white water, stepped almost at once into some kind of hole and felt his nuts shrivel as the water rushed past his waist. He pulled himself onto his board and began to paddle.

It didn't take him long to discover that waves which looked small from the pier got much bigger when you were looking at them from sea level. Getting out was harder than he had expected. For one thing, he kept sliding off the fucking board. He was trying to paddle as he had seen the others do, stroking one arm at a time, but just when he would get himself going in a straight line, a wall of white water would hit him, knock the board sideways, and he would slip off and have to start all over again. His arms and shoulders tired quickly, and when he turned back to the beach to see what kind of progress he was making, it appeared he was no farther out than when he had started.

The point at which the waves rose in smooth hills was growing more elusive by the moment. Still, he kept digging away, his breath coming harder, his strokes becoming weaker. Suddenly, however, the ocean seemed to smooth out, to spread itself in front of him like a huge lake. He dug in for all he was worth and before long he was bobbing with the other surfers in the lineup.

His face tingled from the exertion and his lungs ached. Other surfers sat straddling their boards, looking toward the horizon. Some regarded him with what seemed a quizzical eye. It was amazing how different things were out here compared with what it was like inside. It was peaceful and smooth, the way he had imagined it. A gentle ground swell lifted and lowered them. A pelican flew nearby, skimming the surface of the water. A gull cried above him and the sunlight moved on the water. In the distance he could make out the white flecks of sails and the colors on the distant cliffs of the island.

He tried sitting up and straddling the board the way most of the other surfers were doing. His, however, seemed to tip drastically at the slightest movement. He fell off twice, making loud splashes and drawing looks from those sitting closest to him.

Suddenly, from all along the line of surfers, he began to hear hoots and whistles. He looked outside to see a new group of waves rolling up into long smooth lines. These waves seemed much bigger to him than the others. He struck out for the horizon, paddling now out of fear, afraid the waves would break on top of him, that he would lose his board; he felt too tired out and cold to swim for it. The first wave reached him. He paddled up the face, popped over the crest only to see a second wave even larger than the first rolling toward him. He dug in once more, paddling with arms gone to rubber. To his left and slightly ahead of him another surfer suddenly stopped paddling and swung his board around, pointing it back toward the beach. Ike didn't know what to do. Not only was he apparently going to be hit by the wave, the other guy was now sliding down the face straight toward him.

At the last second, just as the wave was beginning to lift his board, he tried swinging it around, too. Out of the rush and spray of exploding white water, he heard the other surfer yell. Somehow he'd gotten caught sideways in the top of the wave and he was going over.

He came up gasping for air, his arms flailing about him. He was sure his board had gone into the beach, but when he looked over his shoulder he saw it floating only a few yards behind him. How that had happened was a mystery, but he was greatly relieved and began to swim toward it. As he reached the board he noticed the other surfer paddling toward him, the same guy he'd been caught in the wave with.

Ike clung to the side of his board. Maybe the other guy was checking to see if he was all right. He tried to muster some kind of grin but his face felt cold and numb and then he got a good look at the surfer's face and realized something was very wrong. He tried to say something, but he never got the chance. He'd no sooner opened his mouth than the guy hit him. The other surfer was lying on the deck of his board, so the punch didn't have a lot of leverage but it stung anyway. Ike tried to pull himself up on his board, but the guy was punching at him again. One punch landed on Ike's shoulder, another caught him flush on the ear. Everything seemed to be happening at once. He was disoriented from his spill, the cold water seemed to swim in his head, the other surfer was everywhere. Later, when Ike tried to remember exactly what the guy had looked like, it was all just a blur, a red face, white fists, the pain in his ear. And then a wave rescued him. A wall of white water caught him and swept him toward the beach. The board tipped over again, but he hung on. When he resurfaced, he found himself practically on the beach and the other surfer gone.

Morris put him to work in the afternoons, leaving his mornings free to surf. They spent the first few days on the Shovel. The work and getting along with Morris required concentration and by nightfall he was beat. He went home tired and slept. He had looked forward to talking some more with Preston, but the week passed and Preston did not come around. Toward the middle of the second week he began to worry once more.

There was more work and he spent his afternoons staring into the oversize valves of Shovelheads and Panheads, laboring over Fat Bob tanks with Morris's new Badger airbrush, leaving in his wake a rainbow of imron cobwebbing, pearl-silver lace, and candy-blue flames. Mornings were still spent in the water. But he was thinking about time now—two weeks since he'd talked to Preston in his room, a month in town and he still did not even know what Hound Adams, Frank Baker, or Terry Jacobs looked like. He had told Preston he would keep his mouth shut, but now—nothing was happening. It was getting harder to think about the work. He needed another break. And then came the fifth week—twenty-nine days since he'd stood on the gravel at the edge of the road and said good-bye to Gordon. It was the fifth week that brought the swell.

It began with the sound, a distant thunder repeating itself at regular intervals somewhere beyond the hum of the highway, waking him in the night so that he turned for a moment to listen, to wonder, before slipping back into sleep. But in the morning, when the sound was still there, louder than before in the first gray light, he did not have to wonder again. He pulled on his clothes and ran from the room, down the wooden stairs and across the lawn, past the oil well and down the alley, south on Main so he was running toward the ocean and he could see the white water even before he crossed the highway.

The first thing that struck him about the swell was how different it made everything look. He might have been in another town, on a different pier, staring out at a stretch of beach he had never seen before.

The waves did not just rise up out of the ocean in rolling lines, as they normally did. These seemed to come in off the horizon, as if they had marched the whole breadth of the Pacific to pound this stretch of beach. The surface was angry, gray and black, streaked with white. Paddling out appeared an impossibility. The first fifty yards of water looked as if it had been poured from a washing machine. Flecks of foam lay across the wet sand like snowdrifts. As he ran onto the boardwalk, the whole structure seemed to shudder beneath him with each new wave.

He was alone with the swell. Far down the beach he could see the yellow Jeep of the lifeguards. The morning was still and gray, the sun wrapped in a heavy overcast. He walked farther out onto the pier, and that was when he saw them; he wasn't alone after all. At first he couldn't believe it; no one could have gotten outside in this kind of surf. He ran farther. He lost track of them, then found them again. There was no doubt about it. He picked out one, then two more, a fourth and a fifth. The size of the swell made them hard to see. At times they disappeared completely behind the waves. He gripped the rail, damp with spray beneath his hands. They were out there, but as yet, he was pretty sure there had been no rides.

He was nearly even with them now and could see them more clearly: six surfers on the south side of the pier. They stayed together, darting about like a school of fish, apparently trying to get themselves set up amid the huge swells. Occasionally one of them would look as if he were going to take off, only to pull back at the last moment, allowing the wave to peak and pour over, to thunder on through the pier and toward the beach unridden.

The surfers seemed to be having a hard time getting themselves in position. Wave after wave passed them, lifted them and hid them, threw curtains of spray twenty feet in the air as it wrapped around the pilings. And each new set seemed to come from farther outside, forcing them to paddle out farther. Ike was wondering if any of them would be able to take off at all when he noticed one surfer paddling again just ahead of a mountain of gray water. He was paddling hard. The board began to rise, lifted on the wave. And suddenly the surfer was on his feet. It was hard to say how high the waves actually were, but the crest of this one was well over the surfer's head.

The rider sped down the face, drove off the bottom in a powerful turn that sent water spraying in a wide arc from the tail of his board. He drove back up into the face, was nearly covered by a rapidly peeling section. Then he was out of the tunnel, high on the lip, working his board in small rapid turns, racing the wave toward the pier. And then it was over, he had driven through the lip at the last second, just before it met the piling. For a moment Ike lost him in the spray and then he saw him again, flat on his board, paddling hard for the horizon.

By the time the sun had burnt its way through the overcast, there were maybe another half-dozen surfers in the water. They made it outside by staying on the north side of the pier, using the pilings to help shield them from the swell that was moving in from the south. Still, it was risky and Ike saw more than one surfer turned back, more than one board broken on the pilings.

Though few went into the water, many came to watch, and soon the railings were lined with a noisy cheering crowd. The people hooted and cheered for rides. Ike soon found himself cheering along with them. There were cameras set up along the pier now too, a dozen of them, some manned by crews in matching T-shirts that advertised various surf shops and board manufacturers. There were more cameras on the beach, and more spectators, more yellow Jeeps, so that by late morning a kind of circus atmosphere had taken over that strip of the town which huddled about the pier and lined the white strip of sand.

Ike saw the blond-haired surfer, the same he'd seen get the first wave, time and again getting spectacular rides, which drew cheers from the crowd. He had been watching for perhaps an hour when a familiar voice took his attention away from the surf. He turned and found Preston behind him. He was wearing that grimy tank top and the old red bandanna. He looked out of place among the camera crews and surfers who lined the pier. It was a crowd of sun-streaked hair and clean limbs. Preston, with his huge tattooed arms and square upper body, looked more like an extension of the machine gleaming between his legs. The aviator shades were flashing in the sunlight, so that Ike couldn't see his eyes, but his mouth was bent into a large shit-eating grin, as if there was some joke in progress of which Ike was not aware, of which, perhaps, he was the butt. "Thought I told you to leave town," Preston said. Ike felt himself grinning back, not sure about what to say, but glad that Preston had shown up. He supposed that since he'd come to Huntington Beach, Preston was the closest thing to a friend he had. Preston knew why he had come, and that created a link between them, at least in Ike's mind.

"It's big," Ike said.

Preston just looked past him at the waves. "First south of the season," he said. "Takes a day like this to get a wave to yourself anymore; the punks can't get out."

"You ever seen it this big before?"

"Sure. Bigger. I've surfed it bigger. But it's a good swell." Ike was suddenly aware of another sound rising now above the din of the crowd and the thunder of the surf. The tower had apparently spotted Preston and the mechanical voice had begun to whine. "No motorcycles allowed on the pier," the voice said. "Please turn your bike around and walk it off the pier." Preston leaned out into the boardwalk and extended his middle finger toward the tower. The voice went on in its tinny fashion: "Please turn your bike around and walk it off the pier."

Preston just shook his head and began to turn the machine around. The spectators nearest them turned to stare but made sure Preston had plenty of room for the maneuver. "Voice of reason," Preston said. "I think there's been one guy in there for about twenty years. It's always sounded like the same voice to me."

Ike looked up at the tinted windows high above the boardwalk. He decided to start back himself and get some breakfast. Still, it was difficult to tear himself away from the railing and he turned back once more toward the ocean—in time to see the surfer he'd been watching get still one more wave. The guy was easy to spot. He was tall and blond and while most of the others wore full wet suits, he wore only a swimsuit and a vest. "That one guy's really good," Ike said, pointing him out to Preston.

"Your hero, huh?" Preston asked, and the grin had given way to a slightly crooked smile. A moment passed while Ike looked out to sea then back at Preston. "Just don't go getting too sweet on him," Preston said. "He's your man. And that other guy"—he waved toward a dark figure in a full black wet suit with what looked to be red stripes down the sides, sitting farther to the south and way outside—"there's another one for you. Terry Jacobs. He's a Samoan, usually the biggest dude out there." Preston thumped at the pier with his heavy boots and began to walk the bike away, back down the center of the boardwalk, the people spreading to let him pass.

Ike went after him. Preston didn't say anything else; he just kept walking the bike through the crowd. When he had gotten down next to the tower he pulled himself up and came down on the stick. The engine didn't catch and he hauled himself up once more. Ike reached out and grabbed his arm. He grabbed him right on the biceps, on top of that coiled serpent, and it was like grabbing hold of a large pipe. Preston let himself back down and looked at his arm, at Ike's hand. He did it real slow and Ike released his grip. He stared into Preston's shades. "Wait a minute," he said. "You can't let it go at that."

Preston just looked at him. "I can't?"

Ike hesitated. "Well, what about them?" he asked at last.

"What do you mean, what about them? That's them, ace. Two of them, anyway. What do you want me to do, swim out there and have a word with them?" Preston kicked hard and the big engine jumped to life. Just above them the speakers had begun another order—something about *walking* the bike off the pier, but the voice was lost in the roar of the engine. A cloud of pale smoke hung in the air and Ike stood in the midst of it, watching Preston.

"Look," Preston yelled at him. "Let's get something straight. I've been thinking about what you told me. You let me think about it some more. In the meantime, do like I told you, keep your story to yourself. If I come up with anything I think you ought to know, I'll tell you. But remember something. This is not your scene. Can you dig that? You don't know what the fuck goes on around here. And one more thing. Don't ever come runnin' up and grabbin' at me like that. I might pinch your fucking head off." With that he popped the big bike's clutch and was off, right down the middle of the boardwalk with pipes blasting and chrome bars burning and people scattering in front of him like leaves in a wind.

James P. Blaylock

---

from *THE LAST COIN*

Born in Long Beach in 1950, James P. Blaylock moved to Anaheim as a child. He graduated from Magnolia High School and attended CSU Fullerton, where he received an MA in literature. A protégé of Philip K. Dick, he has written twenty-five books, including novels, novellas, and story collections. He is an acknowledged innovator in the fantasy and sci-fi genres and is considered by many to be the founder of the steampunk genre. His short story "Unidentified Objects," set in downtown Orange, was nominated for an O. Henry Award, and "Thirteen Phantasms," also set there, was the first digitally published story to win a World Fantasy Award. Blaylock's novel *The Rainy Season* was named by *Orange Coast Magazine* as one of the "10 essential Orange County books." In 2000, he designed the Creative Writing Conservatory at the Orange County School of the Arts, directing the program until 2013. He continues teaching at Chapman University.

In this excerpt from his 1988 novel *The Last Coin,* Blaylock's unlikely hero, an eccentric collector and Seal Beach innkeeper, encounters an enduring local practice that he finds instructive, both metaphorically and morally, as well as especially resonant for someone on whose coin collecting skills the safety of the world may depend. The Seal Beach Naval Weapons Station and Bolsa Chica wetlands ground the narrative of an otherwise magical, fantastical premise.

I T WAS EARLY evening when Andrew drove along the Coast Highway, listening to an odd rattle in the engine of the Metropolitan. He was entirely ignorant of mechanics, happily so. He didn't have time in his life to meddle with it. There were better things to do, any number of them. In fact, he'd been doing some of them that very afternoon. He'd paid a visit to Polsky and Sons liquor importers and distributors on Beach Boulevard in Westminster, and come away with two cases of scotch, four dozen pint glasses, and most of the items on the list he'd made up out of *Grossman*. The trunk and back seat were full of stuff, and he still had the bulk of Aunt Naomi's money in his wallet. He whistled tunelessly and looked out the window.

The warm weather seemed to be passing. The sky was gray out over the Pacific, and the wind had fallen off. Twilight cast long shadows across the weedy marshland ruins of boatyards and clapboard bungalows. He drove past heaps of rusted anchors and piles of painted buoys and what looked like an old concrete bridge, collapsed now and sunk into the shallows of the Bolsa Chica Salt Marsh. The Seal Beach Naval Weapons Station loomed off to the right, a broad expanse of what looked like pastureland and farmland, with here and there in the dim distances a weapons bunker sitting toad-like and ominous between grassy hillocks. There were broad wooden doors in the ends of some of the hillocks, with grass and canteloupe vines growing right in around the jambs. What lay under the grass and vines was a mystery.

He slowed the car, bumping off onto the shoulder. A knot of people stood around in front of the roadside stand that sold strawberries and corn and tomatoes in the spring and summer, and pumpkins in the fall, all of it grown on government property, which wore the fruits and vegetables as a clever disguise. Hinged sheets of plywood had been dropped across the front of the stand to close it up for the night, so the people—a couple of families with children from the look of it—weren't buying anything. They were clearly up to something else. Another carload pulled in directly behind Andrew, and what seemed to be a half-dozen children piled out and went shouting away past his car, a large woman in a wraparound garment climbing ponderously out after them and yelling them into submission.

Andrew followed just for the adventure of it—something that Beams Pickett would approve of. There was a sign posted, advertising, of all things, a treasure hunt. It referred to a companion ad in the *Seal Beach*

Herald, Pickett's newspaper. The newspaper advertisement no doubt explained the carloads of curious people. Treasures were to be buried, the sign said, no end of them, and the public could come dig for them, on the night of Sunday the 24th, by moonlight. Penlights were allowed, nothing bigger than that, though, and the public could keep what it found. There was a diamond ring, it said, in a hermetically sealed glass box, and a glass paperweight in a wooden box, and tickets for two dinners at Sam's Seafood, which weren't, Andrew assumed, in any sort of box at all. There were five hundred children's toys, and a real treasure chest full of quartz crystals and fluorite and bags of rhinestones and glass beads. No maps would be provided. The public would furnish their own spades.

Andrew recalled such a thing from the past. What was it?—almost thirty-five years ago. It had been a fairly common practice in central Orange County, when vast tracts of houses were routing out orange groves and bean fields, and driving up the price of land so that small farmers couldn't afford to keep it. For a time it had been the fashion for farmers to let the populace spade up their acreage for them. They'd bury rolls of pennies and such, and let suburban hordes do a week's worth of work in a night. It had always seemed an unlikely practice to Andrew, although he approved of the notion because of the mystery and romance associated with digging for spurious treasures in a weedy pasture by moonlight. It appealed to his sense of—what? He couldn't quite define it.

He drove away mulling it over. It made a certain amount of sense two score years ago, when hundreds of farmers owned little tracts of land up and down the roads leading south toward the beaches—just a couple of acres or so—and sold roadside produce to wring out a living. But that was all gone years since, and now what farmland was left was owned by vast real estate companies that, in some indefinable way, let out bits of land for farming in order to gain some sort of nebulous tax profits. Nobody "spaded up" the land anymore.

Still, that didn't mean that there was some sort of secret motive in this moonlight-spading business, did it? He'd have to watch that sort of jumping-to-conclusions. It was too easy to raise people's eyebrows. He suspected, somewhere inside him, that Rose "put up with him" sometimes. In the best possible way, she was conventional. There wasn't any more to it than that. She was conventional; he wasn't. His antics made her tired. He knew that, and he wished it weren't so. But they seemed to inhabit different worlds sometimes, different universes. Hers was neatly mapped out. The streets that seemed to run north and south *did* run north and south, seven days a week, and if a farmer planted pumpkins it was simply because Halloween was drawing near and he could sell them at a profit. Andrew's world was cut with streets that angled and twisted. Fogs rolled through at inopportune moments, seeming to hide the shifting landscape. Slouching farmers planted pumpkins so that the crawling vines would cover hillocks beneath which lay unguessed weapons, cleverly hidden from the eyes of satellites sweeping past overhead, themselves veiled by distance.

And although he was certain that he understood her world easily enough, saw through it clearly, he was equally certain that she had little notion of his. She understood him to be simply frivolous, cockeyed for no apparent reason at all. His enthusiasms were a mystery to her, a closed book. At worst he was stark, staring mad, which didn't, he thought as he drove along, particularly bother him. What was far worse was that she thought him childish, with his coffee makers and his books and his paperweights, his preoccupation with beer glasses and breakfast cereal and his odd car, which, she'd once said when she was angry, no grown man had any business driving. But he was deadly serious about it all. Those sorts of things were the threads which knitted up his world. Pulled out one by one and examined, maybe they were foolish and frivolous things, but if you pulled them all out and pitched them into the dumpster, then what was left? Nothing that was worth bothering with. A lot of airy trash fit for the junkman. That was the truth of it, and Rose didn't quite understand it. She pretended to when he tried to explain it, but in her eyes and in her voice there was something that made him feel as if he were six years old, showing his mother his favorite toy. It made him mad just to think about it.

He drove along feeling half-sorry for himself, neglecting to turn his headlights on. He couldn't tell Rose about Pickett's Caretaker nonsense. It would be evidence of something. Lord knows what would have happened if she were to discover that he'd shamelessly talked two thousand dollars out of Aunt Naomi that afternoon, when what he was supposed to be doing was generally smoothing things over. Now he'd promised a French chef and spent a quarter of the money on exotic liquor, and Beams Pickett was on his way to Vancouver to load up the trunk of his Chevrolet with cartons of Weetabix, charging gas to the company credit card, which Rose had insisted he not use unless it were an absolute emergency. He hadn't *wanted* to give Pickett the credit card, but his wallet had been empty. Now it was full, only a few hours later. That's how life went. It was unpredictable. Just when you thought that the way was clear, that the script was written, wham! there was some new confusion, flying in at the window, overturning chairs.

A horn blared and a car swerved out of the lane in front of him. He'd drifted across the line, into oncoming traffic. He jerked the car back into his own lane, his heart hammering. Rose paid attention when she drove. He didn't, it was true. He couldn't argue with her when she pointed it out. The only human being on earth, she said, who drove worse than he was Uncle Arthur, who was ninety-two.

And she had her doubts about his seeing so much of Beams Pickett. Pickett had developed the reputation of believing in plots and threats, and Rose understood, although she never said it, that Andrew had been contaminated. Pickett believed in the theory that what was obvious was probably lies; the truth lay hidden, and you got at it by ignoring what passed as common sense.

Andrew's mind wandered again as he drove along. He thought about their eventful morning, about the 'possum trick and Pickett's suspicions about Mrs. Gummidge. What was true about Pickett was that he was skeptical of skeptics. He had almost hit one that very morning in a cafe near the pier, after the two of them had dumped the 'possum and went fishing. They had had some luck with bonita, keeping at it until after nine in the morning. Then they'd left the fish in a gunnysack in the back of the Metropolitan and gone in for breakfast at the Potholder. A man named Johnson sat at the counter, sopping up egg yolks with a slab of white toast. They knew him from the bookstore, where they'd attended meetings of a literary society for a time.

Johnson saw through everything. There was nothing that would surprise him. He had "no regrets," he had insisted at the literary society in a hearty, chest-slapping tone, and he'd drained his beer glass at a gulp and smacked his lips. There at the counter at the Potholder he had sat poking at egg yolks and shoving down half a slice of bread without bothering to chew it more than twice. Pickett couldn't stand him, and Andrew could see, as soon as they had walked in through the door, that Pickett was going to go for him straightaway, although what Andrew wanted to do was to nod and sit at the opposite end of the cafe, so as to avoid starting Johnson up. Pickett, braced by four hours of sea air, had wanted to start him up very badly.

Johnson had been reading—old issues of science fiction magazines. He'd come upon an essay that made a hash of Pickett's flying saucer enthusiasm—knocked the pins out from under it, Johnson had said, grinning. He'd nodded at Andrew and motioned down the length of the empty counter. Andrew didn't like sitting at counters. He felt too conspicuous there. But Pickett sat down at once and fingered the menu, grinning at Johnson, who droned along about unidentified flying objects.

"The telling thing," Johnson had said, wiping his face with a napkin, "is that when these things appear, they're always described in the fashion of the day. Do you get me?"

"No," said Pickett.

"I mean to say that a hundred years ago they were a common enough business, weren't they? But they looked like hay wagons, then, with wings and propellers and paddle wheels. I was reading an account of a man in Sioux City, Iowa, who claimed to have seen an airship—this was in 1896, mind you—that was shaped like an Indian canoe with an inflated gasbag above it. It dropped a grappling hook, he said, that caught in the slack of his trousers and dragged him across a cow field." Johnson grinned and laughed to himself, humping up and down with the force of it. He looked sharply at the remaining egg on his plate, as if seeing it for the first time, and then hacked it to bits with the corner of a piece of toast. "A *cow* field!"

"I'm still not certain," said Pickett, "what you mean to say. It's an amusing story, but..."

"Isn't it?" said Johnson, interrupting. "Concentrate, now. It's not difficult to grasp. Really it isn't."

Pickett sat stony-faced.

"You see," said Johnson, waving his toast, "that's how it went in 1896. In 1925 it was the same business, only no canoes by then, no airbags, no propellers. They were those inflated-looking rockets that you see in the pulps. After that it was saucers, and now there's cylindrical ships made of polished metal that go very, very fast. What next? That's the point. It's all fakery, imagination, humbugging. If it weren't, there'd be some consistency to it. That was the crux of this essay, anyway."

"Who wrote it?" asked Pickett, sitting very still and stirring his coffee.

"Asimov. He's hard to argue with. Rock solid logic, from my point of view. Shreds the whole UFO business at a single swipe. What do you think?" He leaned past Pickett to put the question to Andrew.

"Absolutely," said Andrew. "It's a dead issue I should think."

Pickett gaped at Andrew, then turned back to Johnson, heating up. Andrew could see it. Pickett was about to burst. It always happened that way with Johnson. That was why they'd given up the literary society. Pickett would be fired up to have a go at him, and then the conversation would drive him mad, and Johnson would go off grinning, having won.

"Of *course* they keep showing up in different craft," Pickett said. Their breakfasts arrived and Andrew started to eat, but Pickett ignored his. "That's the beauty of it. They don't want to give themselves away, for God's sake. It's a matter of disguise, is what it is. I wouldn't be half-surprised if the aliens who dragged your man across the cow pasture are the same crowd who appeared in the flying egg six years ago over San Francisco. Why not? If they've got the technology to sail in from the stars, then certainly they've got the technology to design any sorts of ships they please. Look at Detroit, for heaven's sake. They can build a truck on Monday and a convertible on Tuesday, just like that. And what's more…"

But Pickett hadn't gotten a chance to finish, for Johnson was suddenly ignoring him, talking to the waitress and paying his bill. He laid a quarter on the counter by way of a tip and then scratched the end of his nose. "Do you know what it was in the airship?" he asked, grinning at Pickett and Andrew.

Pickett blinked at him. "What? What airship?"

"In Iowa—the cow field ship. Pigs. That's what the man said. It was pigs. And they stole his money—a rare coin. That's what he said. I swear it. He was robbed by pigs. Of course, the whole story went to bits, didn't it? It's simple enough. You don't need Sherlock Holmes to piece together the truth. The way I figure it he'd had a run-in with pigs. They were probably out on the road and knocked him into a ditch. That explains how his trousers came to be ruined. And he'd lost money of some sort, probably a silver piece or something, which he shouldn't have had anyway because his wife needed it for groceries. He was on his way to spend it on a bottle, probably. Well, he couldn't just up and admit it, could he? I mean *pigs,* after all. He'd look like a fool. So he made up the story, lock, stock, and barrel: alien pigs, hooks, draggings across cow fields, rare coins. He's a hero, isn't he, and not a fool at all, no longer a poor sod manhandled by pigs." Johnson stopped and squinted at them, nodding his head knowingly. "He lost a pocketful of change in ditch water, that's what I think, and soiled his pants. So he explained it away with the wildest lie he could invent, knowing that the public would go for it. They always do—the wilder the better. But mark me, gentlemen, you can bet that his wife didn't much believe him. Am I right? Yes I am. Right as rain. There isn't a wife alive that isn't ten times as shrewd as the public. What do you think, Andrew?"

Andrew gawked at him, not at all knowing what to make of all this talk about pigs and rare coins. But there was no fathoming Johnson. There was nothing to fathom. Johnson wasn't deep enough. You could see the bottom just by looking into his eyes. "I think," said Andrew, "that if you laid the public out end to end they wouldn't reach from here to Glendale."

"You're a scholar!" shouted Johnson, standing up. "You, too, son," he said to Pickett, and he grabbed Pickett's hand and shook it before Pickett had a chance to snatch it away. "Got to go," he said. "I've got to see a man about a horse. Do you know what I mean? Spaceships—very interesting business all the way around. We'll take this up again."

Pickett started to speak, to get in the last word, to finish what he'd started. "Anyway, as I was saying, convertibles on Tuesday…"

"Yes," Johnson said, setting out. "That's right. Convertibles. Maybe the aliens will be driving convertibles next. Pigs in sunglasses." And with that he giggled and strolled away, letting the glass door slam shut behind him and waving back over his shoulder.

Pickett had left his cold eggs on the counter, Johnson having ruined his appetite. They paid and left, forgetting entirely about the car and the fish and walking the two blocks back to the inn. Andrew tried to bring the subject around to the successful 'possum episode, but his enthusiasm was lost on Pickett, who insisted that he was going to have Johnson killed, that he'd ridicule him in the *Herald,* that before he was done he'd do half a dozen things to ruin the man, to make his life a living hell. That very afternoon, while driving north, he'd compose lovelorn letters in order to publish them in the *Herald* under Johnson's name. "What did you make of the pencil line down the center of his face?" Pickett asked suddenly. "Evidence of insanity, I'd call it."

Andrew shrugged. "Just more of his nonsense. It was best not to ask. He *wanted* you to ask, obviously. He'd probably have had some idiotic explanation prepared, some gag line and we'd be the butt of the joke."

Pickett nodded. "He must have forgotten it, though, if he'd put it there on purpose. Did you see him smear it up with the napkin?"

"He was too fired up about his cow pasture story. You shouldn't work him up so. It doesn't do you any good."

"I'll sell him to the apes," said Pickett, climbing into his Chevrolet. "See you." He started the car up with a roar and drove away toward the

Coast Highway, carrying Andrew's credit card, bound for Vancouver. He'd be gone nearly a week.

It had been the middle of the afternoon when Andrew discovered that he'd left the Metropolitan parked at the pier. He'd jogged back down and opened the trunk. There lay the fish, stiff as papier-mâché ornaments. He had emptied the gunnysack into the dirt of the alley behind Señor Corky's restaurant, and was immediately surrounded by half a dozen cats. He waved goodbye, driving away south to visit Polsky and Sons and feeling generous.

Now here he was, parking the car at the curb, home at last after a hellishly long day. He hadn't gotten around to painting the garage, as he'd intended to, but there'd be time enough tomorrow to tackle it. Haste was never any good. The street was dark, and Aunt Naomi's window was shut against night creatures. Andrew locked up the car. It wouldn't do to start hauling stuff in. He'd wait until Rose went out or went to bed. He'd tell her he'd been to Bellflower to interview student chefs, which wasn't entirely a lie. He'd called the chefs' school, after all, and had gotten the name of a likely graduate, a young Frenchman who had grown up in Long Beach but still had a trace of an accent.

Fog blew in billows now, in between the houses and over rooftops. It would be a good night for some cat sabotage, but he'd probably worked the 'possum angle hard enough already. In fact, he'd been pressing his luck all day long. Maybe he'd go to bed early. That would make Rose happy. It would be evidence that there were traces of sanity left in him. He stepped up onto the front porch, humming, tolerably satisfied with things. Then he jumped in spite of himself to see Pennyman sitting in a rattan chair, smoking his pipe. He looked far too polished and stiff, like a waxwork dummy or a preserved corpse, and it seemed to Andrew as if he had the smell of fish about him, as if he'd been swilling cod liver oil. Pennyman pulled his pipe out of his mouth and pointed at an empty chair. "Sit down," he said.

Charles Wright

LOOKING WEST FROM LAGUNA BEACH AT NIGHT

Born in Tennessee in 1935, Charles Wright attended the Iowa Writers' Workshop and, over the course of his long career, has published poetry, translations, and criticism, including the prizewinning books of poetry *Country Music* and *Black Zodiac*, the latter of which won a Pulitzer Prize in 1988. He taught for nearly twenty years at UC Irvine in its MFA poetry program, and he has served as both poet laureate of the United States and a chancellor of the Academy of American Poets. He is currently the Souder Family Professor of English at the University of Virginia, Charlottesville.

The poem included here is one of a triptych written over the period during which Wright taught at UC Irvine and lived in Laguna Beach. It is from the collection *Chickamauga*, published in 1995.

> I've always liked the view from my mother-in-law's house at night,
> Oil rigs off Long Beach
> Like floating lanterns out in the smog-dark Pacific,
> Stars in the eucalyptus,
> Lights of airplanes arriving from Asia, and town lights
> Littered like broken glass around the bay and back up the hill.
>
> In summer, dance music is borne up
> On the sea winds from the hotel's beach deck far below,
> "Twist and Shout," or "Begin the Beguine."
> It's nice to think that somewhere someone is having a good time,
> And pleasant to picture them down there

Turned out, tipsy and flushed, in their white shorts and their
    turquoise shirts.

Later, I like to sit and look up
At the mythic history of Western civilization,
Pinpricked and clued through the zodiac.
I'd like to be able to name them, say what's what and how who
    got where,
Curry the physics of metamorphosis and its endgame,
But I've spent my life knowing nothing.

Michael Chabon

OCEAN AVENUE

Born in 1963 in Washington, D.C., Michael Chabon published his first novel, *The Mysteries of Pittsburgh,* shortly after graduating from the MFA creative writing program at UC Irvine. Over the course of his celebrated career, he has published two short story collections and eight novels—including *Wonder Boys*, the Pulitzer Prize–winning *Amazing Adventures of Kavalier and Clay*, *The Yiddish Policemen's Union*, and *Telegraph Avenue*—as well as screenplays, children's books, comics, and newspaper serials.

The short story included here first appeared in the *New Yorker* in 1989. Set at the Zinc Café, a downtown Laguna Beach establishment that typified 1980s Orange County yuppiedom, it dramatizes the difficult if hilarious public reunion of a recently separated couple.

IF YOU CAN still see how you could once have loved a person, you are still in love; an extinct love is always wholly incredible. One day not too long ago, in Laguna Beach, California, an architect named Bobby Lazar went downtown to have a cup of coffee at the Café Zinc with his friend Albert Wong and Albert's new wife, Dawn (who had, very sensibly, retained her maiden name). Albert and Dawn were still in that period of total astonishment that follows a wedding, grinning at each other like two people who have survived an air crash without a scratch, touching one another frequently, lucky to be alive. Lazar was not a cynical man and he wished them well, but he had also been lonely for a long time, and their happiness was making him a little sick. Albert had brought along a copy of *Science*, in which he had recently published some work on the String Theory, and it was as Lazar looked up from Al's name and abbreviations in the journal's table of contents that he saw Suzette, in her exercise clothes, coming toward the café from across the street, looking like she weighed about seventy-five pounds.

She was always too thin, though at the time of their closest acquaintance he had thought he liked a woman with bony shoulders. She had a bony back, too, he suddenly remembered, like a marimba, as well as a pointed, bony nose and chin, and she was always—but *always*—on a diet, even though she had a naturally small appetite and danced aerobically or ran five miles every day. Her face looked hollowed and somehow mutated, as do the faces of most women who get too much exercise, but there was a sheen on her brow and a mad, aerobic glimmer in her eye. She'd permed her hair since he last saw her, and it flew out around her head in two square feet of golden Pre-Raphaelite rotini—the lily maid of Astolat on an endorphin high. A friend had once said she was the kind of woman who causes automobile accidents when she walks down the street, and, as a matter of fact, as she stepped up onto the patio of the café, a man passing on his bicycle made the mistake of following her with his eyes for a moment and nearly rode into the open door of a parked car.

"Isn't that Suzette?" Al said. Albert was, as it happened, the only one of his friends after the judgment who refused to behave as though Suzette had never existed, and he was always asking after her in his pointed, physicistic manner, one skeptical eyebrow raised. Needless to say, Lazar did not like to be reminded. In the course of their affair, he knew, he had been terribly erratic, by turns tightfisted and profligate, glum and overeager, unsociable and socially aflutter, full of both flattery and glib invective—a shithead, in short—and, to his credit, he was afraid that he had treated Suzette very badly. It may have been this repressed consciousness, more than anything else, that led him to tell himself, when he first saw her again, that he did not love her anymore.

"Uh-oh," said Dawn, after she remembered who Suzette was.

"I have nothing to be afraid of," Lazar said. As she passed, he called out, "Suzette?" He felt curiously invulnerable to her still evident charms, and uttered her name with the lightness and faint derision of someone on a crowded airplane signaling to an attractive but slightly elderly stewardess. "Hey, Suze!"

She was wearing a Walkman, however, with the earphones turned up very loud, and she floated past on a swell of Chaka Khan and Rufus.

"Didn't she hear you?" said Albert, looking surprised.

"No, Dr. Five Useful Non-Implications of the String Theory, she did not," Lazar said. "She was wearing *ear*phones."

"I think she was ignoring you." Albert turned to his bride and duly consulted her. "Didn't she look like she heard him? Didn't her face kind of blink?"

"There she is, Bobby," said Dawn, pointing toward the entrance of the café. As it was a beautiful December morning, they were sitting out on the patio, and Lazar had his back to the Zinc. "Waiting on line."

He felt that he did not actually desire to speak to her but that Albert and Dawn's presence forced him into it somehow. A certain tyranny of in-touchness holds sway in that part of the world—a compulsion to behave always as though one is still in therapy but making real progress, and the rules of enlightened behavior seemed to dictate that he not sneak away from the table with his head under a newspaper—as he might have done if alone—and go home to watch the Weather Channel or Home Shopping Network for three hours with a twelve-pack of Mexican beer and the phone off the hook. He turned around in his chair and looked at Suzette more closely. She had on one of those glittering, opalescent Intergalactic Amazon leotard-and-tights combinations that seem to be made of cavorite or adamantium and do not so much cling to a woman's body as seal her off from gamma rays and lethal stardust. Lazar pronounced her name again, more loudly, calling out across the sunny patio. She looked even thinner from behind.

"Oh, Bobby," she said, removing the headphones but keeping her place in the coffee line.

"Hello, Suze," he said. They nodded pleasantly to one another, and that might have been it right there. After a second or two she dipped her head semiapologetically, smiled an irritated smile, and put the earphones—"ear buds," he recalled, was the nauseous term—back into her ears.

"She looks great," Lazar said magnanimously to Albert and Dawn, keeping his eyes on Suzette.

"She looks so thin, so drawn," said Dawn, who frankly could have stood to drop about fifteen pounds.

"She looks fine to me," said Al. "I'd say she looks better than ever."

"I know you would," Lazar snapped. "You'd say it just to bug me."

He was a little irritated himself now. The memory of their last few days together had returned to him, despite all his heroic efforts over the past months to repress it utterly. He thought of the weekend following that bad review of their restaurant in the *Times* (they'd had a Balearic restaurant called Ibiza in San Clemente)—a review in which the critic had singled out his distressed-stucco interior and Suzette's Majorcan paella, in particular, for censure. Since these were precisely the two points around which, in the course of opening the restaurant, they had constructed their most idiotic and horrible arguments, the unfavorable notice hit their already shaky relationship like a dumdum bullet, and Suzette went a little nuts. She didn't show up at home or at Ibiza all the next day—so that poor hypersensitive little José had to do all the cooking—but instead disappeared into the haunts of physical culture. She worked out at the gym, went to Zahava's class, had her body waxed, and then, to top it all off, rode her bicycle all the way to El Toro and back. When she finally came home she was in a mighty hormonal rage and suffered under the delusion that she could lift a thousand pounds and chew her way through vanadium steel. She claimed that Lazar had bankrupted her, among other outrageous and untrue assertions, and he went out for a beer to escape from her. By the time he returned, several hours later, she had moved out, taking with her *only his belongings,* as though she had come to see some fundamental inequity in their relationship—such as their having been switched at birth—and were attempting in this way to rectify it.

This loss, though painful, he would have been willing to suffer if it hadn't included his collection of William Powelliana, which was then at its peak and contained everything from the checkered wingtips Powell wore in *The Kennel Club Murder Case* to Powell's personal copy of the shooting script for *Life with Father* to a 1934 letter from Dashiell Hammett congratulating Powell on his interpretation of Nick Charles, which Lazar had managed to obtain from a Powell grand-nephew only minutes before the epistolary buzzards from the University of Texas tried to snap it up. Suzette sold the entire collection, at far less than its value, to that awful Kelso McNair up in Lawndale, who only annexed it to his vast empire of Myrna Loy memorabilia and locked it away in his vault. In retaliation Lazar went down the next morning to their safe-deposit box at Dana Point, removed all six of Suzette's 1958 and '59 Barbie Dolls, and sold them to a collectibles store up in Orange for not quite four thousand dollars, at which point she brought the first suit against him.

"Why is your face turning so red, Bobby?" said Dawn, who must have been all of twenty-two.

"Oh!" he said, not bothering even to sound sincere. "I just remembered. I have an appointment."

"See you, Bobby," said Al.

"See you," he said, but he did not stand up.

"You don't have to keep looking at her, anyway," Al continued reasonably. "You can just look out at Ocean Avenue here, or at my lovely new wife—hi, sweetie—and act as though Suzette's not there."

"I know," Lazar said, smiling at Dawn, then returning his eyes immediately to Suzette. "But I'd like to talk to her. No, really."

So saying, he rose from his chair and walked, as nonchalantly as he could, toward her. He had always been awkward about crossing public space, and could not do it without feeling somehow cheesy and hucksterish, as though he were crossing a makeshift dais in a Legion Hall to accept a diploma from a bogus school of real estate; he worried that his pants were too tight across the seat, that his gait was hitched and dorky, that his hands swung chimpishly at his sides. Suzette was next in line now and studying the menu, even though he could have predicted, still, exactly what she would order: a decaf au lait and a wedge of frittata with two little cups of cucumber salsa. He came up behind her and tapped her on the shoulder; the taps were intended to be devil-may-care and friendly, but of course he overdid them and they came off as the brusque importunities of a man with a bone to pick. Suzette turned around looking more irritated than ever, and when she saw who it was her dazzling green eyes grew tight little furrows at their corners.

"How are you?" said Lazar, daring to leave his hand on her shoulder, where, as though it were approaching *c,* very quickly it seemed to acquire a great deal of mass. He was so conscious of his hand on her damp, solid shoulder that he missed her first few words and finally had to withdraw it, blushing.

"…great. Everything's really swell," Suzette was saying, looking down at the place on her shoulder where his hand had just been. Had he laid a freshly boned breast of raw chicken there and then taken it away her expression could not have been more bemused. She turned away. "Hi, Norris," she said to the lesbian woman behind the counter. "Just an espresso."

"On a diet?" Lazar said, feeling his smile tighten.

"Not hungry," she said. "You've gained a few pounds."

"You could be right," he said, and patted his stomach. Since he had thrown Suzette's Borg bathroom scale onto the scrap heap along with her other belongings (thus leaving the apartment all but empty), he had no idea of how much he weighed, and, frankly, as he put it to himself, smiling all the while at his ex-lover, he did not give a rat's ass. "I probably did. You look thinner than ever, really, Suze."

"Here's your espresso," said Norris, smiling oddly at Lazar, as though they were old friends, and he was confused until he remembered that right after Suzette left him he'd run into this Norris at a party in Bluebird Canyon, and they had a short, bitter, drunken conversation about what it felt like when a woman left you, and Lazar impressed her by declaring, sagely, that it felt as though you'd arrived home to find that your dearest and most precious belongings in the world had been sold to a man from Lawndale.

"What about that money you owe me?" he said. The question was halfway out of his mouth before he realized it, and although he appended a hasty ha-ha at the finish, his jaw was clenched and he must have looked as if he was about to slug her.

"Whoa!" said Suzette, stepping neatly around him. "I'm getting out of here, Bobby. Good-bye." She tucked her chin against her chest, dipped her head, and slipped out the door, as though ducking into a rainstorm.

"Wait!" he said. "Suzette!"

She turned toward him as he came out onto the patio, her shoulders squared, and held him at bay with her cup of espresso coffee.

"I don't have to reckon with you anymore, Bobby Lazar," she said. "Colleen says I've already reckoned with you enough." Colleen was Suzette's therapist. They had seen her together for a while, and Lazar was both scornful and afraid of her and her lingoistic advice.

"I'm sorry," he said. "I'll try to be, um, yielding. I'll yield. I promise. I just—I don't know. How about let's sit down?"

He turned to the table where he'd left Albert, Dawn, and his cup of coffee, and discovered that his friends had stood up and were collecting their shopping bags, putting on their sweaters.

"Are you going?" he said.

"If you two are getting back together," said Albert, "this whole place is going. It's all over. It's the Big One."

"Albert!" said Dawn.

"You're a sick man, Bob," said Albert. He shook Lazar's hand and grinned. "You're sick, and you like sick women."

Lazar cursed him, kissed Dawn on both cheeks, and laughed a reckless laugh.

"Is he drunk or something?" he heard Dawn say before they were out of earshot, and, indeed, as he returned to Suzette's table the world seemed suddenly more stressful and gay, the sky more tinged at its edges with violet.

"Is that Al's new wife?" said Suzette. She waved to them as they headed down the street. "She's pretty, but she needs to work on her thighs."

"I think Al's been working on them," he said.

"Shush," said Suzette.

They sat back and looked at each other warily and with pleasure. The circumstances under which they parted had been so strained and unfriendly and terminal that to find themselves sitting, just like that, at a bright café over two cups of black coffee seemed as thrilling as if they were violating some powerful taboo. They had been warned, begged, and even ordered to stay away from each other by everyone, from their shrinks to their parents to the bench of Orange County itself; yet here they were, in plain view, smiling and smiling. A lot of things had been lacking in their relationship, but unfortunately mutual physical attraction was not one of them, and Lazar could feel that hoary old devouring serpent uncoiling deep in its Darwinian cave.

"It's nice to see you," said Suzette.

"You look pretty," he said. "I like what you've done with your hair. You look like a Millais."

"Thank you," she said, a little tonelessly; she was not quite ready to listen to all his prattle again. She pursed her lips and looked at him in a manner almost surgical, as though about to administer a precise blow with a very small ax. She said, "*Song of the Thin Man* was on last week."

"I know," he said. He was impressed, and oddly touched. "That's pretty daring of you to mention that. Considering."

She set down her coffee cup, firmly, and he caught the flicker of her right biceps. "You got more than I got," she said. "You got six thousand dollars! I got five thousand four hundred and ninety-five. I don't owe you anything."

"I only got four thousand, remember?" he said. He felt himself blushing. "That came out, well, in court—don't you remember? I—well, I lied."

"That's right," she said slowly. She rolled her eyes and bit her lip, remembering. "You lied. Four thousand. They were worth twice that."

"A lot of them were missing hair or limbs," he said.

"You pig!" She gave her head a monosyllabic shake, and the golden curls rustled like a dress. Since she had at one time been known to call him a pig with delicacy and tenderness, this did not immediately alarm Lazar. "You sold my dolls," she said, dreamily, though of course she knew this perfectly well, and had known it for quite some time. Only now, he could see, it was all coming back to her, the memory of the cruel things they had said, of the tired, leering faces of the lawyers, of the acerbic envoi of the county judge dismissing all their suits and countersuits, of the day they had met for the last time in the empty building that had been their restaurant, amid the bare fixtures, the exposed wires, the crumbs of plaster on the floor; of the rancor that from the first had been the constant flower of their love. "You sold their things, too," she remembered. "All of their gowns and pumps and little swimwear."

"I was just trying to get back at you."

"For what? For making sure I at least got something out of all the time I wasted on you?"

"Take it easy, Suze."

"And then to lie about how much you got for them? Four thousand dollars!"

"At first my lawyers instructed me to lie about it," he lied.

"Kravitz! Di Martino! Those sleazy, lizardy, shystery old fat guys! Oh, you pigs!"

Now she was on her feet, and everyone out on the patio had turned with great interest to regard them. He realized, or rather remembered, that he had strayed into dangerous territory here, that Suzette had a passion for making scenes in restaurants. This is how it was, said a voice within Lazar—a gloomy, condemnatory voice—this is what you've been missing. He saw the odd angle at which she was holding her cup of coffee, and he hoped against hope that she did not intend to splash his face with espresso. She was one of those women who like to hurl beverages.

"Don't tell me," he said, despite himself, his voice coated with the most unctuous sarcasm, "you're *reckoning* with me again."

You could see her consulting with herself about trajectories and wind shear and beverage velocity and other such technical considerations —collecting all the necessary data, and courage—and then she let fly. The cup sailed past Lazar's head, and he just had time to begin a tolerant, superior smile, and to uncurl partially the middle finger of his right hand, before the cup bounced off the low wall beside him and ricocheted into his face.

Suzette looked startled for a moment, registering this as one registers an ace in tennis or golf, and then laughed the happy laugh of a lucky shot. As the unmerciful people on the patio applauded—oh, but that made Lazar angry—Suzette turned on her heel and, wearing a maddening smile, strode balletically off the patio of the café, out into the middle of Ocean Avenue. Lazar scrambled up from his chair and went after her, cold coffee running in thin fingers down his cheeks. Neither of them bothered to look where they were going; they trusted, in those last couple of seconds before he caught her and kissed her hollow cheek, that they would not be met by some hurtling bus or other accident.

Victoria Patterson

TIJUANA BURRO MAN

Victoria Patterson was born in Whittier in 1969 and earned an MFA in writing from UC Riverside. Her linked story collection *Drift* established her reputation as a sharp observer of a social milieu defined by an easily assumed sense of privilege, and it was a finalist for the California Book Award and the Story Prize and was selected as of one of the best books of 2009 by the *San Francisco Chronicle*. Patterson is also the author of the novels *The Little Brother, The Peerless Four*, and *This Vacant Paradise*.

The characters in *Drift* include a trophy bride, a brain-damaged skateboarder named John Wayne, a troubled restaurant hostess, and Rosie, the heroine, whose life we see in multiple episodes, beginning in adolescence, continuing through young adulthood, and culminating with her job as a waitress in a quintessential Corona del Mar restaurant. With irony and empathy, Patterson shows young Rosie's vulnerability and precociousness in the story "Tijuana Burro Man." Patterson told us that her tumultuous feelings for Newport Beach—where she attended junior high and high school—still gift her with material.

O N A DRIZZLY wet-cement Thursday, Rosie's second week of eighth grade, her English teacher turned off the lights and made the class look at a slide of Vincent van Gogh's painting *Starry Night* while Don McLean's song (inspired by the artist) "Vincent" played on a tape player. Then they were to look at the slide for ten more minutes, in silence. Miss Deleo said their assignment was "to feel." When the lights came back on, they were to write whatever came to mind. Miss Deleo called it "stream of consciousness."

Rosie wanted to be cool and hate the assignment like the other students—groans and eye rolls. She wanted to be like Heather, sitting at the back of the classroom, green eyes so light they looked translucent, elbow at her desk, chin in palm, staring indifferently at the screen. Heather (every other girl was a Heather, so Rosie preferred to think of her as the green-eyed girl) was beautiful. They'd just come from a school rally. The frequent rallies were supposed to foster school spirit and were a permissible opportunity to ogle: cheerleaders skipping, jumping, cart-wheeling to the middle of the gym floor—whooping and hollering—ponytails swinging, skirts lifting to reveal blue panties, backsides embellished with the school logo: a white-bearded and bare-chested Sea King emerging victorious from the foam of a wave, wielding a trident. Cheerleaders, Rosie believed, proclaimed the requirements of her sex, an exaggerated example, an ideal. But say—just say—in her imagination, she'd been gifted with the looks, confidence, and agility to fling and contort her body before the entire student and teacher population—she could never fake that sort of enthusiasm, *ever*. The green-eyed girl was too cool to be a cheerleader: she always looked bored and this made her superior. Her family was hugely wealthy, exemplified by her wardrobe, and the combination of money and looks put Miss Deleo at a disadvantage: the green-eyed girl didn't really have to give a damn; she simply crossed her legs and the guys wanted her, the girls wanted to be her.

Last year in seventh grade, Rosie had a bad perm. As if that wasn't horrific enough, a photograph in her school yearbook (place the yearbook on a table, let it fall open, and it would land on the picture) had humiliated her. Newport Beach High School encompassed grades seven through twelve, ensuring her disgrace from peers as well as from the five grades above her. In a classroom full of students, it appeared as if the cameraman had yelled, Hey, Rosie!, hers the only face turned to the camera, startled, a *whooshed* fan of kinky hair, a glimmer of metal from the hardwire of her braces. She was pale, but appeared ghostlike because of the flash. The caption under the photograph: What planet are you from?

She'd make sure nothing like that ever happened again, and already had racked up hours naked and supine in the ultraviolet lights of a coffin-like tanning booth at NewportTan, smelling of sweat and chemicals, trying not to tip her protective goggles, ignoring claustrophobic sensations. She never got tan, was perpetually red hued, but it was a start—and her braces had been removed, her perm had died an unmourned slow death; and with the aid of Sun-In and lemon juice, her hair was streaked a dirty blond, coarse and weathered like the surfer girls.

Girls at her high school were so thin their legs resembled arms. Some came back from summer break transformed by breast augmentations and nose jobs. This past summer, in a great panic, Rosie had even persuaded her mother, B, to take her to a plastic surgeon. Her right breast was slightly larger than its mate and she was sure this was a deformity. B had no way of calming her, but the doctor had convinced her that she need not go under the knife and that the incongruity might modify naturally with time.

It wasn't as if Rosie wasn't used to adapting: she'd moved plenty as a child, traveling because of her father's job (Latin Coast representative for Namco Powder Metals Inc.), living in Argentina, Brazil, Colombia. Despite her shyness, her introspective and sensitive nature (Grandma Dot called her The Big Feeling), she was a scrappy survivor, even somewhat of a leader.

When Rosie was in third grade, her father started working for B's father, so that they could settle once and for all near Rosie's grandparents in Southern California. The divorce, three years later, was nasty and scandalous. B asked her father to fire her ex-husband as a show of solidarity, but Grandpa refused, whether out of continued loyalty or as a favorable business decision, Rosie wasn't sure, though knowing Grandpa, she suspected the latter.

There'd been rumors of B's longtime affair with Rosie's new stepfather, Will, a gynecologist and obstetrician, twenty-three years B's senior. And a confirmation, a drunken phone call from Will's ex-wife, answered by Rosie three weeks after moving into their new home in Newport Beach, two days before she was to start the seventh grade. "Look at your birth certificate," Will's ex-wife had said, after expounding on the number of years she'd been married to Will (thirty-four), and her children's (Stanford graduates—two surgeons, one lawyer) shared hatred for B, and (even though she hadn't stated it), by association, Rosie. There was a hint of shame in her slurring voice, "Can you find your birth certificate? I want you to look at it." And then, as if sensing that Rosie was about to hang up in self-preservation, she hung up first—but not before coolly adding, "Your mom's a slut."

Rosie did find her birth certificate, fishing in the avocado-colored file cabinet next to B's dresser in the walk-in closet. The attending physician's signature was Will's, confirming her suspicion: A pregnant B had met Will when she'd traveled solo (not counting Rosie, in utero) to California (from Colombia, Argentina, Brazil?), to deliver Rosie—troublemaker by birth—in a state-of-the-art hospital. It was a large, complicated, indigestible piece of information that she'd been attempting to digest in secret ever since, considering B, Will, Dad, Grandma Dot, and Grandpa weren't keen on heavy discussions, particularly anything having to do with the communal pain of the divorce. All B had told her was that she'd flown to California in her final trimester of pregnancy because she was experiencing "difficulties" (further questioning, futile); that Grandpa had driven her to the hospital and stayed in the waiting area; and that before they'd left for the hospital, she'd taken a shower and shaved her legs (she didn't want to have stubble-haired legs). But Rosie wasn't so sure she wanted to talk about it either, a blossoming of shame—in her fertile imagination, an undeniable responsibility.

Tell the green-eyed girl that her birth had been the catalyst for her mother to meet her lover, subsequently instigating the dissolution of her parents' marriage (not to mention the marriage of the spiteful woman with the slurring sad voice), and she would've been nonplussed. What would it be like to be someone like that? Did she even think about death? She didn't worry. She wasn't sensitive. She looked good. It never occurred to her to ask questions. But Rosie could tell she was dumb.

Last week, after being called on by Miss Deleo, the green-eyed girl had earnestly tried to answer a question about the difference between a first person and a third person point of view: "A third person is someone who has heard something through someone else..." She'd played it off, but not before giving Rosie a secret look. The look said, Yeah, I might be pretty but I'm really stupid. What am I going to do with my life? It was gone in a flash and then she returned to her normal bored and superior posture, and Rosie was relieved: it wasn't natural to be worried for the green-eyed girl.

The slide projector was propped on a stack of books. Rosie's desk was toward the side of the classroom so that she could see the slightest ripples of the screen, a fist-sized rock tied to the end of a cord keeping it weighted down. The song finished, the projector hummed, tittering laughter swept through the classroom. "Shh," Miss Deleo pressed a scrunched index finger to her lips—then quickly withdrew her hand, placing it behind her back. "Ten more minutes. Silence."

B was pretty in the same casual and confident manner as the green-eyed girl. Rosie was doing her best to develop in that direction, but she had a brooding intensity. Grandma Dot said it was like the cloud of dust that circled Pigpen from the *Peanuts* comic strip. And unlike B, who thrived in her new cherry-red Mercedes convertible, wealth hadn't lessened Rosie's anxiety. She envied people who found comfort in material possessions: shallow, naïve, carefree, happy. (Although she did appreciate the "emergency bankcard" Will gave her: stick it in the bank machine and it magically spat out twenties.) She was subject to depressions, insomnia, melancholy, increased by the nagging guilt that she *should* be happy: she could've been born an Untouchable in India, for instance. She'd just read about them in World History. Talk about a shitty fate. She pitied the stupid-wealthy, hated them for their ease, and she certainly didn't want to end up like them. She'd never be able to live under the illusion that owning a Mercedes would make her a worthwhile individual—although she did believe that having perky breasts and a cute little figure might help.

Grandma Dot saw through people across the financial spectrum with a vocal judgment akin to a searing laser beam, often sharing her insights. She usually left Rosie out of her judgments, thank God, because Rosie didn't want to cry. When Rosie had asked Grandma Dot what she would change, if she could change just one thing about her life, Grandma Dot had said: "I wish I'd been more beautiful." "But you are beautiful," Rosie had said, because it was true. And the pictures when she was younger! "Pah," said Grandma Dot, lighting up a cigarette. "Phooey."

Her parents' divorce, in collision with puberty, had amplified a desperate hunger: *love me, love me, love me*—even if I hate you—*love me,* and fulfillment appeared (to a large degree) to be contingent on her physical appeal. When she'd fantasized about becoming a writer, she'd written a story about an ugly librarian who had developed a pen pal relationship with a handsome widower that eventually evolved into a deep love. The man begged the ugly librarian to let him meet her. He wanted to marry her. The ugly librarian worried that the man would take one look at her and run. The ending of the story eluded Rosie: Did love prevail? Or did the widower's love dissolve? Hard as she tried, she couldn't compose a satisfactory ending and had decided not to be a writer (too hard!) soon after.

Miss Deleo stood near the corner, bluish in the light, leaned up against the wall, hands behind her back. Something was wrong with her hands—deformed—fingers scrunched together; she hid them behind her back or in her pockets, made the students write on the chalkboard. She reminded Rosie of a hummingbird, frantic and excited. She probably shopped at JCPenney. Her dress had a bold flower print; her wide belt had stars studded across it. It was her first year of teaching and she had ideas. Was she aware that the students called her Miss Dildo? Her big brown eyes looked on the verge of tears and Rosie wanted to learn for her sake, just so she wouldn't cry. Besides, no one had ever turned off the lights and instructed her to feel.

Rosie rested her head on her arms against the cool of the desk and tried to drop into the Van Gogh painting. She rubbed her fingers against a tiny sentence carved into her desktop, FUCK YOU AND YOUR MAMA, appreciating the crude frank message and the meditative feel of the grooves. She could hear B's voice, "La di da di da—we live and we die and that's it." It bothered her that her stepfather made his living by exploring women's vaginas. After the phone call from Will's ex-wife, she'd come across his medical books, stacked in his office—slick photographs of vaginal disorders, close-up and inside: pink and red and sores and ooze. He wasn't the type of man she expected to steal B's heart: spindly and freckled legs scattered with bruises and burst capillaries, like beads puckered beneath the skin of his calves. A gut. Reddish gray hair, thinned and combed over his shiny head. Large, mottled hands, fingernails broad and slightly yellow, hands that had pulled Rosie into the world (B's legs spread open!), ready or not.

She'd caught him this morning, hunched and smoking a cigarette on the patio, using a paper Dixie cup as a disposable ashtray. "Don't tell B," he'd said, as if B couldn't smell the nicotine on him. He wore thick brown glasses, and there was a perpetual scab near his forehead from all the times he kept hitting his head on the open car trunk, a bag of groceries in hand or one of B's tennis rackets—Oh God!—even when she stood near him, warning him, "Watch your head, Will, watch it,"—*clunk*. She couldn't help but have empathy pains: her stepfather was old and accident-prone; but no matter what, it was impossible to respect a man who wore pink with yellow. When she'd first met him, he wore his green pants embroidered with tiny whales, sprigs of water erupting from their blowholes. Rather than change the way he dressed, B encouraged his bad taste, buying him ties decorated with pumpkins for Halloween or Christmas elves at Christmastime; and they couldn't keep their hands off each other. Rosie's bedroom window overlooked their shower window, and she could see the back of B's head bobbing up and down against the steamy glass. If they weren't having sex, they were asleep, and they were heavy sleepers, possibly from all the sex. She had no memory of affection between B and Dad, whereas Will and B were always touching.

And what about Dad, broken and defeated, living in a gated condominium in Costa Mesa, a man-made creek running down the middle of the complex, ducks quacking. Earnest, sensitive (he, like Rosie, cried at movies), in the process of healing with the help of Jesus Christ, and with the understanding of Lori, fifteen years his junior, a delicious and buxom born-again Christian. Rosie attended Maritime Church with Dad—for Dad—on Sundays, but instead of giving herself over to Jesus Christ, as Dad strongly encouraged, she'd developed a recurrent and involved fantasy: a pack of Hells Angels driving through the huge stained glass depiction of the one and only beatific and bearded J.C., his hands aloft, as if to touch the air, shattering the colored glass, shards of J.C. falling everywhere; Hells Angels wreaking havoc, the church filled with screams and drugs and the choir girls giving sexual favors, ending with her riding off—through the same gap in the window— on the back of a motorcycle with her own personal tattoo-covered savior.

Church was a participatory hypocrisy. One more place where she didn't belong, where the worst thing she could do was be herself. *What planet are you from?* And by the way Dad sometimes looked at her, it was as if he knew that sin was genetic; that she shared not only B's nose and cheekbone structure, but also B's proclivity for extramarital sexual relations. Already a sinner without meaning to be, and in any case, definitely on her way to more sin—in other words, she was doomed. But she was resigned: sinful as her life was, it would never be ordinary. For instance, she'd been flashed twice within the last month while walking near the ocean, both in stark daylight. The first time was from a distance: she gazed toward the rocks and saw a fat, squat man watching her in return, his hand flashing spasmodically at his lap. Two weeks later she took a different walk along the sand. A scrawny older man with wrinkled knees came seemingly from the ocean; he opened the Velcro fly of his wet swim trunks, revealing a patch of graying pubic hair and the curved arc of a pale-veined penis. Both times the men had scurried away like happy little crabs, and although she'd yelled expletives, she'd sensed that she'd gratified them by playing a role. These things didn't happen to so-called normal people.

"Van Gogh," Miss Deleo's voice was wistful, "painted *Starry Night* while in an insane asylum. '*La Tristesse durera toujours,*' I believe, were his last words. Does anyone know what that means?"

No answer. Long pause.

"'The sadness will last forever.'" Miss Deleo waved a cupped hand abashedly in front of her. "I'm sorry," she said. "I'll be quiet now."

Once in a while at Maritime Church, the congregation sang "Amazing Grace," and Rosie would feel *something,* clinging to it as proof: maybe, just maybe, she could please her dad; maybe, just maybe, she could become a Christian. But there had to be more than looking and acting and sounding the same as everyone else. And it was like asking her to believe in Santa Claus, after she'd witnessed her parents putting the presents under the tree. And why hadn't Dad asked her to live with him? Why hadn't he fought for her? Was there something wrong with her? When they drove out of the church parking lot, she'd stick her middle finger up, at her side by the door (where Dad couldn't see), flipping the bird one last time, a heavy mix of guilt and cynicism. Last Sunday, she'd smuggled John Updike's *Rabbit, Run* into Teen Worship, blocking out the Christian rock band, and read hungrily, camouflaging the book inside a Bible. Entering the angst-ridden world of a car salesman, it had occurred to her that she wasn't the only freak. Besides, she concluded, she'd rather be a freak than a Christian.

Miss Deleo flicked on the light switch, her fingers cupped as if holding a tiny chick. Rosie blinked, adjusting to the light, and quickly scribbled three sentences. She thought of the man with no hands: stubs, creases of skin pinched in inverted stars like the ends on a sausage, trying to get something out of his pocket, head down, crouched next to Will's idling Mercedes at the Tijuana, Mexico, border crossing.

Tijuana carried the same designer tennis outfits as the Newport Beach Country Club (Fila, Ellesse, and Adidas), but without the inflated price tags; Will had taken B and Rosie shopping on Monday (only a two-hour car drive from Newport Beach). In the back seat with the plastic bags of clothes, waiting in a line of cars to recross the border, avoiding a look out her back-seat window at the sprawl of human despair, Rosie sat, the sun sending glints of light across her arm like phantom butterflies. And then the man with no hands was tapping a stub against the glass of her window. Her eyes locked into his. Lip and chin tremble, and then she was crying—hot fat tears sliding down her cheeks. He tried to get something out of his pocket, a fruitless endeavor, moved away, merged into the sea of beggars, but there were a thousand other reasons to keep crying, *just look out the window!*—her emotions seeping out without her permission, built up from the reality of Tijuana. The same as when Grandma Dot had taken her to visit her great-aunt at Newport Crest Convalescent, and a woman with no visible chin or neck sitting in a wheelchair had grabbed at her arm and called her Frank, and then Aunt Lydia had kept saying, "When am I going to finally die? When will this finally be over?"—the corner of her mouth crusted with mashed potatoes and spittle. She'd unexpectedly broken into sobs and had to wait in the parking lot for Grandma Dot to finish the visit.

She pressed her cheek against the car window, cool on her skin. Don't look, she told herself. Tijuana all around her, even in the sounds and smells. The tears were coming but she stifled her noise. And then B's eyes caught her in the rearview mirror: she hated when B looked at her impatiently, as if her sensitivity were an ugly troll, and B wanted it gone, out of sight, so they could continue with their contented lives. "What's wrong, Rosie?"

No answer. Lip tremble.

"What's wrong?"

No answer. Chin tremble.

"La di da di da—we live and we die and that's it. Lighten up."

Rosie had her photograph taken that same day, on a burro painted black and white to simulate the appearance of a zebra, although most of the paint had faded. A sombrero, TIJUANA stitched in red thread across the brim, made her forehead itch. She leaned forward, touching the burro's strawlike fur, warm against her hand. He shook off a fly, fur rippling under her fingertips. She knew it was a male burro because of her earlier examination of his leathery, sagging testicles. She tried to convey her sympathies to the young man taking her photograph, and his look showed that he understood. He told her to say "tortilla," her cheeks stiff with an "I'm supposed to smile now" smile. A flash went off and his camera made an agitated noise. Will paid with a crisp twenty-dollar bill, saying the change was a tip. Will and B started walking down the street and she turned to go with them. The man stopped her with a hand to her elbow.

"I need your phone number," he said. "*Teléfono*. For the photograph." He looked her age, already with a wispy mustache. She didn't understand why he would need her phone number when she had that photograph (colors muted, as if covered by a glaze), but he had his look, as if they were in agreement. He handed her a scrap of paper and a pen. Hurriedly, she scribbled her name and phone number. She had the fleeting impression that she was disappointing B, a sharp jab: the lure of an action out of the ordinary. She handed the pen and paper to the man. He was pleased and her sadness lifted at the thought that she had made someone happy. She waved goodbye and ran toward Will and B. They were entering a store with cheap prescription drugs, perfumes, and clothes, and she didn't want to miss out.

They drove back to Newport Beach in silence; she was compliant and tired, spent from her earlier crying jag, watching the sunset bleed across the ocean; they drove past the warning signs for the illegal immigrants making a running break: a yellow diamond shape with the black silhouette of a family, the mother gripping the arm of her daughter (pigtails and ribbons) and pulling so hard the girl's feet left the ground. She searched the terrain: more patrol cars. They drove past the breast-like domes of the San Onofre nuclear power plant, tops covered in bird shit, like frosting on cupcakes. At the tip of each dome, there was a red light blinking slowly—like the bell buoys—not in unison, and never completely off: barely red, and then all lit up red.

And then there was the shrill ring of a phone at two A.M. She picked up the phone in her bedroom at the same time as Will. She could hear

Will's heavy breathing. She imagined his droopy boxers, his red and gray chest hairs.

"Hello," the voice said with an accent. "I need to speak with Rosie."

"Who is this?" Will asked.

"I take picture. She helps me. I cross border. I need place to stay."

She could see the burro's tail swinging at the flies, smell the dirt, hear the children pleading for her to buy Chiclets.

"Hang up, Rosie," Will said, irritated.

She hung up her phone and lay back in her bed, looking around her darkened bedroom. B had let her decorate the room, allowing her "free expression." She'd painted the walls black and taped up advertisements from magazines of scantily clad men. They stared at her with inflated chests and seductive eyes. In the dark, they looked like monsters. She thought about the strangled noise of the camera. B would be mad. Will would give her a lecture; she could already imagine it. Her heart pulsed in her temples—*thump, thump*. She hated the feel of her own blood coursing through her veins. She tried readjusting her head on the pillow. She was a chronic insomniac and this event was more fodder for a thought-infested evening. Bags under the eyes were a beauty detriment. If she didn't look good, she wouldn't belong. She wanted the bed to swallow her. She wanted to disappear. How could a stranger be calling her for help and she couldn't help him? Where would he go? How did he cross the border? Would he be okay? How could she be so stupid? How was she ever going to make it in this world? Grandma Dot had told her to "toughen up." But how was she supposed to do that? Her door opened and Will stood in the doorway. He flicked the light switch. B went back to sleep, no doubt. She would send Will to do her dirty work.

Will sat on her bed, facing her. He had on blue boxers and the tuft of copper hair near his forehead was at attention stance. She felt wide open, lonely and stupid. He smoothed hair from her face, tucked it behind her ear. "No more," he said, but he wasn't angry. He was tired, sorry, concerned. "Jesus Christ, Rosie, you can't go giving our phone number to strangers."

"Maybe he wanted to send more copies of the photo?"

"No more," Will said. There'd been only one other time, when, standing between the bathroom and the kitchen of The Palms, she'd written her phone number on a napkin for a Mexican busboy eight years her senior, simply because he'd wanted to continue their conversation away from the clamor and bustle of the restaurant; but, after a series of aborted phone calls, Will had gone so far as to change their phone number, and she knew better than to argue with him.

"You have to stop," he said.

The bell rang and Rosie looked at what she'd written:

> La di da di da. We live and we die and that's it. Fuck you and your mama.

She couldn't turn her paper in. Papers rustled, backpacks zipped, and she wrote on another piece of paper:

> I don't know. There's the night sky and clouds and stars and moon, swirled together, but it's not messy. I'm sorry he was in an insane asylum. And that he said that thing about being sad forever. Didn't he cut his ear off? He must have been very confused.

Miss Deleo gave her a wet-eyed look as she turned her paper in. Outside the door she could see the green-eyed girl, lip-locked and leg-locked with her boyfriend beside a trash can. And a soft, static, silver-white rain.

Patty Seyburn

GOOD WATER

Patty Seyburn was born in Detroit in 1962. She has earned four degrees, among them an MFA in poetry from UC Irvine, and she is the author of four books of poems: *Diasporadic, Hilarity, Mechanical Cluster,* and *Perfecta.* She is currently an assistant professor at CSU Long Beach.

About the poem "Good Water," from her 1998 collection *Diasporadic,* she told us: "In a way, this poem inaugurated me as a Californian. I grew up in Detroit. Our disasters were mostly man-made. When writing this, I learned about fire and how to control it and how to let it burn—an apt metaphor for being young, which this poem is also about."

for C. V.

When the fires found their way up over the Laguna hills
soon to meet the nothingness left by good-guy fires,
backfires officially set to deprive the wild ones

of bounty, to starve them of fodder, we moved in closer
to watch, eye level to hell, a place where destruction
is so beautiful, you can't help staring. Told that rage

must exhaust itself, that flailing water wouldn't help
until the fire stopped to breathe, we sat on our heels
outside our frangible houses and saw what burns,

which is almost everything natural, as is the burning
itself. And we knew we were faster than the fires,
that some things that hurt us are slow, or seem slow,

or if truly fast, envelop the time before and after,
claiming their turf the way death dog-ears its place.
Where the fire began has long been abandoned,

though we're not sure where that is—the sun always
first to be questioned when some flame gets loose,
as if every fire was borne of a magnifying glass

and we spend our time trying to impress our symbol
on a dead leaf that ends up a smolder, or wanting
to prove that with a lone prop, we could survive

a cold night in the wilderness, though nights
are no longer cold that way, the coolness
one of indifference: Old God tired of pacts,

New One of healing, and now the sky bleeds
with dogs, bugs, warriors, ladles and ladders flung
by Olympians. But you and I can outrun the hour,

the flame's detour around the charred hills, away
from the numbing sea that would shock your limbs
into forgetting how to save themselves, erasing

memory and its pain, pain and its memory: help
we do not need. Our footprints indent the grass.
We watch. Then run. Why not? While we are fast.

Stephanie Brown

THE LOST COAST, CALIFORNIA

Stephanie Brown was born in 1961 and grew up in Newport Beach, where she attended Newport Harbor High School. She has degrees from UC Berkeley, the University of Iowa, and Boston University. She is the author of two books of poetry—*Domestic Interior* and *Allegory of the Supermarket*—and has received fellowships from the Bread Loaf Writers' Conference and the National Endowment for the Arts. She has been featured on the cover of two issues of the *American Poetry Review*, and her work has appeared in six editions of *The Best American Poetry*, as well as in many journals, both print and online. She was the poetry editor of *Zócalo Public Square* from 2010 to 2016, and she currently works as an administrative manager for OC Public Libraries.

In this poem from *Allegory of the Supermarket* (1998), Brown explores perceptions about place, considers what is "lost," and finds both irony and affirmation in sharing the memories and realities of her own region in contrast to those of an imagined or exaggerated one.

These people left. The disappeared from our shores, down south.
The women never look like whores
Never the compromised, damaged nose-job self.
They are helpful, and when I look into their eyes
When I purchase a linen skirt,
They try to look inside. But more afraid than kind.
Stoned Dads, opening the supermarket freezer door.
Baby in the shopping cart, a tie-dyed romper on.
A couple of teenagers beside him—why so quiet everyone?
I don't like it.

"Nature Bats Last" the bumper sticker threatens
Out in the parking lot. But I don't get it.
It took me several days, not just a minute.
The road leads to the stream with abandoned wrecks
Trailers set aside the dry trees and they're old trailers
The trees, of course, are famous for being ancient trees.
I'm sure I would get it, if I listened.
The terrain is dangerous and the road we're on winds up and up,
A steep incline
Trees that would eat you up
Soak you back into the earth—
The environmentalist guerrilla died in her cabin back there,
    last year
We passed the place, someplace we drove by.
We wouldn't think of trying to find someone like her.

When I was growing up the surfers of a certain kind
called our town Zooport or Zoopit (Newport)
What did I know? It was really some kind of paradise
I was a kid   riding the bus through countryside
Eucalyptus trees and hawks   dry brown hills to the sea   glass
    business offices next
Then wide freeways, sprinklered lawns.
It changed from the country into the city.
Some people were sad   Many were too busy   Many were
    making it happen.
Those stoned boys went to Maui or Eureka or Washington
"I saw Hanford   I saw John"
You'd hear every once in a while about someone
A stoned or alky surfer long gone;
My brother's friend said, "I want to feel like I matter
    somewhere—a small town"
He went North
He went to Eureka Shasta Oregon

All those people gone
The hometown a completely different place—
Now you can shop like you're in Paris, New York, Milan.
It's like that: rich and fun.
The women look like whores, the men look strong.

So I vacationed on the Lost Coast
What did they find here, I wanted to know.
What had we lost?
I saw that: vines can grow so thick and tough they can hug a
    house right back.
It's hard to make a living unless you're really rich or used to
    being broke.
The crumbling highway could fall beneath us.
Salt spray on ocean rock delicate spring flower in a field
    under fog—
A natural food store named "The Corners of the Mouth"
Providing Nourishment. It's beautiful there—
Caution cones   the road *is* falling off the cliff.
"Nature Bats Last."
We drove all the way up, but we went all the way back.

Edward Humes

THE LAST LITTLE BEACH TOWN

Born in Philadelphia in 1957, Edward Humes is a Pulitzer Prize–winning journalist who has reported for *Sierra Magazine*, the *Los Angeles Times*, the *Wall Street Journal*, and *Forbes*. He is also the author of fourteen nonfiction books, including the PEN Award–winning *No Matter How Loud I Shout: A Year in the Life of Juvenile Court* and the true-crime bestseller *Mississippi Mud*. His latest is *Door to Door: The Magnificent, Maddening, Mysterious World of Transportation*.

In "The Last Little Beach Town," from the landmark 2004 anthology *My California: Journeys by Great Writers*, Humes gives readers a personal and political tour of Seal Beach—where he still lives with his family—identifying the vulnerability of this charmed locale, which is often overlooked, if sometimes to its benefit.

SEAL BEACH'S RED-TILE roofed, hacienda-style City Hall was built in 1929, but lately part of the lower floor has been rented out to a beauty salon to bring the town a bit of extra revenue. Midway through my work on this essay, I had stopped by to ask about the finer points of town history. Joanne Yeo, who has occupied the City Clerk's office longer than anyone can remember, rummaged under the counter and handed me a little book called *A Story of Seal Beach*.

Now, I had popped in on the spur of the moment after a morning walk on the beach—I had on some old jeans and a sweatshirt and I'm not even sure I had shaved—and Joanne didn't know me from Adam. But when I told her I had run out without my wallet and didn't have the five-dollar purchase price on me, and I started to slide the little book back across the counter, she just waved me off and said, "Take it. Come back and pay whenever you get a chance."

Imagine walking into City Hall in L.A. or Santa Monica or Santa Ana or anywhere else this side of Mayberry and having a clerk (once one finally deigns to saunter over and acknowledge your existence) tell you, *Take it, go ahead, I trust you.* This just does not happen in this century in this part of the world—except, in Seal Beach, it does. This is what we call The Seal Beach Way. This is why few people who stumble on this place ever leave, why Seal Beach gets into their blood, why they move into horrendously overpriced fifties-era tract homes on pint-sized lots and start plotting with architects to add a hideously overpriced extra three hundred square feet of living space—and consider themselves damn lucky to do it. For they have found, tucked inside one of the most heavily urbanized landscapes on Earth, the last little unspoiled beach town in Southern California.

People actually walk here. We leave our cars at home and stroll to the not-Starbucks coffee shop, amble to the Gap-less and Banana Republic-free Main Street, walk our kids to school, or simply put one foot in front of the other until we reach the beach or the market or the playground. Sometimes we even talk to each other along the way, which turns out, after all, not to be unlawful in car-centric SoCal.

Part of the reason Seal Beach has pulled this off is a matter of the company we keep: The town is the first and easiest-to-miss pearl on a string of larger, more prominent beach cities stretching southward into Orange County. It lies at the very top of the chain, abutting the concrete-bedded San Gabriel River that forms a cold, gray border with L.A. County, the famous Orange Curtain. Because Seal Beach lies right on this boundary between the port-city of Long Beach, which years ago trashed its own stretch of coast, and über-Republican, affluent Orange County, non-locals are often confused about exactly which side of the divide claims Seal Beach. The correct answer (philosophically, if not legally) is neither: Seal Beach is proudly not part of LA—the town's founding father, Philip Stanton, formerly speaker of the California Assembly, made sure of that ninety years ago. But it also shares little in common with the planned communities, condo canyons, conservative activism and housing covenants commonly associated with "the OC" (nobody outside of Hollywood scriptwriters and preternaturally attractive twenty-something actors pretending to be teenagers actually calls it that, by the way). You can plaster your garage with a rainbow-hued seascape mural or paint your stucco walls flaming purple or erect a strangely large scale model of a lighthouse on your front lawn and the taste police will not knock on your door here. Seal Beach is militantly untrendy.

Confusion about Seal Beach's identity and location is key to its survival—people who live twenty minutes away aren't quite sure where or what it is, and once you hit the geographically fashionable zones of West L.A., you might as well say you live on the Yucatan—it would never occur to those folks, happily for us, to drive those forty-five minutes south to Seal.

The favored destinations are the beach cities to the south splayed out along the Pacific Coast Highway: Huntington Beach, Newport Beach, Laguna Beach—bigger and better known, all of them, though each has abandoned its roots over time. Huntington Beach replaced its surfer-shack charms with a look best described as Vista del Condo. Newport Beach has become the world's most picturesque outdoor shopping mall and Mercedes dealership. The funky artists' enclave that was Laguna Beach remains the most strikingly beautiful of the lot, homes perched on coastal hillsides in perfect tribute to Mediterranean villas, but the quest for tourist dollars has made its downtown a grid-locked parking lot, and chain-store creep is pushing out personality for purchase power.

Then there is Crystal Cove, which occupies the magical stretch of coastline between Newport and Laguna, one of the main reasons I moved to California. I had flown in for a job interview, my head jammed with a childhood's worth of mythic images accumulated while growing up on the East Coast in the sixties, when the idea of California and paradise were synonymous, all red convertibles and Beach Boys and surfer girls and pale blue skies melting into white-sand beaches. My collision with reality came in 1985, when pollution here was at its historical worst; my naiveté did not survive my very first descent into the Los Angeles Basin. I watched my plane enter a layer of air the color of an old teabag and I just wanted to cash in my ticket and go home. It only got worse when I rented a car, heading south on Pacific Coast Highway starting in Long Beach. I saw a coastal strip marred by one fast-food restaurant and gas station and cheap motel after another.

But then I rounded a curve and the broken promise vanished along with my breath. Stretching out below me was the landscape I had expected, but better: On the inland side, green and brown hills, studded with a few wind-tortured trees and cut by a rugged canyon, rose up from the coastal plain, a herd of cows grazing in the distance. To the right, a graceful, curving arc of frothing Pacific chewed at a virgin white beach pocked with tide pools, and tucked into low, green cliffs, a tiny village of thirties-era bungalows overlooking the water—not mansions, just drafty little houses meant to be used and scraped and repainted year after year in the harsh salt environment, looking as natural here as pieces of driftwood. Back then, visitors parked on the inland side of PCH, then walked through a tunnel under the highway, a glorified culvert, really, and when you emerged on the other side to the sound of waves crashing, the sensation was of having traveled back in time. And seeing that, seeing my mythic California hadn't been paved over entirely, I knew I could move here after all. If there could still be a Crystal Cove, I reasoned, there could still be other traces of treasure spared the axe and bulldozer.

Right.

Today Crystal Cove is a strip mall and a golf course and stack of carefully coiffed and color-coordinated mansions overlooking the non-native vegetation and palms imported to replace the uprooted natural landscape. The beach houses were sold to the state, which promptly kicked all the renters out of their rapidly vanishing paradise, although the grandiose and ludicrous plans to turn the historic old cottages into some sort of luxury hotel never came to pass. Government officials nonetheless congratulated themselves on this abomination, because the landowner, the insatiable Irvine Company, agreed to dedicate a strip of the once-pristine inland pasture and canyon for park use. It serves more as a reminder of what's been lost than a preservation of the cove's past splendors; I find myself avoiding that drive I once sought any excuse to make.

During that fateful drive in 1985, I passed through Seal Beach without noticing its charms, or even noticing it at all. This is because the Coast Highway cuts inland here, three long blocks from the sand, so all you see is an unremarkable succession of gas stations, a strip center, some shops—nothing to pull you in and get you to stop. The heart of Seal Beach, its Old Town section, is hidden from view, but the mile-long stretch of beach neighborhood between the San Gabriel River and Anaheim Bay is a gem. It easily mixes old bungalows with newer-money mini-mansions, throwing together original owners who bought in for nine thousand dollars after the war with newcomers who wish their property taxes were that low. Once I discovered Seal Beach, years after moving to the area, stumbling on another surviving piece of original California, I was hooked.

The center of Old Town is Main Street, a true old-fashioned downtown, where most of the businesses are locally owned and the fanciest restaurant's only dress requirement is shirt and shoes. Business is conducted in shorts and T-shirts; the local congressman can be seen now and then yakking on his cell in his wet suit after surfing.

At the foot of Main Street is the Seal Beach Pier, and the stretch of sand on either side of it is broad and flat and mostly empty. It's a south-facing beach, and the best time to see it, my favorite time, is early afternoon on a winter day. When the sun is as high as it's going to get, it's still slightly in front of you, so that it dazzles the eye when you stare straight out at the water, Catalina Island hazy in the distance, the handful of figures surfing the pier reduced to mere silhouettes. The water becomes monochromatic in this light, a pattern of gray and white circlets, moving sinuously, like scales on a reptile's skin, rippling and sparking in the sunlight, the waves so close together it's impossible to differentiate them, their sound merging into one sustained hiss, the reptile's mesmerizing sigh. Except for sunny summer weekends, the beach is so wide it is possible to be lonely here, to feel small, to not hear the Nokia song chiming in someone's pocket.

It was not always this way. Seal Beach started where its sister beach towns have ended up, the first town served by the Red Car Line, bringing in the beach-bound hordes beginning in 1904. City father Stanton rounded up a pool of investors and built the longest pleasure pier on the West Coast, with fifty-two giant "scintillators" left over from the most recent world's fair erected at the end. These huge light standards, arrayed like a battalion of soldiers staring out to sea, cast brilliant rainbows of light onto the water for night swimming. By 1920, the Jewel Café and the Seal Beach Dance Pavilion and Bathhouse with its ninety-foot plunge flanked the pier and were the talk of the coast, a must-stop for weekend beach goers with a quarter to burn on the trolley, as well as for the stars of the silent screen arriving in their roadsters and limos. Cecil B. DeMille parted the waters in his first filming of *The Ten Commandments* here, as sightseers plied the beach walk on miniature wicker cars powered by electric motors. A giant roller coaster two blocks long towered over all, and celebrities popped into town aboard their private planes, which landed at the Seal Beach Airport, famous for its Airport Club twenty-four-hour casino. Stop by Clancy's Irish Bar on Main Street today and ask one of our longest-lived natives, T-Bone, about it, how he used to earn tips as a kid chocking the wheels of the stars' planes and wiping the motor oil off their windshields in exchange for rides. He loved the old Seal Beach, the splendid pier and the rickety houses and the air of danger, and he decries the "do-gooders" who, with a firm assist from Prohibition and the Great Depression, ground Seal Beach's incarnation as Sin City into dust. The demise of the Red Cars finished the job. Now the old airport is long gone, and the coaster, and the giant Quonset hut with all-night poker inside is just a skeletal foundation by First Street. T-Bone can't afford to live here anymore—he's in landlocked Westminster down the road.

Except for the sky-high cost of its real estate, the town has marched in the opposite direction from its sister beach cities, becoming smaller, quainter, more family oriented over time. Accidents of geography and government have conspired to accomplish this. Bounded on the south by the ocean, the west by the San Gabriel, and the east by the Seal Beach Naval Weapons Station, much of which is now a nature preserve, Seal Beach has almost no room to grow. Some briefly wise city council in the distant past decided to forbid most apartment buildings and duplexes, and so Old Town has remained pristine and stable, a family zone. Except for new commercial development pushing inland past the 405 Freeway, out past Leisure World and the Boeing facility where moon rockets were once constructed and secret spy satellites are now designed, development has been essentially frozen here since the sixties.

When I returned to City Hall a few days later to pay my five bucks for *A Story of Seal Beach,* Joanne had some old photo albums waiting for me. A newspaper ad from 1913 stuffed into the front of one caught my attention. It urged L.A. residents to take the train to Seal Beach and to buy a lot for five hundred fifty dollars (only ten percent down!), so that they, too, could enjoy the city that "has no winter and knows no summer...growing like a weed and sturdy as an oak." The vision, then, was for Seal Beach to become the biggest, brightest, trendiest coastal city this side of the Bay Area. That vision flourished, briefly, then failed, thankfully, but ninety-one years later it is being resurrected.

The city is hard up for cash—there are million-dollar homes, but no money to pick up beach litter or to keep City Hall open a full five days—and so the push for progress, to grow like a weed, long dormant, is rearing up. One of the last undeveloped pieces of land in town, the old Hellman Ranch next to the "Hill" neighborhood above PCH, is now being graded for new homes, the city allowing an ancient Indian burial ground and wetland to be despoiled in its haste to expand the tax base. The most abominable parts of the project—the hundreds of homes, the golf course, the horrendous traffic problems—were long ago killed by public outcry, and Native American monitors now safeguard the artifacts and burial mounds. Only sixty-four houses remain on the drawing board, along with a restored wetland and a nature preserve to keep safe the legion of foxes and waterfowl and coyotes who live there, not to mention the street-savvy skunks who prowl the neighborhood to scrounge cat food and show my wolfhound who's boss. Still, the change will be jarring; the wide, desolate flatlands next to the fragrant eucalyptus trees of Gum Grove Park, where people run their dogs and hike along the old cow pasture and horse trails, will be gone.

More ominously, the city council, after thirty years of resistance, finally voted to put parking meters on Main Street, a sign that Seal Beach's unique small-town feel is truly on the auction block. This is one of the last beach communities in SoCal where you don't have to dig for quarters. Protests came so swiftly and in such numbers that a shocked and awed council soon rescinded its meter vote—but we all sense, now, that it's only a matter of time. After all, a cell phone shop has just opened on Main Street, an absurdly out-of-place beachhead for chain stores. The fact that no customers ever seem to enter the shop has not as yet deterred its corporate owners.

And another parcel of land, the last undeveloped piece of beachfront in Old Town, where a red-brick power plant long ago stood by the San Gabriel and provided electricity used to help construct the Hoover Dam, is now being eyed by developers and many hungry council members who have budgets to balance and who can no longer afford The Seal Beach Way. The neighborhood is up in arms, of course, and may yet prevail, or at least limit the damage, but I can't help but remember Crystal Cove and its vanished paradise, and just how fragile our dreams and myths truly are, at least the ones that count.

Chris Davidson

A QUICK SURVEY OF CONDITIONS

Born in Laguna Beach in 1970, Chris Davidson attended San Clemente High School, earned an MFA from UC Irvine, and now teaches at Biola University. After living in Orange County for most of his life, he recently moved to Long Beach. His poetry and writing have been featured by *Miramar*, *Zócalo Public Square*, *Jacket2*, the *Spoon River Poetry Review*, *Zyzzyva*, *Caesura*, *Spark and Echo Arts*, the *Green Mountains Review*, KPFK's *Poets Cafe,* and other outlets.

In "A Quick Survey of Conditions," published by *Zócalo Public Square* in 2011, Davidson told us he aimed to capture "a version of the Seal Beach house my family and I rented for twelve years, the longest I've ever lived in one place as an adult. I had mixed feelings about living there, as the poem seems to show—in a falling-down house in the midst of wealth and privilege."

> The concrete path goes round the house,
> giving access to all its sides. In summer,
> it's white as salt, at night dulled
> as under a full moon tinted slightly blue,
> like the blue accenting ice in the ocean.
> Around front it lets go a straight
> spur through a lawn of dying grass
> to the street. The neighbors' lawns on both sides
> are lit-up green, and springy, and
> connected to ours by the sidewalk parallel
> to the street absorbing each house's path,
> a creek taking in tributaries and flowing
> or frozen. From above, though I've never been,

the houses with paths like this look like
thought balloons in comics, each house what it—
the street, pale gray space—thinks,
or maybe the street's the bordering void
between panels. The void does the talking here,
friends, and conveys people well-packaged
to and from the aphorisms they sleep in.
This is no complaint. It's where I live.
4th of July the street's released to kids.

Michael Ryan

A VERSION OF HAPPINESS

Michael Ryan was born in St. Louis in 1946. He has written four books of poems, an autobiography, a memoir, and a collection of essays about poetry and writing. He received a BA from the University of Notre Dame, an MA from Claremont Graduate University, and both an MFA and PhD from the University of Iowa, where he was poetry editor of the *Iowa Review*. His work has appeared in the *American Poetry Review*, the *Alaska Quarterly Review*, the *Threepenny Review*, the *New Yorker*, and *Poetry*. He taught previously at the University of Iowa, Princeton University, and the University of Virginia, as well as in the MFA Program for Writers at Warren Wilson College. A long-time faculty member in UC Irvine's MFA program, he is currently the director of its poetry program.

In this work from his *New and Selected Poems*, published in 2004, an outdoor summer concert provides the vibrant setting for considering, and celebrating, the parent-child connection.

for Ellen Bryant Voigt

Tonight the band's Nigerian—
Afro-Cuban, last week; next week, Cajun:
the summer multicultural concert series
in the San Juan Capistrano library courtyard;
two hundred of us, all ages, in the audience;
Edenic evening air and stars: tickets six bucks.
You'd love this music, this place:
the musicians are like poets (they have day jobs)

and they're *good*: they play this music
because they love it, love making it,
love being able to make it—together
(unlike poets?). The sound
each is part of and takes part in
feeds through their collective body
into the next chord and phrase—
into fingers, lips, lungs, even elbows
in the case of the maniac-god on the congas
when guitars and horns cease
and lead singers politely step aside
so that we may witness his five-minute solo
and feel, as they do, the triumph of prowess
over human clumsiness, and notice
who's drumming us into this happy trance.
Now they give us this chance: to notice.
They eye us like parents watching children
unwrap gifts. He sweats not only for us
but also for what against all reason he can do
with whapping palms and shuttling elbows
that engender exponentially beyond his allotted
two of each, because how can one man do this?
Ancient our amazement and this power
that has caused sane men to run point-blank into fusillades
or shuttle themselves, their wives, and their postmarital
extra twenty pounds behind a column of the courtyard portico
to dance beside an eleven-year-old and her mom.
All evening these two have been a joy to notice:
the girl goofing with her dancing, freckled, gangly,
her mom I imagine still her best friend
before the teenage hormonal tsunami sweeps her away
like a beach shack. Mom's late-thirtyish,
bespectacled, frumpy, doing dorky disco moves (like me)

she probably learned riding *her* tsunami
in front of a mirror to Bee Gees songs
with an inconsolable crush on John Travolta
and no clue that happiness might come
someday from a parental talent for pleasure
in what a child can do. I know
your father thought your playing piano for the choir
in Baptist churches in rural Virginia
the pinnacle of achievement.
He loved music but couldn't play it,
so he wanted you to, and you did.
How extreme a child's love is. I guess
we'll do anything to make our parents love us
even if they can't. The ones who can,
though…—ludricous of me
to try to put in words what it does to be loved
like that, but it's still visible
in you, my dear friend. This frumpy mom
shows it, too, as does her girl
despite trials, heartbreaks, and disasters
she may have already and certainly will suffer.
Nobody gets out alive, except in spirit
(the lucky ones), which as you know
can grow through music that couldn't be more
bodily, but translates beautifully.

Martin J. Smith

---

from **DARK MATTER**

Born in 1961 in Birmingham, Alabama, Martin J. Smith is a journalist who says his day job as a newspaper and magazine writer-editor serves as inspiration for his fiction. He is the author of the popular Memory Series of crime fiction and is the coeditor of *Poplorica: A Popular History of the Fads, Mavericks, Inventions, and Lore that Shaped Modern America* and *Oops: Twenty Life Lessons from the Fiascos that Shaped America*. His 2012 book, *The Wild Duck Chase: Inside the Strange and Wonderful World of the Federal Duck Stamp Contest*, was the basis for the documentary *The Million Dollar Duck*, which won both the Jury and Audience Awards at the 2016 Slamdance Film Festival. He worked until recently as the editor-in-chief of *Orange Coast Magazine*.

"Dark Matter" is a fictional story based on the real financial collapse of Dick Dale, king of the surf guitar, whom Smith profiled for the *Los Angeles Times Magazine* in 2001. "I ended up helping him move out of his landmark Balboa Peninsula mansion during a harried twenty-four hours after a court evicted him," Smith recalled to us. "Dark Matter," which Smith wrote for the 2010 crime fiction anthology *Orange County Noir*, is a gothic cautionary tale about a rock star standing at the abyss of his own creation. And, he adds, "It gave me the chance to throw in a live tiger."

I SHOULD HAVE LEFT the minute I gave it to him, should have just tossed the eviction notice across the doorstep and onto the cracked tiles of the old mansion's foyer. A smarter man would have hoofed right back to the Sentra and caught the car ferry off Balboa Island. Me? I stood there like the wide-eyed fan I once was, rooted to the front steps of his formerly grand palace at the island's southern tip. I'd specifically asked for this delivery, just for the chance to meet somebody I once idolized. Now I was staring into the face of a faded nobody with the saddest eyes I'd ever seen. When he answered my knock, he looked like someone peering up from the bottom of a well.

"Been 'specting you," he said, slurring a bit.

"Wheels of justice don't turn so fast, but now you've got the paperwork. Court order came down yesterday."

I resisted the urge to apologize. I'd read everything ever written about him, including the entire bankruptcy file. He could only blame himself for this latest bit of unpleasantness. He'd never stopped living like the star he once was, even if the money ran out years ago. It showed. The fenders on the Porsche out front were rusted through and the canvas top was ripped in three places. The house was the choicest piece of real estate on this tony Newport Harbor refuge, but pretty run-down. His ex, the third, owned it now. The judge gave him twenty-four hours to vacate.

I looked at my watch. "Anyway, the sheriff'll be here this time tomorrow morning."

"Splendid."

He cinched the belt of his robe, raised his highball glass, swirled the ice, and took a sip of something thick and amber— something completely wrong for 9:40 in the morning. His bony chest was unnaturally tan, almost orange, the hair on it white.

"Question for you, sir," he said. "Know anythin 'bout dark matter?"

I'd seen my share of people in denial. I serve eviction notices for the Superior Court of Orange County, California. I am a $15.50-an-hour destroyer of worlds, the death messenger of the American Dream. Nothing surprises me—guys with guns, screeching women, unleashed dogs. It's why I carry pepper spray in a little holster on my belt. But this, this was the worst of it. I'd just delivered a final curb stomp to somebody who'd once meant a lot to me, somebody who'd obviously given up. What was I thinking when I asked to handle this one?

"Dark. Mat-ter," he repeated, working hard to enunciate.

I knew all about his eccentricities. Guy was one of the kings of cock-rock when he was, like, nineteen. So big even a teen dork like me played his first album to death. He was white-hot after that first record, the swaggering lead singer of *the* '70s band. Life was good. Spent millions on anything that moved—cars, horses, women. For years he kept exotic animals as house pets, and claimed some mystical connection to them—right up until Animal Control took them away after his panther killed a neighbor's dog.

Nothing lasts. The second album rose briefly, then sank to oblivion. The third? It was over. The band broke up. That was more than thirty-five years ago, half a lifetime of autograph shows, *Behind the Music* cameos, and the occasional Japanese royalty check. The passing harbor tour boats used to point out his house, but that stopped years ago. No one even called him for session work anymore, because of the drinking. I have this friend who works at *TMZ*, the celebrity scandal show. She said that during his latest divorce, his ex was shopping a video tape that showed him butt-naked on a lawn chair, pasty and late-life saggy, getting blown by a Goth-looking high-school sophomore. Its release actually might have *helped* his career. But my friend told me the show had passed on the tape.

The executive producer didn't even recognize his name.

What do you do when you peak at nineteen? You move to Balboa Island, that's what. You fall down a well.

"Dark matter?" I said.

He stood up straight and squared his shoulders. "Astrophysics. Cosmology. C'mon, *you* know."

He swayed and bumped against the doorframe and motioned me closer, like he was about to share a secret. I stood my ground, but leaned in a little, near enough to smell the booze but far enough to cut and run if he was as drunk and nuts as he seemed. I also caught a whiff of something that made me think of a dirty litter box.

"Can't see dark matter," he said, "'s invisible. But it's *there*."

"Where?"

"All 'round us. Most of th' mass in th' observ-a-ble universe?" He grinned. "Dark matter."

"I'll be damned. And you can't even see it?"

That brought a somber shake of his head, still crowned by that goofy hair-metal cut, improbably black. "But y'see what dark matter *does*."

I took a small step backward. His breath was toxic. "Which is?"

He lit up. Perfect rows of bright white teeth split the weathered skin of his face. "Changes things. Affects things. See, mass has weight, and weight creates grrra-vi-ty." Took his time pronouncing each syllable of the word. "And grrra-vi-ty doesn't lie, man. Doesn't lie." Another wink. "C'mere. I'll show you."

With that he turned from the open door and scuffed down the hall, the soft soles of his UGG boots making a *schik-schik-schik* as he moved away. For some reason, don't ask me why, I followed. Say what you will about celebrity, but there's definitely something magnetic about it. Seductive. Dangerous. No one's immune. Maybe that's what he was talking about? Anyway, as soon as I stepped across his threshold I was thinking, *Dude, you really gotta ask for that raise.*

More than eighty rehab facilities dot the Balboa Peninsula within a mile of this exclusive island; Southern California's celebrities like to dry out in tidy, well-appointed luxury, and by the beach. I'd never been inside one of those, but this place struck me as probably the exact opposite. Piles of stuff everywhere—books, clothes, newspapers. One side of the hall was just drywall, installed but never plastered or painted. The other side was '70s-era flocked wallpaper hung by an amateur. A classic Fender Strat with a snapped neck lay at the base of a stairway leading to a second story, its looping strings holding the pieces together like thin steel ligaments.

"Mind your way right here," he called back over his shoulder, side-stepping something. It looked like a mound of shit the size of a football.

When I got closer, I realized it *was* a pile of shit.

"Whoa," I said, and stopped.

"Cheers," he said, lifting the glass again as he moved off down the hall. "Best to let it air-dry a bit."

He waved me on, turning left toward a sun-filled room facing the harbor's main channel. "Right in here."

My father taught me caution in all things. He lived life by the Law of Worst Possible Consequences and communicated it to us daily. An unbuckled seat belt would lead directly to death. So would a carelessly placed skateboard, improperly inflated tires, or an incautious remark to the wrong cop. To be honest, it's probably why I gravitated to a career wreaking legal vengeance on people who live too close to the edge. Still, something irresistible was pulling me around the corner into the unknown, into a room filled with cast-off dorm furniture.

The space itself was a realtor's wet dream. Vast windows overlooked the main channel of Newport Harbor. Electric Duffy boats slid past, and the mast and mainsail of an enormous passing yacht briefly dominated the view. Here was a daily parade of all that the Good Life could offer, no longer within reach from this ringside seat.

No matter how ramshackle this castle, the thought of losing it must be torturing the king.

"Sweet," I said, crossing between a battered couch and a shredded La-Z-Boy recliner, which lay on its side in the middle of the room. It looked like a toy tossed aside by a giant child.

I joined him at one of the windows. "You've lived here a long time, right?"

He drained his drink before answering. "Three albums. Three marriages."

He turned away from the view and headed for the bar across the room. That's when I noticed her.

She was stretched out in a claw-footed tub, gray and glassy-eyed and naked except for a pair of strappy red-stiletto heels. Maybe early forties, with the look of a tired old groupie. She had stringy, damp blond hair on her head. The dark roots were the same color as the fluffy patch between her legs. He'd half-filled the tub with party ice he must have bought last night or early this morning at the 7-Eleven on the peninsula. A dozen crumpled plastic ice bags were piled at one end. Best guess: she hadn't been there long; for an ongoing obsession, he'd be using dry ice.

I tamped down my clutching fear. I'd never seen a dead body before.

"Sh-she may need help," I managed.

Absurd, I know. My other option was to just crap myself and run.

"Who?" he said, his back to me, pouring himself another drink.

I pointed to the tub even though he wasn't watching. "Her."

When he turned around, he was stirring his drink with the index finger of one hand. He did that for a long time without saying a word, without even looking at the chilling body in the middle of the room. Suddenly, he seemed to notice her.

"Hoo boy," he said, cheerful, as if he'd simply neglected to introduce her. "Dam'nest thing, that."

"She definitely doesn't look okay."

"Oh no. She's definitely not." He took a sip. "No par-medics necessary, 'm afraid."

Time to go. I sidestepped toward the hallway.

"Wait," he said. "Her...this...tha's not what I wanted to show you."

"Dude," I said, "this is seriously fucked up."

"I *know*!" he said. "She comes by th' house to party, then overdoses. Self-control's sush a problem with some people."

She didn't look like she'd been killed. No blood. No bullet wounds or knife holes. No bruises at her throat. Just the waxy gray corpse of a woman who'd stopped by to party.

On ice.

"When, um..."

"Lass night. She found my coke and jus'...overdid!"

"Jesus," I said. "I'm sorry."

"Me too! Terrific talent, that one." He winked. "Not a kid anymore, but she sure knew how to work it."

I struggled for words. "Sorry for your loss."

"But now y'see what I mean 'bout dark matter?"

I sidestepped again toward the hallway, quietly unsnapping the plastic holster of my pepper spray as I did. "Not really."

He reached into the pocket of his robe. When he pulled it out, I saw something black in his hand and swallowed hard. Who carries a gun in their bathrobe? Nobody sane. He seemed as surprised as I was to see it. He slid it back in and fished into the robe's other pocket. Whatever he pulled out of that he pointed across the room toward me. The widescreen beside me blinked to life.

A TV remote.

"DVD," he said, "'s a Science Channel thing on the cosmos or some such, 'bout dark matter. Been watching it all mornin', tryin' to sort this out. All this shit slidin' toward th' center, t'ward me. I mean, where do I go from here? M'whole comeback thing?" He nodded to the dead woman. "This'll complicate plans a bit."

A bit?

"You said it was an accident. I can't imagine they'd—"

He waved my words away like gnats. "So I'm listenin' to this show, about how dark matter's invisible, but y'know it's there cause it has gravity, 'cause it pulls things into its orbit. All sortsa things. And I'm thinking, see, how *I'm* sort of like dark matter."

I said nothing. He sensed my confusion.

"Shit happens, you know? To *me*. All the time. I always seem to land right in the middle of it. And I had this..." He paused to enunciate. "...epi-phany. I just wanted t'show somebody."

I looked at my watch again. Made a point of doing so. "Really gotta get back."

"Won' take long. Wanna drink?"

"Can't."

"I told you to stay."

Those final words were hard and sharp enough to cut glass, scary, the dopey-drunk voice completely gone. I stared at him until something flashed in the corner of my eye. My first glance to the left registered nothing. The second registered something that didn't compute at all. Why would a full-grown Siberian tiger be standing in the doorway, right between me and the only way out of the room?

Things started to add up. The giant shit pile in the hall. The suffocating litter-box smell. Even the shredded La-Z-Boy, which I suddenly realized was just an overworked scratching post.

"Really need to get going," I said.

"Pussy, sit!" he called out.

The tiger didn't move, just kept its intense yellow eyes fixed on me. It filled the door frame.

"Sit!" he commanded.

I sat back on the window ledge, just in case he was talking to me. Slowly, the tiger sat. Head level. Ears back. Gaze steady.

"That's Pussy!" he said. "Raised 'er right here. Took 'er in as an orphaned cub, had 'er a year." He wandered across the room and scratched the tiger between the ears. "Harmless old bird now. Mostly. No sudd'n moves, though. Big cats never lose those instincts. Don't want 'er thinkin' yer a threat. Y'sure don' want her thinkin' yer wounded."

My body was flushed with primal juices. Every nerve was on fire. "It lives here?"

He shook his head. "Refuge. Up in Ventura. Snuck 'er out yesterday and drove 'er down in my panel van, brought 'er in after dark." He gestured grandly around the room. "We lived here together once. Happy days, y'know, and I jus' wanted her to see the place again, b'fore…well, you know."

"I see."

"Figured we'd spend a li'l time together before the big move." He held an index finger up to his pursed lips. "Don' tell the neighbors."

"Not a word."

"Nice people, but they'd go apeshit. Always do." He tipped his glass toward the bathtub. "Course, now there's this situation."

"Complicated, like you said."

"I *still* generate a lot of grav'ty, even if I'm invisible."

"I'm sure you do." I don't know why, but I added: "I played *Ani-Mosity* to death when I was a kid. Great album."

"Thanks."

I'd kicked into some weird survival mode, desperate to say anything that might get me out of this. He hadn't threatened me. I didn't think he was capable of violence. On the other hand, I was in a room with a dead groupie, a live tiger, and a desperate armed man who was drinking heavily before 10 a.m. Things were beyond weird already.

"I even liked the second album."

THE SANTA ANA MOUNTAINS AND THE CANYONS

Close by stands the tiny cottage, with its green blinds, its numerous porches and outer doors. Near the dwelling, supported by nine slender posts, is a square roofing of live-oak branches laid thickly together. The posts are twined with water ivy and other climbing vines. The space sheltered by this canopy is the dining-room. In the center stands a large table, at which we have just taken a delicious breakfast of coffee, hot rolls, fresh cheese, and thick white honey from the apiary, in sight across the creek which flows down the cañon. For this dining-room Nature wove the carpet. Disdaining cotton or wool, she made it of the earth, and took pleasure in the thought that the feet of men and women can never wear the staunch fabric thread-bare. Feet may come and feet may go, but that carpet will wear forever.

—EMMA H. ADAMS, FROM "IN THE SANTIAGO CAÑON,"
TO AND FRO IN SOUTHERN CALIFORNIA, 1887

Henryk Sienkiewicz

from IDYLL IN THE SANTA ANA MOUNTAINS

Nobel Prize laureate Henryk "Henry" Adam Aleksander Pius Sienkiewicz was born in Poland in 1846 and is most famous for *Quo Vadis*, one of the many historical novels he wrote after a career reporting on his extensive travels in the United States. In 1876 he arrived in what would become Orange County with Helena Modrzejewska (soon to become the internationally famous stage actress Helena Modjeska) and her husband. Sienkiewicz lived in both Anaheim and Anaheim Landing (now Seal Beach) and chronicled his adventures, which included hunting, meeting Native Americans, hiking in the Santa Ana Mountains, and observing the blossoming of Modjeska's theatrical career. His engaging, exuberant, digressive, and informed tales of travel and winning escapades were composed as letters written home to Polish newspaper readers.

In these excerpts from one such letter, "Idyll in the Santa Ana Mountains" (1876), we see his careful yet enraptured reporting, along with his sociological observations and a tone of self-congratulation consistent with the ethos of the joyful wanderer (in this case one accompanied by a dog and a "tame badger" that he calls one of "nature's exceptional adventurers"). Here Sienkiewicz surveys the natural and human landscape and explains the spirit and character of canyon life.

THE SANTA ANA MOUNTAINS, from which I am sending this letter, constitute the southern part of the enormous range that stretches in scattered masses and under various names from Oregon all the way to southern California and to Mexican Sonora. I came here from Anaheim Landing together with my host Max Neblung. We arrived late at night, but this night, being my first spent in a wild and completely uninhabited region, left an unforgettable impression upon me.

We had stopped with a certain squatter, Jack Harrison by name, who reminded me of Robinson Crusoe, for he lives all alone in a tent with a dog and rifle as his sole companions. My neo-Robinson was a gentleman no longer young, about fifty years of age, whose appearance was such that if I had met him on one of my expeditions, I should have reached for my revolver without hesitation. He was dressed in a flannel shirt, trousers made of the skin of fallow deer, and a tattered Mexican hat whose ragged brim covered a bearded and threatening face. As soon as Max introduced us to one another, the squatter shook my hand firmly and, uttering the usual "Hello," he departed immediately for the ravine to light the fire and to prepare our supper. Max and I proceeded to unsaddle our mustangs, which we had tied to a tree with long lassos. The horses started to munch clover that was growing luxuriantly under the oaks, while we, having lighted our pipes, sat in the tents waiting for supper.

I began to examine my surroundings. Black, piled-up masses of mountains enclosed the valley whose only outlet to the north and south was the bed of a deep mountain stream. The region seemed to me extremely wild and gloomy. Rocky cliffs hung over the valley in huge, titanic blocks, thrown up as if with confused fury one upon another. It seemed to me that at any moment these blocks might break loose and crash to the bottom of the valley. The bright night increased still further the wild extravagance of all these forms. The moon's beams threw a silver ribbon around the edges of the rocks whose black, motionless silhouettes were etched against the illuminated background with strangely severe clarity. The sounds of night heightened still more the grim spell of the environment. In the rock crevices covered with trees, wildcats wailed threateningly and hoarsely; now and again an owl hooted; at times the horses neighed. My dog, unaccustomed to such commotion, raised his muzzle towards the moon and began to howl. My tame badger clambered up determinedly on my knees as if from fright. As for me, I was intoxicated by all this and in a state of complete ecstasy. Although

I had galloped about thirty miles on a wretched nag and felt as though not a bone in my body was left intact, nothing in the world would have induced me to follow the example of Max. He had spread a blanket in front of the tent, lain down on it, and fallen asleep.

When you travel eastwards from Anaheim in the direction of the mountains and your horse crosses the wide, sandy bed of the Santa Ana River, you recognize that you have left the pale of civilization where land is divided up and constitutes private property, where society is governed by the laws of the United States, and where all relationships are regularized. Government lands begin on the other side of this river. They are only sparsely inhabited by squatters and Indians, and for the most part are still unoccupied and awaiting the pioneer. The only law in this territory is the terrifying lynch law which can best be defined in these words: not merely a tooth for a tooth, an eye for an eye, but for every assault against an individual or his property, there is but one penalty—the rope. But owing to the integrity and decency of the squatters, it is never applied.

These lands are divided into so-called claims, that is, square sections of 160 acres. Actually this division is not exact, for no surveyor ever set foot on the remote, mountainous wastelands. The law allows each American or candidate for naturalization to take this set amount of land for his use, on condition that he pay the government $1.50 per acre within a ten-year period. After the expiration of this period of use, the land becomes unconditionally his own property which he may sell, bequeath, or rent; in a word, he may do with it what he pleases. The obligation to pay the government exists only on paper, for, in reality, a squatter who occupied unowned land, cultivated it, and erected buildings upon it, although he has not paid a cent, cannot be ousted by any law.

In view of such liberal terms and the ease of taking up land without legal obstacles, and in view of the almost fabulous fertility of these valleys covered for the most part with age-old forests of oak, platan, and laurel, one might expect that squatters would come swarming and teeming in; but such is not the case. I have already mentioned the main cause—lack of people! Undoubtedly a large penniless mob of immigrants with nothing to lose would descend upon the place were it not for the enormous distance between the Eastern states and California. Furthermore, the cost of the journey from New York, Philadelphia, Washington, or Boston, not to mention Europe, is the equivalent of more than two claims.

As for the Americans living in towns, they are all businessmen, that is, people engaged in industrial or commercial affairs, who see no material gain from settling in the mountains and on empty wastelands. Aesthetic reasons such as picturesque scenery, solitude, undisturbed peace, and life in the bosom of nature, these are things for which a true Yankee will never pay a nickel. What's more, there are no roads leading into these beautiful mountain valleys.

The Spanish name *cañón* means, speaking precisely, a gorge. When such a gorge widens abruptly or gradually so that it forms a spacious dale surrounded by an amphitheater of mountains, enough space is thus made for cattle raising, beekeeping, and even farming. But most often such clearings lie deep in the mountain chain and only the bed of a stream serves as an entrance. It is simply a large crack, or as it is called in the Ukraine, a *yar*, at whose base water roars over stones. Its sides consist of cliffs rising perpendicularly sometimes two or three hundred feet.

Nothing is more grim than the gullies of such streams. At the bottom reigns eternal twilight since the fertile tops of the cliffs are covered with trees whose branches often meet each other over these streams and hide the sky from the traveler's eye. In places wild hops, wild grapes, or liana reach out from bank to bank, join together, become entangled, strangle each other with their arms, forming such thick festoons of greenery that daylight passes through them with difficulty. Sometimes the traveler is under the impression that he is moving along some underground passage. Wherever blue sky can be seen through a chink above, the cheering sight is disturbed by the whir of the wings of vultures, ravens, and eagles, and by their gloomy cawing that fills one with sadness and foreboding.

From the depths of such crevices after sunset there resound those ominous cries and roars which are unbearable to nerves unaccustomed to them. When the sun is extinguished on the peaks, all the wild beasts come down to drink water from the streams. First come the deer, antelopes, then Rocky Mountain sheep with sickle-like horns almost touching their backs, and small white-flecked mountain goats. Behind them come the rapacious animals of the mountains. The silver and red cougar crawls quietly in the twilight like a greyish snake. From a rocky crevice the lynx raises his head and rolls his fiery eyes. In the trees sneak grey wildcats. Now and again there comes a distant sound of stones falling down the steep rock face. It is the grim tyrant of the mountains, the grey bear, plodding along with heavy steps as he goes to plunge in the stream, his huge frame fatigued by the heat of the day.

In many places the stream beds are so blocked with various size rocks that it is impossible to cross either by wagon or on horseback, especially since the stones are always covered with wet and slippery moss. In winter during the rainy season and in spring during the general flooding of the waters, the streams become bursting torrents, and at that time the inhabitants of the canyons are completely cut off from the rest of the world. As a result, they are compelled to live a rough life in the canyons and not even to dream of the comforts of civilized life.

To be sure, where the canyons widen, the valleys are beautiful and fertile. It is easy to reach and to occupy them, to find a spot as yet unvisited by man, and to say to oneself: this is mine! As on a desert island, no one will dispute your right to ownership. While it is simple enough to take up the land, it is not easy to live upon it. A squatter is usually a poor man, without a wife or children, a lonely individual. Such a person comes to the mountains, chooses the canyon that pleases him most, and says to himself: "I will settle here." But to settle, you must build a house. The squatter does not ordinarily own any tools other than an ax, a saw, and a drill. There is plenty of timber for a cabin, but how do you commence when all around you whispers a virgin forest of century-old trees whose trunks are several feet in diameter and whose tops are lost somewhere in the clouds? A huge, black oak grows next to a white-barked plane tree; next, a grey oak; then again, a hickory with such a hard grain that the ax rebounds from it as from a stone; further on grows a laurel. Everything is so tied in snakelike knots of liana, so intertwined, so crowded, that the forest seems to be one solid, indestructible mass. Imagine what hardships the settler must endure to clear a place for a cabin and a yard, to cut down and drag away the gigantic trees. Later, in building the cabin, what enormous strength is required for one person without help from anyone else to lift into place one log after another, one rafter after another. For thinner trees it is sometimes necessary to walk a mile or two and then to drag them along the spiteful bed of the stream. At the same time you must carry on your back a heavy rifle without which you dare not move, first of all for protection, and secondly to kill something to eat. It is obvious that the mere construction of a cabin is almost too much for human strength. Therefore, it is not at all surprising that squatters are very few in number. Those embarked upon such a life are either wanderers from abroad who, having arrived without a knowledge of the language or any financial means, and unwilling to be dependent, have no other alternative; or they may be shipwrecks from life pursued by the law, or unhappy souls seeking solitude, or finally, nature's exceptional adventurers who value such rugged independence above all earthly treasures.

But just as a shepherd sorts out his sheep and removes the weaker ones from the flock, so in similar circumstances does life sort out the squatters. Weaker individuals fall in the unequal battle. Thus, squatters are generally men of great physical strength and of uncommonly tough spirit. It could be said that civilization has sent out her most robust members to clear the way for her in the virgin forests. Stronger yet are the qualities of those squatters in the territories inhabited by wild Indians, but their attributes are outweighed by their faults which make pioneers of progress extremely dangerous men. Bloody conflicts with the redskins and the need to use a knife or a revolver at any moment develop wild passions and cruelties in them, as well as coarseness verging on brutality, while the uncertainties of tomorrow give rise to recklessness. To be accurate, a squatter from New Mexico, Arizona, or the Indian Territory is not a settler, but a lumberjack. Gathered into groups of a few dozen men, these squatters search out virgin forests untouched by the ax, and not really caring whether the timber belongs to the Indians, or to the government, or even to private companies, they cut it down, form it into rafts on the waters of the Red River, Rio Colorado, or Rio Grande, and float it to the nearest towns. After selling the timber, a squatter with his pockets loaded with twenty-dollar gold pieces abandons himself to drunkenness and absolute idleness in the town or the nearest tavern until he has lost his last penny, and then, poor as a churchmouse, he goes back to the wilderness. I need not add that this life is often full of very bloody incidents.

Theodore Payne

---

from *LIFE ON THE MODJESKA RANCH IN THE GAY NINETIES*

Born in England in 1872, Theodore Payne was a horticulturist, gardener, landscape designer, and botanist who made his name in Southern California teaching the region about its own abundant native plant culture. New to the county and only twenty-one years old, he began work as the head gardener for Madame Modjeska at her estate, Arden, in what is now the Silverado region. Payne happily recalls his three years there in his memoir *Life on the Modjeska Ranch in the Gay Nineties*, published in 1962, when he was ninety years old.

A thoughtful recollection of his own journey, the memoir is both an enthusiastic immigrant's story and a classic of horticultural science. As a piece of scholarship, it greatly contributed to the study of Southern California ecology and profoundly influenced natural resources management policy.

N ESTLING AGAINST THE hillside beneath century old live oak trees in the beautiful Santiago Canyon about 20 miles east of the town of Orange stands a low white bungalow, the former home of Madame Helena Modjeska, the great Polish actress who spent so much of her life on the American stage.

Today the grounds are surrounded by a tight wire fence with a padlock on each gate and a great dane warns you not to try to enter. Unless you are a friend of the present owner or can persuade the caretaker to open the gate, you are not going to be able to view this interesting and historic spot except to get a glimpse of the house through the trees. The place is somewhat overgrown with shrubbery, the lawn has disappeared and there are not as many flowers as in former days. But to me it still holds many pleasant memories and my mind harks back to a summer day in July of 1893 when first I set eyes on this charming spot.

I was a young man then, 21 years of age, just arrived from England and looking for a job. I had received a thorough training in the nursery and seed business, so upon reaching Los Angeles it was only natural that I should look up the different seed stores and nurseries here. In this way I became acquainted with James H. Denham, a Scotchman who owned a seed business on Main Street just south of 2nd Street. Mr. Denham took quite an interest in me from the start and promised to try and locate some work for me. I got a job picking apricots at $1.50 a day but this only lasted a short time. One nurseryman offered me a job budding fruit trees if I could wait till September. Then one day Mr. Denham said, "How would you like to take a position as gardener on a private estate?" He went on, "Madame Modjeska, the famous actress, wants a man for her place in the Santa Ana Mountains, the pay is $35.00 a month with board and room." I told him I was not a gardener but a nurseryman. The latter's work was to propagate young plants and trees, while the former's was to grow these plants on to maturity and bring them into flower or fruit. But if he thought I could qualify, I would be willing to give it a trial. So I decided to take the job.

Now, working in Denham's seed store was a man named Jones and when he heard that I was going to the Modjeska Ranch he tried his very best to discourage me. He said it was a terrible place, that they had a lot of Mexicans and Indians there and they would just as soon kill you as not. The foreman on the ranch was murdered last year, he said. If you go you had better carry a gun in your hip pocket. This kind of took the wind out of my sails. Mr. Denham had told me what a beautiful place it was with such fine people. I did not know what to think. I was really scared. But please remember, I was only twenty-one, having spent my 21st birthday at the World's Fair in Chicago, on my way to California. I was in a strange country and 6000 miles from home.

I talked the matter over with my friend, West Cove, who had come out from England with me and also John Watts, another Englishman who lived in Hollywood. Then the three of us went down to Harper and Reynolds Hardware Store and selected the first and only revolver I ever owned. I fully expected to be a real westerner and carry it in my hip pocket continually.

On the morning of July 18, 1893, with some misgivings I took the Santa Fe train for El Toro which was the nearest station to the Modjeska Ranch. Arriving at El Toro depot, I was met by a Polish boy named Johnnie Hare, with a buckboard and team of horses. Then a ten mile drive through rolling land, foothills and mountains brought us to the Modjeska Ranch. The horses' hooves made quite a resounding noise crossing the wooden bridge over the creek, then we swung up the driveway and stopped in front of the house.

Madame Modjeska and her husband, Mr. Bozenta, came out to welcome me. They were very nice, democratic kind of folks. He was a former Polish nobleman and his full name was Count Karol Bozenta Chlapowski, but here he preferred simply to be known as Mr. Bozenta.

After unloading some provisions which he had hauled from the depot, Johnnie Hare helped me with my luggage and showed me to the bunk house which was down by the creek. One of the first things he said was, "Where are your blankets? You know, on ranches in this country all the men furnish their own blankets." This was news to me and of course I did not have any. However, Johnnie was good enough to lend me a blanket and got another one from one of the men. Then the first time he went to town I gave him some money to buy a pair of blankets for me.

It was haying time and the men did not come in for lunch but at the evening meal I met them all. The foreman was a German named John Ruopp, a fine looking man, rather tall with blond hair and beard. Two other Germans, one named Heinke, a middle-aged man, the other Edward Ziegler, a lad of seventeen who had left Germany before reaching that age in order to avoid having to serve in the army. This was a common practice among German boys in those days. A Frenchman, George Rock, that does not sound like French but it appears he changed his name after coming to this country as a boy, the same as Johnnie Hare, the Polish lad had changed his. Then there was an American, Sid Williams, and a Mexican, Joaquin Serrano. This made up the ranch crew. The cook was an old Mexican, Jesus Soto, and there was also a Mexican woman who worked around the house. Now that I was added to the list, six nationalities were represented round the table, quite a cosmopolitan group, and also quite a peaceful looking lot. And, by the way, we ate all our meals out of doors under a beautiful arbor of grape vines.

Where were the wild Indians Jones had told me about? True, I was a little suspicious of Joaquin at first but I soon found him to be a really fine fellow. His family owned the next ranch and he had come over for a few weeks to help out with the hay. The hay, here, I found, was made out of oat or barley straw. This was entirely new to me. Where I came from hay was always made of grass or clover, but I had many things to learn in this new country.

I soon found I had no use whatever for my revolver except to amuse myself by shooting at ground squirrels in the evenings when taking a walk down the canyon.

The ranch consisted of a little more than 400 acres, devoted mostly to cattle raising. There was some grain land, about 30 acres of olives, a small acreage of oranges and grapes, together with an apiary of about 120 hives of bees.

The house, a low rambling bungalow, was designed for Madame Modjeska by Stanford White, the celebrated New York architect and built sometime in the eighties. It is one of California's historic spots and many world famous people, including Ignace Paderewski, were entertained here. In front of the house were spacious lawns, two fountains, a large rose garden and flower and shrubbery borders. Then, a little farther up the canyon, was a good sized vegetable garden, the maintenance of which was also a part of my duties.

I soon found I had plenty to do to take care of all of it. Of course, everything had to be irrigated and this constituted the principal portion of the work in the summertime.

The water supply came from the stream in the canyon. A dam had been constructed in the bed of the creek about a mile and a quarter up the canyon and the water carried from there in wooden flumes to a reservoir on a hill back of the house. From here it was piped to different parts of the grounds.

The Mexican woman who worked in the house had a little boy about ten years old named Domingo. The first Sunday I was there he and I went for a walk up the canyon. I was enchanted with the beauty of the scene; the rugged, rocky peaks on either side, the winding trail crossing and recrossing the creek so many times. That beautiful little stream of clear water poured down over boulders forming miniature water falls fringed on either side with trees. Although the grass had pretty well dried up, here and there a late wild flower, like godetia, was still in bloom. At every turn in the canyon a new vista opened up; it was intriguing. I felt as though I must go on and see what was around the next bend; something seemed to draw me on and on. I had never experienced anything like it before and in my joy and enthusiasm I began to run along the trail. Then, all of a sudden, I saw something lying right across the path. I knew instinctively that it was a rattlesnake. I could not stop so I jumped high enough to be sure and clear it. I called back to Domingo to look out. He said it was a rattlesnake and he would kill it; but before he could find a good big stick the snake had made its escape.

About a week later I killed a small rattlesnake in the garden and during the two and a half years I lived on the ranch I killed a good many more. In fact, when I left there, I had fourteen snake skins, mostly rattlers. In those days it was quite a fad to make ladies' belts of snake skins and I had four made up and sent them home to England.

One of the first things I discovered after coming to work on the ranch, was that we had to wash our own clothes. This was a job for Sunday morning and the procedure was to take a round wash tub, a cake of soap, a board and a brush. Then go down by the creek, build a fire and heat a tubful of water, throw the clothes in the tub, then take them out one at a time, lay them on the board and scrub with the brush, rinse out in the creek and hang up to dry.

Our clothing requirements were very simple and consisted principally of a pair of blue overalls and a shirt. In fact, no one thought of wearing any other kind of clothes. If you were going to visit one of the neighboring ranchers or one of the beekeepers who lived in the different canyons, or perhaps ride over the trail to Silverado Canyon to see the pretty young school teacher, you would simply put on a clean shirt and a clean pair of overalls, then you were all dressed up. No one ever thought of wearing cloth clothes unless he was going to the city.

In the fall, Mr. Ruopp hired an Indian to come and chop a supply of firewood. His name was Antonio and he brought with him a squaw whom the boys called Cachora (lizard). I don't know what her real name was. An old house a short distance away, on the other side of the creek, was provided for them to live in. We soon made a deal with Cachora to do our washing. Antonio would come over and collect the clothes and take them home. After they were washed he would bring them back and collect from each one of us the amount due. It worked out fine and we were all glad to abandon our Sunday laundering by the creek.

One day I went over to the shack where Antonio and Cachora lived and there on the windowsill was a long row of bulbs of the soap plant or amole. I asked Antonio what they were for and he said, "Amole, amole." "Yes," I said, "I know what you call them but what do you do with them? Do you eat them?" "No, no," he said, "Washy, washy." To my great surprise I found that the old squaw washed all our clothes with these roots. You never saw a better job of laundering anywhere, the clothes were spotlessly clean.

In the Santiago Canyon it gets pretty hot in the summertime and I found it a little trying at first. I had to put in long hours to keep up with all the work, nevertheless I enjoyed it. One thing that interested me very much was the large number of swallowtail butterflies which flitted around the garden, also the little hummingbirds. We had swallowtail butterflies in England though they were rather rare, but the hummingbirds were entirely new to me and I never got tired of watching them dart so rapidly from flower to flower.

Madame Modjeska used to come out and walk around the garden every day. She was passionately fond of roses.

In the afternoons Madame and her friends would generally occupy chairs or hammocks on the lawn under the oak trees and read and chat or do fancy work. Later in the afternoon they would go horseback riding. Madame rode a bay horse she called Orlando.

This was a fascinating place and such lovable people to be associated with. Besides the natural beauty of the scene the whole air seemed charged with gaiety and romance. It was indeed a new experience for me and sometimes I wondered if it were not all just a beautiful dream.

Terry E. Stephenson

---

from **SILVERADO'S LURE**

Terry E. Stephenson is often called the first Orange County historian. Born on a farm in Texas in 1840, he arrived in Santa Ana at age four. He grew up in the county, becoming an editor and part owner of the *Santa Ana Register* (now the *Orange County Register*) and served as county treasurer through much of the Great Depression.

A leader in the early years of the Orange County Historical Society, his many publications include *The Shadows of Old Saddleback: From the Day of the Dons Down Through the Years When Pioneers Built Their Cabins Among the Oaks and Sycamores*, from which "Silverado's Lure" is excerpted. When it was published in 1948, after Stephenson's death, the legendary Southern California journalist Phil Townsend Hanna described it in his foreword as "history coupled with natural science" and "the work of an earnest layman, intensely devoted to the eminence, the land within its dominion, and the tales of great enterprise and reprehensible knavery that it has witnessed."

SILVERADO CANYON—THE NAME itself almost tells its story of mining days. It pictures mines and wealth; it portrays tales of hope and faith in search of silver. But the name does not tell us the story of many vanished and shattered dreams. It does not tell the story of broken fortunes and broken bodies, the toll that was exacted by this beautiful canyon in days gone by.

Famed ghost cities of the desert and of mountain fastnesses furnish unending tales of romance of the West. In those places swaying walls and weather-torn roofs mark the old-time mining camp long since deserted. The Sierra Santa Ana, too, has its ghost cities—two of them,

Silverado and Carbondale in Silverado Canyon. Some of the California-built whitewashed structures erected in Silverado in its mining days are still standing and in use. Where Carbondale stood there is not a shack, not one timber upon another to mark the location of stores and post office, and the dwelling places of those who delved deep in the earth.

Along the Silverado eager miners in search of wealth drove in their tunnels. Prospectors combed the mountainside and canyon bottoms in search of signs of precious metal. Six-horse teams hauled out coal and ore, and dreams of wealth seemed certain of realization.

The same beautiful turns in the road, the same alder-bordered stream, the same oaks, the same towering, brush-covered canyon sides that enchanted the miners of fifty years ago hold yet their charm untarnished and undiminished. There is in the Silverado an atmosphere of contentment, a haze of quietude, and everywhere is beauty of landscape; truly, a canyon made to satisfy the longings of an artist's soul rather than a place to be torn to pieces.

Long before American settlers came into the Santiago canyon, of which the Silverado is a branch, this canyon was well known to the Spanish Californians, as, of course, it was known to their Indian predecessors. To the early Spanish-speaking white men it was Canada de la Madera, translated Canyon of the Timber. By them an ox-road was broken through. Perhaps it was no more than a trail, yet it served as a road for the Californians who went into the upper reaches of this canyon for pine timber to be used in joists for their adobes.

It was thus as an already explored canyon that Canada de la Madera was found when J. E. Pleasants and Sam Shrewsbury pioneered in the Santiago, first known to them in the early '60's. These men were followed by others seeking homesites. The level valley below and much of the mountain lands were privately owned through Mexican land grants, and succession to Spanish and Mexican land grants. What government land there was open to location lay mostly in the mountains, in rugged canyons, with here and there a grassy flat, bits of ground where a few fruit trees could be planted, where a cabin could be built and an apiary, a barn and a corral and various other buildings crowded in from time to time.

Goats were raised at nearly all of the ranches, and for years vied with bees as the principal industry. The hides were marketed in San Francisco, the meat in valley towns. Among the homesteaders was Sam Shrewsbury, who added lime-burning to bee-keeping as a means of livelihood, hauling his product oftimes as far as Los Angeles. There was the Harwood place in Ladd canyon, a lower branch of the Silverado, and in the main canyon was John Bleeker, son of a Boston mariner and a Spanish mother, who lived at what is known today as the Holtz place. Above were the Alford and T. B. Julian homes.

Wild game was everywhere—grizzly bears that came down from the high ridges to feast on honey torn from the bee stands, mountain lions that preyed upon the goat herds, foxes, coyotes howling at night upon every hill top, deer in every wooded draw and quail at every turn of the winding road.

Only now and then were the ranches disturbed by bears or mountain lions, mere diversions in a life of extreme contentment in a rugged land of wild beauty. The breezes stole softly through the branches of the oaks and sycamores, rustled the quivering leaves of the alders along the tumbling creek, and swayed the brushy blankets of the steep mountain slopes covered deep with sage and sumac and scrub oak. Though an occasional winter storm brought a dash of snow, the climate was always satisfying. The settlers believed there was none to compare.

Thus it was, a quiet canyon with hardly a half-dozen mountain homes in it, when one day in the fall of 1877 Hank Smith and William Curry, both of Santa Ana, hunting in the upper mountains, came upon some rock that looked to them like silver ore. An assay was reported as showing the rock to be a blue and white quartz carrying silver to about $60 per ton. These two men staked a claim that they called the Southern Belle, and soon ran in a tunnel some fifty feet. They took their time about their work, as they both had affairs to attend to in Santa Ana.

Finally, they decided to locate another mine, which they called the Santa Clara. They hired F. S. Luce to run in a tunnel, he to receive a one-fifth interest. Previous to that time, however, an article was published in a Los Angeles paper, heralding the discovery in Madera canyon. This newspaper report brought a rush such as has been seen in many a canyon in every part of California. Within a week between 250 and 300 men had hastened into the Silverado, which was the name given to the place at that time by men who thought the old name Madera was altogether unsuitable to portray the glorious developments just ahead for this canyon of silvery promise. Eventually no less than 500 locations were made in this mountain area, organized as the Santa Rosa Mining District.

The whole mountain range was covered with prospectors. At that time, it should be remembered, silver was up in value, and a silver mine was something very much to be desired. Times had been hard in Los Angeles and throughout Southern California, and the Silverado was looked to with hope and enthusiasm as the source from which the coffers of the banks would be soon replenished.

Creaking wagons, some of which had come across the plains, spring wagons, carts, dilapidated old surries and shiny rigs from livery stables clashed over the rocks at the crossings, and sweating horses dragged the outfits over the rough roads into the new-found El Dorado. Scores of men shouldering their packs walked into the new mining country, seeking wealth and adventure. Lumber, hauled in from Santa Ana and Anaheim, which were then straggling pioneer villages, was sold from the wagon.

Hasty camps were struck along the creek. Tents were everywhere. Scores of men lived throughout the summer and winter beneath the trees, without shelter, seldom disturbed by storm or cold.

In a remarkably short time, the whole canyon was staked out. Gradually, the excitement steadied down, and work of development was begun. With an eye to business, P. A. Clark, a real estate man from Anaheim, quickly laid out a townsite at the Forks, where Pine Canyon on the south joins the main canyon, and called it Silverado. He wrote to Washington about the things that were happening in the canyon, and asked that he be made postmaster at the new town he was starting in the midst of mines and miners. His request was granted. The sub-divider had no difficulty in disposing of lots.

Carpenters hammered away early and late, and a village quickly came into being. It was not long before the correspondents for the Los Angeles newspapers were sending in enthusiastic stories relating the fact that Silverado had grown to be a town with three hotels, three stores, a post office, two blacksmith shops, two meat markets in which venison competed with beef, and seven thriving wide-awake saloons, inevitable in mining camps of early California.

Into the canyon J. D. Dunlap came as a deputy United States marshal, armed not with pick and shovel but with a warrant for the arrest of a man wanted for crime. The man he sought was gone. Instead of a fugitive from justice, the deputy caught the mining fever. His location was high on the southern ridge up toward the grassy area. His mine, first as the Dunlap, later as the Bluelight, became the best known of all the Silverado mines.

Christopher Isherwood

_____

from *DIARIES*

Christopher Isherwood was born in England in 1904 and educated at Cambridge. A novelist, short story writer, memoirist, and fervent adherent of the Vedanta branch of Hindu philosophy, Isherwood is most well known as the author of *The Berlin Stories*, which was later adapted into the musical *Cabaret*. An enthusiastic immigrant to California, he lived in Santa Monica for decades.

His friendship with British historian and philosopher Gerald Heard led Isherwood to often visit Trabuco College, founded in 1942 by Heard and fellow British writer Aldous Huxley to promote the study of comparative religion, prayer, and meditation. In 1949, the Trabuco campus was donated to the Vedanta Society of Southern California and became the Ramakrishna Monastery, known for its silent meditation room, broad vistas, and gorgeous gardens and paths. In this passage, Isherwood refers to Heard and his own cousin, builder Felix Greene, who designed the campus.

IT WAS DURING this visit that I first saw Trabuco. It was a big ranch lying about twenty miles inland, under the mountains. Its very name indicated its loneliness: nothing noteworthy had happened in that area since a day in the seventeenth century, when a Spanish soldier had lost an arquebus there—a "trabuco." There is something weird about the emptiness of these South California uplands. The foothills and creeks and woods look deceptively tame and inhabited. You could wander for miles, always expecting there'd be a ranch house around the next slope, just out of sight, with a little town beyond. But there are no towns, and very few houses, in the whole neighborhood. A local architect named Van Pelt (who was also the designer of the house Chris Wood had bought in Laguna) had evolved, with Felix Greene and Gerald, a long, straggling building: a series of cloisters which mounted, in flights of steps, the slope of a little hill. The total effect was beautiful. The buildings fitted perfectly into the landscape. Gerald said they reminded him of a small Franciscan monastery in the Apennines.

You entered a big courtyard which was also an orchard, planted with fruit trees. To your right were garages, toolsheds, and the pumping house; a long, low dormitory for married couples; and the circular meditation hall, which had no windows and was built on three levels, so as to hold the maximum number of people. You entered the cloisters through a pair of big wooden gates, with a bell turret above them. All along the cloisters were bedrooms and bathrooms, comfortable but very plain, with built-in closets, and a minimum of furniture. At the top of the cloisters were three big rooms, a library, a living and dining room, and a kitchen. When you were in the courtyard, your view was bounded by the irregular line of red tiled roofs against the sky. But when you opened the big gates and entered the cloister, you found yourself at the edge of a hill, looking away over the woods and hollows to the distant ocean.

When I first saw Trabuco, a great deal was still lacking, but the buildings were there and inhabitable—a miracle in itself, considering that this was wartime. Felix Greene had worked all winter, with his superhuman energy, collecting materials, bullying contractors, grabbing the last available supplies of wood and metal fixtures before the government froze them. Trabuco was three-quarters his creation, physically—ideologically also—for I soon began to realize that this place, this institution, was altogether in excess of anything Gerald's timid conservatism had ever planned or wished. The snug little anonymous retreat for four or five people, "Focus," had been swallowed up by "Trabuco College," which was capable of holding fifty. Already, Felix was talking of a printing press to issue pamphlets, and was planning next year's seminars. For the present, Gerald went along with all this, a little dazed, a little unwilling, but tremendously impressed and excited. It seemed to me that a new cult, Heardism, was being born, with Felix, a sunburnt and smiling Eminence, holding the real power behind the throne.

Such, however, was far from Gerald's intention. However much he might enjoy the limelight, the prestige of leader, I am sure that his intentions were sincerely democratic. He spoke repeatedly of Trabuco as a "club for mystics"—nonsectarian, nondogmatic, strictly experimental, a clearinghouse for individual religious experience and ideas. Its members were to be colleagues, not masters and disciples, superiors and inferiors. I suppose this was an impossible ideal—maybe even an undesirable one. The Quakers have maintained a large degree of democracy (though they do have elders or "weighty Friends") but only at the price of diverting their attention from really businesslike mysticism to social service: their standards of meditation are low and vague. The Swami, on the other hand, would have said, "Nonsense, of course they must have a teacher": he would only have questioned Gerald's suitability for the job. But, at Trabuco, it was Gerald or no one. And so, eventually, inevitably, it was Gerald.

Chris regarded Trabuco with a kind of wistful amusement. He was like a child who does and yet doesn't want to play with the others. His status was that of a sort of honorary outcast. He could go there whenever he liked—for the afternoon—but he wasn't really welcome: Felix was heartily polite to him. When the building fund ran out, Chris had contributed several thousand dollars, and this made things extra awkward. "Well, anyway," he'd say, with his twisted, little boy's grin, "their kitchen belongs to *me*." At that time, Gerald was commuting regularly between Trabuco and Rockledge Road—a fact which made for further embarrassment, since several members of the college knew and disapproved of Paul. Just how Gerald spoke of Chris and his affairs when he was up at Trabuco, I shall never know: but the general effect of his remarks must have been deplorable—for the Hunters and many of his other friends regarded Chris with horror, and sympathized with Gerald as one sympathizes with the victim of an unhappy and impossible marriage. Chris knew this, and took it very well and humorously, without the least humility or resentment. From this time onward, I began to like and respect him enormously. With all his babyish weaknesses, he was a living demonstration of the one cardinal virtue Gerald lacked— charity. Also, I began to realize that I had never once heard him tell a lie. The truth—however shameful or embarrassing—seemed to blurt itself out of him, accompanied by a nervous, apologetic laugh.

Jo-Ann Mapson

from *HANK AND CHLOE*

A third-generation Californian, Jo-Ann Mapson was born in Fullerton in 1952, graduated from Troy High School, and earned an MFA in poetry and prose from Vermont College. For many years she taught at UC Irvine Extension, CSU Fullerton, and Orange Coast College. She now teaches in the low-residency MFA program at the University of Alaska, Anchorage, and lives in New Mexico.

Mapson is the author of eleven novels and one collection of short stories, many set in California and the Southwest. In the passage excerpted below, from her first novel, *Hank and Chloe*, a drive from the unincorporated equestrian wilds of Orange County inspires a reverie about their past.

A NSWER THE DOOR after midnight and you might as well set a place at the table for trouble—Chloe Morgan's first thoughts when the knock came. Hannah, her shepherd, let out an initial throaty growl from her nest of blankets, then thumped her tail in the dark for the all clear. Tugging the horse blanket from her bed, Chloe padded barefoot across the rough plywood floor.

Rule one: You were damn careful out here in the middle of nowhere. Hugh Nichols let a select few live in the slapped-together shacks on his two hundred acres; he'd be damned if he'd sell out to developers so they could fling stucco around his land. But when it came to just who got to stay and who didn't, he was mercurial. You did nothing to make him question his decision. Few of the shacks had electricity, but Nichols had tapped into the county water, so it wasn't all that bad. Rig up a hose and you could take a cold shower. If you wanted to read after dark, you could light a hurricane lamp—oil wasn't expensive. Living here was safer than the streets had been, when she'd lain awake in her truck till dawn, fearful of every noise. Each night since she'd moved here, she said a silent prayer of thanks for the roof. So far the county had left them alone, but she wasn't naive enough to think it would last. Who knew? You did what you could and then you moved on.

She walked quietly through the dark and rested her cheek against the plywood door. "What do you want?"

"You got a call."

The voice was Francisco Montoya's, who lived nearest to the pay phone and the main house, where Nichols slept off his legendary drunks and fought with a series of women he believed were after his considerable bankroll.

Bad news could always wait. "Tell whoever it is to call back in the morning."

He tapped louder now. "Chloe, you got to wake up. Mr. Green from the college. His mare is foaling. He asks for your help."

She cursed softly to herself. "Okay, Francisco, thanks. Go on back to sleep." Naked except for the blanket, twelve hours' work under her belt and only two hours' sleep, she wanted to go back to bed and the respite of unconsciousness. Earlier, the night air had smelled like rain and her truck tires were showing steel. Now Phil Green's mare was giving birth. So what? Did he want her to share in the joy of it? She despised foaling—the utter mess it could turn into, the way owners got stupid with pink or blue birth announcements, and all that crepe-paper nonsense. Too often she'd seen tiny hooves lacerate the vaginal wall, an ignored infection rack fine horseflesh until death came like an awkward blessing. The heartbreaking view of twins haunted her still—she'd sworn off all that—simply tried not to think about it and get on with her own work, teaching people to ride. But Phil was a good friend. He hadn't begged—he never would.

Out her only window, she watched the reflective stripes on Francisco's jacket dim as he trudged back up the hill to his own place. Home was an old tow-along silver Airstream, complete with electricity he'd jerry-rigged off a truck battery. Constantina was pregnant again, and their four-year-old daughter, Pilar, was just out of County Med with a winter bug that had turned into pneumonia. Out here a lot of things could level you, but Francisco and Constantina were illegals. They lived in fear of illness. The expense and the lack of proof of citizenship were more nightmarish than enduring the sickness. Once in the hospital, anything could happen. Social workers didn't help any, separating everyone. So they took care of each other out here, circled their wagons when there was trouble, recycled scrap aluminum, fed each other's animals when money was tight.

Hannah sat obediently by Chloe's side, snapping at some unseen insect. She had slim pickings in winter. Chloe shut the door, lay back down in bed for a minute, cursing motherhood, winter rains, the night in general. Then she got up, threw a pink sweatshirt over a denim miniskirt and found her tennis shoes, the only pair of footwear dry enough to be of service.

"Go get in the truck," she told the dog, and Hannah flew out the door, down the fire road, and into the bed of the old Chevy Apache, her bent tail folding beneath her like a flag at dusk. The truck started on the second try, a good omen. Chloe drove out of the compound without her headlights so as not to wake any more of the squatters than she had to.

Forget reason and plausibility, there were times Chloe swore she heard voices out here. Not babbling or devil tongues, human voices. Once she figured she wasn't crazy, she decided maybe they belonged to people who had died long before, whose very lives had been erased by time and progress, but who weren't quite done speaking their piece. On nights like these when she drove through the canyons in darkness, half asleep, on the watch for deer crossing, she heard them the clearest. *Hermana, hija…*They called her back from swerving off the highway, kept her awake. Tonight they were saying, *La yegua sufre…tocala…*She kept the windows rolled up and didn't stop for anyone. You didn't need a newspaper story to learn the wisdom of the road—everyone was suspect —everyone had an agenda. But that didn't stop her from stealing side-long glances at two hitchhikers, noting their hopeful grins, the echo of

others who seemed to single her out, speak to her. *¡Date prisa, por aca!*
She would have liked the company of another warm body, even if they
never touched or spoke. Just someone along for the ride. Like Fats had
been, Fats Valentine. *Stop it.* Her life was singular now, since his death.

There, past the junction at Cook's Corner, as she waited for the traffic light to turn, she watched two bikers stumble out onto the tarmac.
That character with his thumb out—his face held an echo of Fats's smile.
Probably dangerously drunk, his liver halfway to cirrhosis. The other guy
had the jutting brow of a Neanderthal and probably a survival knife to
match every outfit. Forty years ago, he might have been an immigrant
orange picker, his overalls thick with the labors of a night spent smudg-
ing, hope suffusing the weariness in his bones as he rounded another
row of trees in the glistening frost. But the trees weren't there anymore,
were they? A whole town surrounding the giant, nearly new university
had sprung up like concrete circus tents. Still the words whispered in
her ear, the breath faintly erotic as it tickled her neck flesh: *Nunca ser-
emos vencidos. Este niño representa mi sufrimiento, y mi esperanza...*

She shook her head drowsily and in the distance before her saw the
freeway, a trickle of moving cars. Stay awake, she commanded herself.
Phil Green needs your help. No good for anyone if you fall asleep and
crash someplace like Irvine. You think the city fathers would name a
street corner after you? No way, sister. Scrape you up like the rest of
the trees and pour concrete for a new foundation.

But under the hard shell of highway she felt something else press
against her tires. Prerememberances she could not possibly know, yet
did. The faint outlines of roadhouses from sixty years ago shimmered
before her eyes like heat mirages. She heard bits of tinny music from
an old upright that had traveled the plains in a covered wagon, losing
a few strings to the desert animals who thought they might make fine
nesting material. Old music, simple, prim love songs asking permission
to court and woo. People who weren't there. Visions. The result of some
kind of brain irregularity you developed, deprived of sleep and adequate
protein? All she knew was they had to do with the earth somehow, a
past so charged with promise that it couldn't quite give up its grip on

the present. Not that it was unpleasant; she never felt lonely. She saw them shimmer in those heat mirages; they were in serious desert now, land not in the least fertile, no longer preoccupied with rain but resigned to the stasis of hot waiting. All those faces—what did they want to tell her? Didn't the people coming west sense that they'd never leave? Why not go back to what they knew? A certainty of weather, seasons that descended like ritual? What promise drove them on? Was any struggle worth it? *To stay alive. Bear children to increase the tribe.* Some notion. Underneath that notion another surfaced, equal in weight: Someday they would each have to give up with grace.

It was raining hard now, the water hitting her windshield at an angle. The wipers were just about useless. She slowed down to help the old tires gain purchase on the slick highway. It was a twenty-minute drive to the junior college. A couple of hours might go by in an instant, seeing to that mare. She craned her head out the window to see if it was clear to change lanes. She hadn't brought her work clothes. She would have to drive back home, hopefully have time for a quick nap, get dressed for work. She worked at the Wedler Brothers Café from six to three-thirty, its sole waitress, but Rich didn't need her in until nine today—a miracle. He'd been promising to break in a new waitress for a relief shift, and after several who quit in their first hour, he'd found one he swore was a jewel: Lita. Whatever kind of name that was, Chloe hoped she would work out, didn't have those fifteen-inch-long fingernails or a penchant for the color black. If she smoked the same brand of cigarettes that would be nice. They could bum off each other.

She exited the freeway at the old Fairview Road, driving past all the sleeping houses in the subdivisions. Used to be that this road led straight into the fairgrounds. The extra-wide lane was designed for horse trailers and cattle trucks. They held a swap meet here every weekend now—cars and hundreds of vendors forming an outdoor mall. This was the last stretch of county to be paved over and civilized. Slowly the college was following suit, phasing out whole departments that seemed impractical and leveling anything that resembled the California style of architecture in favor of blocky, two-story brick buildings. She drove the back way through the service roads and parked in a handicapped slot near the Agriculture building. Outside her car she was immediately drenched—the rain's signature to the storm. After it quelled, she whipped wet hair from her face and hustled toward the lighted barn. Inside, after nodding hello to Phil, she straddled the prone chestnut mare, her skirt hiking up nearly to her crotch.

"Well?" Phil's face was pulled tight. The trouble light hanging from a nail on the barn wall flickered across his damp forehead.

"I don't know anything yet." She checked pulses, gum color, respiration. "How long has she been prone?"

"A couple of hours. I thought she was just getting comfortable. But then I couldn't get her back up. She's not going to make it, is she?"

"I'm not a vet, Phil."

"But you've been around this before. I can handle it. Tell me."

Chloe smiled, stretched her hand over the horse's neck to give his shoulder a pat. He sighed with relief, and immediately she felt sorry she'd given him any kind of gesture that could be mistaken for hope. Truthfully, it looked like no good; the mare was nearly beyond fighting, committed to lying down and apathetic when Chloe goosed her. With all those textbooks, all his telling students how it's done, had Phil missed the early signs of trouble? Not likely.

She stroked the mare's muzzle and her hand came away bloody. What the hell was that about? She wiped her hands in the straw and cedar shavings.

"I waited too long, didn't I?"

"Probably had nothing to do with it."

"So?"

"Phil, this is a grace time. What we do is call in a vet, stand here, and hold a hoof."

"And watch the lights go out."

"Maybe." She stepped over the horse and took his hand. His calluses nearly matched her own. She wished she could erase his pain, but it was beyond her, beyond just about anything short of a miracle. Cross fingers, she said to herself. Pray.

Andrew Tonkovich

REELECTION DAY

Born in Lynwood in 1960, Andrew Tonkovich studied with poet Peter Carr at CSU Long Beach and with Oakley Hall at UC Irvine, where Tonkovich currently teaches writing. His short stories, essays, and reviews have been published in *Ecotone, Faultline*, the *Orange Coast Review*, the *Los Angeles Review of Books*, and *The Best American Nonrequired Reading*. He hosts the literary arts program *Bibliocracy Radio* on Pacifica's KPFK in Southern California and is the longtime editor of the *Santa Monica Review*. He lives in Modjeska Canyon.

In this ghostly civics parable, Tonkovich constructs a fabulist's political allegory situated in the rural environs of the Santa Ana Mountains. "Driving Santiago Canyon Road, the juxtaposition of white memorial crosses and election signs struck me," he recalls. "I embraced the idea that came to me: exploring civic responsibility and its imagined, contrived boundaries."

One of the penalties for refusing to participate in
politics is that you end up being governed by your...
    —PLATO

THE ARRIVAL OF the first voter stirred the poll workers that late morning Election Day, as it would, the regular trio of friendly local lady volunteers, jolly underemployed or retired civic do-gooders waiting for representative democracy to show up at the canyon's Parks and Rec trailer, though it stirred them only gently at first. The voter was an attractive and familiar-seeming woman in her mid-thirties whose uncomfortable resemblance to a dead ex-soldier—a local single woman raped and beaten to death in her home outside the canyon and then buried, sloppily, a hundred yards from the bike lane of the rural road—was passing, as they say.

Except that it did not pass, it arrived and then remained there at the polling place with her, with the three clerks and the official county precinct inspector in the modular prefab community center and its welcome station, cardboard voter booths, large topographic map of the outlying canyons area, the ancient wide-open-faced clock on the wall, and the faded plaque commemorating the nation's long-forgotten bicentennial.

Anyway, thought the inspector, what was it with these macho killers of girls and women, that they could bludgeon and fist and cut and shoot but could not take just a little extra time, please, to dig an only slightly deeper, safer grave? Was it that they wanted to be found and found out, discovered and punished that much more quickly, buying or selling or trading some time in a minutes-per-inches equation, and of course in the meantime exposing the body to animals, the sun, insects?

She strolled in, this first voter, wearing a camo uniform and high boots, and stood there, resembling herself. Dark hair wisped from under her cap, her posture straight. None of the crew of old-lady poll workers or the inspector did much—theirs was a slow and deliberate routine which always seemed to portend more, if elsewhere, and in a vaguely if confidently imagined democratic future—and so they did the same just now.

The inspector, an overweight and generally resigned but otherwise happily retired high school principal, puzzled momentarily over her arrival, and then hesitated before speaking. It was a habit born of three decades of careful, tempered nonreaction. He was a conscientious, lonely man with a mostly forgotten ex-wife and no children of his own, worn to easy complicity and gentle, humane acceptance after a career spent looking for so long after other people's kids—an effort that had required, always, reconciling the compulsory and the unanticipated.

There was mild confusion at her appearance, some little electrical-level reflexive flinching, as when wasps or bees occasionally find their way into a room, and then relief—as almost immediately following the lady soldier were four bikers, easy to identify with their middle-aged masculine girth and black leather vests, flag bandannas, shiny chaps, beards, and tattoos. Playing dress-up as cowboys or Indians or Nordic sci-fi road warriors, all dreamy revisionist heroics and self-mocking bravado, except who could be sure it wasn't totally sincere? They were happy each weekend to burn fossil fuel for no good reason, to drive too fast, to pass cars on a blind curve. Proud to exercise their privilege and poor judgment. Meaty fellows with straight day jobs, ex-wives, children. Or drug dealers and genuinely dangerous criminals, who knew? They were old and fat, and yet in their costumes they were somehow elevated or transformed, immortal even, and so proud and oblivious in their childishly happy self-regard, too. Helmets? Required by law, but resisted on principle. They favored the spiked Kaiser Wilhelm, the World War II Nazi, or sleek, streamlined robot wear. So, death, regardless!

Then, after the biker dudes, one by one, underneath the American flag hung above the front double doors, right there into the official polling place entered a dozen bicyclists, road racers, *tap-tap-tapp*ing in their special cleats, peeling off their tiny cycling gloves, securing their fancy polarized sunglasses on the zippered collars of their tight, too-colorful, mosaic-patterned racing jerseys. Have you noticed the thighs on these guys—the inspector thought to ask his poll clerks but of course would not out of professional courtesy—their shaven legs, their skeletal, insectlike posture from wearing those shoes, tight pants, their bulges and contours and muscles? The inspector began to look away, embarrassed at his curiosity, not to mention the failure by unavoidable comparison of his own portly man-body—all of what he had become now held up somehow with no effort from him, by a belt and support arches, and contained in an oversized shirt. Yet his embarrassment at the grim, bare polling place, at his own obvious shortcomings, was tempered by the quiet, the strangeness, of these arrivals.

He heard—could it be?—a horse whinny outside. He stepped to the open door and saw, dismounting, an old Mexican man, skin brown as baked mud. The fellow tied the big animal to the railing on the handicapped access ramp and hobbled in, wearing dusty work boots and a faded western shirt, his broad, big hat perched behind his head, held in place by a thin lanyard of twine. He might have been blind, so open and broad was his gaze—or somehow all-assuming, as if he had been there before.

The three little children arrived next, a girl and a boy, carrying their sister in a car seat elevated between them. The infant whimpered, but was, everybody could see, a good baby, a sweet baby, a little girl-child wearing a pajama costume meant to resemble, no, to transform the human infant into a pink and white domestic animal, a cow or a pig.

Immediately behind arrived the children's father, his eyes still proud, but so lonely and lost, carrying a backpack and diaper bag. He was tired, clearly, but occupied generously, conscientiously, with his kids, his responsibility to citizenship, the kind of grown man who seems to live and act by good example, and around whom his kids—anybody's—could feel safe, content, assured.

As if the little family—missing, it seemed, a mother—were not enough just then, as if in mocking mimicry of his sober example, as if characters in a cartoon Noah's ark, in walked two grizzled old-timer miners, spelunkers, explorers of caves and caverns at any rate, dusty and weary-looking fellows in thick denim and wearing metal hats, tiny lamplights affixed to their visors. After them, a brief pulse and no more, two hunters, a pair of bearded fellows in orange vests with matching rifles slung behind their backs. The inspector was fairly sure weapons were not allowed in here, at a voting place, but he would have to double check.

Finally, two more visitors walked in—a thin, dark man and woman, purple-black hair, small, precociously matching native people who could have been composed, thought the ex-principal, out of the illustrated imaginings of a grade-school California state history book. Juaneño or Cahuilla or Chumash were the names of the people who once lived in what is today Orange County—hard to guess but indigenous for sure, dressed as if in a pageant of celebration, but unsmiling, wanting, as in *lacking,* not *desiring.*

And so they all just stood there, this headcount assembly of insistent civic engagement, not taking a seat on the old, oversized church pew shoved up against the wall, not speaking at all. It was ten A.M. according to the too-large if friendly face of the clock on the wall, a relic from the days of more vigorous state spending on the future.

They'll all need to show proof of residency, thought the inspector. Recite their names, addresses convincingly. Offer some evidence of eligibility. Prove somehow that they have a right to be here. Except the children, of course. Asking the grown-ups outright would be awkward, but somebody needed to do it. Yes, that was *his* job. He could ask them to please, everybody, line up in front of the respective box of ballots organized on the table, the one corresponding to your last name: A–I, J–R, S–Z, an old lady sitting at each. He could pretend to recognize them, welcome them as familiar neighbors or friends, fellow citizens, though all were complete strangers to him except, somehow, the soldier woman.

"Fellow citizens," he thought to himself. Perhaps this was how to begin his little speech, his welcome, his orientation, his public service announcement. He'd read, taken notes, practically memorized the handbook from the State Registrar, provided by the county. At the training they'd done elderly, handicapped, hearing and visually impaired, ADA; Spanish-language, Vietnamese, Chinese, Korean, and the rest of them; wrong polling place, noncitizens and illegal aliens—er, "undocumented persons"—felons, fake IDs, possible voter-fraud perpetrators—almost unheard of but lately a big deal on Fox News. But nobody had mentioned these, what he now took—reluctantly, as you would—to be representatives of old Nixon's "silent majority" and, before that, Homer's, showing up at the inspector's—why his?—polling place, seeming to intend to interfere or, worse, participate.

And then, finally, he recognized her, because he could not deny any longer who she was, who any of them were. His mind now placed the lady combat veteran, beyond doubt or inference or speculation, however still impossibly. She was the leader, clearly. U.S. Army, Sergeant. Combat vet, Iraq, medaled and honorably discharged, but then murdered in her apartment back home by her non-boyfriend roommate, a large man, three hundred pounds. And she was so tiny in person. Working days at some shitty job, enrolled at the community college in night classes, her body beaten, head crushed, found between the scenic road and the creek bed, just a few hundred yards away from here, at the mouth of the canyon and, yes, barely covered in sand, gravel, dirt. She'd been easy to find, if you knew where to look. The police and their dogs had found her once the killer told where, generally, to search, the bastard.

The inspector had been seeing her photograph for so long that now it was difficult to look at her. First, on the Sheriff's Department's missing person poster and then in alerts from the local community e-mail network, in the newspaper, and on TV. Later, he'd seen her portrait up on an easel at the side of the road—done in pencil or charcoal as if by an artist at a theme park or carnival, maybe the pier—with her official armed-services photograph framed in plastic butterflies, and a small American flag and a plaster Virgen de Guadalupe standing guard, a faded wreath of silk flowers, notes and ribbons and mementos left with it, stuffed animals, all at her—what had been quickly coined by the newsmakers—"makeshift memorial." He didn't know what to do now. He stepped forward. He saluted.

She approached the first box, ignoring his stupid gesture, ignoring him altogether—a relief.

Garcia. That was her name. Or Gonzalez. Lizbet Garcia. Liz. Elizabeth. Isabella. Something like that. He was embarrassed to not remember, embarrassed to ask, and just plain embarrassed at his own behavior so far. He looked at her. She'd been a good-looking woman. Still was. Healthy, nice skin. Excellent figure. He looked for wounds. Not a scratch on her.

He smiled, and nodded her toward the first line. Dear old Bea Nelson, sitting at a folding chair behind that first row, looked at him without discernable curiosity or alarm, thank goodness, not seeming yet to recognize the woman, not seeming to have recognized the—what was it?—unlikelihood, momentousness, threat—of the arrival of the whole strange crew. The inspector was now beginning to wonder—not how they were what they were, that was problem enough—but how it was that they had all gotten here at the same time.

Or was it that Granny Bea, as she liked to be called, was polite, kind, unflappable, and understood just exactly what was happening but also could not, would not, respond, because that would be impolite or inappropriate or, even, insane?

Meanwhile there was the immediate, the quotidian, to occupy them. This was official, governmental, after all, a constitutional right, but with rules. It turned out that the bikers were mostly registered at addresses far away, some in other counties. The inspector recalled his poll-worker training, his administrative bag of tricks. There was a procedure for this, a default. So he issued them all provisional ballots, which was right and fair—if also completely wrong—and seemed to satisfy them.

He was pretty sure there was going to be a problem here, but someone who knew, somebody downtown with real power, would figure it all out later. Or so he told himself. The old Mexican man had been naturalized, had last voted for Kennedy, go figure. Luckily, they had bilingual voting instructions for him. Kind, generous, unflappable Granny Bea handed him a pamphlet. She was indeed a cheerful, kind, good person. Or she was clueless. It didn't matter, not now, and he was grateful, either way.

He wasn't sure about the Indian couple, if they were a couple, and was glad when they quietly accepted their ballots and followed the ancient *vaquero* toward a voting booth.

The band of cyclists organized their own high-tech helmets, gloves, water bottles, and backpacks in a tidy pile, entering their respective booths one at a time, in the same elegant choreography he'd seen in that impressive group dance they'd performed on the highway every weekend morning. Water seemed to drip from one of the bags. Certainly nobody was going to say anything about that.

The young, sad, proud father asked Connie Peterson and Alice the ex-librarian if they could watch his children, please, and of course the ladies were delighted to, and then the fellow stepped inside a booth himself. They were all of them quiet and disciplined, thought the inspector, even the children, who seemed to understand why Daddy was there. He wished everybody who voted was as focused and cooperative.

The whole thing lasted forty-five minutes, suggesting that the voters were also careful with their responsibility to fill out the ballot correctly, that they were educated and well prepared. The bikers waited outside for their companions to finish. The cyclists stood at one end of the trailer, sipping from their water bottles, stretching, slipping their gloves back on, clicking their helmet straps into place. Then out they went, the dead, walking and riding and racing back, he presumed, as the murdered woman soldier, to their respective places of rest—unrest, interrupted rest. He's seen these places marked nearby as shrines by the side of the scenic state route that connected the boulevard through the rustic canyon, connected the suburbs to the new toll road to the open-space corridor, to the past, or somewhere further, clearly.

Their ballots were now all in the ballot box. *His* ballot box. There was red and white tape on it, sealed, as it should be, except of course not. He could not get in there, not even if he wanted to. There was nothing that he could do at all now except affirm to his superiors the clearly sketchy, dubious, and totally unacceptable decision he'd made about these "provisional ballots"—God, who was he kidding?—and then let somebody else at headquarters, yes, at the county, make sense of it all. It was only, what, two dozen votes? True, an unacceptably high number of irregular ballots cast, especially for a small rural precinct with fewer than ten times that total, but, again, he had done the right thing, followed the protocol. What else could he do? That's what provisional ballots were for, after all.

The provisional voters themselves were gone, disappeared. The heavy-duty ceiling fan in the modular circulated dusty, warm air, making its chunking sound, only calling further attention to the indoor meteorology, or climatology—he could not find the right word or idea—maybe atmosphere? It might as well be raining. This was meant to be a safe—even hallowed—place, with its acoustic ceiling tiles and ballot box with its official seal. The flag seemed to be trying to make things right, its positioning above the entrance encouraging, supporting the premise of it all. But what next, Abraham Lincoln?

He tried not to make eye contact with Granny Bea, Connie, or Alice. And, thankfully, they did not, as he expected, ask questions or burst out in relief. Besides, what could he even say? Perhaps they also did not know what to say or, worse—as he now suspected regarding Bea—they might not have noticed. But perhaps this was for the better.

A new couple walked in, healthy-looking, handsome, middle-aged professionals, husband and wife, well-dressed, cheerful, and white. The old girls knew them right off, recognizing them as local residents, thank God, and greeted them with smiles and encouragement.

Two real, sentient, qualified, ready-to-vote members of the American electorate, whatever that meant now, stopping at the community center on their way to late lunch breaks, or making it the end of an early day, taking or giving themselves their constitutionally protected time off, whether lawyers or bankers or administrators. They provided their names, addresses. Easy. They laughed and spoke, and time and expectations seemed to have caught up with their arrival, and the three poll workers and the inspector too, after the departure of the provisionals. The day was restored and reaffirmed, if somehow too easily, the anticipated outcome perhaps still possible.

They left, and after a few dozen more voters throughout the day, the inspector almost—but not quite—wondered whether the lady soldier and her congregation had even been there at all, and then it was late afternoon, and then early evening.

Everything else, everybody else, checked out, no complications, and they too disappeared one at a time into the booths to punch in their votes on the electronic machines, to emerge a few minutes later from their booths bearing a receipt, to receive a small oval sticker with Old Glory waving on it reading I VOTED, to thank the crew, to seem to celebrate some modest satisfaction at having fulfilled this civic obligation.

And that was it for most of the rest of Election Day and night at the precinct polling place in the canyon: the usuals, regular voters, locals, mostly rushed, a few lingering to chat in mutual satisfaction at the routine performance of this familiar ritual of representative democracy. A short, early dinner break—take-out brought by Connie's husband, eaten in half-hour shifts—then nightfall, and soon it was closing time, eight o'clock. Extremely low turnout, yes, two- or three- or four-an-hour average, but that was to be expected and, besides, so many in this community, a majority in this precinct, voted by mail.

A van arrived, driven by an official from the county, a solid young black fellow wearing an ID badge identifying him as ELECTIONS COORDINATOR, seeming to fulfill the expectations of his official labor. A friendly, efficient civil servant on a tight schedule. The inspector said nothing to him, and the young guy departed with the equipment in the locked vehicle, taking the signature log with him, and of course the voting machines. The inspector was left with only the three faithful civic volunteers, booths to take apart, the flag to fold, chairs to stack, and tables to put away. By way of acknowledging their bravery, he again said nothing about the unusual visitors to the three Fates assigned to him by the county, hoping they wouldn't either.

Instead, he thanked his charming crew, reminding them to expect a small check in a month or so. That was unnecessary, as they knew the drill. He hoped, he said, truly, that they'd all work together again. It was difficult for even him to ignore what he assumed sounded clumsy and false in his recitation of the speech he'd been required to deliver. Perhaps they did not hear it, or chose not to. They all wished each other a good night, and then he was alone.

The visit that morning had been fleeting, and now things were back to their tidy, hopelessly normal and jolly permanence. Or not. He'd wait and see. A good enough thing perhaps, the quiet, as the effort of organizing the day had been exactly what he could afford to expend only every two years, plus the occasional special election. Those had even lower turn-outs than today, a phenomenon which seemed commensurate with and reflective of the failure of the Republic generally, its light lately dimming, the shrill antagonists of cooperation, the ungenerous, and the steady cynics gaining on the ideal, smothering it, nearly snuffing it out except for on Election Day, which arrived, however shabbily, like a parade of misbegotten clowns, sad but happy but so very sad. The day was irresistible still, sentimental, an enduring—if barely—ritual of low-stakes commitment.

He looked around the place, made one last survey of the empty room. He turned off the fan, closed the windows. One of the cyclists had dropped a single glove, the kind with fingers half-missing. He picked it up, stuffed it in his pocket, feeling like a criminal hiding evidence. Certainly no one would be back for it. Certainly he should have said something to somebody about the early-morning voters. He would be contacted, maybe. Or maybe not.

He turned off the lights, locked up, returned the key to the lock box. He drove in the direction of home, but found that he needed to stop on the way, pulling over, lights left on, engine running, to get out at the familiar shrine on the shoulder. His car door open, he moved quickly, dropping the glove at the foot of the biggest of the six or eight homemade white crosses, next to a bicycle wheel and other memorials of the notorious big accident there, fading and rotting markers with paint peeling, no names left on them anyway. So it didn't seem to matter, except that he'd tried, perhaps even succeeded, who knew? It might be the right one, but he had gotten rid of it, at least, returned it, if that's how you wanted to see it. And he did.

Tired from the long day, the inspector fell asleep on the recliner in his living room after too much red wine and satisfyingly greasy leftovers, the classical music radio station on. When he woke the next morning well before dawn, too early, the station played Mozart, too loud. He turned off the Requiem Mass in D Minor—this morning annoying, disappointing, and mocking—and switched on the TV news, made coffee, got the newspaper.

Front page, above the fold, in caps, were the allegations, complaints, accusations: voting abnormalities, massive anomalies, possible fraud, demands for a recount, thousands of ballots under scrutiny, suspicion all around, and more than a few local races likely to be contested as a result.

Sunlight forced itself through the cracks between the living-room shades and the glass. He left them down, glanced at his answering machine. He'd anticipated a call, a visit, even an arrest; now more so. For sure a message, however pointless or angry, from HQ. Nothing so far. Maybe never—as, clearly, his had not been the only precinct. So said the TV news. Stories of similar troupes visiting polling places, with disagreement over what other inspectors and poll workers, other voters had seen, and the story all over AM talk radio too. An argument, a scandal which would indeed throw into question more than suffrage, fair elections, whatever the opposite was of voter disenfranchisement— overenfranchisement, retroactive enfranchisement?—but the actual governing of districts, counties, cities across the state.

He read multiple articles, then went online for more, and there were plenty. Meanwhile, the chatty TV news crews did their best, offering up performance art—exaggerated and manufactured alarm, titillation, celebrity fuck-ups, local weather, sports, and traffic—yet seeming this morning to be doing more than only their miserable, shiny jobs. This was somehow so very serious, even possibly sincere. They tried, in between the updates, to reassure with lame, half-hearted, nervous jokes about Chicago and zombies, but still seemed genuinely shook up, more so than during the riots or police chases, the wildfires or earthquakes.

Experts were brought on, interviewed: witnesses, law enforcement, poll workers. Accounts were corroborated. Photographs of voters alleged to have been seen were located and frozen in place on the screen. He thought he recognized her, the sergeant, before her picture disappeared, replaced by a snapshot of a new stranger, a high school yearbook photo, a man or woman cut out of a group shot. Why didn't people bother to get good photos of themselves, anyway?

The details suggested a pattern. As they came together, events pointed to a completely logical, if nonetheless totally impossible and completely unacceptable, story.

The announcers went to commercials, came back, offered "breaking news" that turned out to be nothing, interrupted each other, reported that precincts nearest cemeteries, mortuaries, and mausoleums had been most affected, most "impacted." But other places, too. "Our top story this morning," began every sentence, and, almost immediately, on the screen appeared the words SCANDAL and ELECTIONS HIJACKED, a cartoon of Ms. Blind Justice with her scales, flying icons, alarming graphics of ballots stamped with a question mark.

There were maps in the background, with different colors to indicate precincts, pinpoints and connecting lines, radiating seismic concentric circles, most of it nonsensical. Nobody—as the news readers repeated over and over—actually knew much at all, though none of them would stop talking, would they?

It quickly became clear that provisional ballots cast would indeed dramatically change the outcome of elections: candidates chosen or recalled, bonds funded, local measures passed or not, school board races lost and won. Serious consequences, as if the more obvious ones were not serious enough. Yet nobody seemed quite ready to confirm that, to speak out loud the voters' identities, their status, the singular and remarkable existential characteristic of those suspected, involved, whatever. Wrong to speak ill, or criminal, of "provisionals," as they soon came to be named by media, authorities, the governor, and the secretary of state.

A door slammed outside. A white TV news van was parked in front of the inspector's house. A reporter got out and made her way to his front door. He took his home phone off the hook, ignored the knocking and then his cell, set to vibrate. He watched it buzz on the dining room table, then skitter along to the edge and fall off, onto the carpet. He did not move, waiting for her to leave.

And so it began, with the political parties and their spokespeople, the candidates and attorneys, all arguing with each other on television and, by that afternoon, in the courts. He was glad to be alone. The TV people outside gave up after a half hour and the inspector found himself going out, for no real reason, driving out of his way on a transparently contrived errand to the supermarket, not fooling himself, knowing exactly why, but embarrassed to admit it out of doubt and fear, out of the possibility that he was on to something.

And, yes, there was the same TV van, parked at the roadside memorial for the dead lady veteran. He slowed his car. The young reporter holding a microphone stood at an uncomfortable distance from what remained of the tattered shrine to the dead woman, reciting questions, it seemed, while a cameraman kneeled, shot his footage up close, closer, braver, and the tiny flags on the shrine composed in a broken halo of ruined color and crippled motion whipped painfully in the breeze over the portraits, mementos, plastic flowers, statue, and ribbons.

There was clearly an interview going on, if one-way, the reporter posing questions to no one, to herself , to the missing dead woman, to anybody overhearing, and the cameraman doing what he had to do, perhaps ignoring these weird circumstances or playing along, as was often required. As you would if you were employed to do this, obligated, if you had been asked and then agreed to document this work of locating the missing principals, tracking down the witnesses, but instead found yourself at the scene, the stage—an impossibly big one—but with none of the players on it, an empty set, if a set nonetheless.

The framed official color photograph of U.S. Army Sergeant Elizabeth Gonzales, because that was in fact her name—he read it there now, clearly, remembering it at the same time, the way you do—had turned chemical pink in the sun after six weeks, yellow and faded lime green where there once had been gorgeous dark hair and deep brown eyes and ruby lips and bright white teeth, a blue service uniform, the red and blue of Old Glory draped behind her.

And no, that was absolutely *not* the woman, the voter he'd met yesterday with her delegation behind her. She'd been alive and vivid, beautiful albeit quiet, perhaps angry or only very disciplined, military-courtesy style. This was only a photograph of her, an image, after all. She couldn't possibly be here herself—couldn't they see that?—not now, not there, under or above or below, nowhere in this vicinity.

Still, if you were a news reporter, where else would you go to find her? He'd had to check the spot himself, hadn't he—so there it was, corroboration. It made sense, as a first step, eliminating other possibilities. It made no sense. But he'd done it, to be sure. To be sure. Unsure.

And so he drove on a few yards, past the news-crew pair and the memorial. The classical station played the requiem again, or perhaps it was still on, the same piece, or the DJ had forgotten to hit a button or abandoned the studio. The inspector turned it down low and stopped to watch in his rearview mirror, hoping that a further detail might be revealed, about how exactly the dead sergeant and the others, possibly hundreds, possibly thousands of them, had done it, had claimed their loud, impossible, formerly silent majority, or at least so profoundly confused the weak arithmetic of what passed for representation. One man or one woman, one vote. One ghost, one vote.

They would seem to have changed everything, you could see that, every premise and lazy expectation about how life was lived in our fragile but clumsy democracy, about presumed rights and responsibilities, and then they'd disappeared: all in plain sight. Well, not plain at all—and now nothing would be the same, as everyone had said so often, so easily. Not ever again, and certainly this time, at last, really "not the same," different than the way the assassination of JFK had once made things not the same, or the moon landing, or 9/11, or the economic collapse.

Another loud, if as yet unspoken, observation, offered uselessly to no one, to whoever else was out there, others, whoever else would already be seeing and understanding. He said it out loud anyway, slowly: "Nothing will ever be the same." It could mean anything, really, and not necessarily a bad thing. For the first time in his life, his career, his lonely citizenship, he was way ahead of the curve, the first sailor to sight land, spot the wildfire, see the tsunami approaching the shore.

There was no point in reports or interviews, in ringing a bell or calling headquarters. It had happened now, finally, no going back. And why, exactly? Not for religion or for revenge, not for punishment, no. They had not been cruel, not bloody or scary or mean. His voters had been polite, agreeable. *Better* people.

Removed from the rolls, they must've been waiting there all along, hiding by the side of the road—like robbers in the bushes, like trolls under bridges, behind pillars or trees like a Highway Patrol of the Dead, until yesterday, Election Day, not clear how many or for how long. Not missing but missed, you might say, absent. Overlooked or unaccounted for. And then, on the first Tuesday of the month, they'd come back, together, unanimously, to add their voices, insist themselves back in. They'd studied, and we'd been forced to take their pop quiz—a tenth-grade civics or government class exam, a literacy test—and failed, and they'd gotten the franchise. Ours.

The familiar staccato of warning came on the radio. Perhaps this would be the official announcement. But no, only "This is a test of the Emergency Broadcast System. In the event of an actual emergency..." He turned it off.

The sergeant and her comrades, he thought, having committed their fraud upon the living, a felony for which they would never be prosecuted, had taken our presumed hegemony, that was the emergency—if a slow one. They'd stolen the default privilege of living, breathing, of irresponsibility, and failure to participate, too: what so many had abandoned or ignored, taken for granted, failed to esteem. It was funny, really, but not funny *ha-ha*. Still, the inspector had to laugh. Like someone was forcing him. Like he was living as a punch line in a joke, a prop in a skit, a big dumb giant in a fairy tale.

He'd long admired the eccentric political science teacher at school, a colleague who wore a bowtie with sincerity and yet seemed to live and breathe irony and politics simultaneously, a genuinely happy man unshy about marching around with both practically stapled to his sleeve. The teacher, Winston was his name, had taped a bumper sticker to the window of his office, "Oh, no, not another learning experience," and the quote from Plato about the problem of not personally participating in politics, and the inspector thought now to himself, "Oh, yes, oh, yes, oh, brother, yes!" and knew exactly where to go next, understood that he would have to learn, and suffer, and experience, just like everybody else. There would be more to corroborate, and very soon. But he'd get a sneak peek, a preview, just down the road.

He clicked on his turn signal, accelerated, and drove off, perhaps a half mile, to the next site. Others would also be on their way, piecing together what was up, perhaps responding less curiously at this point, less generously. He'd been on the front line, seen firsthand the provisionals' gentle, non-violent breaching of the protocol, of the rules of the natural order too, and he had been okay with it. But what would the rest of the living, breathing human electorate make of the claim by the super-powered provisionals on the living, the bored or the stupid, all—so far, every woman, man, child—as yet having managed to avoid speaking of it, talking about it, admitting?

And how would he and the others in authority be treated, having acceded, given in, failed to even report what they—he—had witnessed or suspected they were witnessing, but must have clearly understood was happening? What should he have done at the polling place, anyway? Asked them to leave, challenged them, disputed their eligibility—to vote, to breathe, to walk—and, what, called the cops?

Sure enough, there they were, up ahead: a crowd, a constituency. Some cause, theirs. Some campaign, boy. Not mourners, but an angry assembly. A lynch mob, but with nobody there to kill. Cars were lined up on the gravel shoulder, both sides of the narrow country road, people with signs, maybe fifty, and no doubt more on the way. One nut with a shotgun, other guys with shovels. He could not figure their politics, and it probably didn't matter. Old, young, women and men, hippies and buttoned-up business types, where had all of them been yesterday? But here, now, bipartisanship at last!

The spot itself was a mess. Desecrated. Erased. They'd already torn up the memorial to the cyclists, tossed it all over the steep embankment: the single racing road-bike tire painted white, helmets festooned in flowers, water bottles decorated in glitter and puffy hot-glue letters and hearts, bright lanyards and faded photographs, a jersey or two, flags, flags, and more American flags, and, there it was, on the top of the pile, the single glove he'd left himself only last night as these people slept.

He performed a careful but quick U-turn, headed back home, shaken. A police car, lights flashing, passed him going the other way. Then another.

He found a strange car parked in front of his house, somebody at the wheel. After he pulled into his driveway, she emerged—a young, tired-looking woman, her outfit sloppily thrown together, as if she'd been living in the vehicle, or driven all night. He was both nervous and relieved—of course he knew her immediately—and invited her inside.

He made them coffee, found cookies, and let her talk: about what she knew that he knew, about her widowhood, the beautiful, gone children—especially the infant—the four well-maintained giant red papier-mache hearts she'd painted and hung on oak trees at the site, not far from the gas station and roadhouse at the junction just a mile away. They'd been visiting from out of state, headed for Disneyland, the beach.

Drunk driver. She showed him pictures—of the kids and of her handsome husband. The man wore that same sweet, difficult look of duty tempered with something almost like satisfaction.

The inspector had of course driven by this display of hers a few times himself—though it was off his usual route—where the wasted teenager had smashed into their minivan, the woman thrown from the vehicle, yet surviving. The dumb kid too. It made no sense, her being alive and her husband and babies dead, she said. Everybody knew that.

So, yes, here she was, in his living room. Why again, exactly?

Because he'd seen them, and that was all that she wanted, everything she wanted. A report of what he'd seen, imagine that. How were they? Democracy, elections, voting, about these specifics she did not care. Well, she cared, sure, but her husband hadn't even been that political. She only wanted to show the inspector her photographs, to show somebody, to corroborate, to weep of course, to drink coffee and eat cookies with him this morning before the TV news van came back once again, which it had; she'd been out front to see it cruise by.

Nobody else knew, not quite, not yet. They had only a few minutes, she said, and he trusted her. She wanted only to be with him, quietly, and then she'd go. And he agreed, because he knew, even then, that they would all eventually track him down, wouldn't they, the rest of them: the relatives, the boyfriend or girlfriend or mother or father or friends or coworkers of Sergeant Gonzales, U.S. Army, all the children and lovers and wives and husbands and friends of the cyclists and bikers and drivers and hunters, perhaps even the old, very old, ones whose claims would be so much more complicated, perhaps confused but, still, completely understandable and meant to be respected. He was the elections inspector, after all, and that was his job, and he would be glad to do it.

So the retired high school principal and the heartbroken widowed and abandoned mother, they were the first two people to figure it out completely that late morning, if by *figure it out* you could mean *understand* or *explain* or *comprehend* well enough to at least tell the story, which they would, and tell it first, when the TV van did come back, about the nature of this campaign of resistance, its inevitability and its demands, which should, after all, have been so obvious for so very long.

The provisionals, they would explain, were hard to tell from the living, from the eligible. They looked like us, dressed like us. Who were we kidding? They *were* us, or had been. They would have to be asked to stop, sure, but kindly, if firmly, and not before they were apologized to, or otherwise made to count. They would need to be spoken to as if we were speaking to one another. No, better than that, with more empathy and with more kindness. And there would have to be a new election, a better one.

And in those minutes that they had together, the inspector did indeed tell her everything he remembered and more, going through each moment of the morning before, offering comfort, he imagined, practicing. Oh, yes, practicing. Nothing would ever be the same—and for that, you could choose to be grateful.

SANTA ANA
AND ORANGE

The Santa Ana rancho, which was originally granted to the Yorba family, has been cut up and sold out into tracts upon which thousands of happy homes may now be found, including the towns of Santa Ana, Orange, and Tustin City, three of the prettiest and most prosperous places in California.

—*SANTA ANA HERALD*, DECEMBER 31, 1881

Victor Villaseñor

from *RAIN OF GOLD*

The son of Mexican immigrants, Victor Villaseñor was born in 1940 in northern San Diego County, on the Carlsbad ranch where he still lives. For the first five years of his life, while his parents worked he was cared for by his Yaqui grandmother, whom he cites as a major influence. After dropping out of high school, he went to Mexico for several years, and it was upon his return at age twenty that he began writing. His first book, *Macho!*, was published in 1973 under the name Edmund Villaseñor. He wrote the screenplay for the 1983 film *The Ballad of Gregorio Cortez*, based on the Américo Paredes book *With a Pistol in His Hand*, but he is perhaps best known for his 1991 autobiographical novel *Rain of Gold*, which tells the tale of a young Mexican couple who flee the violence of revolutionary Mexico for the challenges and promises of the United States. Villaseñor has written numerous books, both fiction and nonfiction, including, most recently, the memoir *Revenge of a Catholic Schoolboy.*

This chapter from *Rain of Gold* takes place in 1920s Santa Ana, where, in 1929, the author's parents were married.

THEY'D BEEN IN Santa Ana for almost a year when Doña Guadalupe insisted that they were doing so well that Lupe could go back to school. After all, education was their only hope of ever really getting ahead.

At school, Lupe was put in the third grade—even though she was going on fourteen—and the other students teased her because she was a head taller than all of them. But she'd been teased at school before and so Lupe ignored them and worked so hard that she was moved up to the seventh grade within three months. Her long hours of studying with Manuelita back in La Lluvia de Oro had given her an enormous amount of self-discipline.

Late one afternoon, Lupe came home from school to start dinner for her family, who were still out working, when there was a knock on the front door. Lupe cleaned her hands on her apron and went to the door.

"*¿Sí?*" she said, opening the door.

"Excuse me," said the small, tired-looking old man, taking off his sweat-stained hat, "but is this the house of the Gomez family?"

"Yes," said Lupe, "it is."

"And you come from La Lluvia de Oro, no?" he asked.

"Why, yes, that's right," said Lupe, taking a better look at the man, wondering if they knew him.

"Oh, thank God!" said the man, his tired eyes taking on new life. "I was so afraid it would come to nothing again."

"But what are you talking about?" asked Lupe. She stood half-a-head taller than the man and she felt as awkward as she always did talking to men who were so much shorter than she.

"Please," said the man, "I don't mean to be a bother, but could I please have a glass of water?" He swallowed. "I've come a long way on foot, you see."

"Why, yes, of course," said Lupe. She closed the door and went through the tiny living room into the kitchen and got him a drink of water in an old chipped cup and came back to the front door.

Lupe was tired. She'd had a hard day at school. Her new teacher was a man and he'd kept her after school to help her, but she had felt very uncomfortable with him.

The old man was sitting down on the steps when Lupe reopened the door. He didn't look well at all. Quickly, she handed him the cup.

"Oh, thank you," said the man, gulping down the water. "That saved my life. Now tell me, is your mother's name Doña Guadalupe?"

"Well, yes," said Lupe, "but really, I don't see what—"

"And your father's name is Don Victor?" he interrupted.

"Yes, that's right," said Lupe. "But I don't think that we know you, *señor.*"

"Oh, no, not me," he said, standing up, and his chest filling with power, "but you do know the love of my life, your sister Sophia. I'm her husband."

"Sophia? My sister?" said Lupe. "But she can't be your wife. She was killed at sea years ago."

"Oh, no," said the man. "Sophia lives!"

Lupe's mind went reeling, pounding at her temples. For the last year their mother had been going crazy, praying every night for them to find their lost sister. Everyone else had given up hope, including Lupe.

"Tell me," said Lupe, still not believing this man, "and what does this Sophia of yours look like?"

"Why, just like you, but shorter," he laughed. "You must be Lupe, no?"

Lupe's legs went weak. "Then, Sophia didn't die," she said, beginning to cry. "She's really alive!"

"Oh, yes!"

"And her little Diego?"

"He's fine, too, and so is Marcos. And we have one more of our own and another one on the way."

"Where?"

"In Anaheim," he pointed, "just up the road six or seven miles." He stood up as tall as he could, then he bowed to Lupe. "Francisco Salazar *a sus órdenes!*"

That same afternoon, when Lupe's family came home from the orchards, she quickly told them the news and introduced them to Sophia's husband, Francisco. Doña Guadalupe gripped her chest, thanking the heavens, and they all got into a neighbor's truck, along with Francisco, and drove to Anaheim.

And Sophia came to them, plump and older, but still very much alive, rushing out of her home with her two boys and another in her arms. "Oh, Mama!" she screamed, grabbing their mother in her arms.

It became a time of miracles, of hugs and kisses. Sophia took Lupe into her arms, then Victoriano, Carlota, Maria and their father. She just couldn't stop hugging them and kissing them. It was one of the most exhilarating moments of Lupe's entire life. A dream come true, a gift given to their family by God Himself.

Then they all went inside, and Francisco put on an apron, just like a woman, and went to work. "You people talk, and I'll make dinner for all of us!" he said. He began making tortillas as if he'd made them all his life, cooking the meat and vegetables at the same time.

"And all these years," cried Don Victor, "I've been blaming myself for your death, *mi hijita,* thinking that you'd died in that ship I put you on."

"Oh, no, Papa," said Sophia. "I never even realized that you people thought I was dead. You see, when you put me on that boat, Papa, I didn't have any food, expecting that they sold it on board. But I was wrong; they didn't have anything. Not even fresh water to drink. So I had to get off the boat just before they sailed. And it wasn't until two days later, after I'd bought provisions, that I boarded the next ship."

"But didn't you know that the other boat capsized?" asked her father.

Sophia shook her head. "No, I never heard about that until months later because, well, I was out at sea at that time and I had enough problems of my own."

Sophia stopped and started to laugh, and Lupe saw a strange mixture of anger, yet joy come into her eyes. "Oh, those wretches," she said, laughing lightly as she smoothed out the apron on her lap the way their mother always did. "Do you realize that they robbed me the first night I was on that boat while I slept with my baby? It was terrible," she said, still laughing. "Why, they had us all stacked up like cattle, and by the time we got to land, the whole ship smelled of human waste."

She laughed, shaking her head, and Lupe realized that this was something that her family always seemed to do when they spoke of the terrible misfortunes that they'd suffered. They didn't get angry or upset, like so many other Mexicans did; no, they smiled and laughed as if even these bad fates had been handed to them by a mischievous but good-hearted God.

"Oh, it was difficult for me," she continued. "I'd come with all that gold from La Lluvia but, by the time I got to Mexicali, I had nothing. But, well, what could I do? I was a woman alone."

"So what did you do?" asked Maria, no doubt thinking about herself now that she was without a husband, too.

"Well, getting to Mexicali I sold my earrings and wedding ring, wanting to get American dollars so I could get across the border. But the money changer tricked me, by giving me useless currency from the Revolution. Oh, I argued with him, Mama, as hard as you would have, to give me back my earrings and wedding ring. But he told me to get out of his place or he'd call the police." Sophia's eyes danced with fire. "But not before I knocked over one of his elegant vases," she said, laughing. "And then that night my fortune changed. I met some people who were going across the border, and I became friends with a woman and her husband. I told them my story, and they took me in as part of their family, and I had Marcos in the camp where they worked. Then I got contracted along with them to work in the cotton fields on the American side of the border."

"Where?" asked Victoriano. "We worked in the cotton fields when we first got across, too."

"Oh, I don't know," said Sophia. "I was lost."

Sophia continued her story, and she told them how they'd been transported out of the town of Calexico in big trucks, going across tracts of flatland for hours. Then that night, they came to a ranch and she was given a little house to share with the family that she'd come with. The next day, they were at work before daybreak. Sophia left Diego and her infant with the woman who had befriended her, and she worked with the woman's husband in the cotton fields all day long. Within a few days, Sophia and the woman's husband became the two best cotton pickers in all the fields.

"I did, too!" cut in Carlota. "Victoriano and I were the best in all Scottsdale, Arizona! We even beat the big Negroes from Alabama," she said.

"You, too?" laughed Sophia. "Well, I'll be. It must be because we've always been quick of hand."

"And we're quick because we're short!" said Carlota.

"All right, go on," said Dona Guadalupe. She knew why Carlota had said that. Ever since Lupe had gotten so tall, Carlota picked on her.

"Oh, yes, where was I?"

"Picking cotton," said Lupe, "with that woman's husband."

"Oh, yes, well, there we were, and I thought we were becoming rich because we were doing so well, until at the end when we went to get paid."

Sophia stopped and, for the first time since she'd been talking, Lupe saw her sister get angry with rage. But then her husband, who'd finished with the tortillas and was now feeding the children dinner, came over and took her hand. Lupe saw her sister's eyes go soft with love. It moved Lupe's heart to see such tenderness between a man and a woman.

"You see," said Sophia, "I was in line to get paid along with the other people, but when it came for my turn to get my money, the fore-man gave me only half my wages. Oh, it still makes me so mad, I could scream," she said.

"Calm down, *querida,*" said Francisco. "It's done now, it's done."

"Thank you," said Sophia, holding her husband's hand. "Well, anyway, then I said to the foreman—his name was Johnny—'But why do you do this? I made more money than this.'

"'Move aside,' he told me, 'I have other people to pay.'

"Seeing all the people behind me, I moved aside, but I didn't leave. No, I just stood there, waiting until the last man was paid.

"'Well, I see you waited,' Johnny said to me.

"'Well, of course,' I said, 'you still owe me half my wages.'

"'Are you married?' he asked me.

"'No,' I said, 'but I don't see what that has to do with this.'

"He stood up. He was a big *pocho* who could speak both English and Spanish and liked to brag that he'd been born on this side of the border. 'If you had a husband, I'd give him your money for you,' he said, 'but since you haven't got a husband, I can't give you any more money than I've already given you.'

"'But why not?' I asked.

"'Because you made too much money, and the other men will get angry at me if I give you as much as you made.'"

"'But I earned it!' I yelled at him. 'I worked hard for it!'

"'Yes,' he said, 'I know you did, but these men have families to feed.'

"'But so do I! I have two children!'

"'Yes,' he said, 'but you should be married. It's not right for a beautiful woman to be alone.' Then I'll never forget, he came around the table and smiled at me and said, 'Look, I'm a good man and I make good money, so marry me, and I'll take care of you and your children.'"

"I couldn't believe what I'd heard. I was so outraged that I began to cry. But the fool didn't know who he was dealing with. So he took my tears to be weakness and drew close to me, saying in a very nice voice what a decent man he was and how much he'd been loving me since the first day that he'd seen me.

"Oh, Mama, I tell you," said Sophia, turning to their mother, "that man had absolutely no idea how we'd been raised by you. 'You're no decent man!' I screamed at him so loudly that all the camp could hear me. 'You're a bully, and a coward, and you have no idea of how to treat a lady!' And saying this, I turned and walked away.

"But then that same afternoon, the trucks came and loaded the people up to take them to the next ranch. You see, the cotton was done where we were, so it was time for us to go. But, when I tried to board the truck, the driver said I couldn't go on his truck. I went to the next truck and was told the same thing. The man I'd been working with said it was an outrage, and he tried to get me aboard the truck that he and his family were on, but the driver only threatened to take him off his truck, too. So he had to think of his family and keep quiet.

"After the trucks were gone, I was all alone on that ranch with the foreman and this old lady who kept the main house. Oh, I tell you, I thought it was the end of the world for me.

"Then that night, to make matters worse, the old lady came to my house and said, '*Mi hijita,* I don't know why you're so upset. It's a very good offer Johnny has proposed to you. He's rich. He works all year round for these big farmers on both sides of the border. I say, give your thanks to God that you're so attractive that such a man came forward and made you an offer like a gentleman. It could be worse, you know. He could have just grabbed you and used you like it's happened to me so many times.'

"Oh, I became so enraged! No human was going to break my will. I'm your daughter, Mama! So I grabbed the old lady, pushing her out of my house, but then she began to cry. Can you believe that? And she told me that she'd get in trouble if she went back without having talked me into marrying Johnny. Poor woman. So I let her stay, and we talked some more and I proposed to her that we run away together."

"'But where will we run to, child?' she asked me.

"'Down the road!' I told her.

"'But which road?' she asked me.

"'That one,' I told her, pointing to the road in front of the ranch.

"'But that road goes nowhere, child,' she said. 'There are hundreds of roads crisscrossing all over these flat fields. I've come out to this ranch three seasons already, and I still don't know where I am.'

"And suddenly, I realized that she was right. I had no idea where I was and, in the heat of the day out in those treeless fields, a person could easily die of thirst. Also, I had a child to carry, and the land was perfectly flat in all directions. There were no hills or high ground to show you where you were. It was like being lost in the middle of the ocean, I swear.

"That night Johnny came by again and said, 'Listen, honey, be reasonable and accept my offer. I'm rich, and I ain't so bad to look at, either."

Carlota laughed. "He really called you 'hoe-ney,' just like an *americano*?" she asked, laughing all the more.

"Well, yes."

Carlota went into hysterics, yelling. "Hoe-ney! Oh, oh, oh, hoe-ney!" And she continued laughing until her eyes watered.

Everyone just looked at her, wondering why she thought this was so funny. But then they, too, started to laugh, breaking the tension of this awful story.

"Anyway, to go on," said Sophia after Carlota calmed down, "Johnny went on and told me, 'Look, be reasonable; you got nothing, and I promise you that I'll take care of you and your two sons for the rest of your lives.' Then he gave some candy to Diego and played with Marcos, trying to show me what a good man he was.

"'Look, yourself,' I told him, 'if you were really a good man, like you say you are, then you'd pay me my money and take me to town in your truck so I could clean up and buy a dress and look really pretty for you. Then, there in town, where I'm free to decide, you can ask me if I wish to marry you. But not here, where you have me trapped like a prisoner. Because, believe me, no matter how much you try to impress me here—even by playing with my two sons—I know it's all false!'

"And I got up, screaming at him and telling him that he was a bad man, trying to take advantage of a woman alone. And I pushed him out of my house, hitting him with my fists, but he only laughed, telling me that I was the prettiest woman he'd ever seen, especially when I got mad.

"The week passed, and every day he'd come by and propose to me, and every day I'd throw him out. But then, the second week, he closed the doors to the little ranch market so I couldn't get any food to eat. By the third day Diego was so hungry that he was crying all the time. That's when I knew that he was the devil, and a woman has absolutely no chance in this world without a strong man.

"Late that same afternoon, I was holding my children, praying to God for a miracle, like you always taught us, Mama, when I saw this—excuse me, Francisco, but this is what I thought when I first saw you—an old man coming up the road, and he looked like he could barely walk.

"Getting to the buildings, he glanced around, saw no one, and began to search around. He found the water trough where the livestock drank but, instead of taking a drink, he just laughed and jumped into the trough, with his clothes and all. He looked so funny splashing around, that I began to laugh like I hadn't laughed in months. But hearing my laughter, he jumped out of the trough and began to run.

"'No,' I yelled after him, 'don't run! I need your help.'

"'My help?' he asked, pointing to himself.

"'Yes. Please, come back here.' But he wouldn't come. So finally I had to go out and get him."

"But why should I have come back to her?" said Francisco, laughing goodheartedly as he stood by the stove, cooking. "I'd been bitten by the dogs on the last ranch, so no one was going to catch me this time."

"But I got hold of him," said Sophia, "and brought him back to my little house and fed him the last of our meager soup that we had."

"I was starving," said Francisco. "I'd walked all day and hadn't eaten; it was a great feast for me."

"Then I told him my story and he became so red-faced with what I thought was anger," said Sophia, "that I was sure that he was going to go up to the main house and massacre Johnny when he got home."

"But she was wrong," laughed Francisco uproariously. "I was so scared that I was just trying to keep the food down that I'd eaten so it wouldn't come up on me." He laughed again. "So getting my food back down, I said to her, 'Well, then, I better get out of here quick! Because if he finds me with you, he's sure to beat me up.'"

"'Beat you up?' I said to him. 'But it's me he's mad at, not you!'"

"I finished my bread and got up to go," said Francisco. "'I'm going,' I told her. Oh, I was scared."

"I didn't know what to do," said Sophia. "Here was my miraculous prince sent to me by God, and he wanted to run away. So I looked at him and his balding head and his big scared eyes; I remembered how he'd jumped into the water trough with his clothes on, and my heart went out to him. 'Okay,' I said, 'let's go then, I'll go with you.' So he helped me get my things, and we left immediately.

"We followed a cattle trail across the fields, and he carried Marcos most of the way—he was much stronger than I'd expected. We traveled for three days, and every night we found plenty of water. Francisco trapped rabbits and we ate well. By the time we came to town, I knew I loved this man, Francisco Salazar, very much. He was a good man. And he respected me, and he was so funny. He reminded me of you, Papa, especially with his thinning hair."

Everyone else laughed, including Francisco, but Don Victor didn't think it was funny. He mumbled something under his breath, turning uneasily in his chair.

"So in the town of Brawley, we got work at a ranch together, and we worked side by side for several months and made good money; then I decided to marry him."

"Just like your very own mother!" said Don Victor, jumping to his feet. "There I was, free as a bird, a finish carpenter making good money, when she came into my life with two children and married me, just like that, too!" He laughed and laughed and went across the room and gave Francisco a big *abrazo*. "Welcome to our family, Francisco; may God help you! Because I can't! These women are tyrants! All of them!"

And so they ate the food that Sophia's husband had prepared, and it was delicious. The tortillas were round and perfectly cooked. Maria got so excited about Francisco's cooking that she couldn't stop complimenting him.

"I swear it, you're the lucky one, Sophia," said Maria. "You lose everything and still come up with a prince! Oh, if only I could be so lucky."

"Francisco has a friend, Andres, that he works with," said Sophia.

"Can he cook?" asked Maria.

"He taught me," said Francisco.

"Then it's settled, I'll marry Andres," said Maria. "He's mine!"

They all howled with laughter.

The following afternoon, they all gathered together by the orchard behind their rented house in Santa Ana. Lupe helped Victoriano dig a hole so that they could plant the lily bulbs they'd brought from La Lluvia.

"Let us pray," said Doña Guadalupe, "for I promised God that I'd plant my beloved flowers the day that we found Sophia. And we've found her."

The sun was going down as Lupe and her family knelt down on the rich, dark soil and gave their thanks to God. They were far from home and they'd been fearful that God hadn't come with them. But they had been wrong. God lived here, too. This land, this country, was filled with God's grace as surely as their beloved canyon had been full of miracles.

They bowed their heads in prayer, and the right eye of God turned to liquid flame, disappearing behind the orange trees in colors of red and yellow, as round and golden as the fruit hanging in the dark-green trees.

MacDonald Harris

---

from *SCREENPLAY*

MacDonald Harris was the pen name of Donald Heiney, who was born in
South Pasadena in 1921, grew up in San Gabriel, and lived much of his adult
life in Newport Beach. After serving in World War II, he earned a BA from
the University of Redlands, followed by an MA and a PhD from USC. In 1965
he joined UC Irvine as an original faculty member, cofounding its esteemed
MFA program. He wrote sixteen novels, including the National Book Award–
nominated *The Balloonist*. Since his death in 1993, much of his work has
made its way back into print, championed by British novelist Philip Pullman.
His novel *Herma*, set in Orange County and featuring a Madame Modjeska–
like character, was recently reissued with a foreword by novelist Michael
Chabon, one of his former students.

First published in 1982, the novel *Screenplay* was brought back into
print in 2014. The story is a gauzy, creepy overlay of 1920s cinematic life
onto the present reality, featuring a weird but empathetic loner character
whose privilege and remove is challenged only by the impossibly erotic and
idealized unreality of the silver screen.

SANTA ANA WAS a sleepy little county seat. Everything was covered
with dust and only one street was paved, a few black cars parked
on it with their noses in toward the curb. There were awnings stretched
out over the shops and the few loafers in sight were trying to stay in
the shade of them as best they could. A dog lay in the middle of Main
Street and we drove around him. There was a single movie house, a
block or so from the business district and next to a Chinese laundry; it

was called the Electric Theater. We were out of town and in the open country again in five minutes.

From here it was only ten miles or so to the beach. Over to the left were some brown hills, and ahead, as we went on, the sea gradually came into view with the sunlight sparkling on it like a thousand tiny diamonds. We went through Costa Mesa, the last town before the beach, and wound down a hill past a rather disreputable-looking roadhouse. Here we came out on a bay, and beyond it were the Newport dunes stretching along the coast as far as the eye could see. We crossed an arm of the bay on a narrow bridge and set off across the dunes, an endless expanse of sand carved by the wind into elaborate mounds and hillocks, with clusters of weeds growing here and there in crevices where the rainwater collected.

After we crossed the bridge the road turned into a pair of wheel tracks and then dwindled away entirely. The expanse of sand was unbroken except for the tops of some trees showing over the dunes in the distance. As we came closer I could see they were palms. I drove toward them over the dunes, the loose sand scrunching and shifting under the narrow tires of the Ford. I imagined stopping the car and getting out and resting with Moira in the shade of the palms. If there were trees there must be water too, and there would be grass and it would be cool. As though I were recalling a distant and almost forgotten happiness from another life I remembered sitting with Moira on the grass by the Old Mill Stream. I pulled down on the hand throttle to make the Ford go a little faster.

Then we came up over the top of a rise in the sand and we could see the palms only a short distance ahead of us. There was a small crowd in the shade of the trees and scattered around on the dunes near them. The camera was set up on its dolly, with boards for it to roll around on so it wouldn't get stuck in the sand, and there was a folding chair for the script-girl. Everybody else was standing around smoking cigarettes.

I pushed the throttle back up and the Ford slowed almost to a walking pace, wallowing and pitching as it crawled over the uneven surface. But I had to keep it moving a little or the wheels would sink into the sand. I stared out through the windshield, watching the scene ahead of me grow larger until it almost filled the screen of glass in its metal frame. I didn't look at Moira. Finally I heard her saying, "You couldn't turn around in this sand anyhow."

I stopped the car near the trees and shut off the magneto switch. In the silence I was aware of the murmur of voices and of the faint crepitation of sand as people walked back and forth on it. Moira got out of the car, untied the scarf around her head, and shook her hair free. I went on sitting there in the driver's seat for a while, and then I got out too.

The grips were setting up a tent that seemed to be made out of old scarves and Persian carpets, a long elaborate affair higher at one end than the other. I noticed for the first time that there were a dozen or so mangy-looking camels standing on the other side of the trees, where they had been out of sight as we came across the dunes in the car. The reflector-screen men were setting up their screens to point into the tent, which had its front drawn up and folded back so that you could see into the interior. Near it was a prop well with a wooden bucket in it, worked by a primitive windlass. The extras were all standing around in Bedouin garb. Well, here we were. It was the stupid thing about Arabs, as Moira had put it.

Reiter, who was standing by the camera, took off his hat and wiped his head with his handkerchief. The planes of his skull, gleaming with moisture, shone in the sunshine. He put the hat back on and strode around waving everybody toward the set with his riding-crop, as though he were shooing geese. "Okay, let's go!" he shouted.

I started to turn back toward the car, but Reiter gave me a light blow across the back of the legs with the crop—just a friendly tap. "Over this way, Alys. Come on, come on, everybody. We've got to get moving on this thing! What's the holdup?"

"*Pirate of the Dunes,* Take Four," said the script-girl, looking at her book. "The Expedition stops at the Oasis."

Reiter looked around through the crowd and caught sight of Moira. "Where've you been anyhow? Get your ass over there and climb on a camel. Where's her pith helmet?"

"Pith on you, Reiter," said Moira under her breath.

The costume-girl fitted a topi onto Moira's head and bent down to apply a quick touch of the comb to the curls that emerged from it.

"Fine, fine," said Reiter. He turned to a couple of grips standing next to him. "You guys get out there with the rakes and smooth out the tracks of that Ford. The only thing worse than shooting in sand," he said, "is shooting in snow."

Tom Zoellner

THE ORANGE INDUSTRIAL COMPLEX

Born in 1968, Tom Zoellner grew up in Arizona. He studied history and English at Lawrence University, earned his MA at Dartmouth, and worked as a journalist at a number of newspapers. He is the author, most recently, of *Train: Riding the Rails That Created the Modern World—from the Trans-Siberian to the Southwest Chief.*

A professor at Chapman University, Zoellner composed the following essay especially for this anthology. It offers a helpful, provocative, and elegantly constructed survey with stories of the rise and fall of an entire industry, one that captures nearly all of the big Orange County themes: labor, trains, commerce, and the diminishment of agriculture, with nods to so many influential people and their eponymous place names.

ALL FLESH IS AS THE GRASS. This dour wisdom from the Book of Isaiah is also true in reverse: all plants are as flesh. Crops of the fields, like the humans who tend them, have their day and die.

For seventy years, the defining "grass" of Orange County was its namesake product: the sweet fruit that hung from relentless furrows of trees serrating the county from top to bottom. A group of well-off Protestant migrants from the Midwest tried to bring small-farm values to new nineteenth-century business with the size—and a dose of the heartlessness—of a Southern rice plantation. They managed to create an economy unlike any other in America, as well as a vast tablecloth of waxy leaves, windmills, and dirt farm lanes, all cloaked on chilly mornings in a manmade, frost-defying haze of oily smoke.

The citrus trees left long shadows. Orange County's modern-day preference for large tracts of single-family homes, the exploitation of

Latinos as laborers, the decentered urban carpet, the bland mass culture, the self-conscious expression "California Dream," the thirst for youth and cosmetics, the Iowa-like probity: all of these local distinctions can be traced to the time between 1870 and 1950 when the orange was monocultured king, and the local economy arranged around it.

A first irony: oranges aren't native to California. The sweet variety called mandarin emerged in China and Vietnam around the time of Confucius in 500 BCE, then crossed with a related fruit called pomelo. Jews used a hard and sour breed called citron for rituals in the Feast of Tabernacles; the Moors of North Africa are thought to have brought it in the eighth century to Spain, where it softened and sweetened through hybrid speciation to something resembling the Valencias and Washington navels we eat today. During the fifteenth century, scurvy-wary Spanish sailors brought these seedlings to what is now California, and small groves of sweet oranges were planted on the grounds of the missions that Junípero Serra created in his path up the coast.

But the local birthplace of Orange County's signature business is less picturesque and not even in the county: it's a lonely stretch of Alameda Street south of Fourth Street, at the scruffy edge of downtown Los Angeles, where the only landmarks today are a row of cold-storage seafood warehouses, a weeded-over set of railroad tracks, and a liquor distribution warehouse. No plaque marks the spot where an Anglo trader planted the first set of orange trees for a commercial purpose in Southern California.

That man was William Wolfskill, a Kentucky native who had drifted to Mexico as a mountain man and gotten involved in the frontier liquor business. He and a partner sold jugs of grain alcohol mixed with red pepper and a dash of gunpowder under the name "Taos Lightning"—a booze so vile it could "peel the hide off a Gila Monster," in the words of historian Marshall Trimble. Wolfskill married his way into Mexican citizenship, and while passing through the dusty village of Los Angeles on the way to blaze a trail to the Pacific from Santa Fe, figured that Southern California's climate would support a citrus trade.

He acquired seeds from Serra's thirty-five trees that grew near the Mission San Gabriel Arcángel and planted them near his farmhouse. There he grew rich exporting his juicy food up the coast by horse cart to the gold-rush camps near Sacramento. By the time of his death in 1866, he owned two-thirds of the orange trees in the state.

Wolfskill's son and business heir Joseph thought even bigger. He understood that local markets were never the future of the California orange; the real money lay in shipping them to places where the fruit was an exotic species, a subject of rumor and fascination. Such was the intention of the first railroad shipment of oranges to St. Louis in 1877, in a single boxcar stacked high with crates stamped "Wolfskill California oranges." In the lore of the California citrus trade, this was like the voyage of the *Discovery*, because new technology was about to make orange growers fantastically rich.

The ice-bunker car, which kept oranges cool with air blown over ice, debuted on the nation's railroad tracks in 1889—the same year the California legislature approved the formation of Orange County as a separate political entity, and both the Southern Pacific and the Atchison, Topeka, and Santa Fe feverishly extended their tendrils down to the brand-new farming boomtowns of Anaheim, Orange, and Santa Ana, where the land was flat and gloriously empty. Huge fortunes could suddenly be made railing oranges east for customers eager to taste this high-priced exotic dessert.

The Southern Pacific Railroad also doubled down on hype, popularizing the slogan "Oranges for Health, California for Wealth" and sending promotional trains to state fairs across the Midwest featuring traveling lecturers, glowing booklets, and free samples for locals to enjoy. Unlike heartland cash commodities such as wheat, corn, or oats—nutrient-dense but visually humble grasses—the California orange had an erotic maternal shape, and origins in the sun-splashed Mediterranean instead of gloomy steppes. Citrus sales doubled across the Midwest over the next decade, and some of the new consumers were persuaded to try out the California ranching dream for themselves.

These enterprising landowners tended to be Protestant, wealthy, middle-Western and middle-aged, and looking for a reinvention in the warm sun of a far land. This was, in the words of local antiquarian Charles Fletcher Lummis, "the least heroic migration in history, but the most judicious […]. [I]nstead of gophering for gold, they planted gold."

The first job of a gentleman orange farmer was finding porous alluvial soil and nearby mountain ranges to provide shelter from restless Santa Ana winds. The best places were known to be immediately southwest of hill slopes, parallel to the wind and resistant to the "frost pockets" of stagnant cold air that could freeze the fruit off a tree in a single night. To best catch the sun's rays, orange seedlings were planted twenty-six feet apart, in militaristic rows set north-to-south.

He also needed a screen of eucalyptus or poplars to protect the young buds from being blown off the trees in high winds, and cornstalks wrapped around the bases of the trees to protect them from animals.

There had to be a local water cooperative with a system of ditches and canals, run by a foreman—known as a *zanjero*—who kept a strict accounting of when the sluice gates were opened and for how long. He also needed to be patient, because trees didn't grow on trees. They had to be nurtured in seedbeds, carefully planted in rows, and then left to mature for at least six years. But once a tree matured, it produced at least eight hundred pounds of oranges—ten boxes' worth—which had to be carefully clipped from the branches without nicks that could admit bacteria.

He needed a full complement of the bulbous metal devices known as "smudge pots," which were set on the edges of the groves and set to burn used oil and rubber tires on winter nights so as to create a layer of thick smog over the trees, blanketing them from the bud-killing frost that tended to creep inward. Some of the more well-appointed ranches had electric thermometers in the fields that would set off an alarm inside the house in the middle of the night if the temperature dropped below freezing.

Most importantly of all, he needed a cheap labor base from April to November to pick and sort the fruit if the orchard was big enough.

The first field-workers were Chinese or Japanese, many of them former tracklayers who traded in their hammers for a canvas shoulder bag and a tall ladder. They also dammed rivers and dug canals that proved indispensible in the later prosperity of the region. The Chinese, in the words of one approving employer, were "industrious, peaceful, never drank and kept cleaner in body than the Indian did."

Mexican nationals gradually took the place of the Asians. Their wives typically worked in the packinghouses that sat astride the railroad tracks—measuring oranges with metal hoops, washing them in soap and water, treating the greenish ones with ethylene gas to warm their color, wrapping the fleshy spheres in thin paper stamped with a brand label, and arranging them into wooden crates plastered with colorful labels idealizing and eroticizing their own image and labor: buxom young women cradling sacks full of equally voluptuous oranges, against a backdrop of snowy mountain peaks and the spires of semiruined Catholic churches. The caricatures were so resplendent that many of these labels were framed and hung as artwork in distant living rooms.

The real life of the Latino fruit picker or packer, of course, was not so picturesque. Wages were about two cents per box picked, and workers lived in rows of squalid shacks next to the canals. Orange resident Ken Schlueter, whose father owned 625 trees in the city when he was growing up in the 1950s, recalled being sent out to work alongside the Mexican crews, his well-to-do father's way of imparting a work ethic. They would bring him homemade tacos that they had heated up with hot coals buried inside the earth. He always felt outdone on the ladders, for his coworkers were rapid and precise, fleecing each tree from the top on down, making the oranges rain down to the earth in a cannonade of soft thuds. "Their hands were in constant motion," he told me. Harvesting oranges was a far more labor-intensive enterprise than stripping an Iowa farm of corn and wheat. "One acre here took as much work as a hundred acres in the Midwest," said Schlueter.

In brand-new settlements like Pasadena, Pomona, Riverside, Orange, and Santa Ana, the transplanted citrus elite like the Schlueters and their families found a "new El Dorado" and built Victorian houses, libraries, churches, and small opera houses—recreating the cities of a more established America, according to familiar patterns. A group of German immigrants from Ohio founded St. John's Lutheran Church in the city of Orange and built a pink and gray Gothic Revival sanctuary in 1913 that would have looked entirely at home in a cozy suburb of Cincinnati. The citrus trade was, said William Andrew Spalding, "an industry suited to the most intelligent and refined people."

But instead of seas of wheat or corn around them, there were phalanxes of the fragrant trees—once viewed as a romantic gift of the Spanish padres, produced now for the more Yankee virtues of thrift, industry, and bulk commodities. Orange County became, in the words of historian Phil Brigandi, "one vast orchard, dotted with little towns." Folded between the chain of tourist villages on the Pacific Coast and the range of the Santa Ana Mountains to the east, the county was a matrix of groves, dirt roads, windmills, and canals: "wall-to-wall trees," in the recollections of Ken Schlueter.

An immigrant from Ohio named Frank Nixon came out to the new town of Whittier, married a local Quaker woman, and took a grubstake from his father-in-law in 1912 to plant nine acres of oranges and lemons at the settlement of Yorba Linda, where he also built a kit house purchased from a lumberyard. The thirty-seventh president of the United States, Richard Milhous Nixon, was born in that house and later recalled a "hard but happy" childhood swimming in a nearby canal and listening to the sound of train whistles in the night. They were poor, he said, but they didn't know it, and the work was as vigorous as it would have been on any corn farm in Nebraska. Frank Nixon had chosen his land poorly: there was no windbreak from the Santa Anas and the ground was hard clay, which he refused to soften with fertilizer. Frost and poor yields wiped him out, and he retreated with the family to Whittier in 1921 to run a gas station. .

But cars didn't move the money; trains did. The Santa Fe and Southern Pacific Railroads, hubbed in Los Angeles around a mini-city of cold-storage warehouses, linked this archipelago society of sweet fruit to the rest of the country. The polycentric foundations of modern

Southern California were laid down through this interconnection between the orchards and their bulk storage: a network that would later provide the skeleton of the modern freeway system.

Typical among the Tom Sawyers who arrived for Orange County's second act was Charles C. Chapman, who had been an ambitious young seller of apples next to the railroad tracks in his Illinois hometown. He later operated a telegraph and had made a good living writing and publishing local histories across the Midwest. At the age of forty-one, he moved to warm Los Angeles for his wife's health and bought a "sadly neglected" grove near Placentia, almost as a hobby. When he wanted to visit it, he rode the Santa Fe Railroad to Fullerton—a town where he would later become the Republican mayor—and peddled his bicycle eight miles out to the oranges.

What made him atypical was his willingness to take creative risks in crop cultivation and sales. Chapman figured out that, unlike the Washington navel oranges which dominated the business, Valencia oranges could be left on the trees an extra six months after ripening and then shipped east in August—a season in which buyers were not accustomed to seeing oranges.

He also cut down on spoilage by insisting that his pickers wear leather gloves and cut the stems with rounded-tip clippers in such a way as not to leave small gashes that eventually harbored mold and could spoil an entire crate. After he shipped an initial carload of fruit back East at the end of the summer of 1897—a rail voyage that recreated Joseph Wolfskill's famous shipment to St. Louis—he made a huge profit and Valencia orange trees soon took over the inner folds of the coastal plains.

Chapman created a brand with an especially sumptuous crate label, featuring a ridiculous fantasy landscape of snowy peaks, palm trees, cactus, and, in the foreground, a group of portly Catholic monks inspecting a freshly picked orange with amazement and delight. *Scientifically grown*, proclaimed the advertising. The iconography and the brand name, Old

Mission, were plucked directly from the hype surrounding the novel *Ramona* by Helen Hunt Jackson, which told the story of a mixed-race Indian girl growing up on a ranchero. The romantic portrayal sparked a touristic craze for Southern California and its vanilla-Mexican curios.

Chapman's fame grew in this atmosphere. The trade press ran fawning stories on him, and one editor offered him $50,000 cash for the privilege of selling oranges for two years under the Old Mission brand. (Chapman declined the offer.) "He is indeed the ORANGE KING, not only of America but also of the world," proclaimed the *Fruit Trade Journal* in 1905. Chapman molded himself into a Southern California version of Ben Franklin, making himself both eminently useful to those around him and phenomenally rich.

Chapman joined the boards of hospitals, banks, and Christian missionary societies, married a pretty young second wife from the church choir, got himself elected mayor of Fullerton, founded a newspaper, and built a rambling thirteen-room mansion. He even persuaded the Santa Fe Railroad to build a branch line out to his orchard. Despite never having gone to college himself, he put forward nearly half a million dollars in a nationwide fundraising challenge to revive the fortunes of a moribund Bible school and rebrand it as Chapman College (a name he swore was chosen by the trustees without his knowledge). His interest in Christian education was topped only by a young orange farmer named Charles Fuller, who used the oil-drilling royalties from his orchard in Placentia to put himself through Bible school. He went on to host a radio show called *The Old-Fashioned Revival Hour* and founded the influential Fuller Theological Seminary.

Chapman's own evangelism on progress and American values was a regular crowd-pleaser at the California Valencia Orange Show, a kitschy 1920s carnival called a "fairyland of fruit" by the *Santa Ana Daily Register*. The child-friendly show embodied much of the exuberance and goofiness of the Jazz Age: fake Arabic minarets, models wearing bathing suits, high towers of fruit, parades and floats, congratulatory phone calls from the president of the United States.

This fair was the public face of the California Fruit Growers Exchange, a powerful oligarchy that functioned as a seller's ring. Truly independent farming had never worked out very well in Orange County. In the early days, a grower had no choice but to sell his crop to any number of agents representing the packinghouses who would estimate a price based on what they saw on the trees—and this price was often a result of collusion. Some Orange County growers were persuaded to sell their fruit on consignment, which meant that if it showed up in Chicago as spoiled pulpy mush, they got nothing in return. Brokers could also falsify their spoilage reports and deal contraband oranges on the black market.

Fed up with the disorganized system, a number of powerful growers formed the exchange in 1905 to share packinghouses, codify grading standards, and stabilize prices. It functioned like a nonprofit, owning no property and selling no shares, but it commanded enormous power, employed a national network of salesmen, and paid huge telegraph bills. They pooled the annual crops of Washington navels and Valencias from various districts around Southern California and sold them in bulk. Train schedules and deliveries were coordinated out of a high-gated office on Glassell Street in downtown Orange that looked more like a Middle Eastern temple than a place of business.

Despite the pro–small business rhetoric of most growers, this was not lassiez-faire economics at work, nor did it really resemble a Jeffersonian democracy of small landholders. This was, in the words of historian Laura Gray Turner, the essence of "managerial corporate capitalism." Led by a dapper ex–US Department of Agriculture man named G. Harold Powell, the exchange functioned as a legal monopoly that happened to be exempt from antitrust laws; fewer than two hundred men owned plots of more than one hundred acres. The Orange County elite made the decisions and controlled the prices.

Charles Chapman was one of the notable holdouts: he feared the brand power of Old Mission would be diluted if he had to sell through a single channel. But like the CFGE, he was not above bending the rules of free enterprise and engaging in outright market manipulation. "It was early evident that California citrus could not, without protection, successfully compete with foreign fruit, especially from Italy and Spain," he wrote in his autobiography.

In 1908, Chapman and several associates lobbied the House Ways and Means committee for a one-cent-per-pound tariff on European oranges, which opened up the ports of Boston and New York to his higher-priced goods. And when he got news of a shipment coming across the Atlantic in spite of the stiff duties, he played hardball. "When a consignment of foreign fruit came into the harbor and was offered for sale, a sufficient amount of our fruit was offered on the market to depress it or break it"—usually about one hundred train cars "donated to be sacrificed on these markets." Like a generation of nineteenth-century monopolists before him, Chapman and his allies also pressured the railroads for special-rate deals. When the tariff again came up for reconsideration in 1913, Chapman made a special plea for the "fostering care that our Government has always been good enough to give new industries." California thus muscled its way into Eastern iceboxes.

The rise of the CFGE and the era of Big Fruit came with a wave of orchard consolidation and the end of the "gentleman farmer" way of life in Orange County. Yet it ordered the market in times of uncertainty, created new year-round markets, and made large investments a little safer. Oranges were still a notional product, ranking nearly as frivolous and childlike as candy. There were up to five million orange trees in Southern California by that time, serving a national appetite that could turn fickle at any moment.

In the early decades of the twentieth century, Orange County faced an imbalance dreaded by every manufacturer: an overabundance of product not matched by rising demand. The ad agency of Lord & Thomas—and its in-house poets—dreamed up a campaign to boost sales that played off popular fear. The disaster of the Spanish flu epidemic during World War I had made Americans more germ conscious than ever. But the pasteurization process had recently made it possible to rid a beverage of bacteria.

Lord & Thomas came up with the slogan "Drink an Orange" to promote the simple but excitingly novel idea of having a glass of juice at breakfast—adding a morning eating ritual, in liquid form, which had been practically unknown before. Breakfast was "a habit meal," said the agency, not prone to much variance from day to day. And in that morning ritual was the possibility—if not the expectation—of daily consumption of a fruit thus far regarded as a dessert delicacy. "Its delicious juice is as invigorating as it is palatable," said Charles Chapman in one of his many speeches, "giving to man increased nerve power and a clear brain."

Orange County's liquid product took on the name of an earlier CFGE brand called "Sunkist," which evoked in a single phrase what had been portrayed in all the kitschy art on all the wooden crates over the years. The name graced billboards across the nation, educational films passed out to public schools, huge neon displays in Times Square and Coney Island. "Thanks to admen," wrote historian Jared Farmer, "the sweet orange completed its trajectory from fruit of the gods to the aristocracy to the bourgeoisie to the average Joe." Vitamin C would not be isolated in a laboratory and clearly understood until 1932, but the mysteriously healthful qualities of orange juice were all over the press.

The word Sunkist became so popular that the CFGE adopted it as the new name for the organization and stamped it directly on the oranges in black ink. Oranges, and orange juice, had found their direct competition not in other fruits but in sugared beverages like 7 Up and Coca-Cola, and Sunkist found its marketing strategy in the bright colors and salutary qualities of its product. Though it was not fizzy, it emerged from nature and not from the bottling plant. The advertising for Sunkist got so thick, wrote historian Douglas Cazaux Sackman, that nearly 1,500 Manhattan retail stores and soda fountains had bright-orange advertisements plastered in their windows. At Christmas, a cartoon Santa Claus offered an orange as the "most *healthful* gift."

Some of the local connotations of "Sunkist" were not nearly as radiant. In 1936, more than two thousand *naranjeros* decided they had had enough of poor working conditions and put down their round-tipped clippers in an attempt to strike. But their uprising was doomed from the start. The local press, including the *Santa Ana Register*, portrayed them as disloyal saboteurs similar to the IWW Wobblies who had tried to organize factories around the time of the outbreak of World War I. According to historian and journalist Gustavo Arellano, one of the pickers bit a policeman's arm, Mexican strikers were thrown in jail, and the Orange County sheriff gave "shoot to kill" orders, deputizing American Legion members to guard the orchards with shotguns. Hecklers broke up union meetings and police threw tear gas canisters through the windows.

The lawyer and journalist Carey McWilliams was appalled at the head-cracking he witnessed and coined the term "Gunkist" to describe the danger and violence roiling in the sun-splashed orchards. "Under the direction of Sheriff Logan Jackson, who should long be remembered for his brutality in this strike, over 400 special guards, armed to the hilt, are conducting a terroristic campaign of unparalleled ugliness," McWilliams wrote in *Pacific Weekly*. In the end, growers agreed only to minimal wage hikes and no union.

As labor tensions reached fever pitch, the California orange empire was already wilting from a series of cultural and economic blows. The colorful crate labels had begun to shed their fanciful Raphaelite iconography in favor of the simple word "Sunkist" across a blue background; with the advent of chain groceries and cardboard boxes in the 1950s, the crates themselves became a memory. Tired of the industry's smog—even uglier and more pervasive than the growing encroachment of car exhaust—municipalities all over the Southland began outlawing the smudge pots lit aflame on the edges of orchards on cold nights. A disease with the poetically clinical name of "quick decline" ran through the orchards, turning trees into dead sticks within a week. The blight spread through the ground, traveling root to root, and one sick tree could ruin all of its neighbors. Ken Schlueter recalled digging deep trenches around healthy trees, trying to keep them from dying.

And the most unstoppable force of all, even worse than quick decline: newly prosperous young couples sought detached ranch homes —a slice of the California good life—for themselves in the peace and prosperity of the early 1950s. Ten acres of orange trees started looking like a sucker bet compared to forty new houses on quarter-acre lots. Schlueter's father gave in and sold out after the city incorporated his property and raised his taxes.

In 1953, the movie studio chief Walt Disney acquired 160 acres of orange and walnut trees on Harbor Boulevard, right off the new Santa Ana Freeway, with more profitable ideas than agriculture. The Stanford Research Institute had studied land growth patterns and real estate models and told him the spot was an ideal place for a new amusement park, whose design was based on a railroad fair that Disney had seen in Chicago five years prior. The bulldozers went to work on the morning of July 16, 1954, and the rise of Disneyland on a vanished bed of citrus was the highest-profile land conversion yet of what had already become an unstoppable change.

Within a decade, the citrus business hastened its move to the Central Valley, near towns like Visalia and Tulare, where land could be bought for a fifth of the cost. Orange County became a residential instead of agricultural satellite of greater Los Angeles—celebrating its namesake crop with bas-relief concrete displays on the noise-dimming walls of the Garden Grove Freeway, and a few remaining acres of symbolic trees that historical preservationists had to fight to keep. The "fruit frost service" reports disappeared from KFI radio.

Only locals who know what to look for today can see the faintly visible archaeology of the orange empire—from the Anaheim Orange & Lemon Association Packing House turned into a food court to the Santiago Orange Growers Association building on a quiet street near the railroad tracks, waiting for Chapman University to find a re-adaptive use for it.

The Orange Industrial Complex lasted seventy years—which the Bible holds to be about the natural lifespan of a human being, the metaphorical flesh. It ultimately succumbed to the changing technologies of agriculture and the shifting economies of real estate that spelled a natural fate for the plantations. The same forces, in other words, that helped create them.

While the trunks of the last orange trees were burned and mulched decades ago, they left imprints that go deeper than the name of the county or the bulbous image on its seal. The echoing imprint of the citrus business can be perceived in the tract subdivisions whose geometry matches the acreage of the orchards they replaced; within the segregated neighborhoods of Anaheim and Santa Ana, where the Latino grandchildren of the *naranjeros* live on the disadvantaged side of a racial rift as pronounced as anywhere in the Deep South; within the volubly conservative editorial page of the *Orange County Register;* within the cultural emphasis on overt displays of wealth and youthful voluptuousness as fetishized and misleading as any rural maiden pictured on a crate label.

Critics of Orange County look at the orchard-sized subdivisions, or the vast consumerist rectangles of South Coast Plaza, the smoked-glass office parks with grassy berms and bottlebrush trees out front, the chintzy Spanish Mission architectural vocabulary, the feeder avenues as wide as rivers, and declare the whole scene bland, monotonous, and corporate. But so were the orange plantations they replaced, if not more so.

Near the center of the college that Charles Chapman helped endow, and where I now teach, is a statue of our founder seated in an easy chair. He leans slightly forward as if telling a story or giving a piece of advice. A dwarf orange tree grows behind him. Carved on the back of this memorial are words from his autobiography that describe the business strategy that vaulted him to prominence:

> I knew from experience that there were periods when citrus fruits were entirely absent from markets in the East, and I believed that if I could get oranges to customers during those periods I might develop a really profitable trade. So I took my courage in my hands and delayed any Valencia picking until long after all the other varieties had gone. Then we shipped

[our oranges on] our first experimental [railroad] cars. The response was beyond my greatest expectations. The "trade" eagerly accepted this new variety, which was solid, juicy, long-keeping and delicious.

Words on stone monuments are not usually so practical and specific. But this inscription perfectly symbolizes what the promise of Orange County represented for an earlier generation. Civilizations both great and small are founded on economic schemes more than high moral purpose. That usually comes as an afterthought, or a luxury of hindsight.

For seventy years, Orange County once stood for the harnessing of nature, the manipulation of distant capital markets, the production of sensual pleasure, the unapologetic mythologizing of an abundance not shared by all (especially those who picked the fruit), enjoyment of material success, the dependence on the Lord's constant blessings of warm sun, cheap land, and frost-free air. The county was a place that its citrus lords perceived to be free of history, leaving them free to make their own. And they left us the orange-ghosted world we live in today.

AUTHOR'S NOTE: A common tourist habit is to imagine what the scene might have looked like in a previous era, especially in older parts of the world. How did the coast of Virginia look to those English sailors, for example, or the cliffs of Capri to a Roman solider? This exercise is especially difficult in Orange County's flat parts when you try to see through the wide-boulevard monoculture of Del Taco and Ralph's into a time not yet a century ago when the roads were all dirt and the sun was blocked out by a mathematically precise forest of orange and lemon trees.

The trees are all gone now—*sic transit gloria citri*—but they molded the county into what it is today in the aspects we celebrate and also those held up as regional jokes or stereotypes. There's a reflexive tendency to think of our orange-ranching era in a golden light, perhaps because of the lost ethic of physical work or the pleasing taste of the fruit, but the reality was often contradictory and difficult. So it's important not just to envision the vanished trees but to see them for what they really were.

Linda Thomas

ORANGE, 1951

Linda Thomas was born in Orange in 1946 and graduated from Orange High School. She attended Fullerton College before transferring to UC Irvine, where she earned a BA in English and an MFA in fiction. Thomas taught at Irvine Valley College for thirty years, and she now volunteers as a naturalist docent with the Audubon Sea and Sage Society. Her poetry has appeared in the *American Poetry Review*, the *Blue Mesa Review, Faultline*, the *Hawaii Pacific Review*, and *The Ear*, where the following poem was published in 1988.

She introduced "Orange, 1951" as follows: "A native of Orange County, a white girl growing up Catholic in the 1950s on the southwest side of Orange, California, and an elementary school student at Holy Family School—I was paradoxically an outsider immersed in the traditions of the Mexican American people who lived in my neighborhoods and attended my school and church. In this poem, I use the images of those years to remember my hometown."

> The year the Pope announced the Blessed Mother
> assumed bodily into heaven
> I believed in America,
> on summer evenings just past dark
> that hour before the blinds fall
> when sprinklers sprayed the sidewalks
> and the paperboy swerved and
> shot what little news we needed
> at the front porch screen.

A dark window of eucalyptus
separated our block from Cypress Street
where shafts of yellow light
fell out of tarpaper houses
and foreign voices sang full-mouthed,
rackety as laughter
or the sound of a homecoming.

What slipped through the trees those evenings
and leaned on windowsills
that hour before the blinds fall?
When through the window
a brown woman stirs a skillet in America,
her religion a stack of tortillas,
her children a circle of stars.

Mona Ruiz

---

from *TWO BADGES*

Mona Ruiz was born in 1960 and grew up in Santa Ana, one of five daughters of Mexican immigrants. Her childhood, adolescence, and young adulthood, which spanned her experiences as a gang member and then later a Santa Ana police officer, became the subject of her book *Two Badges: The Lives of Mona Ruiz* (co-written with Geoff Boucher). She frequently tells her life story to civic groups and students.

In this excerpt from her memoir, Ruiz's early impressions of law enforcement anticipate her later intellectual and emotional struggles to understand the roles of both police officers and gang members in the community— a situation that, for her, is further complicated by her affection and respect for her father.

I WAS PROBABLY JUST four years old when my father first showed me the Soldiers of Christ. The images are a jumble in my mind now, vivid and lasting, but dreamlike when it comes to the details. The moment seems almost magical now. We lived on Golden West, in a house with a wide porch and a huge tree that my sisters and I climbed almost every day. Our home was an old wood-frame house. The rooms stayed cool in the long summers beneath a shady elm that towered above it and stretched its branches over the entire yard. My father and I were inseparable in those days. Each afternoon, as a hazy dusk would start to cool off the neighborhood, my father would return home from work. I would be waiting for him, sitting on the front steps and watching the corner for the first glimpse of his hulking 1955 Buick, a red and white beauty that was his pride and joy. My father, Raymond Sandoval, was a construction worker in those days, and he filled my world like a giant.

On one late afternoon, my father and I walked up Golden West toward the corner market to buy an ice cream. I remember my father held my hand as we walked. His fingers were rough from work but the grip was always gentle. Ahead, we saw a commotion. A car, one of the barrio's many lowriders, was parked at the curb and blocked in by two police cruisers, their blue lights flashing. All along the street, residents were stepping out into their yards and staring, shading their eyes from the setting sun.

There were two boys, but I don't remember them too clearly. They looked like most of the other young boys in the neighborhood with their short, black hair, white t-shirts and the baggy pants with sharp creases ironed in. There were two other men, too, but they didn't look like anyone I knew from the barrio. They were huge, they seemed to tower like trees over the boys, and their angry shouting had turned their faces beet red. Both were blond and wore uniforms and badges. Their size and voices frightened me.

"Don't be scared, *m'ija*," my father said. He was leaning down, close to me, and his hand held mine tighter. "They won't hurt you. Do you know who they are? They are the police…"

The word had only a vague meaning for me. I had learned by then, I think, that the police were the people who help you when you're lost and that they were friendly, but these men terrified me. The boys looked like rag dolls as the burly officers shoved and spun them and scolded in their deep, booming voices.

My father was still talking in hushed tones. "They have respect. They help people and they have respect, that's what's important. And they don't take anything from these…these stupid *cabrones*!"

Dad wagged his finger at the two gang members, who were now sitting on the curb with their heads hanging. Father always told me the gang members were full of themselves, too selfish to amount to anything good. He hated the way they strutted and showed contempt for elders, and through the years he would repeat his lectures about the dead-end road offered by gangs. I didn't understand much of that, but I solemnly nodded anyway. My father was the center of my world then, and if he said the boys were bad people, then they were bad.

"Listen, *m'ija*," he said, his strong hand clamping on my shoulder. "The police are like Soldiers of Christ. Do you understand? They do God's work here on Earth."

My father went on, talking about the example police officers set for all of us, the way they risk their lives for a just cause. I couldn't take my eyes off the two men. One of the officers was bent, his hands on his knees, and yelling into the face of one of the boys again. I wondered what the two had done, why God was mad at them.

"Police officer, it is a good job," my father said as if he were thinking out loud. The crowds on the sidewalk were thinning out. The street show was almost over, but my father and I did not move.

"I always wanted to be a police officer, *m'ija*. But someone like me...no, not me, I lack an education. These hands are good only for hard work, yes? But you, someday, you should be a police officer. To show people that a *Mexicana* can do a good job, too. For respect, for honor, for your *raza*..."

The words didn't make sense to me. Me? How could I be one of them? Why would I want to? I couldn't even imagine talking to those fearsome men. One of the boys was getting pushed into the police car, and my eyes locked for a moment with one of the officers. I instinctively drew closer to my father's leg and he chuckled. Then Dad tugged at my hand to follow him as he walked up the street, toward the market. I looked back over my shoulder, back toward the flashing blue lights, trying to see more of these Soldiers of Christ, these brutal angels whom my father admired so much. I wondered: Were they ever children like me?

I would see many things during my years on the streets, horrifying sights of pain and despair and even death, but for some reason that first glimpse of the conflict between police and gangs has always stayed with me, just as my father's words did. If the police were Soldiers of

Christ, what did that make gang members? And, if the cops were truly agents of a greater good, how could I justify the corruption and excess I would eventually see among their ranks?

It was simpler when I was a little girl sitting at the knee of my father, Raymond Sandoval. He made everything clear with his wise words, and I was the focus of his teachings. He loved all of my sisters, of course, but we shared a special bond that began when he named me Ramona Sandoval. He gave me a form of his name because I, like him, was the second born among my siblings. To be the second, he often told me, meant I had an extra responsibility to my family, just as he felt he has always carried.

My father saw his older brother, Paul, die as a teenager on a stormy day. The two were working for a man who owned walnut trees in El Modena, and Paul was killed in a flash of blue when his aluminum tool grazed power lines running through the branches of a tree. The other men shouted for my father to stay back, but he ran to Paul's still form and cradled him as he died. He promised Paul he would tend to the family.

"I had to grow up then, *m'ija*," my father often told me in hushed tones. I would close my eyes and see him there, beneath the rolling black clouds and rustling trees, holding his brother. Paul was limp, his arms out to the sides so his body looked like a cross. To my child's mind, it was a bolt of lightning that killed this mysterious uncle, a bolt that transformed my father into a sad but strong adult. In my mind, I fully expected that someday some similar transformation would happen to me.

My father was wrestling with the grief of his brother's death when he left Orange County, staying for a time with his cousins in Cardiff and then moving down to Mexicali to join his own father. A year went by before he could return to California, when he met up with his sister, Jenny, in San Diego. Jenny was dating a man named Lupe, and she introduced Raymond Sandoval to Lupe's teen sister, Elvera. It was love at first sight, my father said.

Raymond was in his thirties, and while Elvera's parents allowed them to date, her father said he would forbid them from getting married. But that did not matter to my parents. They were in love. They ran off to Santa Cruz to marry and, after saving up money, they set down roots in Santa Ana, a city about thirty miles southeast of Los Angeles.

My father raised me as if I were his son. We worked together in the musty workshop he set up in our old garage, listening to Motown music and the mariachi songs that always made me giggle. In the late afternoons, as the sweet smell of my mother's cooking signaled dinnertime, I would watch the street, waiting for that huge red car to round the corner.

We were always a big family. My oldest sister was Maryann, and after me there was Lydia, Roni and Sandra. I was born in 1959, and in the sixties my four sisters and I watched the world from our barrio in central Santa Ana. (Later, as I was nearing adulthood, there would be more siblings—Margie, Isabelle and Raymond Jr.—to bring the household to ten.) I was always closest to Lydia, bounding off together for some new adventure while the rest of the sisters played with dolls. But while I was a tomboy, more comfortable roughhousing than playing house, Lydia enjoyed being at my mother's side, learning cooking and all the difficult, endless skills it takes to keep a large household going. I was mesmerized by car engines and tree climbing, while Lydia's daydreams were devoted to motherhood and her own family. Maryann was bookish and quiet, always the smart one, and always fascinated with the ceremony and solemn magic of church. As she grew older, she talked a lot about becoming a nun. And, in those days when I was a youngster, Sandy was always the baby, the target of our teasing and, maybe because of that, always a little spoiled by Mom and Dad. We were all different, even in appearance. Maryann was slender and dark with frizzy hair and almond-shaped eyes. I always had light skin and reddish hair, while Lydia had dark skin and wavy, black hair to match her black eyes. Roni looked just like Mom, with caramel-colored skin and big, brown eyes.

Lydia and I were happiest climbing and swinging on the huge tree that dominated our home's lot. The tree was the center of our games, the finish line and the starting point. We would play hide-and-seek around the trunk and the branches would play games with the echoes, making us wonder where everyone else was. We would wrap our arms around it to see if we were growing, testing and resting ourselves against it.

Lydia and I loved to wrestle, even with our male cousins, Edward and Andy Elizalde. Many afternoons were spent going toe-to-toe with these two, the youngest of the Elizalde brothers, and their family was a fixture in our lives. Each weekend, they were either at our house or we would make the five-minute drive to their home. Eddie and Andy had two older brothers, who seemed huge and intimidating to us in those days. Their names were Ricky and Jesse James Elizalde, and they were far too wrapped up in their teenage concerns to spend much time with their young cousins. Eddie and Andy would tease and tangle with us, but Ricky and Jesse seemed to belong to a different world with their glowering faces, slicked-back hair and sullen expressions. Later, I would learn much about that world.

Everything in my youth revolved around family, both our household and the extended family that seemed to reach throughout the city. My sisters and I were all different, but all close, brought together by two hard-working parents who strived to give us the best they could. It was not easy. We never had much money.

My mother was always the organizer of our household, keeping tabs on our finances and, remarkably, finding ways to stretch my father's paycheck to cover the cost of the whole family. She was also a master of making time for all of us in those days, juggling the duties of the house with tending to her girls. Looking back, I don't know how she did it.

I knew little beyond Santa Ana. Although I lived only a fifteen-minute drive from the beaches in Huntington or Newport, we rarely went. That was a different world, a white world, mostly. We did go down to San Diego each summer, a big Fourth of July vacation for us to visit my mother's family. I remember my sisters and me, all ponytails and summer clothes, piling into the car for the drive, which was less than three hours but felt impossibly long to a group of children. Going to San Diego would always feel like a dream: We would leave so early that my mother would dress us all and my father would carry each of us, sleeping, to the brown station wagon, like sagging bags of flour in his arms. Later, maybe about 6 a.m., I would wake up in the back seat, speeding down Interstate 5, well on the way. I'm sure my parents preferred it when we were sleeping. While Maryann would play quietly with her paper dolls or comic books, Lydia and I invariably would get bored and turn to tormenting poor Roni, staring or poking at her until she collapsed into tears. My father would get so angry, he'd threaten to take us all back home. We'd turn our attention to coloring books for awhile, but two freeway exits later we'd be back to trouble.

My mother always dressed us to match. One year, I remember, we had bright yellow outfits, cool cotton with bell-bottom pants and a garish daisy floral pattern. We went to the big fair they had in Solano Beach, and I can still recall my sisters weaving through the noisy crowd and past the rides in those bright yellow clothes.

On the way home, weary from sun and all the hot dogs, we were far quieter. We would whine about leaving San Diego, but then it was always such a relief to get home. It always felt like we had been gone for months.

Our neighborhood seemed so vibrant and alive in those days, and so very different from what it would become in the decades since under the eroding pressures of crowding and crime. But it would be many years before I ever detected those woes. When I was a child, my worries went only as far as my yard and could all be solved by the wave of my father's hand.

I was always a runt. But father taught me that size is no excuse for fear or losing. He knew that our blue-collar neighborhood would eventually throw challenges at me, so he taught me how to protect myself, how to throw a punch. He also told me that God looks out for people in the right. If you stand up against people who do evil things, God will be on your side, so have no fear. Often, after dinner, I would sit in his lap and listen to his words about right and wrong, good and bad, held in his arms and feeling safe as I drifted off into a light sleep.

Again, it was so simple to a child's mind and so reassuring. In the years to come, those lessons would seem like a bad joke to me, but as a young girl they made me brave.

As I said, my oldest sister, Maryann, was different from me. She was very bright, always finding the classroom success that eluded me, and she was shy and reserved. That made her a target for a pair of bullies down the street who tried to imitate their older brothers' thuggery by preying on anyone they could. I hated bullies, and when I saw them knock the books from her hand one day as she walked home from the library, I threw my books down and shoved the boy and kicked him in the shins. I was eight or nine, and the boys were ten-year-olds. But my father had taught me that boys were never supposed to hit girls, it was a rule of honor, and I was furious at the bullies for flouting that rule. My sister was kneeling on the sidewalk, picking up her books, as I shoved and kicked wildly at the two stunned boys. The world went red for me, washed away by my anger. I held nothing back. It would become a familiar sensation that would carry me through many fights, although afterward it often left me more frightened of myself than any foe.

Trips to the library or the market became a gauntlet for my sisters and me. The bullies were not deterred by my wild combat; if anything, it provoked and shamed them into teasing us more. Fighting became familiar. The fights were really just wrestling matches. No one ever got hurt, but I got used to the reality of hitting people, trying to hurt them. As bad as it sounds, I came to enjoy it. The release and the competition suited me, and as long as I believed I was in the right, I never felt guilty about fighting. And I was good at it.

My father's hatred for the gang members was driven by his belief that they were lazy, disrespectful and shamed our people. The gangs flew in the face of his strong work ethic and love of tradition. He proudly detailed his family history, his roots spreading back to Spain. He spoke with admiration of simple people who through sweat and dedication made their dreams come true for themselves and their children. History was sacred to him, and the gang members, the *vatos,* were all about today, the satisfaction of the desire of the moment, be it for beer or drugs or rowdiness. Raymond Sandoval was no saint during his youth, I know, but as he grew older and shouldered the burden of a family man, his spite for the gang members and their predecessors, the *pachucos* of the earlier generations, also grew. If his dream for me was to become a police officer, then his greatest fear was certainly that I would fall into the gang scene. It is ironic, I suppose, that both of these visions would come true.

My father told my sisters and me that the gangs promised only shame and danger for a young girl. As an adolescent, I heeded his warnings, the same way I listened to all his words. Still, I was mesmerized by the colorful characters who strutted through the neighborhood with an air of confidence and menace. Because my father called them evil, I would glare at them, made brave because I knew I was in the right. But it was not easy to despise them as my father did. They often seemed to do nothing wrong and their cocky antics made me curious. It was hard to hate them, too, because more than a few of them were family.

Nothing is more important than family, nothing is more binding than blood. If there were a lesson my father hammered into me, it was that I should do anything to protect the people who shared my name and past. I should be willing to die, he often said solemnly, sending a chill through me. But what about the cousins and uncles who clearly were on the side of the gangs? It confused me and, I knew, presented my father with a frustrating problem. He would not turn his back on the homeboys in our large, extended family, nor did he want his daughters to embrace their ways. It was a hard road for my parents to walk.

Once, when I was perhaps eight years old, loud banging on our front door and the insistent barking of our dogs, Chopper and Pandora, woke me in the middle of the night. Half asleep, I pulled myself up and padded past my sister's bed to the hallway. I made my way to the top of the stairs above the living room. Below, I could hear voices, my parents and someone else. Peeking around the corner, I saw my father helping a stumbling figure through the front door. As the man collapsed to the couch, my mother locked the door and closed the curtains hanging at the front window. As my eyes grew accustomed to the dim light, I recognized the man on the couch: It was my cousin, Jesse James Elizalde. A few years later, I would realize that Jesse was a neighborhood celebrity of sorts, one of the founders of F-Troop, the gang that liked to believe it ruled Santa Ana. Like his historical namesake, Jesse James was a popular rogue, an anti-hero for the youngsters who admired his cocky troublemaking. But that night I did not know all that, I only knew that he was family and that he ran with the people my father did not like. He was bad, but he was blood.

It was hard to hear what my father was saying, but I could tell he was upset. Jesse was breathing hard and his teeth were bared, like an animal or someone in pain. My mother gasped and said something in Spanish when she saw the large crimson stain soaking Jesse's shirt, just above his waistline. Outside, the sound of sirens made the dogs howl even louder. Jesse rasped something about "no place to go" and my mother brought towels and water to him and started cleaning his wounds. My father began to pace in the room, shaking his head. I could not understand what was happening, but I sensed that Jesse was in trouble and was looking for help. I craned my neck to see what my father was doing, but then I quickly jerked back into the darkness—for a moment it looked like Jesse had turned toward me. When I worked up the courage to peek again, my cousin's head was down, watching my mother clean his wounds. Despite the blood, I could see the famous Jesse James Elizalde was now smiling.

That night, holding my breath and hiding in the shadows, it was impossible to imagine all the pain and loss that he and his friends would cause me and just about everyone I knew. Maybe my father knew, maybe that's why he had so much anger for the fun-loving gang members. To a young girl's eyes, though, Jesse and his friends seemed more and more like cool and exciting figures. I still believed my father's warnings about the gang, but my resolve was already slipping, giving way to a giddy infatuation. Soon, the warnings in my mind would evaporate altogether. No one knew, but fate was about to strike my father down and, once he fell, his second-born daughter would also begin to tumble.

Aracelis Girmay

SANTA ANA OF GROCERY CARTS

Born in Santa Ana in 1977, Aracelis Girmay earned a BA at Connecticut Col-
lege and an MFA from New York University. Her poetry collections include
Teeth (2007), *Kingdom Animalia* (2011), *The Black Maria* (2016), and a
collage-based picture book, *changing, changing* (2005). She won the Isabella
Gardner Poetry Award and was a finalist for the National Book Critics Circle
Award. She is currently an assistant professor at Hampshire College and
teaches in Drew University's low-residency MFA program. In 2015 she won a
Whiting Award, given to emerging writers on the basis of early accomplish-
ment and great promise. She lives in New York and Massachusetts.

Featured on PBS's *Bill Moyers Journal*, this poem from *Teeth* explores
and celebrates Santa Ana and Ruiz's family history there.

> Santa Ana of grocery carts, truckers,
> eggs in the kitchen at 4 am, nurses, cleaning ladies
> the saints of ironing, the saints
> of tortillas. Santa Ana of cross-guards, tomato pickers,
> bakeries of bread in pinks & yellows, sugars.
> Santa Ana of Cambodia, Viet Nam, Aztlán
> down Bristol & Raitt. Santa Ana.
> Boulevards of red lips, beauty salons, boomboxes, drone
> of barber shop clippers fading tall Vincent's head, schoolyards,
> the workshop architects, mechanics.
> Santa Ana of mothers, radiators, trains.
> Santa Ana of barbecues.
> Santa Ana of Trujillos, Sampsons, & Agustíns,
> Zuly & Xochit with their twin lampish skins.

Santa Ana of cholas, bangs, & spray.
Santa Ana of AquaNet, altars,
the glitter & shine
of 99 cent stores, taco trocas, churches, of bells,
hallelujahs & center fields, aprons,
of winds, collard greens, & lemon cake
in Ms. Davenport's kitchen,
sweat, sweat over the stove. Santa Ana
of polka-dots, chicharonnes, Aztecs, African Fields', columbianas,
sun's children, vanished children. Santa Ana of orales.
Santa Ana of hairnets.
Patron saint of kitchens, asphalt, banana trees,
bless us if you are capable of blessing.

When we started, there were cousins & two parents,
now everything lost has been to you.
The house, axed, & opossums
gone. Abrigette & her husband John.
& the schoolyard boys underneath the ground,
undressed so thoroughly by your thousand mouths, Sana Ana,

let that be
enough.

Emmy Pérez

HALLADAY STREET

Emmy Pérez, born in 1971, was raised in Santa Ana and graduated from Saddleback High School. She received her BA from USC and her MFA from Columbia University. She is the author of two poetry collections: *With the River on Our Face* and *Solstice*. She is currently an associate professor at the University of Texas Rio Grande Valley, where she teaches in the MFA creative writing program and the Department of Mexican American Studies. She has lived on the Texas-Mexico border, from El Paso to the Rio Grande Valley, since the new millennium, and she visits her family in Santa Ana as often as she can.

Pérez grew up near Halladay Street in Santa Ana, the site of this poem, which appears in her collection *Solstice*, published in 2003.

> The men notice the slight swelling
> of her chest. The street breathes:
> a mirage of gasoline
> flooding ghosts of orange groves.
> To be a man is to detect
> bodies as they soften.
>
> She checks her reflection
> in the chrome of his car. Holds still
> while strangers scout a path
> halfway to her sky. It is good
> to have much cake on your behind.
> They want to drop silverware; bring food to lips.
>
> Mouths and hands join together; she ought to

say a prayer to Our Lady of Guadalupe.
Light candles for her bowed head.
Use cushions for knees. Kneel. Stained
glass keeps the sun out. A hymn flutters
through exhaust pipes. Outside, wildflowers
bloom through cracks of stone. Worms appear
in puddles of last night's rain.

...She smiles for mother as bolillos bake into boats.
They will slit them, fill them with meat.
Plums ferment near the ocotillo fence.
Under skins, flesh hums—capillary, sweet.

Karen An-hwei Lee

ON TRISTEZA LIGHT IN SANTA ANA

Karen An-hwei Lee was born in 1973 in Boston. She earned an MFA from Brown University and PhD in English from UC Berkeley. She is the author of four books of poetry, including *In Medias Res*, winner of the Norma Farber First Book Award. Her book of literary criticism, *Anglophone Literatures in the Asian Diaspora: Literary Transnationalism and Translingual Migrations*, was selected for the Cambria Sinophone World Series. Lee has taught at Vanguard University in Costa Mesa, has received a National Endowment for the Arts grant, and is a voting member of the National Book Critics Circle. A resident of California for almost two decades, she currently lives in Santa Ana.

The poem that follows appeared in *Pool: A Journal of Poetry* in 2014. The word *tristeza*, translated from Spanish as "sadness," describes an aphid-borne citrus virus capable of causing the widespread destruction of orchards. Lee told us that after moving from Northern California to Santa Ana, she "sensed the earth's grief as morning light, orange-drenched, broke over the OC fairgrounds to the south and ocean waves to the west: the color of light [bearing] witness to vanishing orange groves in Orange County, reaching even to the parched orchards of the Inland Empire, evoking the *tristesse* of migrant workers."

> On a crazed world of raining glass—
> > there is no marriage
> > there is no fiscal crisis
> > there is no estranged fiddler
> splitting pear-shaped lutes in a luthier's workshop
> on the other side of the globe
> > in a Maolan karst forest.

On the sides of *el camino*, orange trees—
       there is no outsider to a love triangle
       there is no unrequited moon
       there is no sour root-stock
wilting in the blight of *tristeza*,
       aphid-borne virus—

No tristesse on a *miércoles* evening
when we spy an *estrella* in the sky
       of blue gas-flame.
Santa Ana, a new year of no oranges,
       no one weeping in groves
       no one setting up camp with fruit-pickers
       no one praising *tristeza*.

Lisa Alvarez

AT THE LAST BOOKSTORE

Lisa Alvarez was born in 1961 in Inglewood and grew up in and around Los Angeles. A graduate of CSU Long Beach, she earned her MFA from UC Irvine and is currently a professor of English at Irvine Valley College. Her poetry and prose have appeared in *Codex Journal, Faultline*, the *Green Mountains Review, Huizache*, the *Santa Monica Review*, and *Truthdig*. Alvarez coedited *Writer's Workshop in a Book: The Squaw Valley Community of Writers on the Art of Fiction* with the late Alan Cheuse, and she codirects the annual Community of Writers summer conference in Squaw Valley, California. She lives in Modjeska Canyon.

This poem, published in *Zócalo Public Square* in 2015, describes a visit to the legendary Bookman bookstore in Orange. That sanctuary of worn paperbacks can be hard to reconcile with both the easy abundance and violence observed on the drive home. The poem's angry yet hopeful conclusion speaks to the contentious, unresolved history of Orange County's suburban milieu, which is never far below the surface—if it's below it at all.

> At the last bookstore, Anne Frank still smiles
> on the shelf,
> marked down to sell.
>
> No one is buying tonight.
>
> Down
> the
> road

beyond the miles
of cinder block walls
hiding
suburban backyards
the bricks
the color of old bandaids

comes the bright tumble
of perennial California citrus
oranges, lemons, grapefruit
swollen on the branch
and smashed
on the sidewalk

a careless harvest

down that road

past the fruit no one is hungry enough to pick
to eat

someone
keeps spraypainting
a swastika
on the county-owned storage trailer
as big as a railroad car
parked forever
on the canyon road.

Someone else keeps spraypainting over it.
A spray of fury: black
  white
          black
  white   black.
Both are so diligent.

Kristen Leigh Schwarz

EMPEROR OF UMBRELLAS

Kristen Leigh Schwarz was born in 1983 in Harbor City and received her MFA in fiction from UC Irvine. Her work has appeared in the *American Literary Review*, the *Saint Ann's Review*, and the *Santa Monica Review*, where the following story first appeared in 2015. Schwarz lives in Los Angeles and works for the Los Angeles Alliance for a New Economy.

Santa Ana's iconic water tower makes an important cameo in this short story told by a resilient if nearly beaten hero working in a silk-screening warehouse. A rush order of umbrellas inspires our hangdog narrator's vision of an imagined oasis of cooperative post-scarcity culture in which a gorgeously diverse group find themselves working together, all brave immigrants in an old, new world.

O N WEDNESDAY AT 5:30 PM, the sun still raking the world, I stood outside the shop with José and Rick and wanted to scream *yow* like a coyote.

Every other night, for months, our print jobs had gone to eight or later, depending on the number of color screens, number of shirts or cards or decals, number of guys. Any other night, a thousand story-less Santana nights, it'd be dark out, and I'd be tripping home over the cracked sidewalks, blinded by the headlights of cars and the unicorn-infrequent buses, visually frisked by other pedestrians and wishing myself into our kitchen and my hand into a can of olives.

But not Wednesday. Wednesday, I stood near a renegade sprinkler head, and I huffed the summer smell of hot soaked sidewalk, the smell of three hours of freedom.

Two blocks away, the amber Western sun poked out from behind the water tower, hugging it like a hazy jazz club light clinging to the black form of a chanteuse—Nuestra Madre de Posibilidades—brass section slinging to life as she ascended the stage, laying everyone out in dizzy, imaginative longing, until the moment when the spotlight would ignite her face and burn away all her alternate dimensions.

The power of backlighting is the power of hope. The power of spotlighting is the power of truth.

I was familiar with this water tower, a hoisted white hut. I knew it read *Welcome to Santa Ana* in cursive on the opposite side, the truth side. Every day, Alex, my brother, got to read it on his drive home from his law firm. It marked the place where he crossed from his daytime reality back into our nighttime one. In between me and those scrawled words, I'd long wondered whether there was anything inside that tank. Was the water tower an honest tower? A swimming pool suspended on stilts populated by Santana ghosts in Afterlife swimwear? Or had it been dry for decades?

California was turning into beef jerky, so if that tower really did hold water, it'd be worth more than gold, more than lives someday.

Yixiang, our boss man, who went by "Charlie"—and it made me nervous, calling an Asian guy Charlie in this country, I'd seen documentaries—Charlie had called the shop Monday from the Mongolian Barbecue place and said *prepare yourselves.*

A nutritional supplement company in a green glass tower off Jamboree was going to be hosting a four-day convention next month, and a man in an office had made a decision: corporate logo umbrellas as party gifts for all the attendees. Silk-screening these umbrellas was going to be our job.

They're expecting 350 people. You ready for this?

Pinning the phone against my shoulder, I'd crossed my arms and my eyes at José. Charlie had a way of making jobs sound overwhelming, maybe so we'd feel good when we finished them and then forget, in the middle of our self-congratulating, that we didn't get paid shit.

I'd worked in the shop for two years, and I saw no need to *prepare myself*. Even though we were a small outfit, 350 wasn't a scary number.

And we'd printed onto objects other than paper and shirts before, even if we hadn't done umbrellas specifically. We did seat cushions for a tech company's Angels night. Foam fingers for Valley High's boys' varsity basketball, *Go Falcons*. Even baseball caps for a kid's funeral, a couple months ago, which hurt us in the chest even as it turned out to be a bitch of a job: fabric too thick, too textured, too curved, all the detail of the print bleeding out like the kid himself. They should've gone with embroidery, but the family couldn't afford it.

Usually, if a job was hard, we'd take turns spitting the nastiest shit about the client we could conjure. Our first round of ruined foam fingers had the boys' varsity basketball team sucking every drippy dick in Orange County, Tijuana, the Vatican.

With those hats, though, we couldn't even talk. It was five hours of angry, impotent silence. Rick's brother knew the kid. We went out to a bar together after work, something we had never done before, and as we drank our beers, the silence continued, our table the eye in the happy hour storm.

Screening the Herbalife logo onto an umbrella might hold some challenges, but it wouldn't make us question the fairness of the universe quite like running a squeegee over "Remember Daryl Salinas 1985–2001," over and over. Younger than my baby sister Rosa, and it hurt, hurt in the chest.

Around three on Wednesday, we *prepared ourselves* the way we always prepared. We blocked and burned out and pressure-washed the screens, dragged over the ink buckets and squeegees, and braced down everything in the vise frame we'd built from clamps and two-by-fours.

José and Rick and I gathered around the press, wiping our foreheads. Air thickened in the shop from the morning, when it felt too thin and cold to breathe, to the afternoon, when the room bloated and the corrugated metal siding was hot as a stovetop. Last week Bill, the guy we never saw because he worked on the weekend, came to the shop to pick up a check and showed us a scar on his arm from where he'd accidentally leaned against the siding. *Third-degree burn. Touch it, the hair's all gone.* Since then, as each day wore on, we crowded toward the middle even as we called each other out for being babies.

Santana was already on water rationing for the summer, like it had been last summer, except that this year we were rationing by early May instead of mid-June. Lawns let go long ago.

In the future, if life in California proceeds according to precedent, rationing won't help us. The desert aches to take it all back, you can feel.

When the sun finishes wringing the last moisture out of the land, reducing it to one endless cramped muscle, if that water tower really does hold water, everyone will come looking for it. We'll have to wall off Santana from the dazed would-be conquerors, and defend our water Mad Max-style from the legions of the thirsty. A call will go out in the dusty streets when it is time for the final showdown, *Stick your knives and your pistols in your belts, pansones,* and off to the tower we'll ride to guard the water from the gathered invaders outside the wall. We'll roll up in trash trucks and dusty Cadillacs and circle the base of the tower like a wagon train in the laser of the undead sun, voices of the desperate rising from beyond the fortified bricks like color from hot asphalt.

We printed the first umbrella together. Then we propped it up on a chair and examined it. It had been an awkward effort, angling the spokes out of the way of the press, which chomped down on the umbrella like a bird eating an insect.

Jose stroked his goatee like a villain. Rick squinted. Despite the process, the logo was clean, and single color, so no concerns about overlap. The edges were sharp, and the mustard color contrasted well. It was a good piece, we decided, something nice enough to make the suits feel appreciated, and something they would actually find useful if they were from anywhere but here.

Then, as we scrutinized the wet gloss of the logo and began considering the other 349 umbrellas, José started laughing.

My throat jumped. I started laughing too.

"Did you just—"

"Shiiit."

Rick nodded and walked in a circle, "Uh huh, uh huh, uh, huh."

We couldn't close the umbrellas until the logos dried, or else they would smear. The logos wouldn't be done drying until tomorrow. Closed, 350 umbrellas were like 350 burritos, 30 to a box, twelve white and unassuming boxes leaned calmly, anonymously, against the back wall. Open was a different game.

We cleared as much out of the shop as we could. We hauled all the ink buckets out to the back patio, stacked them up on top of our spray-painted test stencils, and laid the smoker's chair across the top. We went back inside with only what we needed for the job.

We started the pile of opened, printed umbrellas in the back corner, next to the patio door, as far from the front entrance as possible. At first, we were careful about leaning the umbrellas on each other so the damp logos wouldn't touch anything, either the wall or other umbrellas. By fifty, we had given up carefully arranging them.

By one hundred, we were staying at our stations and chucking umbrellas on the pile from the press. It took technique since the umbrellas wanted to catch air, to sail off into the wall or dive prematurely into the ground. We patented a move, an upward stab and fling that had the highest success rate, the greatest accuracy. Our RBIs sky-rocketed. Our short résumés grew in our heads.

Two hours later, we had backed the press up against our exit, and 225 umbrellas, their awkward wings jammed open, surrounded and towered over us, a dense, twitching jungle of silent red animals reaching all the way to the fluorescent tube-lights. We were on the umbrellas' turf now.

We stood in a line outside the front door.

"Nothing else we can do today," laughed José. "Good thing the door opens out, man."

Rick reached inside the shop and retrieved the phone off the wall. Beyond him, a couple umbrellas bristled like a nest of spiders. José lit a cigarette, and we both kept chuckling, high from lofting open umbrellas into corners, then jamming them into cracks, from feeling outnumbered and a little paranoid, surrounded by too many of the same gangly object. He huffed out little puffs of smoke like a train, which made us laugh harder.

"Yeah." Rick was explaining our situation over the phone to Charlie, who was offsite at another one of his six businesses, probably the dry cleaner's. Charlie cleaned our shirts for us for free once a month, kept us looking fresh. He even cleaned and pressed my brother Alex's lawyer suits. Charlie got wound up a lot—with six businesses, what could you expect—but he hooked us up in these small ways. Rick and José and I were all lurching around inside the immigrant's echo chamber, trying to become artists even though we had no idea what being an artist looked like or how we could get paid for it. In the midst of our *tormenta* of insecurities, Charlie treated us well enough to get us to stick around and throw minimal tantrums, even though the money was shit. Not enough to cover much more than my portion of rent and food, hardly anything to kick over to Rosa. Nothing for Mom, who was coughing carcinogens back home in Zacatecas. Al would recall these financial failures to me whenever we got in a fight, which was whenever it was time to send the money order.

So I wasn't lawyer material. But at the shop we got starched Dickies, our own custom business cards, and on Fridays, fat plates of greasy noodles from *Charlie's Mongolian Emporium*.

He was like us, Charlie. He showed up in Santana ten years ago with no papers, a handful of names, and a lingering sense that doom was at his heels.

Rick shouldered the handset and crossed his arms, the phone cord trailing out of sight into the maw of the shop.

"Yup. We done 75 each, and now there's no room for other jobs, no room for us even. You gotta come see the place, man. Eh!" Rick jabbed a finger at José and me. "Charlie says he told you to prepare."

José and I had already lost it. We were hyenas on the gravel.

"*Que demonios* prepare? What could we do?" José choked, eyes watering. "Rent a bigger building? Tell you what, son, tell Charlie if it rains tomorrow, then we'll be fucking *prepared*."

We caved in, leaning on either side of the rusting, broken grill we had parked next to the pressure washer. José lifted the lid and stuffed his cigarette inside with the others.

"What are we even doing here, man?" he yelled.

We were still laughing, but something in his face, a part that couldn't be isolated and studied, looked suddenly sad, and my laugh jumped a hundred feet away from me. I could hear it going, but it no longer felt like mine. José slammed the cover closed.

Charlie had hauled the busted grill over six months ago, a misguided offering from his failing ribs emporium. Charlie loved the word "Emporium," put it in the title of every endeavor he could. He said it made him the Emperor of his businesses. He was building dominion over the material world, one piece of merchandise at a time. We had talked about silk-screening him a sweatshirt for his birthday with a list on the back: *Charlie Cheng, Emperor of: Day Old Donuts. Stain-Free Prom Dresses. Medicinal Herbs.* Now it also would have to say *Emperor of Umbrellas.*

In the Great Drought to Come, when the march on the water tower happens, Charlie will be inside the wall with us. His love for the wall will be prideful and uncomplicated, since his people built the best wall in history, and since he never had to climb over or crawl under one to get here. Top down on his Mercedes, parked in the one spot of shade the water tower offers, bullhorn in his face, he'll be screaming orders in Mandarin and Spanish as José, Rick, and I peg wall-climbers with T-shirt guns. *Get back on your side.*

My friends and family, dressed in the appropriate apocalyptic clothes, will stand in a line beside us:

Uncle Eddy, the first of us to make it stateside, sporting an eye patch, and Mamacita, his ragged parrot, perching lookout on the tower above us.

Baby sister Rosa, in heavy metal jeans she'd already ripped up for looks long before The Drought.

Alex in his dress shirt, sleeves rolled up, wearing a sash of M-16 shells like Mr. America.

And Cheryl, his white girlfriend, still immaculately groomed somehow, crossing her arms and staring at the back of Alex's head, disgusted and aroused.

The voices of the invaders will die off, and we'll stand, nervous, looking sidelong at each other before training our eyes again on the wall. The whoosh sound of the wide sky will build and build. Then we'll hear the sudden slam of some big concerted effort, maybe a truck, against the wall, ramming the adobe bricks we'd made with dust and sealed with spit.

The wall will crack, but it will stand.

We will run to it, checking the braces, and we'll feel those presences on the other side, hear the low growling of the retired Irvine cops and the fluttering of Anaheim's ragged theme park mascot suits, smell the $120 hair products of the Newport Beach bums and the heady turpentine of the Laguna Beach painters, those artists born with money and time. Their frenzied panting will rise up like a cloud of locusts. In that moment, standing between the wall and the remains of California's water, we will be reminded again of the cruelty of human geography. It would be a first for Familia Alvarez, to have the luck to start out on the right side of a wall, free of the desiccating desire for a shimmering oasis and the pursuant compulsive, endless, featureless journey toward that oasis, our irrelevant moral compass dragging in the sand behind us. It would be a first, to have the luck of belonging.

Light pinged off the water tower, and the broken sprinkler continued wasting what we had left. Fucking *umbrellas, paraguas benditas,* closing down the shop and kicking us out into the summer heat, giving me these golden hours before Rosa would need dinner, before Al would come home coke-fried from his nine hundredth deposition, before Mom would call with the obligatory medical updates.

Whatever I did with my time would be my secret—if I told Al, all he'd hear would be how I lost three hours' wages.

All we ever did was prepare.

Behind me, still on the phone with Charlie, Rick said, "You gotta come by the shop, man. It's beautiful."

THE FLATLANDS

Running down around the towns along the shore
When I was sixteen and on my own,
No, I couldn't tell you what the hell those brakes were for.
I was just trying to hear my song.

Jimmy found his own sweet sound and won that free guitar.
We'd all get in the van and play.
Life became the Paradox, the Bear, the Rouge et Noir
And the stretch of road running to L.A.

Pages turning,
Pages we were years from learning,
Straight into the night our hearts were flung.
Better bring your own redemption when you come
To the barricades of heaven where I'm from.

—JACKSON BROWNE
"THE BARRICADES OF HEAVEN," 1996

Jessamyn West

---

from *HIDE AND SEEK*

Jessamyn West was born into a Quaker family in 1902 in Indiana, moved to Yorba Linda at age six, and grew up near her second cousin, Richard Nixon. A graduate of Fullerton Union High School and Whittier College, she worked at various jobs, including as the society editor at the *Yorba Linda Star* and as a teacher in a one-room school in Hemet. The author of eighteen books, West is best known for her historical novel about the Civil War, *The Friendly Persuasion*, which was made into a film starring Gary Cooper and nominated for a 1957 Academy Award for Best Picture.

West's relationship to Orange County features in some of her fiction—in particular the classic young adult short story collection *Cress Delahanty* and the novel *South of the Angels*—but it is especially prominent in her 1973 memoir, *Hide and Seek*. The following selections from *Hide and Seek* recall her youth in rural Orange County in the early twentieth century, when local children swam in the "crystal clear" water of the sycamore-shaded Santa Ana River, a defining ecological feature for a child growing up in the basin between the foothills and the Pacific Ocean.

WE MOVED OUT to Yorba Linda at Christmas time. The rains had been early that year, and there was a good stand of barley on the hillsides that had been cleared and planted. Later, in school in Yorba Linda, we sang a song called "Barley Is King." I thought that it had been composed especially to honor the barley fields of Yorba Linda. And I still think a tall stand of blue-green barley is the lordliest of crops. Beside barley, oats are frilly, wheat blunt, rye overcomplicated, alfalfa lowly. The bearded barley is king.

We moved into the house Papa had built for his family. I don't know where he had learned carpentry, and perhaps he hadn't. We had built as the pioneers did: on the brow of a hill, where the redskins could be seen as they mounted their attack.

Wind, not savages, was the danger in Yorba Linda. Our two-story house was the first obstacle to confront the Santa Ana in its 100-mile sweep in from the Mojave Desert. Papa propped up the house with plants on the west side. On the worst nights he bedded us children down in the cement weir box (no water in it yet), and he and Mama slept on the hay in the cow shed. In time the beds in the uncarpeted upstairs bedroom marked the floors with permanent scars of their frequent east-to-west roll.

Perhaps, without knowing it, Papa's principles of construction were sound. He built as earthquake-proof houses are now built: buildings that can roll with the shocks. The wind might push, but the house could give.

Everyone knew when a Santa Ana was coming. First, the air was unusually clear and still. Then, in the east, just visible at the Pass of San Gorgonio ninety miles away, a smudge the size of a hand would appear. This was the tower of dust and sand the approaching Santa Ana was pushing before it.

The Santa Anas scared me. I waited in the night for the next gust to blow the house over. I also loved them and their force: the traveling beds, the bounding tumbleweeds, the scream and whine of the wind around—and through—our unbattened house. An unplowed land is virgin. A land without wind is dead.

A small wind blowing down through the canyon behind me sends some of the cottonwoods' few remaining gold coins into the band of passing gold. I don't suppose that this little down-blower has a name; but I do know that because it is blowing downward through the canyon from the mountain behind me it is a foehn, a fall wind, the most dangerous wind in the world for flyers. The Santa Ana is a fall wind and is listed among the world's dangerous foehns. I was elated when I found my old childhood bed rocker so honored. I wished I had known when the tumbleweeds blew about us and Papa packed his children into the weir box that we were being endangered by something world-known and scientifically classified.

Half, maybe more, of the delight of experiencing is to know *what* you are experiencing. Would falling in love be as great or as painful if you had no name for your emotions? Or knowledge that others had suffered through the same attack? Without knowledge, you might think your racing pulse and distaste for food the onset of the measles.

Without knowing, I thought the Santa Ana was a little Yorba Linda disturbance, unknown elsewhere. I never expected to see it listed with the "*Yamo orshi*, foehn of the steep valleys of Japan," or with the "*Reshabar*, lusty and black out of the high Caucus."

I don't know why I have always been so excited by the names of the world's winds. I understand why one wants to know the names of what he loves. "A man" is not the same as "Thomas Jefferson" or "John Keats." Naming is a kind of possessing, of caressing and fondling. I supposed this is as true of winds as of human beings. If you love wind, you want the intimacy of touching your tongue to the syllables of its name: monsoon, williwau, chinook, mistral, choclater, sirocco; westerlies, line squalls, black rollers. I feel them as I write their names, I push against their strength; my cheeks burn with them, my hair streams from me!

If you live in California, as I do, and love the wind, you will of necessity have to love some pretty nasty blowers. In Southern California the Santa Ana will sandblast the paint from your car in thirty minutes. It will push a brush or forest fire ahead of it at the rate of a mile a minute. Nevertheless I love the sound and feel of these great destructive blowers. Above San Francisco, the norther, while never the equal of the Santa Ana, howls through eucalyptus windbreaks, unbroken, and with the sound of surf against rocks. It comes around the corners of houses with the heartbroken whine of a ghost shut out.

Thoreau loved what the wind *did*; if it had never blown through the telegraph wires, forming what he called his wind harp, I don't know that he would have mentioned it. He loved the earth as it was; and water did not have to flow or air move for him to appreciate it. But the air moving through the telegraph wires sent him into a real ecstasy: "The telegraph harp again. Always the same unrememberable revelation it is to me...I never hear it without thinking of Greece. How the Greeks harped upon the words immortal, ambrosial! They are what it says. It stings my ear with everlasting truth. It allies Concord to Athens and both to Elysium. It always intoxicates me, makes me sane, reverses my view of things. I am pledged to it. I get down the railroad till I hear that which makes all the world a lie. When the zephyr, or west wind, sweeps this wire, I rise to the height of my being."

I understand Thoreau's feeling for his harp music. I often sat in the barn in Yorba Linda and listened to barn music as the wind squeezed itself, wailing, through the cracks in the barn. But I never thought of this sound as music. I thought the sounds I heard were the voice of the wind.

People who consider themselves "real" music lovers have pitied poor Thoreau, his own chords "trembling divinely" as he listened to the wind blow through telegraph wires. The telegraph harp, they felt, was a sorry substitute for the Boston Symphony. Actually the world is not that either-or. Something blows through telegraph wires and barn cracks that can't be heard in the Pastoral Symphony or *La Mer*. Above all it is something accidental, something that Thoreau's ear (and mine) composed as it went along.

Unless Thoreau heard the wind, and especially as it blew through the telegraph wires, he hadn't much to say about it. He is, of course, a connoisseur of water: its color, its depth, its taste, its function as mirror, its transformation as ice, its use for bathing and fish breeding; but he is with water as he is with air: it doesn't have to move to please him.

Thoreau was a great one to take nature as he found it. Walden was a pond, and except when wind-whipped, it was still and unmoving. It is the nature of a pond to be quiet. Thoreau accepted that quiet. He never asked hawks to sing or whippoorwills to become predators. He didn't kick against the prick.

I would never, if I could choose, live beside a pond or a pool or a lake or a reservoir. Thoreau was never tempted at Walden's edge to shake his fist and say, "Don't just sit there. Do something." Still waters, especially the waters of the great man-made lakes, so-called, which are really reservoirs, make me feel that way. I know the good that reservoirs do, but I don't really care to look at them. They are caged animals; a zoo where the animal is a dead river; a snake of enormous sinuosity of muscle, stripped of its rippling skin, bunched up, pegged down, movable only when man lets gravity take hold of his captive.

The river I write by was once a dangerous animal. I am living in the midst of reminders of the Colorado's strength—mountains moved by it; canyons dug by it. It has been tamed, if not killed. It can no longer move mountains and houses, kill people and animals. Instead, properly chlorinated, it will quench the thirst, fill the swimming pools, and cool the radiators of Los Angeles County's millions. Would I have Angelenos parched, their pools empty, their engines hot? No. But I don't have to admire the look of what that quenching, filling, and cooling has done to the river that flows past my window.

I don't know why the names of the great winds of the world move me so much more than the names of the great rivers. Astrologically this is wrong. My element is water, not air. Perhaps I am a true Californian in this respect. There is so much more wind than water in California that I have decided to live in the element that I possess.

All Californians *should* be river lovers. Without our rivers we would all die. As it is, our rivers are all—because we love them so much—dying. We will not let them run away from us into the sea. We cage them behind our mile-high dams. We build dams the way the Aztecs built pyramids; then we flock to them for weekend devotions, which are almost religious and *are* sacrificial. Each Saturday and Sunday, as on the steps of the pyramids, youths and maidens are sacrificed on the sacred dam waters: beheaded by outboard motors; knocked cuckoo by blows from flying water skis; drowned when stamina proves weaker than ambition. Even the no-longer-young are sacrificial victims: dead from a surfeit of beer and pizza, in six feet of intended drinking water.

Water in California has become a superhighway (the superhighway is our true sacrificial altar). It is a surface upon which a vehicle can be propelled at high speed. It has become in many ways a super-superhighway. The surface of water is not worn by travel and does not have to be repaired, so you pay no highway taxes for the gas you put in your Chris-Craft. Water is cooler than asphalt in summer and not much wetter than asphalt in winter, so as a year-round roadbed it has great advantages, to say nothing of the novelty: going fast on land is an old story to everyone in California; going fast on water is a new sensation, because the recently built damns now make it possible. The superhighways that lead us to the lakes are clogged on weekends as people with boats hasten to the super-superhighways to experience the sensation of (and perhaps become one of the sacrificial volunteers to) speed on water.

There are no laws against the explosive noises of water vehicles. Water encourages and justifies a minimum of clothing. And water travel, provided you can swim and are not decapitated or mangled by flying solid objects, does have another distinct advantage over asphalt: it opens up in case your craft turns over.

Yesterday afternoon I saw a boat on the river that made me stare: motorless, silent; a rowboat, with two middle-aged men, fully clothed, sitting in it and using oars. They were not fishing. They were just ahead of the mud hens. Perhaps they were helping the hens in their job of rolling up the sheen of the westering sun? They appeared to be watching the sunset. They were out of the past. They were stranger on the river than a horse and buggy on the road.

The trailer is perched two feet from the edge of the bank of the Colorado. The river flows six feet below. The curtains are not drawn, and my lights are reflected like goldfish on the crests of the ripples.

When I was young I knew two rivers, and I'm not sure which was more real to me: the one I had never seen or the one near at hand in which I sometimes swam.

The river I had never seen was the Wabash. Mama played and sang of it: "Through the sycamores the candlelight is gleaming on the banks of the Wabash far away." Grandpa and Grandma's white house was far from the banks of the Wabash, but when Mama sang, I saw *it*, beneath the sycamores, lighted by coal oil, not candles.

Sometimes it was summer, and lightning bugs flitted around the chinaberry tree and I could smell Grandma's cinnamon roses and door-yard lilacs and flags. Sometimes it was winter, and snowflakes, curled like goose down, floated about the house. Winter or summer, I imagined myself standing outside the house, but not excluded or lonesome. Inside I could see the fire on the sitting-room hearth, and I could smell the wood smoke. And when I was tired of looking inside, I looked down at the unknown river, the river Mama sang about, the "Wabash far away." It was a big river, thick and slow, but it never stopped moving. On its banks lived those we had loved and left behind us: the poor benighted Hoosiers.

The river I knew was the Santa Ana. I thought about it less often when I was a child than I did the Wabash. There is no need to think about what you possess. There never was a river more suited to children than the Santa Ana. Winter was another story. Then, at the time of heavy winter rains, the Santa Ana (this was before it had been molested by man) could rise up and take out bridges, drown cows, and flood the towns of Anaheim, Placentia, and Yorba.

In summer you had to lie down in the river and roll over if you wanted to get wet all over. The water was crystal clear, and it flowed over sand that was sometimes gold, sometimes silver. Beer cans, tires, and plastic containers had not yet been invented. Summer, the sand, the water, children in old overalls and castoff dresses. The Santa Ana had one thing in common with the Wabash: sycamore trees grew on its bank. The river's waters were dappled by the shade of the big sycamore leaves; the mottled tree trunks appeared to reflect the dappled waters.

The minute Papa and Mama arrived in California they began traveling. They had never read Thoreau. They didn't know he had written: "What need to travel? There are no sierras equal to the clouds in the sunset sky. Are these not substantial enough?" No, said Papa and Mama, they are not substantial enough. We want the Sierras.

They didn't get the Sierras at once. They traveled in the beginning by nonmechanized horsepower: Diamond and Chinopsee hitched to surrey or spring wagon. We went to the Santa Ana in the spring wagon.

All Californians travel toward water: toward the sea; once toward the rivers; now toward the rivers impounded and called lakes; toward snow, which is frozen water. And even when Californians head toward the desert, they do so more to marvel at the presence of swimming pools and fountains than to play in the sand.

Papa and Mama were no exception. They went to the "Santa Ana," which was the river. They went to Newport Beach, which was the sea. They set out with four children, traveling pies, shoeboxes of beef sandwiches, and foot-and-a-half fig newtons. Sometimes, not often, they traveled on Sunday. Occasionally they stayed overnight. They always took a trip on the Fourth of July, on Memorial Day, on Labor Day; they made excursions during spring vacation; on Christmas they drove to Big Bear or Baldy or Mount Lowe to see the snow.

The three big children rode on the backless, springless seat of the spring wagon. If we got tired we could lie down on the wagon floor and take a nap. Papa, Mama, and the new baby, Merle, who had been given a fancy name like all of us, rode on the front seat, which had a back and springs. Merle was to be Mama's last chance to produce what she had always wanted: an Indian-nosed, black-haired, bronze-faced baby like the man she had married. With Merle she missed totally: he had red hair, blue eyes, a big pug nose, and fair, freckled skin. He was never called anything but Rusty.

When we got to the water we swam. In the shallow, golden Santa Ana we were handled like princelings of a rich realm by the warm, gentle water. Sometimes a current would lift my dress to the waist, and, bloomerless (bloomers held too much water to wear swimming), I saw with pleasure my white minnow-shaped body, dappled with the shadows of sycamore leaves.

We were not princelings on the beach. There we were buffeted and pounded and scared. I, at least, was scared. We slept on the beach, and I could feel the earth tremble as the great waves struck the shore.

Ann Stanford

THE RIDERS and DONE WITH

Ann Stanford was born in 1916 in La Habra and graduated from Fullerton High School. She earned a BA at Stanford University and two MAs and a PhD at UCLA. She taught at CSU Northridge for twenty-five years, influencing a generation of poets and writers. In her long career, she published eight poetry collections, two plays, a biography of the poet Anne Bradstreet, and a translation of the *Bhagavad Gita*, in addition to editing a landmark anthology, *The Women Poets in English*. She died in 1987, and, starting in 1988, USC has awarded a poetry prize in her name.

"The Riders" was first published in *Variegation: A Free Verse Quarterly* in 1952 and appears in Stanford's first book, *The Weathercock* (1966). Her childhood friend Eunice Harris (née Launer), to whom the poem is dedicated, assured us that it references their early childhood in La Habra in the 1920s, when Stanford's home on Hiatt Street was "surrounded by mustard fields." Harris told us that in summer Stanford's parents would rent a cottage near the Balboa Pavilion, and that that is the beach mentioned in the poem. Harris added that when Stanford composed the poem, they each had three children who played in the "long grasses" in La Habra. The poem "Done With" appears in Stanford's second collection, *The Descent*, published in 1970.

THE RIDERS

For Eunice

We made castles of grass, green halls, enormous stem-lined rooms
And sailed in trees.
Close to the backyard fence
We dug a cave.

We never finished it,
But there was plenty of time for moving that last foot or two of earth.
It was an eternity till Christmas.

Do you remember the yellow fields
We tussled through, small mustard petals clinging?
And the hikes on Saturday up to the grove of oaks?
Plenty of time then, and dark came down before we were home.
They were out calling and searching.

There was a winter year and a summer year.
The last was for beaches.
Salt wind over the gaudy pier,
And things moved faster.
You on the yellow horse, I on the dun.
One way the sea, the battleship,
The pier, the fishers leaning by the rail,
The ferris wheel,
And turning still
The shoddy mermaid painted on the wall.
Up and down we laughed and caught the rings.
And one was gold for summer.

Then summer was gone, and the horse bunched warm ripples
Trotting through orchards down to the practice ring.
His eyes were like suns, when he changed his gait
Faster and faster till the trees blurred and the sky
And there were only posts and the wind and the packed earth
And the warm beast gathering and springing.
How to get off, how to escape!
At last I fell, but it was no better.

The earth turned under my back
Swift, swift, we turned out of day to night to day again,
Light and shadow from a picket fence.

And the planet whirled on the sun, a swift carousel.

Our heads grow grey, our children laugh in the long grasses.

DONE WITH

My house is torn down—
Plaster sifting, the pillars broken,
Beams jagged, the wall crushed by the bulldozer.
The whole roof has fallen
On the hall and the kitchen
The bedrooms, the parlor.

They are trampling the garden—
My mother's lilac, my father's grapevine,
The freesias, the jonquils, the grasses.
Hot asphalt goes down
Over the torn stems, and hardens.

What will they do in springtime
Those bulbs and stems groping upward
That drown in earth under the paving,
Thick with sap, pale in the dark
As they try the unrolling of green.

May they double themselves
Pushing together up to the sunlight,
May they break through the seal stretched above them
Open and flower and cry we are living.

Gustavo Arellano

from *ORANGE COUNTY*

Gustavo Arellano was born in Anaheim in 1979 to two Mexican immigrants, one of whom, as he often notes himself, entered the United States illegally. A graduate of Anaheim High School, he studied at Orange Coast College, later transferred to Chapman University, and eventually earned a master's degree in Latin American studies from UCLA. At the *OC Weekly* he created the award-winning syndicated column "¡Ask a Mexican!" and is today the magazine's editor. In restaurant reviews, feature essays, cover stories, radio interviews, and more he has become a go-to national commentator on Orange County. The author of *Taco USA: How Mexican Food Conquered America* and a consultant for the Fox animated sitcom *Bordertown*, Arellano teaches at CSU Fullerton and Chapman University.

In the following excerpt from his 2008 memoir *Orange County: A Personal History*, Arellano tells the story of Orange County's transition from a place of romantic nineteenth-century legend to the land of "citrus dreams" and then finally to an ocean of tract housing. He explores the forgotten history of the farm laborers' Citrus War of 1936 and celebrates its principal chronicler, California historian Carey McWilliams. From Anaheim to Orange, San Juan Capistrano to Irvine, Arellano surveys the construction of new dreams and the erasure of the old.

IN THE EARLY 1960s, the Anaheim City School District released a fifty-seven-page booklet titled *Living in Orange County*. School officials published it in response to the hundreds of children who were entering Anaheim elementary schools in those years, part of an American inmigration to Orange County that was turning the area from farmland and small towns to the American Dream.

Living in Orange County's protagonists were Diane and Don, siblings from Fresno who had never been to Southern California. When Diane asked her mom if Anaheim was a big city, the mother replied she remembered Orange County from a trip long ago, when it was tiny. Now was different, however: "In fact, I think Orange County is the fastest-growing area in the country."

A brief history of the county ensued, written for children but equally relevant to their newbie parents. Diane and Don, meanwhile, zipped from one landmark to another, concluding their tour in Newport Beach. "I think Orange County is just about the best place in the whole world to live!" Don proclaimed as the book ended and the surname-less family drove home to their new Orange County lives.

The most inappropriate passage in the book, however, occurs when Diane asks her mother if Orange County continued to harvest oranges. "There are still many orange groves," replies her mother. "However, houses now cover much of the land that used to have orange trees. There are many motels and places to eat. More and more apartment houses are being built. There are many big shopping centers."

To placate any new Orange County residents who might want to see those orchards, *Living in Orange County* contained a full-page picture titled "Typical Orange Grove in Orange County." Rows and rows of orange trees spread across the frame in the photo, all the way to foothills. If you squint, you can make out the ghostly images of farmhands out in the groves, fixing an aquatic ditch.

The inclusion of such an agrarian reminder jars with the rest of the small book, which devotes itself to modern, grown-up Orange County. But the message was clear: no matter what happened to Orange County, no matter how much development might sprout in the region, those large, fragrant trees that contributed so much to the county's status had a guaranteed, cherished place.

Forty years later, that promise is almost gone.

Consider the quarter acre or so of orange trees on the corner of Santa Ana and Helena streets in Anaheim. Every winter, their fruit hangs from the branches, bright and plump, awaiting pickers. But the grove is almost always quiet, save for pedestrians who trail their hands along the chain-link fence that keeps the trees free from trespassers. And so, the fruit falls to the ground and rots.

Nearby, in a vacant lot that was an orange grove not even five years ago, new town homes await their sale. More are on the way. Cars buzz by, oblivious to the orange grove, the fenced-off living history. Before the luxury houses came, you could walk into this orange grove, no questions asked, and pick a ripe, golden Valencia straight from a branch. Not anymore. Razor wire now tops the chain-link fence, and a gate stops people from entering at will. If you ask the men who repair cars in the factory next door if they can let you in, they run you off with a growl. Construction tools lie nearby. This was once a mere piece of a massive orange grove that covered hundreds of acres. But it won't be long before this, one of the last orange groves in Orange County, too, falls victim to Progress.

Down the street is the Sunkist Packing House, the same place where my grandfather packed oranges in the 1920s. Touted as state-of-the-art when first opened, the building is now a historical landmark, one of the last citrus packinghouses in Southern California that didn't meet the hard swing of a demolition ball. It also has no use. The last oranges were packed here in the 1950s; today, it's a furniture warehouse. The windows are broken or boarded up. The only functioning area is in the back, where the packinghouse's original icehouse served the surrounding neighborhood's beer-cooling needs decades after the last orange crates were loaded. The icehouse shut down last year.

Kitty-corner from the packinghouse stand faux New York City–style brownstones. Up the street are lofts and a new Cuban coffeehouse—never mind that few Cubans live in Anaheim. Other properties—bars, houses, used-car lots—are condemned but await gentrification.

Orange groves still exist in Orange County—the Kimberly-Clark campus in Fullerton has one fenced off, and orange trees sway just off the 5 Freeway in Irvine and near the Orange-Riverside county line. Drive around long enough anywhere in Orange County, and you'll see the irregular, waxy leaves of the tree peek out of backyards. But they're illusions: fewer than one hundred acres total from a high of more than sixty-five thousand acres in 1948.

The most prominent reminders of Orange County's past citrus dreams mock you on the 22 Freeway. A couple of years ago, county supervisors authorized billions of dollars for an expansion and beautification project. The expansion succeeded, and cars can now zoom on the 22 most hours. The beautification angle consisted of connecting soundwalls with concrete pillars every hundred yards or so, etched with bas-relief oranges, fleeting reminders of the fruit that satiated a nation and made America first notice Orange County. Those are *our* oranges—who cares if they're fake. The past must always be present, or at least its illusion, lest the dream finally wither.

When I was a student at Chapman University in Orange during the early 2000s, hanging on the walls of Beckman Hall—a four-story glass structure that housed the school's business program—were dozens of orange-crate labels. They were collector's items and truly gorgeous, each representing a particular packinghouse, all portraying the same theme of health and heaven on the Pacific coast. The Mission Brand featured a group of befuddled monks examining oranges, with a Spanish-style home in front of acres of orange groves and Old Saddleback—the ridge made by Santiago and Modjeska peaks—in the background. Others used pretty women, genies, Indians, to sell their fruit. The labels function as artifact, as history lesson, as economic ambition. Propaganda functioning as projected dreams. Orange County as Nirvana.

To understand Orange County, you must accept the Cult of the Orange Crate. From its settlement by the Spaniards until today, residents have emphasized that they're creating a spectacular civilization, a County on the Hill: one that attracts but also inspires others to copy. The PR strategy has succeeded for over a century, even if its projected image never fit neatly into reality. Doesn't matter; if we say we're wonderful, you'd better believe it.

The mythmaking began as soon as Spanish conquistadors set the foundation for Mission San Juan Capistrano. Its caretakers deem it "the Jewel" of California's mission system and claim that half a million tourists tour the mission's grounds each year to marvel at its rose gardens, its restored golden retablo, and the ruins of Great Stone Church, the final resting place for about forty Indian converts who were unlucky enough to be praying when a giant earthquake leveled it in the 1800s. But the mission wasn't always so revered—for a while, it served as the home of Juan Forster, an English immigrant who purchased the mission along with most of present South County from the Mexican government for $710 in 1844. Forster returned the mission to the Catholic Church in 1864, and the Church began restoring the buildings, mainly because the mission's chapel was the last existing structure where Father Junípero Serra had officiated over Mass.

Mission San Juan Capistrano's long-lost luster and relative isolation tickled the mind of Johnston McCulley, who published *The Curse of Capistrano* in 1919. This novella debuted Zorro, the mythical hero who sparked a celebration of a nonexistent California past where Spanish dons entertained guests for nights, and Manifest Destiny was applied only to the Indians. There is little mention of the actual mission in *The Curse of Capistrano*—actually, just one: the villain Pedro Gonzalez remarks he broke a sword "while fencing at San Juan Capistrano," which he occasionally guards. McCulley never fully explains why Zorro is called the Curse of Capistrano, just that the town is "where he began this wild life of his, and for that reason the Curse of Capistrano he is called."

Douglas Fairbanks filmed a version of the short story in 1920, changed the name to *The Mark of Zorro*, and the exciting Capistrano that the movie sparked became an American obsession. "The Zorro myth presented a Southern California that never existed," wrote Kevin Starr in *Material Dreams: Southern California through the 1920s*, "a material dream of chivalry, romance, swordplay, and roses rising up against a creamy white Andalusian wall."

For Fairbanks to pick this tale to film wasn't too surprising. During the silent era, filmmakers flocked to Orange County to use its diverse topography for shooting. No film save for *The Mark of Zorro* actually set its story in Orange County, but the big names filmed here—D. W. Griffith was supposedly the first, and following him were Mack Sennett, Harold Lloyd, Buster Keaton, and Santa Ana native Roscoe "Fatty" Arbuckle. Parts of Cecil B. DeMille's original *The Ten Commandments* were filmed in Seal Beach, while *All Quiet on the Western Front*'s horrific trench warfare was actually played out on the sandy slopes of Corona del Mar. Even Fairbanks's wife, Mary Pickford, married her first husband in the mission chapel, an occasion commemorated with a mission-owned painting.

The mission staff were smart—its newfound fame via Zorro grabbed people's attention, but more was needed to keep it. They found a lasting attraction in birds.

For centuries, swallows returned from their winter nesting grounds in Argentina to the Capistrano area every year around March 19. The small birds nested all around the area, not just the mission, but the annual rite intrigued the locals. In 1930, the mission published *Capistrano Nights: Tales of a California Mission Town*. One of the stories included was "The Mission Swallows and How They Arrive Every Year for the Feast of Saint Joseph." According to the tale, a padre was walking through Capistrano near the mission when he saw a shopkeeper destroying a nest of swallows. After realizing that the shopkeeper wanted to kill them, the father announced to the birds, "Come on, swallows…I'll give you shelter. Come to the mission, there's room enough there for all!"

The holy man wasn't named, nor did authors Charles Francis Saunders and Father St. John O'Sullivan provide a date for the anecdote, but the idea that small birds returned every year on the same day to the mission because of a priest's goodwill struck a chord with Depression-weary America. "I am safe in saying that Capistrano's charm needs no such crutch to support it." St. John O'Sullivan (not a saint) wrote about the swallows, "Every month the moon blesses the ancient pile with a mystical beauty that is sufficient of itself."

Nevertheless, the mission needed money. On March 19, 1939, the mission welcomed the media to record the return of the swallows. "Sure enough," wrote *Time* a week later, "sharp at 5:56 a.m., 40 minutes after sunrise, a lowering cloud appeared on the horizon, grew bigger and bigger until it all but blotted out the Mission sunlight, making the air loud with the beat of thousands of narrow wings. Suddenly, while the rest flew on to the canyons beyond, a great segment of the swallow cloud broke off, swooped down on the Mission." Tourists have flocked from across the world ever since.

It's also part of mission lore that this same broadcast inspired Leon René to pen "When the Swallows Come Back to Capistrano." As with the actual incident the song uses as a metaphor for unrequited love, the origin of its lyrics is a bit of a lie. The popular version of the story goes that René heard a broadcaster say the swallows were returning to Capistrano that morning and penned the song in admiration of the critters. But René disclosed to a Louisiana genealogical publication a couple of years ago that he got the idea for the song after his wife didn't cook breakfast fast enough. "Maybe when the swallows come back to Capistrano," he told his wife, "I'll get my breakfast." Liking the line, he wrote a couple of stanzas for it; summarily impressed, the wife made breakfast. With his appetite satiated, Rene finished the song's music and lyrics. "When the Swallows Come Back to Capistrano" became a World War II–era smash—Guy Lombardo, the Ink Spots, and Glenn Miller recorded it, further promoting a tranquil, appealing Orange County to an America in need of peace.

While Capistrano tied Orange County to an idealized past, its booming agricultural industry promoted a profitable, appetizing present.

The region's soil had always provided fragile bounties. The families who originally owned Orange County—the Yorbas, Ontiveroses, Avilas, Rioses, and others—made their fortune by herding hundreds of thousands of cattle, fattening them on the nutritious grass of the county and the replenishing waters of the Santa Ana River. This industry attracted Richard Henry Dana and other Americans to Southern California in the decades before the Mexican-American War. But lethal combinations of floods and droughts largely destroyed the ranchos by the 1850s, and litigating American businessmen eager for the Californios' holdings drove many toward bankruptcy. The vintners who started Anaheim saw bumper grape and wine harvests during the 1860s, but the colony teetered on bankruptcy in the 1880s when blight destroyed nearly all the vines within a year. Over the coming decades, Orange County boasted walnut groves, sugar beet crops, lima bean fields, and sheep and cattle herds that ranked among the largest in America, only to see each collapse within years. It was to citrus, specifically the sweet, sturdy Valencia orange, that most of the county's farmers quickly tied their fortunes.

Charles C. Chapman, an orange grower and descendant of Johnny Appleseed, wrote a history of the young industry in 1911. One passage in particular embodies the determinism of that era's county leaders:

> Indeed, the Divine hand has been lavish in bestowing upon all Southern California, and upon Orange County in particular, rare natural advantages, perhaps greater than those enjoyed by any other section over which the flag floats. The magnificent mountain ranges not only form picturesque scenery and giant bulwarks to guard the fertile valleys, but are our great natural reservoirs. Our coast is washed by the boundless Pacific. Our climate is faultless. In fact, it is not too much to say that as to fertility of soil, the charming climate and the scenery with its grandeur and beauty, it is not surpassed the world around.

Multiple stories purport to explain how entrepreneurs introduced oranges to Orange County, but the one endorsed by the County of Orange Archives credits Dr. William N. Hardin of Anaheim with planting the first orange tree in 1870. Hardin, the story goes, had two barrels filled with rotten Tahiti oranges from which he saved the seeds and grew trees. Sounds like yet another unverifiable fable, no? Indisputable, however, is that orange trees took well to the county. "By the blessing of nature, Orange County had the lion's share of the summer crop [of oranges] when the consumer was thirstiest," wrote UC Irvine professor Gilbert G. González in *Labor and Community: Mexican Citrus Worker*

Villages in a Southern California County, 1900–1950, his 1994 history of Orange County citrus pickers.

The rise of refrigerated railroad cars in the 1880s allowed citrus farmers to ship their edible gold across the country, and California growers hawked their wares and homeland at country fairs and expos. "On crates and at garden shows, oranges were presented as pure products of nature that would provide instant contact with California's therapeutic environment," wrote Douglas Cazaux Sackman in his *Orange Empire: California and the Fruits of Eden.* But more than just provide a dreamscape, the oranges also filled national stomachs and county coffers, accounting for two-thirds of the county's agricultural profits during the 1930s and one-sixth of the country's Valencia orange crop.

Orange County groves became renowned, thanks not just to the fruits but the ornate labels on every packing box. What the labels, farmers, and civic leaders never highlighted was the means of production: Mexicans. A mix of whites, Filipinos, Chinese, Indians, and Mexicans had picked the initial harvests in the late 1800s, but by the 1920s orange growers were arranging to bring in as much Mexican labor as possible. Citrus camps sprouted across the orange groves, and the growers created Americanization programs for their wards. Men picked the crop; women sorted them at packinghouses. Even children joined in, grabbing any low-lying fruit or those that the older men dropped. The growers nicknamed them *ratas*—rats.

This arrangement was generally fine until June 1936, when about twenty-five hundred *naranjeros* representing more than half of Orange County's citrus-picking force dropped their clippers, bags, and ladders to demand higher wages, better working conditions, and the right to unionize. Their demands didn't sit well with the orange growers or Sheriff Logan Jackson, himself the owner of a grove. Jackson and his fellow growers colluded with the district attorney's office, the Board of Supervisors (which had the previous year outlawed picketing in Orange County), and local police agencies to crush the strike. Freshly deputized private guards arrested Mexicans en masse and raided striker meetings with tear gas and ax handles. The growers asked the American government to deport the Mexican consul who sided with the strikers and asked immigration authorities to deport the same men the growers gladly overworked just weeks earlier. After a month of virtual civil war, the strike ended—the *naranjeros* earned a small raise but not the right to unionize.

The 1936 Citrus War is ignored in most histories of American labor, largely because it's almost nonexistent in the annals of Orange County, both during the actual strike—when local newspapers ridiculed strikers and interviewed only angry police officers and growers—and in its history books. Even the most diligent researcher will be hard-pressed to find *any* mention of it in Orange County scholarly anthologies. A 1975 *Los Angeles Times* retrospective noted the paucity of information about the strike, calling it "one of the least-chronicled incidents in the history of the citrus belt." "It still is not mentioned in polite histories," an unnamed professor told the *Times*. "It was not a very pretty thing, but it tells something about where this county has been."

It's telling that the strike's best chronicler was Carey McWilliams, the great progressive journalist and longtime editor of the *Nation*. In 1939, he published *Factories in the Field*, which, alongside John Steinbeck's *Grapes of Wrath* and Dorothea Lange's Okie portraits, toppled California's carefully cultivated reputation. One of the book's sections, titled "Gunkist Oranges," was adapted from an article of the same name McWilliams wrote for *Pacific Weekly* at the height of the Citrus War. The Orange County strike, McWilliams wrote in the article, was "one of the toughest exhibitions of 'vigilantism' that California has witnessed in many a day....Under the direction of Sheriff Logan Jackson, who should long be remembered for his brutality in this strike, over 400 special guards, armed to the hilt, are conducting a terroristic campaign of unparalleled ugliness."

McWilliams added in *Factories in the Field,* "No one who has visited a rural county in California under these circumstances will deny the reality of the terror that exists. It is no exaggeration to describe this state of affairs as fascism in practice."

Even years later, McWilliams couldn't shake the strike. In his 1946 *Southern California: An Island in the Land*, he remembered being "astonish[ed] in discovering how quickly social power could crystallize into an expression of arrogant brutality in these lovely, seemingly placid, outwardly Christian communities.

"In the courtrooms of the county I met former classmates of mine in college, famous athletes of the University of Southern California, armed with revolvers and clubs, ordering Mexicans around as though they were prisoners in a Nazi concentration camp."

The Citrus War had a profound effect on McWilliams, according to his biographer, Peter Richardson. He points to a passage from his book *American Prophet: The Life & Work of Carey McWilliams*, a 1940 interview in which McWilliams said, "I hadn't believed stories of such wholesale violation of civil rights until I went down to Orange County to defend a number of farm workers held in jail for 'conspiracy.' When I announced my purpose, the judge said, 'It's no use; I'll find them guilty anyway.'"

"McWilliams saw a contrast between the fruit-crate-label version of California and ugly labor practices," Richardson told me for a 2006 story I did on the 1936 Citrus War. "It fed his notion that there was this bright, pleasant surface to California life, but it had an uglier underside. The Orange County citrus strike struck a chord for him because it was so obviously unjust."

After suppressing the strike, the growers went back to reaping millions. But the oranges didn't last. In the 1940s, a virus infected the county's groves, killing trees by the thousands within weeks. Farmers named it Quick Decline, but the Mexican pickers called it *la tristeza*—the sadness. As more people began moving into Orange County, farmers found that their groves turned a better profit as lots to be sold and built on. Once beloved and all-powerful, King Citrus died a quiet, fragrant death.

Tract housing soon spread across these orchards and other farms in Central and North County, and cities enshrined their agricultural past with fairs and festivals—La Habra has a Corn Festival, Garden Grove celebrates the Strawberry Parade, and Tiller Days are what they hold in Tustin. But it was time to show the country a new Tree of Life.

Tract housing wasn't an Orange County invention—if anything, it copied what was happening in suburbs across the United States from Levittown to Lakewood. The idea of master-planned communities, though, reached it apotheosis both for old and young in Orange County.

Planned communities are actually old hat in Orange County. In the 1920s, while traveling from San Diego to Los Angeles, Ole Hanson passed through Orange County and was immediately enamored with the land between the Orange–San Diego county line to San Juan Capistrano—hilly, seamlessly sweeping into the Pacific or toward undeveloped wilderness. Hanson was a celebrity of sorts, having crushed a citywide strike in 1919 as mayor of Seattle and unsuccessfully sought the Republican presidential nomination in 1920.

This son of Norwegian immigrants bought the property and announced he was going to create a new community: San Clemente, named for the island within eyesight of the Orange County coast. In 1928, it incorporated as a city and pronounced itself a Spanish Village by the Sea. Drawing on the cult of Zorro and the mission already associated with the county, Hanson structured the ordinances so that all houses and businesses were built in a Spanish-revival style—whitewashed, red-tiled roofs, with flowery street names such as Avenida del Mar, Avenida Califia, and El Camino Real. The lots sold out within a year, and San Clemente opened up Orange County beachfront to the possibility of more than just sand and waves.

Twenty-eight years later, Ross W. Cortese envisioned a different kind of reverence for old times. In 1956, the developer built Rossmoor, an unincorporated community between Los Alamitos and Seal Beach that was one of the country's first walled-off neighborhoods. Then, after a conversation with Los Angeles's Cardinal Francis Mcintyre about the housing needs of the elderly, Cortese decided to create a city specifically for seniors. He opened Leisure World Seal Beach in 1962, America's first planned community for geezers. Critics accused Cortese of building a "geriatric ghetto," but the demand was there—he sold the community's six thousand houses within a couple of years.

Cortese wasn't finished. The same year he opened Leisure World Seal Beach, Cortese bought about thirty-five hundred acres from the Moulton Ranch, pastureland that encompassed most of what today is Laguna Hills and Laguna Woods. Here, he built another Leisure World twice the size of the original. He went on to build five more across the country before passing away in 1991. By then, senior housing communities were an accepted part of American life. "The idea was so beautiful that we put it to work," Cortese told a reporter a few years before his death. "It just took off like a bomb."

Cortese chose Orange County for the experiment because he viewed it as "the new development frontier." Orange County landowners in the undeveloped south were also realizing the potential of their properties. In 1959, the University of California asked the Irvine Ranch for land to open a new university. The ranch occupied almost one-fifth of Orange County, from the Cleveland National Forest all the way to the Pacific, a swath so huge its owners set up a water system company historians claimed was "the largest private water system ever built in the United States and, possibly, ever built in the world."

By the time UC regents made their proposal to the Irvine Ranch, it was no longer in sole possession of the Irvine family. The company's board of directors refused to part with any land, much to the anger of Joan Irvine Smith, granddaughter of the ranch's founder, James Irvine. She publicly revealed the no vote to the public, hoping to embarrass the Irvine Company into charity. In the face of public resentment, the company hired UC's architect, William Pereira, to design a model community around a planned university. He envisioned self-sufficient villages, but the housing market demanded Pereira build more than what he wanted. As it expanded, the small town incorporated as Irvine in 1971.

The same boom was happening even farther south, in Rancho Mission Viejo and Rancho Trabuco, the hilly lands in South County that weren't San Juan Capistrano or San Clemente. The family in control, the O'Neills, decided to sell ten thousand acres in the late 1950s to a group called the Mission Viejo Company, a badly mangled translation of the ranch's original name, Mision Vieja (Old Mission). One of the company's principals was Donald Bren.

If you want to blame same-look suburbanization for the downfall of America, if you hate the Orange County method of micromanaging communities and cities down to every blade of grass and molting salamander, blame Bren, whom the *Los Angeles Times* named the most powerful person in Southern California a couple of years ago, saying, "Simply put, Orange County looks like Orange County—much of it uniformly manicured and catering to the high life and high tech—because of the influence of Bren." Imagine Gatsby combined with John Muir, Howard Hughes, and Rockefeller, and you still can't match the mysterious pomposity of the man.

Bren was the stepson of Claire Trevor, the Academy Award–winning actress who first became famous for her role as a prostitute opposite John Wayne in *Stagecoach*. After a stint in the marines, Bren returned to Southern California and began building houses in Orange County. After seeing Mission Viejo turn into a community within a couple of years, Bren sold his interest in the Mission Viejo Company and developed on his own for a while. In 1977, he and other investors bought a one-third share in the Irvine Company; a couple of years after that, Bren bought out all shares.

Under his watch, the Irvine Ranch turned, in just forty years, from a place to raise cattle into an ever-spreading blob of meticulously managed communities. Professors called Bren's Orange County one of America's "key laboratories of contemporary urbanism, a giant theme park," and *BusinessWeek* described Bren as "the last of the California land barons." One former employee described it thusly: "Other developers build homes. The Irvine Company builds cities." Despite such an overarching presence in shaping modern Orange County, Bren is aloof, a reclusive man who former secretary of the interior Bruce Babbitt described as "presid[ing] over his holdings like a Spanish grandee, attending to every detail, down to the placement of individual palm trees along the medians and open spaces." Don't bother trying to learn more: Irvine

Company drones must sign nondisclosure statements, and Bren only agrees to interviews when guaranteed positive coverage.

Bren's success with Irvine kick-started suburbanization south of Irvine. By the 1980s, a new term entered the Orange County lexicon: *South County,* code for the newness south of the 55 Freeway where wealthier people relocated to escape their parents' decaying North and Central County neighborhoods. The county experienced a new wave of city incorporations—from 1988 until 2001, eight cities joined Orange County, almost all of them indistinguishable from one another.

The developers who transformed the county replaced the Californios of old to become modern dons. Newspapers, lifestyle magazines, and society pages hail these men as visionaries, as the area's superstars. It's not surprising that perhaps the best historian of the development of Orange County is First American Title Insurance, which has shot pictures of Orange County for almost a century.

Tens of thousands of people migrated from across the United States to the creations of Bren and others, just slightly below the hundreds of thousands who moved to Orange County during the post–WWII housing boom. The sameness of these fresh burbs—many governed by strict homeowner associations that micromanaged everything a resident could do to their abode, from the color of the paint on the door to the type of plants on the front lawn—earned widespread derision from the rest of the county. "While the wives of Orange County may not be the home-oriented drudges that Ira Levin described in his 1972 novel, the new towns could serve as model communities for the distaff side of Stepford," the *New York Times* harrumphed in 1983. No one in Orange County minded—instead, they hailed their newfound image as perfect towns governed by benevolent builders.

These new communities have spurred envy in older Orange County cities, which have strived to redevelop themselves in South County style since the rise of Irvine. Anaheim is embarking on an ambitious plan to incorporate high-rise towers for live/work purposes around Angel Stadium and the Honda Center (where the Anaheim Ducks play hockey).

Santa Ana is embarking on similar measures—ironic, since every Orange County city is desperately trying to reinvent itself before becoming another Santa Ana, America's worst-case Mexican scenario.

The county seat had always fancied itself the center of Orange County and still does—last year, city officials spent more than $1 million to refurbish a water tower next to the 5 Freeway and paint it with a new slogan: DOWNTOWN ORANGE COUNTY. But in reality, per a 2004 study by the State University of New York's Nelson A. Rockefeller Institute of Government, the city is the toughest place to live in the United States. Santa Ana boasts other ignominious distinctions. One of the most Spanish-speaking in the United States. Youngest. Most immigrant-heavy. Most Latino. Fattest. Densest. For these reasons, Santa Ana ("Santana," as pronounced by the city's Latino supermajority) is a dirty place in Orange County, the brown blight no one wants to discuss.

Santa Ana officials are trying their hardest to get over this Little Mexico reputation, investing millions of dollars into lofts, museums, and artists' villages in an effort to "diversify" (read *de-Mexicanize*) the city and make it "safe" for all the South County residents. But the efforts are largely for naught. Even now, with an all-Latino city council—the largest such city in the United States—the city tries to pretend it's a Bren fiefdom, part of the Gunkist memories, not content with its reality as the Lower East Side of Orange County.

Santa Ana is lesson, warning, and code word in Orange County for cities that don't pay close attention to the folks moving in. Poverty? Can't exist in Orange County.

But one little wrinkle won't stop other people from aspiring to an OC paradise. In China, developers opened their very own Orange County in 2003, filled with town homes modeled on neighborhoods in California. "As in the case of its namesake," the *New York Times* duly noted, "Orange County (China) is mostly a haven for conservative lawyers, businesspeople and celebrities, looking for a peaceful place to rear children." The dream never withers.

Don Drozd

CHALK DUST

Don Drozd was born in 1949 and spent his early years in and around northern Orange County. He graduated from Servite High School and received a BA from UC Santa Barbara in 1971 and a JD from UCLA in 1974. For twenty years Drozd has been the general counsel for the Orange County Employees Association, representing public employees throughout the county in, as he told us, "the fight to provide fair wages, quality healthcare, and secure retirements for working people and their families." He has published poems along with plenty of appellate court briefs and opinions.

   "Chalk Dust," he told us, "covers a lot of childhood territory revolving around myths and loss of innocence, including the true story of a fellow St. Bruno Catholic School student friend choking on an apple and suffocating." The poem appeared originally in *The Ear* in 1992.

Wednesday mornings Father Landis said mass inside
The Sunkist packing house, all brown board and barn roof.
We sat on sacks of lemons and walked back to classrooms
School green, even the Venetian blinds.

I sat beside Louis (silent "s") Garcia, row six, seat six.
We memorized catechism definitions and Catholic words,
Like "encyclical" and "ecumenical," and prayed to St. Pius,
Patron saint of schoolchildren. We waited for God to deliver

Vocations, and Sister Carmella kissed her rosary.
Chalk dust rose on plaster Jesus dressed in straw.
Quill-thin fingers blessed our class and the awful power
Of the trinity dissolved, pushed outside at recess.

Foursquare lines like scoured pans, perfect brick,
Asphalt cracks, flour-face boys single file,
Water spilling out porcelain fountains.
St. Francis flew from a thousand foot pole.

Sister Carmella's cheeks, squeezed round in starched white,
Almost filled her eyes, and her habit flapped
Across the playground like some unwenched sail.
But when she blew her whistle, we listened like larks.

We beat Leffingwell, the public school, in flag football.
We wore cotton scapulars and holy medals on silver chains,
Symbols of our mission, child crusaders for Christ.
Led by Sisters of Mercy, our lives were certain and clear.

One Wednesday we were playing basketball.
Bobby Saylor swallowed a whole apple.
A fireman blew in his mouth and yelled at him to breathe
And we all whispered, "Breathe, Bobby."

During the Black Mass, I stayed outside the sacristy.
Sister Carmella touched my shoulder with those fingers,
But I just listened as the whole school sang
Hymns to roses, his open casket.

Mitsuye Yamada

THE FOUNDATION

Mitsuye Yamada was born in 1923 in Fukuoka, Japan, while her parents, both first-generation Japanese Americans, were on an extended visit. When the family moved back to the United States in 1926, they settled in Seattle, Washington. During World War II, they were taken to the Minidoka Relocation Center, an internment camp in Idaho. Yamada and her brother were released after formally renouncing their allegiance to Japan, and she attended the University of Cincinnati and earned a BA from New York University and an MA from the University of Chicago. She went on to teach at Fullerton College, Cypress College, and UC Irvine, where the Mitsuye Yamada Papers are now located. In 1980 she helped found the group Multicultural Women Writers of Orange County. Yamada has written and contributed to several books, including *Desert Run: Poems and Stories* and *This Bridge Called My Back: Writings by Radical Women of Color*. She appears with Chinese American poet Nellie Wong in the seminal documentary *Mitsuye and Nellie: Two Asian-American Woman Poets*. A tireless activist for civil rights and social justice, she served on the national board of directors of Amnesty International USA.

"The Foundation" is a poem from *Camp Notes and Other Writings*, Yamada's landmark 1976 debut collection. Its speculation about wildness and growth was inspired, she told us, by the early 1970s grading of land dedicated to the construction of new buildings at Cypress College, where Yamada taught. In it we recognize both the regret and anticipation often related to development and progress.

This could be the land
where everything grows.
Bulldozers had sifted up
large pieces of parched woods and
worthless rocks.
Bilateral buildings
to be are not yet.

Meanwhile on this dust
I counted seven shapes
of sturdy greys and greens
some small and slender
vertical parallels.
No one planted them here with squared T's.
Some weblike tentacles reaching out
toward rounded rotundas.

Molded by no one.

Here
starshaped with tiny speckles,
are these the intruders in my garden
of new seedlings?
My garden carefully fed and fettered?
Of course.
I pronounced their execution
with a pinch of my fingers.

But here
among myriad friends
they flourish in weedy wilderness,
boldly gracing several acres
of untended land.
Tomorrow they shall be banished from their home.

And watered by many droplets
of human sweat
will sprout another college
where
disciplined minds finely honed
will grow
in carefully
planted rows.

No room for random weeds.

Jim Washburn

from **VISIT HISTORIC BUCOLIC ORANGE COUNTY**

Born in 1955, Costa Mesa–based Jim Washburn has written about music and popular culture for the *Los Angeles Times*, the *OC Register*, the *OC Weekly* (of which he was the founding executive editor), *Rolling Stone, Reader's Digest*, and more. He coauthored *Martin Guitars: An Illustrated Celebration of America's Premier Guitarmaker* and *The Wheel and I*, the autobiography of Orange County recreational-vehicle magnate and philanthropist John Crean. Washburn has also curated exhibits at the Fullerton Museum Center, including two specifically on the history of Orange County's popular culture: *The Orange Groove: Orange County's Rock Music History* (2004) and *Lay Down the Boogie: OC in the Disco Era* (2012).

The following selection is an excerpt from a talk Washburn delivered at the 2012 Off Center Festival, held at the Segerstrom Center for the Performing Arts in Costa Mesa. In it Washburn recounts his personal and political coming-of-age in the 1960s, with a special focus on the cultural—and especially musical—history of the county. Beginning with a title fairly drenched in sarcasm, Washburn's memoir builds to a cautiously empathetic assessment of the places that made him.

I N 1964, MY family moved from La Puente to Buena Park, a big jump up the social ladder for us, since they hadn't even invented rungs yet in La Puente. To me, the move mostly meant I had to find new places to buy my 45s and comic books.

We lived in the Highland Greens condo community, on Ginnis Green, one block from Glengarry Green, as all the streets had names from the Scottish Highlands. What were they thinking? It was right off

Beach Blvd., 12 miles up from the bonny Pacific, across the street from the Big T Golf Course, flanked to the south by a field where everyone dumped their garbage and to the north by dirt clod cliffs strewn with Standard Oil derricks.

Greyfriar's Bobby wouldn't have lasted ten minutes on Beach Blvd., where the green Asbury Co. gravel-hauling trucks were notorious for mean drivers who would swerve toward kids walking along the dirt curb, or blow their horns to scare you into crashing your bike.

I had to walk that way to the Mayfair Market and Johnny's Speed and Chrome. Johnny had all the stuff to trick out your hot rod or dune buggy, or, if you were ten, all the cool Weird-O and Rat Fink T-shirts.

A lot of shop owners ignored their young, cash-poor customers, but not Johnny: "Hey, kid, you got any money?"

"No."

"Then get the fuck out of my shop!"

There was usually something going on up there worth risking the Asbury trucks. One day I hit the parking lot just in time to see a guy ram his Impala into a phone pole outside the Tastee Freez. A crowd gathered. Some tried and failed to pry the driver's accordioned door open. Blood streamed down his face from a long gash near his hairline, while he blubbered behind the wheel, "She doesn't love me anymore! I don't wanna live! Let me die!"

A young woman whom I presumed to be the girl in question stood by the side wall of the Tastee Freez, holding a milkshake and seeming embarrassed by the whole thing. It confused the hell out of nine-year-old me. I wondered what about a girlfriend could ever make a guy want to do that, though time certainly answered that one for me.

Another occasion, Little Oscar's Wienermobile was parked outside Johnny's. Again, unless you're too old, you might not know that the Oscar Meyer company once thought you'd eat more hot dogs if a midget in a chef's hat told you to.

They sent Little Oscar to appearances in the Wienermobile, a hot dog bun on wheels from which a wiener jutted at a very optimistic angle. I like to think that, late at night, Little Oscar drove that wiener back and forth into the holes of the giant donuts that graced Southland donut shops.

I pulled up on my Huffy Stingray to find that Oscar wasn't making a personal appearance. He'd just come from one at the La Mirada Unimart, and he was definitely off the clock, a stogie wagging from his five o'clock shadow as he complained, "Johnny, these fuckin' kids, I tell ya…"

Rounding out this mini-center was a single-chair barbershop where the drunk owner would watch cartoons while nicking your ear, and a little Italian spaghetti and meatballs joint. I was friends with the owner's son, whom I envied no end because his family was so broke they lived in the restaurant. My friend had to sleep in a leatherette booth every night, with a backlit Hamm's beer sign behind him, one that looked like water flowing down a stream. I thought he had the coolest life ever.

Just up Rosecrans from this idyllic abode lay Bellehurst, one of the north county's most elegant communities, or it would have been if the developer's financing hadn't failed. You'd have one or two spacious finished homes amidst a block of skeletal frames with maybe one room suggested by drywall, on concrete foundations already encroached by weeds. It was like one more example that adults really didn't know what the hell they were doing.

I never saw the Bellehurst Werewolf, but my future brother-in-law did: a stringy, bearded tramp in tatters who'd scamper after kids on all fours. I don't know what my sister saw in the guy. Sorry, I was talking about the werewolf. Some thought he was a genuine werewolf, and you had better wear your silver St. Christopher medal up there after dark. Others said he was Old Man Bellehurst, who'd gone crazy when his money ran out. Most likely it was just some hobo with a penchant for loping.

No one called them homeless then. They were hobos, up from the railroad tracks just south of Malvern. They congregated in a mini-canyon right near Beach Blvd., where they'd conduct their Sterno-based endeavors beside a small stream that was probably Highland Greens' runoff. Hoot mon!

I'd mainly see them in the nearby field where people dumped their trash. Buena Park had curbside trash service, but a lot of folks in town had moved from the Deep South, and old habits die hard.

To me, the hobos were competition at the dump. We were all scrounging for the same unexhausted hairspray cans: me to use them as flamethrowers or to explode in one of the dump's eternal trash fires, while the hobos wanted the cans to maintain their crazy-guy hair or something.

Some summer days, when the wind blew hot from the west, you'd smell Dairy Valley, and never have to wonder why it was called Dairy Valley. In 1965, that smell mixed with the smoke of the Watts riots. We kids stood on our carport roof at night watching the angry flames, thinking, "Wow, there's someplace worse than Buena Park."

It had its merits. Even without going anywhere, things came to you: The Helms truck full of breads and bear claws; the Good Humor ice cream truck driven by a wizened guy with about five tooth stumps in his mouth; the Saturday morning bookmobile full of adventure. Nearly every week, a Sears truck stopped on our block, delivering neighbors' credenzas, TV sets and everything else that wasn't an electric guitar for me.

I'd walk to Knott's sometimes, and wander its horse-trod streets. Off its beaten path, sort of behind the Chicken Dinner Restaurant, was a courtyard with a motorized diorama boxed in rough stone, of a nasty little devil inside turning a crank that rattled a copper sheet, creating a rumble to accompany the plaster volcano behind it. It was troubling to a kid because it had no reason to exist, yet adults had made it.

You could wander Knott's for free until 1968, when they fenced it off and started charging admission. Walter Knott claimed they had to, to keep hippies out. Hippies are like weevils. They get into everything. The Knotts' fear of hippies made them a fortune.

Across from Highland Greens, the Big T burger shack had a jukebox that often had "Little Latin Lupe Lu" blasting from it, with a pulsing bass line and husky lyrical gibberish like, "She's my mashed potato baby, little Latin Lupe Lu." It was *fantastic* to a kid, because it too had no reason to exist, yet adults had made it.

The record was by two Orange County guys, on a little Garden Grove label. Righteous Brothers Bill Medley and Bobby Hatfield were some of the first artists to attain escape velocity from OC.

Which was odd: OC was still largely an agrarian place—known for oranges, lima beans, sugar beets, celery and such—and the population was abundantly white, and partial to country music, if they had made time for entertainment at all. Hatfield and Medley were white guys singing black music, to which they'd been introduced by LA R&B radio and by a trio of real Santa Ana brothers, Rick, Barry and Butch Rillera, who had formed OC's very first rock and R&B band in 1955.

Of Mexican and Filipino descent, they weren't satisfied with the world they'd been given—one where the eldest brother Rick could come home from serving in Korea to find that he and his new wife couldn't buy a home in most parts of Santa Ana, because they were "restricted neighborhoods."

So, emulating the music they heard on B.B. King 78s and Hunter Hancock's R&B broadcasts, they created their own better world.

This was uncharted territory in OC, and the Rillera's Rhythm Rockers had to promote their own gigs, booking Anaheim's Harmony Park Ballroom on off nights. While Harmony Park typically hosted country and western bands, the Rilleras were soon drawing mixed-race crowds.

One night while the Rilleras played a Cuban instrumental, LA R&B singer Richard Berry was backstage, writing in his notebook. The next week he asked the Rilleras to repeat the number, sang his fresh lyrics atop it, and the ur-garage-rock classic "Louie Louie" was born.

Berry released a record of it that didn't do much. A few years later, the Northwest band the Kingsmen did a raucous, mumbly version that was an electric thrill to a kid, and an enduring international hit.

That's pretty much the story of American culture: People of color get a good thing going, and then white people horn in on it.

This was not my observation when I was eight. I just loved that amplified racket. Much of that was due to Clarence Leo Fender, who was born in a barn outside of Anaheim in 1909, and wound up making the guitars, intended initially for country musicians, that Jimi Hendrix rode into outer space.

Leo's guitars and amps democratized music, giving a louder voice to the working man, from the south side of Chicago to the streets of Bakersfield, where thanks to Fender any trio with a few hundred bucks could make as much racket as an orchestra.

His instruments came along at the same time as another creation: teenagers. Formerly regarded as remaindered children or larval adults, teens came onto their own as a social force in the 1950s, with their own look, movies, music and financial clout.

Parents weren't expected to like a record like "Little Latin Lupe Lu" or "Louie Louie." They were out of the loop: the records spoke straight to kids.

As a curious side note, "Louie Louie" was actually investigated by the FBI, on the rumor that its mumbled lyrics masked obscenities. Along with suspecting communists under every bed, the right-wing mindset in OC and DC feared the corrupting, brainwashing influence of rock music on America's youth. If a congressman was in the news claiming that rock and roll was a communist plot, he was probably James Utt or other of OC's representatives.

To that stiff generation, the most subversive message might be that it's great to be alive. Rock did tend to spread the abandon.

The Rilleras, with their flashy Fender gear, became the first rock band to play Disneyland. They were regulars at the Coke Terrace and other stages there, making them also the first live rock music that tens of thousands of kids ever heard, who all returned to their hometowns intent on rocking.

Chances are that the first songs they learned were "Louie Louie" or another OC-born number, "Pipeline," penned in 1962 by two fifteen-year-old Santa Ana High School kids, Bob Spickard and Brian Carman. Hardly playing for six months, they went into a Downey recording studio with their department store guitars—upgraded to Fenders once they made some money—and cut "Pipeline," which became one of the biggest instrumental hits of the 1960s, and certainly the most popular surf music recording.

That was another youth-specific form of music, born on the county coast. In 1961, Dick Dale emerged from the briny Pacific, glistening, speaking of himself in the third person, and holding a gold metal–flake Stratocaster. He plugged it into a Fender reverb unit and hulking Showman amplifier, and lo it was good. He created a musical rendition of the sea that was startlingly more alive than Debussy or Ravel's. It wasn't just music. It was sensation. Dale's rumbling, reverb-saturated sound put you right in the middle of the curl with him.

On short order, Dale and other surf bands were packing Balboa's Rendezvous ballroom and other music spots. One band, the Chantays, were Santa Ana High School kids who had only been playing for a couple of months when they got together in a Santa Ana bedroom and wrote "Pipeline," which became a worldwide hit.

There was a whole other scene going on here, too: folk music. Starting in 1958, clubs started springing up all over: Café Frankenstein, Sid's Blue Beet, the Prison of Socrates, the Golden Bear, the Paradox and other rooms featured touring folk and blues artists, and were a place where local guys like Jackson Browne and Tim Buckley could learn their stuff.

When Sunny Hills High student Jackson Browne stole a bicycle, my friend had to get his dad to get it back, because Mr. Sensitive back then was known as a "hard guy," meaning he smoked and had bangs, and you didn't mess with him.

Folk was such a big deal that even Disneyland had a hootenanny night, in Tomorrowland, where the green room was the now long-gone 20,000 Leagues Under the Sea attraction.

Most local authorities and parents adopted a tolerant attitude towards kids and their music. Our politicians might rail against the stuff, but for the typical county conservative it was a given that everybody had a right to make a buck. Let these kids have their dances.

That attitude took a sharp turn in the late '60s, when Vietnam, drugs, college revolt and the fear of hippie communes drove a bloody wedge between the generations.

Maybe it's because America's built on stolen land that we fear in turn that someone's always after our Lucky Charms. Where once a white majority worried about Irish and Mexicans, by the late '60s that fear focused on their own children who had gone hippie.

They were everywhere. Tim Leary holed up in Laguna Canyon, where the open-secretive Brotherhood preached LSD and hash, and supplied the goods. There was a Marxist hippie bookstore on the Balboa Peninsula. Half the towns had head shops or underground record stores. There was a rock festival at the OC fairgrounds, with the requisite mud-wallowing hippies, and a love-in at Fullerton's Hillcrest Park, or, as the *Orange County Register* headline put it: "Communist Dupe Negroes Invade Park."

In 1970, hundreds of hippies converged on Disneyland for "Yippie Day," intended to "bring the reality of Vietnam to America's fantasy-land." Yippies (members of the Youth International Party) did manage to raise the Viet Cong flag over Tom Sawyer Island's fort before being rounded up by hundreds of cops in full riot gear. For years after that, you couldn't get into Disneyland if you had long hair.

Across the street at the Anaheim Convention Center that year, poor crowd control led to a rock concert riot, where 382 cops were called in from 19 cities to battle kids. Rock music was banned from the arena for years.

I knew squat about the OC music scene or politics when I was eight in 1964, but by 1970, I knew plenty. I'd been to that fairgrounds "Newport Pop Festival" in 1968 when I was thirteen, and learned that hippies could be real litterbugs. That same year I saw Cream at the Anaheim Convention Center, forced to wear my Penney's burgundy suit with clip-on tie because my stepdad thought, "Concert? Cultural event!" How hippie chicks resisted my allure, I don't know.

My interest in music led me to the counterculture politics in the *LA Free Press* and *Rolling Stone*. A reference to Lenny Bruce in an interview with the Hollies in a *Hit Parader* magazine bought at the Mayfair Market was enough to turn me on to his paperbacks and arch worldview. Friends and I frequented Laguna's Sound Spectrum record shop, Fahrenheit 451 bookstore and fabled Mystic Arts head shop.

By this point, my family had upgraded to Newport Beach, to Harbor View Homes, where if you stood atop your roof, you couldn't see the harbor. But you couldn't see Watts either, and people liked that.

Newport was the land of idle pleasure and of new money that smelled old. At Corona del Mar High School, we had exactly one black student, and we *jetted* him in: an exchange student from Africa. My stepdad wanted us to host an exchange student, until he learned he couldn't force them to do yard work.

We didn't have the Bellehurst Werewolf there, but something else haunted the neighborhood. For wont of anything else to do, I used to ramble through the field near the tract, just off MacArthur Blvd., behind the old Irvine Co. ranch house where architect Bill Pereira's offices were. That's where the master plan that was to pave over Irvine was born.

A hundred yards or so behind that one day, I rounded a rock abutment that had a little waterfall—this one supplied by Harbor View Homes runoff—and saw the tip of a tail vanish behind the rock.

I went around the other way, trying to get a glimpse of what it was, and was suddenly facing a king-sized mountain lion. I read later in the *Daily Pilot* that he'd been sighted for years, coming down from the hills when water and game was scarce. All I know is it was lucky this lion believed the propaganda about us being the dominant species, because I was so dumbstruck he could have devoured my pancreas without so much as a mild rebuke from me.

He's gone. The field is gone. I'm still here, and the pavement goes on forever.

Lorene Delany-Ullman

---

from ***CAMOUFLAGE FOR
THE NEIGHBORHOOD***

Born in Costa Mesa in 1957, Lorene Delany-Ullman lives in Orange County
and teaches writing at UC Irvine, where she earned an MFA in poetry. She
was a founding member of the long-running Casa Romantica Reading Series
in San Clemente, and her work has appeared in the *Santa Monica Review,*
TAB: The Journal of Poetry and Poetics, Prime Number, Sports Literate,
Stymie, Lunch Ticket, AGNI 74, and *Warscapes.*

In *Camouflage for the Neighborhood,* a collection of seventy-one short,
untitled narrative prose poems, she traces her childhood and offers adult
impressions of Orange County. Connecting the culture and economics of
militarism to everyday life, in these selections Delany-Ullman revisits sites
including a playground with a fighter jet, a group of munitions bunkers at
the Seal Beach Naval Weapons Station, and the World War II–era dirigible
hangars of the former Marine Corps Air Station in Tustin, the largest free-
standing wooden structures in the world. *Camouflage for the Neighborhood*
won a Sentence Book Award in 2011.

Clocks stopped. Even in grayscale, the destruction wasn't
lost. A child's lunchbox tied to ash and bone. What were
we—seven or eight years old when Mrs. Risko exposed us
to the photographs of Hiroshima? I had nightmares; my
mother called the principal to complain.

* * *

Alongside the freeway, rows of weed-covered bunkers.
Not fallout shelters. Each mound a cache of munitions—

warheads, missiles, bombs, stockpiling since World War
II. The Naval Station shares its boundaries with an estuary,
home to three endangered species—the California least
tern, Belding's savannah sparrow, the light-footed clapper
rail—their refuge along the Pacific Flyway. Here, wetlands
and weapons.

* * *

One-fifth of my hometown was once an army airbase.
Eager cadets became pilots, navigators, and bombardiers.
After V-J Day, the land and buildings were converted
into schools, the county fairgrounds, and city hall. Land
banking made men rich: lima beans and celery, cleared
from the fields, were replaced by tract houses built on
raised foundations. Our streets had Irish names: Watson,
Dublin, and Shamrock linked into a three-block loop. We
didn't live in a Cinderella home with scrollwork and fascia
board. Our house was basic ranch. From the front porch, we
had a peek-a-boo view of Disneyland's Matterhorn and its
fake snowcap until everything civic sprawled. Next-door, a
German physicist with five children. What frightened me
was the mad Italian woman, her grappling hold on her
young son too strong. Hollering for my mother, she broke
down on our steps late one night. Her husband and parents
hauled her away. Around the block, a retired marine raised
and saluted the stars and stripes at 0600.

* * *

No skyline. It used to be like Mayberry—small town,
southern California where the words "town" and "city"
are interchangeable by law. Poised atop a coastal tableland,
sixteen square miles, today it's an edgeless city.

My dad was driving us home from a camping vacation when Apollo 11 landed in the Sea of Tranquility. From the car radio, we heard Armstrong as he walked the moon. I was scared of what he'd find there.

* * *

We called it the airplane park. Near the swing set and the seesaw, Jane and I danced the length of its hot fuselage, skipped across its wings—what we fingered was not the military crest or the missing cannons from the nose, not the dogfight near the Yalu River, but the sea of yellow sand below, the milk-and-water sky above the Navy jet beached in our lot.

The town's first park, now full of vagrants and homeless, still hosts the venerable fish fry every May. Carnival rides and raffles. The day after last Christmas, teenaged boys shot three dozen paintballs at a homeless man sitting at a picnic table, reading. Left him blind in one eye.

* * *

The seventeen-story hangars once sheltered lighter-than-airships, blimps on coastal patrol for a Japanese invasion, but to first graders the wooden structures seemed monstrous. How tiny we were inside a building with its own weather. A colonel escorted us across the wide runway; we saw a mirage—soldiers quivering in the distance.

Jon Wiener

from **INSIDE THE NIXON LIEBRARY**

Born in 1944 in St. Paul, Minnesota, Jon Wiener is a professor emeritus of U.S. history at UC Irvine and the host of a weekly public affairs show on KPFK radio, as well as a contributing editor to the *Nation* and host of its weekly podcast "Start Making Sense." His research and legal battles led famously to the release of FBI surveillance records on John Lennon, as well as two books on the political life of the singer. Wiener's other books include *Historians in Trouble: Plagiarism, Fraud, and Politics in the Ivory Tower* and *How We Forgot the Cold War: A Historical Journey across America*.

Born in Yorba Linda, Richard Nixon opened his first law practice in nearby La Habra, and during his presidency he established a residence in San Clemente that became known as the Western White House. Following his scandalous years in office, both UC Irvine and his alma mater, Duke University, declined to house his presidential papers, which were eventually placed in the Richard Nixon Presidential Library and Museum in Yorba Linda. In 1990, Wiener recounted for the *Nation* his first visit to the then newly opened and privately controlled facility, challenging the unabashedly pro-Nixon narrative suggested by its design and embracing the opportunity to present an alternative tour of the political life of a president born and raised in Orange County, once an outpost of his particular variety of combative conservative politics.

THE $21 MILLION Nixon Library in Yorba Linda, California, which opened in July 1990, takes visitors on a twisted trip down memory lane. From Helen Gahagan Douglas, whom he defeated in the 1952 race for California Senator, to E. Howard Hunt, participant in the Watergate crimes, the effort made here to reshape popular memory is more sweeping, more relentless, more sophisticated and more expensive than that undertaken by any other president.

The dedication was a cheerful occasion. While an audience of 50,000 sweltered under the desert sun and CNN broadcast the proceedings live, former Treasury Secretary William Simon spoke of Nixon's "lifelong commitment to peace and freedom"; Ronald Reagan said "the world is a better place—a safer place—because of Richard Nixon"; and President Bush asked, "Who can forget how much he endured in his quest for peace in Vietnam?" The people watching at my house yelled something like, "How much did the Vietnamese endure?" but CNN didn't hear; anchorman Bernard Shaw called it "a grand day." It made me wish gonzo journalist Hunter Thompson had also been on the program, calling Nixon "a Born Loser...the predatory shyster who turns into something unspeakable, full of claws and bleeding string-warts, on nights when the moon comes too close." But instead TV preacher Norman Vincent Peale wrapped things up.

Calling this a "library" is misleading; the place has no books or documents. Officials have promised to open a basement archive in 1991 to contain primarily pre- and post-presidential papers. Nixon, alone among presidents, has been denied control of his presidential papers by an act of Congress. After he resigned and was pardoned, he signed an agreement with Gerald Ford's General Services Administration allowing the destruction of some of the papers and requiring the destruction of the White House tapes. An outraged Congress passed a law taking control of the materials away from Nixon and giving it to the federal government. The disgraced but defiant ex-president then challenged the law before the Supreme Court and lost. Even today library director Hugh Hewitt says Nixon's papers were "stolen" from him.

The Nixon presidential papers and tapes now rest in Alexandria, Virginia, where the National Archives has been working at declassifying them, but Reagan-era budget cuts slowed the process. Since 1978, when the processing began, 4 million pages have been released, along with 12½ hours of Watergate tapes; that leaves 40 million pages and 4,000 hours of tape that have not yet been processed. Nixon's lawsuits have blocked the release of 150,000 pages of documents. Library officials say their basement archive will include photocopies that will constitute "a complete collection of key presidential documents"; scholars and journalists respond to that claim with understandable skepticism.

If the library is weak on archives, it is strong on video: visitors get to see Nixon's 1952 "Checkers" speech, in which the weepy vice-presidential candidate labored to exonerate himself of charges of corruption with maudlin references to his dog Checkers and his wife's "respectable Republican cloth coat." (Visitors are not told that columnist Walter Lippmann called the Checkers speech "the most demeaning experience my country has ever had to bear.") Next come the 1960 Kennedy-Nixon debates, featuring a brief glimpse of the 5 o'clock shadow that many believe lost Nixon the election. To recreate the original experience, viewers watch in a 1960 living room—an upscale one, with Reader's Digest Condensed Books on the mantel. Visitors also get to see Nixon's unforgettable 1987 eulogy for Ohio State football coach Woody Hayes (but only if they get there by 10.30 in the morning). In the opinion of museum director Hewitt, none of these videos will be as popular as the tape of Nixon's daughter Tricia's wedding, which is shown at 10.45.

The "Hall of World Leaders" is one of the best, with life-size bronze statues of de Gaulle, Adenauer, Churchill, Sadat, Golda Meir, Mao, Zhou Enlai, Khrushchev and Brezhnev posed as if they were all at the same cocktail party. By touching a video screen, the visitor can learn what the library guide calls "their thoughts on Nixon." The thoughts contain few surprises: de Gaulle, for instance, does not describe Nixon as "head of...the racist, fascist pig power structure" (as Bobby Seale did) but rather as "one of those frank and steady personalities on whom one feels one could rely in the greatest affairs of state."

"Richard Nixon: Hiss is your life," Nixon biographer Garry Wills once wrote. Nixon, a member of the House Un-American Activities Committee in 1947, pursued Whittaker Chambers's espionage charge against Alger Hiss, a prominent New Deal figure; Hiss's conviction for perjury propelled the formerly unknown Nixon into national prominence. The Hiss case is featured in the library; visitors to the museum arc told that Hiss's Woodstock typewriter convicted him when samples typed on it were found to match documents Chambers said Hiss had given him to transmit to the Russians. The library display includes a replica of Hiss's Woodstock, and library officials told the *Los Angeles Times* that the original Hiss typewriter is kept in a vault in the library basement. Could it be true that Nixon has the Hiss typewriter? Most of the artifacts in the library are on loan from the National Archives; I asked archives spokeswoman Susan Cooper about the typewriter in the Nixon Library vault. "It's not ours," she said, "not the National Archives'." It turns out that it isn't Hiss's either: the typewriter was returned to Hiss after his trial and is now in the attic of filmmaker John Lowenthal.

The claim that Nixon has Hiss's typewriter in a vault in the library basement adds another bizarre chapter to a forty-year saga. At the time Chambers charged Hiss with espionage, the typewriter on which Hiss was said to have typed the documents was missing; Hiss claimed it would prove him innocent. Despite a massive FBI effort to locate the typewriter, the Hiss defense found it and presented it triumphantly to the court, only to learn that it matched the Chambers documents. Ever since that time the Hiss defense has claimed that the typewriter was used to frame him, that the FBI manufactured a phony duplicate Woodstock to match the Chambers documents and left it for Hiss to find—a type of fabrication that even Hiss critic Allen Weinstein acknowledged "had become standard procedure in the repertoire of espionage agencies by the time of the Second World War." For forty years the debate has focused on the authenticity of the typewriter Hiss introduced at the trial; now it seems that in the Nixon Library vault there is a second phony Woodstock. Needless to say, the "forgery by typewriter" theory is not presented in the library display. One visitor to it commented, "Isn't that something! I remember hearing about the pumpkin deal, but I never understood what it was about."

Other exhibits include the "Domestic Gifts" section, where one can see the Colt .45 pistol Elvis Presley gave Nixon when he visited the Oval Office in December 1970. The Elvis gun is surrounded by crocheted miniature doll hats, an electric football clock and a rock in the shape of Nixon's profile. In the official White House photo of "the President and the King" on display in the museum, Nixon wears a tweed suit and Elvis sports a flowing cape and a huge gold belt buckle. The photo has sold 31,000 copies—an all-time record for the National Archives; unfortunately it's not for sale at the library gift shop. Nor does the library reproduce Elvis's letter seeking an appointment with the President, volunteering to enlist in the war against drugs: "The Drug Culture, the Hippie Elements, the SDS, Black Panthers," he wrote, "do *not* consider me as their enemy."

At the end of the exhibits comes the "Presidential Forum," where a touch-screen video monitor allows visitors to "ask" Nixon questions in what is billed as a "Face-to-Face Dialogue." He "answers" on an immense video screen. This proved to be something of a disappointment; you "ask" by choosing questions listed under topics such as Watergate, the Vietnam War and "the media." The system contains 300 answers, drawn either from past interviews with Nixon or from statements he recorded recently in a studio. The list invites visitors to ask Nixon, "What is the source of your passion for peace?" A question that is not on the list is, "Are you a crook?"

The museum's Vietnam display is its most reprehensible. It doesn't mention the fact that during the mid 1960s Nixon was the country's leading hawk, constantly attacking Johnson for not escalating the war. It barely mentions the 1970 invasion of Cambodia or the nationwide student strike that followed and the Kent State killings. It doesn't show Nixon calling campus demonstrators "bums," or the father of Allison Krause, one of the students killed at Kent State, replying on national TV, "My child was not a bum." It doesn't mention the illegal surveillance, harassment and prosecution of antiwar activists under Attorney General John Mitchell. Instead, visitors are told the antiwar movement consisted of "a violent minority" that "used force and intimidation to stifle debate; they used bombs to proclaim their message that there should be no bombing; they took lives while professing that they were trying to save lives."

The library's Watergate display, a dark, uninviting corridor filled with small print, shows that Tricky Dick is alive and well in Yorba Linda. Before the library opened, officials repeatedly told reporters three key Watergate tapes would be played in their entirety for visitors. One tape is available; its most significant portions have been deleted. It's the 18½ minute gap all over again. The "smoking gun" tape, recorded July 23, 1972, reveals that Nixon approved a plan to have the CIA tell the FBI to stop investigating Watergate. In the Nixon Library version, however, a narrator explains that what Nixon really said was, "The best thing to do is let the investigation proceed unhindered." Why that would bring Barry Goldwater and the Senate Republican leadership to advise Nixon to resign is not explained. The Watergate room leaves out a few other things. It doesn't mention Nixon's use of the FBI, CIA and White House "plumbers" to harass, spy on and punish those on the President's "enemies list." It doesn't mention the criminal convictions of Nixon's senior aides for carrying out these actions. It doesn't mention the resignation of the disgraced Vice President Spiro Agnew. Most incredible of all, it doesn't mention that Gerald Ford pardoned Nixon for his crimes. Instead, the Watergate affair is described the way Nixon has always described it: not as a systematic abuse of power but as a single act, a second-rate burglary carried out by overzealous underlings without his knowledge, followed by a partisan vendetta in which Democrats sought to reverse the "mandate of the 1972 election" by forcing him from office.

Nixon can get away with all this because it's his museum, financed completely by private donations from rich friends. His is the only privately run presidential library. The Kennedy and Johnson libraries run by the National Archives contain virtually no criticism of their subjects, but it's inconceivable that a National Archives–run Nixon Library would delete key portions of the Watergate tapes. Anyone with $21 million can build a museum and fill it with lies about what he or she has done—that's what it means to live in a free country.

Tom Vanderbilt

THE GAUDY AND DAMNED

Born in 1968 in Lake Forest, Illinois, Tom Vanderbilt grew up in Wisconsin. A journalist and editor, Vanderbilt's work on technology, science, and culture has appeared widely in such publications as *Artforum*, the *Financial Times*, the *London Review of Books*, *Rolling Stone*, *Slate*, *Popular Science*, and *Wired*. He is the author of four books, most recently *You May Also Like: Taste in an Age of Endless Choice*.

In 1994, when Orange County declared bankruptcy due to bad investments by its aptly named treasurer, Robert Citron, Vanderbilt traveled to the region as a journalist. Here is his giddily skeptical and sarcastic report for the *Baffler*, the nation's leading anti–business culture magazine. After visits to the *OC Weekly*, the Crystal Cathedral, Coto de Caza, and Newport Beach, his sketch of the economic and cultural life of Orange County in the mid-1990s spares no one.

> *California is a place in which a boom mentality and a sense of Chekhovian loss meet in uneasy suspension; in which the mind is troubled by some buried but ineradicable suspicion that things had better work here, because here, beneath that immense bleached sky, is where we run out of continent.* —JOAN DIDION

Sоменоw the pursuit of the American Dream is always most poignant in California. When it crashes here, it seems to do so with epochal fury, and no place has experienced a more fiery crash than Orange County, California, the storied locus of virile, "B-1" Bob Dornan conservatism and entrepreneurial might. Here, in this theme park of a county (the theme, as one tourist brochure put it, is "you can

---

have anything you want"), the meeting of boom and loss played itself out in the daily papers: The *Orange County Register*, the most reliable barometer of local opinion, ran stories only pages apart that contrasted life under the penumbra of bankruptcy against the place in the sun that we had always known Orange County to be. Tales of personal depression and "bankruptcy blues" cast a shadow on the passing parade of upbeat economic indicators that everyone else seemed to be enjoying.

Nowhere was that "uneasy suspension" more strikingly manifested than the Crystal Cathedral, the immaculately-maintained headquarters of televangelist Rev. Robert Schuller, set in the modest, Eisenhower-era suburb of Garden Grove, where the John Birch Society once sold its pamphlets in the Knott's Berry Farm amusement park, and where Newt Gingrich's book sells briskly in the Richard M. Nixon Memorial Library and Birthplace. The Cathedral, in the shadow of Disneyland, is a metaphorical motherlode in the otherwise inscrutable terrain of post-suburbia. Walking through the parking lot, past the silver railings and concrete of the private family gardens ("offering the finest in memorial property"), my first thought was of the Cathedral's fidelity to the environment outside. Designed by Philip Johnson, it is an immense building of white steel trusses and glass-paneled walls. Its mirror exoskeleton glares crisply, like any one of the corporate headquarters ringing the highway interchanges near Irvine. Flanking the Cathedral is a giant "Tower of Power" made up of steel tubes thrust upward into the sky, terminating in a set of sharp, jagged points, their metal surfaces glimmering menacingly in the sun like a phalanx of missiles at a desert military installation. Inside, a smooth piece of crystal set in a larger mass of unpolished rock rotates under glass like a jeweler's display in Fashion Island, one of the county's more exclusive malls. An inscription marking the fortieth anniversary of the Crystal Cathedral (1955–1995 A.D.), which is situated nearby, reads like a distillation of the history of suburbia itself: "This was also the era of the birth of television, the building of nuclear weapons of warfare, an age of hope and fear."

The Cathedral is a sprawling "megachurch," with all the trappings of mass entertainment: indoor stadium-style seats for 2,862 (but not—at least not yet—skyboxes), Sony JumboTrons adjoining both sides of the pulpit, and an array of broadcasting equipment used to beam Schuller's "Hour of Power"—the country's most popular religious program—to its estimated three million weekly viewers. Just past the church entrance lies the "Drive-In Worship Center." On that day it was an empty parking lot, but each Sunday it swarms with Schuller's vehicular flock, who watch from their cars as the Cathedral's 90-foot-high doors slide open; a peculiar homage to the preacher's first house of worship, a drive-in movie theater. In the gift and book shop one may find Crystal Cathedral cocktail napkins and keychains, a "Motivational" book section, and myriad postcards and t-shirts bearing Schuller's copyrighted homilies, the most popular of which seems to be: "Tough Times Never Last, But Tough People Do!" Unlike his more inflammatory neighbor in Anaheim, the Rev. Lou Sheldon of the Traditional Values Coalition, Schuller is interested less in morality and sin than a libertarian inspirational uplift, designed to soothe those who have reaped the rewards of success and console those who haven't yet, hinting broadly that economic salvation is just round the corner. It's a message worth millions of dollars a year from viewers, and one that he delivers across the country in places like Flint, Michigan, where he is shown in Michael Moore's 1989 film *Roger and Me* pronouncing his regenerative slogans to a room full of unemployed autoworkers.

In a local library, I found what was perhaps, in light of the county's fiscal catastrophe, the most ironic piece of the Schuller merchandising empire, a slim volume called *The Power of Being Debt-Free,* written by Schuller and an undistinguished economist. After thanking Milton Friedman, Arthur Laffer, and a number of others in the introduction, Schuller notes that the book began over a dinner with Robert and Elizabeth Dole. The national debt, it seems, had been vexing him, so he set about drafting a recovery plan based on his self-help doctrines; the book, accordingly, is a litany of exhortations and bold pronouncements, a forest of exclamation marks interspersed with statements like: "America is a superpower with superpeople who have superpotential for superproductivity."

But outside the library, Orange County seemed gripped not by "super" anything but rather the less empowering dynamic of "hope and fear." Under the bankruptcy, the county seemed to inhabit a dual world; one a gray dystopia of uncertainty and falling property values; another, the accustomed bright and buoyant showcase of affluent citizens who were forming start-up software firms in small industrial parks and shopping at Coach and Hermès. It was home to one of the country's most profitable Mercedes-Benz dealers, yet ominous talk loomed of massive cuts in bus service to help bail out the county—and just how would those nannies and gardeners from Santa Ana make the daily commute to Big Canyon Villas or Belcourt? In Orange County, such paradoxes run deep and jagged like irrigation ditches: Only there did it seem to make sense that the soft-spoken and earnest editor of the new "alternative weekly," itself housed next to those software firms in a commercially-zoned office park, would meet me for lunch wearing a three-piece suit, and then drive me in his BMW to a cafe at "the Lab." Known as the county's "anti-mall," the former canning factory is a perfect fabricated bohemia—with rusted post-industrial debris as strategically chosen as the "environmental" music at the county's real malls—made possible through the generous cooperation of a local surf/skate-wear tycoon.

Popular ideas of Orange County still revolve around gated communities, golf villas, yacht clubs, and European signature boutiques. The picture is of a sylvan suburban paradise—just a shade less blanched than Sun City—where places like Coto de Caza, an equestrian rising-property-value preserve of the rich, stretch for miles along the breathtaking backdrop of the Santa Ana Mountains. Media coverage of the bankruptcy focused on this sort of opulence fixedly, with a stream of TV dispatches from high-end Newport Beach shopping centers, where the point that Orange County was a "wealthy deadbeat" could be driven home more effectively. But a twenty-minute drive replaces the glimmering things of F. Scott Fitzgerald's imagination with the cluttered barrios of Santa Ana, the shabby procession of strip malls selling fish tacos and "$1 Chinese food," and the repeated binary clusters of attached homes (from $85,900) in Tustin Ranch for what Richard Ford once called "starter people." Minus its two or three wealthiest enclaves, it has been pointed out, Orange County barely makes the state's median income level.

And yet it's certainly easy to find pockets of privilege and prosperity in Orange County, places where the better-off can cocoon in relative safety as everyone else frets about the ground-level impact of the "Citron crater." One night in Newport Beach, I rode to dinner on the thirty-foot yacht of a Corona del Mar investment banker. As we motored slowly through the still waters of Newport Harbor, past the former estates of John Wayne and Gene Autry, past the second or third homes of international industrialists, the banker would turn away from the wheel every so often, pointing with awe to one of the multimillion-dollar vessels resting in their exclusive berths. "That boat cost more than God!" he would gush, conjuring up immediately the entwined supplication to religion and money that Schuller's ministry also seemed to suggest. Returning to the dock, the banker's assistant asked if I had enjoyed the ride, and then, gesturing to the panorama of bobbing boats and harborfront property, said with a smile, "See, not all of Orange County is bankrupt."

Greg Bills

from *FEARFUL SYMMETRY*

Greg Bills was born in 1965 in Midvale, Utah, and holds a BA in English
from the University of Utah and an MFA in fiction from UC Irvine. He is the
author of two novels, *Consider This Home* and *Fearful Symmetry*. His stories
and essays have appeared in *Brothers and Beasts: An Anthology of Men on
Fairy Tales*, the *Fairy Tale Review*, the *Redlands Review*, and the *Santa Monica
Review*. He is currently a professor of creative writing at the University of
Redlands and lives in Los Angeles.

In this excerpt from *Fearful Symmetry*, published in 1996, the narrator
considers the ideologies of self-celebration implicit in the design of a curious,
once-innovative architectural landmark: a 1990s shopping center in Costa
Mesa called Triangle Square. Recently renamed "The Triangle," it situates
Bills's story of desire, narcissism, sexual obsession and, yes, a love triangle.

TRIANGLE SQUARE WAS a cunningly designed multilevel complex
nestled in the acute angle of the intersection of Newport and Harbor
Boulevards. The development did not possess the necessary critical mass
to become a shopping mecca like South Coast Plaza, but it was too
capacious and pretentious to be properly designated a strip mall. It was
sleek, upscale, vaguely glamorous. I parked in the tiered garage, which
was located at the center of the Square's design, and after checking my
watch to plan for Irena's eventual arrival, I toured the attractions.

A series of open-air escalators glided up beneath a whitewashed,
red-tiled canopy held aloft by a series of pillars. On the top floor there
were movie theatres, trendy Mexican and Italian restaurants, a yogurt
store, and other concessions. On the ground floor were the bookstore,
coffeehouse, and shops. At the far end of the structure was a giant

sporting-goods store, a flagship, full of expensive, elaborate, self-congratulatory display—interactive vitrines, life-sized statuary, numerous computer terminals, and banks of video monitors celebrating exertion and litheness—a corporate shrine, a mausoleum of fitness. There was also a giant music and video store and a virtual reality game room. Beneath all this, on a basement parking level, a subterranean supermarket glowed pristinely. Inside its cavernous hall, long aisles of product stretched back, separated by unusually wide expanses of hygienically polished floor tile. As in the sports store and the music store, the goods simultaneously shimmered with freshness, vibrated with novelty, and posed with almost incantatory quietude, with sepulchral perfection.

I walked off the escalators and through a food court arranged with tables, chairs, and black-framed windbreaks like Japanese screens in canvas and clear plastic, then down another set of escalators onto street level, where I paced the perimeter. I admired the façades and the vistas; they were all attractively wrought. The governing principle was postmodern, but like the pun of "Triangle Square," the ironies had been normalized by familiarity. Outsized, "weathered copper" lanterns dangled from hooks over the central court; Spanish styles from mission and adobe to Moorish were plundered for gewgaws; magnified decorative motifs loomed from the walls, while vestigial cupolas, domes, and minarets bloomed above. But all these borrowings and juxtapositions offered no commentary, only pleasures. Postmodernism was dead as a philosophy but alive as a palette of tropes. I could not imagine Triangle Square at fifty years, at seventy-five; I could not imagine that the architects had considered its persistence either. The sporting-goods store would make a cool nightclub in five or ten years if the parent company reckoned with deficits and decided to clear out. But in twenty years the whole enterprise would seem somewhat embarrassing. For the present, however, I was charmed by its mixture of the timeless and the obsolete.

When I looked down to eye level again, I found myself between a square fountain platform and the inescapable Gap outlet. The clothing stores in the Square all focused solely on leisure: besides the Gap, there was a store for outdoor wear, one for ready-to-wear casuals, a T-shirt vendor. The clothes on display promised sport, play, fun, and activity, as did the posters for coming movie attractions, as did the array of romances and spy thrillers in the bookstore windows. As I strolled towards the bookstore, I heard the spirit of the place, of Orange County, the combined voice of its architecture, its merchants, its concealed history (of what had been razed to make way for the new). It muttered from the elevated planters and the benches of glazed ceramic tile, saying: Here is a world you need never leave, here are pleasures and products and sustenance without consequence. There is nothing beneath the surface, no subtext to disturb; there is no end. It told me that I would be young forever, that I would never die.

Anh Chi Pham

THE PICTURE

Born in Vietnam in 1972, Anh Chi Pham left in 1979 as a refugee. She grew up in Orange County and graduated from Brown University. She has published several short stories, received a Fulbright fellowship and two Pushcart Prize nominations, and is currently a yoga, movement, and meditation teacher based in Orange County.

Observing that the U.S. war on Vietnam was possibly the most photographed conflict in history, Pham composed a series of stories based on iconic images associated with the war and its aftermath. What follows is her fictionalized version of a famous 1999 incident involving a video store owner's much publicized display of the Vietnamese flag and an image of Ho Chi Minh inside his shop, located in an enclave of Westminster known as Little Saigon. "The Picture" first appeared in the *Santa Monica Review* in 2004.

LILY DIDN'T WANT to go, but she had to. Her father was one of the organizers of the demonstration. In Little Saigon, the owner of a video rental store had hung a picture of Ho Chi Minh in his shop. News of his display spread; immigrants and veterans crowded the parking lot, holding signs and waving flags. They stood behind the metal barricade, glaring at the Vi-Tek Video storefront. The owner's shadow could be seen behind the smoky glass. On the window was taped a picture of an old man with a silver goatee.

A few blocks south, Lily and her father sat in traffic. He tapped his cane against the side of the door as they inched forward. He looked at his watch and exhaled. Lily hadn't seen her father this animated since the stroke.

"I can walk from here," he said. He reached to unbuckle himself.

"No, Dad." She blocked his hand from the seat belt lock. "I want you to bring your wheelchair in case you get tired."

"I can sit anywhere if I get tired." He pushed her hand aside.

"But you'll get frustrated if you can't move around," she said.

"Who raised you to be my mother!" he pouted.

Despite his complaints, Lily knew her father liked being doted upon. She looked at him sulking. The left side of his face still drooped, but his speech was back to normal.

When she turned into the strip mall south of Vi-Tek Video, Lily saw a KTLA news van and media people setting up for the day's work. Across the street, the demonstrators chanted. Lily couldn't help thinking that they looked like ghosts, with their hollow eyes and extinct flags. After all, Ho was long dead and the Berlin Wall had fallen.

In the parking lot, some of her father's friends from the Vietnamese Chamber of Commerce greeted them. They helped him out of the car and took his wheelchair, but he refused to sit in it.

Lily told her father that she would wait for him at the Little Paris Coffee Shop. His friends were disappointed that she wasn't coming. She apologized, saying that she had to study. Her father asked them for the rundown of the activities. Lily watched as they walked toward the demonstration. Her father was in the middle, he moved effectively with his cane. To his right, Mr. Lai pushed the empty wheelchair.

She sat down with a *café sua da* and opened her organic chemistry textbook. She read her problem set. Outside, riot police arrived to protect the foolish man and his shop. Cars crawled along, honking in agreement or frustration. A man in a Ford Bronco screamed, "Fucking gooks!"

She heard what could have been her father's voice on the bullhorn. She couldn't make out what he was saying, but she didn't need to. Ever since she was a little girl her father had taken her to demonstrations of some kind or another: she sang the old national anthem at Tet Festivals; she handed out name tags at Army reunions and served punch at the Vietnamese Anti-Communist League planning meetings. Her father had notoriety in these organizations. Strangers whispered when he entered a room. He had been Chief of Police in Saigon.

In the coffee shop, a trickle of customers ordered sandwiches and tapioca drinks. A couple wore cheap shoes and acid-washed jeans. Next to them, a well-dressed girl ordered the special sandwich in perfect English. They watched the demonstration across the street with detached curiosity. The owner, a chubby woman, complained bitterly about the drop in business. "I have four kids to feed," she complained.

Lily moved to the back of the shop to concentrate on her problem set. She didn't see when the police had entered the man's shop. She didn't hear the cheering when they came out, carrying stacks of videotapes. She didn't know what was happening until her father returned and told her the police had closed the store for copyright infringement; the owner had duplicated hundreds of Hong Kong movies.

"And the picture?" she asked.

"The landlord removed it," he said with satisfaction.

When they arrived home, Lily's mother reminded her that all her sisters and their families were coming for dinner; even Rose was here for the weekend. Rose was the third eldest, the one that no one in the family could figure out. She went to school back East, became an artist, but no one was sure of what. She did a bit of everything. Once, Lily saw a performance at UCLA. Rose posed and preened on stage against a backdrop of projected images: aircraft carriers, combat scenes, school girls in white *ao dais*. Lily thought it was melodramatic, but she saw Rose's boyfriend at the time watching her; his eyes shone with puppy adoration.

Lily's mother was de-veining prawns. Inside the sink, a box of frozen calamari lay next to a large mollusk. Its feet sagged like a miniature elephant trunk. Lily often wondered who discovered that sea snails were edible.

"Could you clean the guest room?" her mother asked. Lily used it as a study, which meant that it was littered with books, papers, mugs, and McDonald's apple pie wrappers.

Rose pulled up in a white Neon; her hair had been cut short and highlighted red. She wore gigantic Jackie O. sunglasses, a black tank, black cropped pants, and red stilettos. As Lily and her mother stood by the front gate to greet Rose, Lily laughed at how out of place her sister looked in their neighborhood of square lawns and look-alike houses.

Rose dropped her bags and hugged her mother and sister. Lily put her arms around her sister awkwardly. Rose learned this custom from her friends, from being away so long.

Inside, their father was on the phone, still talking about victory. He nodded at Rose, who he had not seen in almost a year, and continued his conversation. Rose seemed offended at his disinterest, so Lily told her about the demonstration, the picture of Ho Chi Minh.

"He's a communist," their mother piped.

"That's not a crime," Rose said, as she poured herself a glass of water.

Their father gave Rose a disapproving look behind her back. Before she said anything else, Lily grabbed her by the elbow and escorted her to the guest room.

"Dad helped organize the demonstrations," Lily whispered.

"Doesn't he have anything better to do with his time?" Rose asked.

Lily gave her a condescending look: "Just humor him, OK?"

Plates of thin-sliced beef, shrimp, squid, and sea snail covered the table. In the center, a pot of vinegar broth boiled. The tart steam floated in the air, tickling nostrils. Lily passed a bowl of the dipping sauce, shrimp paste with pureed pineapple, lemongrass, garlic, and chili. The children ate at a separate table. Their mothers had already made little rolls for them, just beef and shrimp for Jessica and Jon, but Hien, who was only four, ate everything: the calamari, the sea snails, the pungent sauce. The three men sat on one end of the table and the five women the other; the men drank beer with ice, and the women drank 7-Up. The men talked about politics; the women, the food.

"Dad, have you thought about why that man put the picture up?" Rose asked. She took a bite out of her fondue roll.

"Because he's a communist, Thanh," her father said, using Rose's Vietnamese name.

"Yes, but why would he advertise it?"

"I'm not sure. You would have to ask him."

"Well, it seems like a lot to do about nothing," Rose said. She finished her roll.

"Nothing? Do you think the freedoms that you have here cost nothing?"

"That's not what I said."

"Stop it. I want a peaceful dinner," Rose's mom interrupted.

Lily kicked Rose under the table.

"This is delicious, Mother," Rose said. She smiled and made another roll.

Her father took a sip of beer.

To break the tension, Hien's mother asked Rose about her plans.

"I'm part of an exhibit in LA. The reception is tomorrow if you guys want to come," Rose said.

"I don't understand art," their father said.

"Well, I'd like to go," their mother offered.

"Me, too," Lily said.

With some prodding, Lily's father decided to join them.

After dinner, Rose and Lily went out to the garden to smoke. They stood underneath the fig tree. Its layered branches and broad leaves covered them from the house.

"Have they caught you yet?" Rose asked.

"No, they don't know," Lily said as she took a drag.

"Oh, they know," Rose laughed.

Rose took out a plastic bag filled with her smoking accoutrements and started to roll a joint. Lily wanted to stop her from smoking the joint now, but she knew Rose wouldn't listen to her. Lily poked her head between some leaves to look back at the house. Everybody else was still inside. Some of their father's friends had arrived and could be heard laughing.

"He looks terrible," Rose said.

"He's fine. He hasn't been this active since the stroke."

"You have to take that wheelchair away from him. He'll just rely on it and then really become a cripple."

"When did you become his physical therapist?" Lily asked. She was the one who had been driving their father to therapy for the past year.

"I'm sorry," Rose said. She took a toke and handed the joint to Lily.

"How's school?" Rose asked.

"Not good. I might flunk out."

"You're not serious."

"If I don't pass Orgo this quarter, I'm on academic probation."

Rose took another drag and said unconvincingly: "You're smart. You'll do fine."

They giggled at the belly-flop of an encouragement.

"Well, you didn't want to be a doctor anyway," Rose said.

"Thanks, that's really reassuring."

Rose patted Lily on the shoulder.

"Maybe you should take some time off. Figure it out," she said.

"What would I do with my time off?" Lily said.

"Whatever you want. You're not stuck being a goody-two-shoes for the rest of your life," Rose said.

"Is that what you think I am, Miss Flaky Artist?"

"Goody Two Shoes," Rose said and shoved Lily.

"Flaky," Lily responded, bumping her back.

When they were younger, Rose and Lily shared a bedroom. During the summers, when the lights were out and the window was opened, a soft breeze stirred and Rose would tell stories about Vietnam, about Tet and how it was a month-long celebration, about the attic of their grandfather's store filled with candles, funerary money, and a fine layer of dust and incense powder. Rose told stories about their grandfather, who Lily had known only through letters and photographs, about how once when they played soccer, his slippers flew away as he kicked the ball, or about the white sand beaches with water so salty and warm you could float in it. During those summers, Lily fell asleep dreaming of a Vietnam of moon cakes, paper houses, dancing dragons. Rose's stories were her only link to the past; everything else about Vietnam she learned from television.

The first time Lily saw the picture, she was seven. Rose and she were up late, watching a Vietnam War documentary on PBS. That night, the topic was the Tet Offensive of 1968. Their parents were already asleep and their older sisters, who worked as nail stylists, were in their room, plucking eyebrows or performing any of the endless beautifying regimes that Rose found tedious and Lily could not yet understand. The glow of the television filled the room with an eerie light. On the screen, they saw tanks level houses, men carried away in stretchers. Then, the image changed to show a South Vietnamese soldier holding a handgun. He was younger, but he had the same build, the same economical way of holding himself. He walked up to a prisoner, a man in a plaid shirt with his hands tied behind his back, and shot him in the temple. The sound of the handgun boomed, leaving silence in the room.

"Turn off the TV, Lily," Rose commanded.

In the following days, Rose went to the library and borrowed books about the War. She brought back photocopied pictures and chapters about the Tet Offensive. She seemed to be looking for something, some way to understand the past. After a week, she finally mustered the courage to ask him, but he was curt, elusive.

It was the first in a series of fights that led to their estrangement and Rose's absence from home. During her senior year in high school, Rose got into the Rhode Island School of Design and her parents did not want to let her go. They fought about it all spring, but she sent the acceptance letter to RISD anyway and declined all the local schools that her parents preferred. When her parents found out, they refused to pay for RISD. Rose took out more loans, worked two jobs that summer, and when August came, packed her bags and left.

When the day arrived, Rose's friend showed up in a beat-up Mustang to take her to the airport. Her mother cried, but she and her father were unemotional. He told her that if she left she wasn't allowed back in the house again. Rose responded by carrying her bags outside. Lily watched her family from the living room window. Her father stood on the front lawn watching Rose drive away. He seemed like the loneliest man in the world.

Lily and her mother supported her father out of the car. Because the sidewalk was too uneven from the roots of an old sycamore tree, they held him by the elbow toward the gallery. The foyer of the library at school sometimes displayed paintings and sculptures, but beyond noticing colors and shapes, Lily was not sure what else to make of art. As she signed the guestbook, she heard Rose ask their father if he remembered the photograph she showed him many years ago. He said he did. Then, someone shouted Rose's name and the woman pulled Rose into a circle, passing her from person to person. Rose introduced their parents and gestured toward Lily. Their parents nodded politely, but Lily could tell they were uncomfortable. Her father seemed tired from last night's festivities.

After the pleasantries, Rose took their father by the hand and led him toward the far wall. Lily could make out a black and white painting behind the backs of strangers. As they got closer and people fanned out, she could tell that it was the picture of the execution. Rose had reproduced the image hundreds of times and arranged them into a large quilt. Next to it was a caption. Instead of referring to the War, to public opinion, to the circumstances around the shooting, the caption read simply: "Father, at Left."

Linda Purdy

WAITING FOR THE LIGHT TO CHANGE

Linda Purdy was born in Orange in 1943 and earned a BA in English from Whittier College and a Master of Library and Information Science from CSU Fullerton. Her poetry and prose have appeared in *The Ear*, *Faultline, International Harvest*, and the *Santa Monica Review*, and at the Smithsonian Photography Initiative.

Purdy's fiction envisions challenging moments of everyday life, and in the piece that follows, it is the matter of how to respond when witnessing a police chase. Composed with both heartstopping realism and deadpan hilarity, the only fictional part, Purdy told us, is the letter to the traffic sergeant: "That's the part I *wish* were true," she said. The story appeared in the *Santa Monica Review* in 2010.

LOIS WAS LOST in the beauty of the sunlight on the waxen magnolia leaves as she waited in a left turn pocket for the light to turn green. Her 1990 smoke-blue Mercury diesel was the only car waiting on this May spring day in Tustin, where the man-made world of her nondescript Southern California neighborhood seemed oblivious to the larger universe it inhabited. Her neighborhood was a grid of streets named for the wives of developers. Charlene Circle to the north, Priscilla Drive to the east, Nadine Loop to the south, and Judy Way to the west were the boundaries of her tract, Deer Run, where the only deer were the lighted deer that decorated the lawns at Christmas, plugged into a generator so their heads could bob up and down, imitating the pastoral grazing of real deer.

Lois was enthralled by the flickering light on the big, shiny magnolia leaves of the trees that rose from a backyard enclosed by a cinder block fence, built to drown out the noise of the four lanes of Red Hill Avenue, which ran north and south, as an alternative to the 55 freeway. Lois marveled how light from a star ninety-four million miles from Earth could send sunbeams across the heavens, land on the waxen magnolia leaves in Tustin, California, and make the trees grow, through photosynthesis. "Natural law is all we need," thought Lois as she waited for the light to change, one eye on the traffic signal, the other on the glory of the sunlit leaves.

Red Hill Avenue was named for a real local landmark in Tustin, a small hill, probably with a deposit of iron in the soil, which marked the divide between the higher elevations of Tustin and the flatlands, where Lois lived. A center divider on Red Hill Avenue, planted with low-maintenance greenery, separated its four lanes. The divider jogged inward at the intersection of Red Hill Avenue and Walnut Avenue, where there were no walnut trees, creating a pocket for those turning left. Lois's diesel Mercury was the only car waiting in the left turn pocket, waiting for the signal to go through its long cycle. The two north-moving lanes to her right were bumper to bumper with traffic, also waiting at the red light. The Toyotas, the Nissans, even the BMWs all looked alike, as if inspired by the shape of a potato. That monotony made the magnolia leaves and the sun even more spectacular.

Lost in reverie, when Lois heard the wail of sirens, she took a few seconds to realize that she was a sitting duck in the left turn pocket. The screaming sirens sounded mean and fierce, as if they were after the Crook of the Century. The wail was coming from the south behind her, and the congested lanes of northbound cars to her right had no room to yield. Lois knew that her car was not visible to the oncoming posse, and that to the galloping suspect in a tan panel truck and to the police cars in pursuit, the left turn lane would seem like clear passage to continue their good-against-evil high-speed chase. To be caught in a police chase after contemplating the miracle of photosynthesis seemed like a non sequitur, but life can be very rude. Lois prepared to die as the image of the tan panel truck got bigger and bigger in her rearview mirror.

The left turn pocket was now a pocket of time and space where the impossible of impossibles happened, a miracle as improbable as photosynthesis. When the clumsy panel truck saw her, the driver turned sharply to avoid her and his truck leapt the center divider into the lanes of oncoming southbound traffic, and then all three of the pursuing police cars did the same. Like a nightmare, each screeching police car, with its jukebox of flashing lights, loomed in Lois's rearview mirror, and then, as if by cue, each leapt the center divider, becoming airborne, like horses leaping a hurdle in an equestrian show, landing on two wheels, righting themselves, and then speeding into oncoming traffic in pursuit of their prey. One thought went through Lois's head during these few seconds: "I have a full tank of gas." This called her back to Earth.

As the fourth wailing police car approached in her rearview mirror, Lois finally broke the law and got out of the way, as necessity trumped her rule-bound mind; she was the obstacle here. She swung a wide right turn from the left turn lane onto Walnut, and then right on Charlene Circle, left on Priscilla, another left on Judy, then a right into her home at 1492 Nadine Loop. She parked in the driveway, still not sure why she had escaped a rear-end collision four times in a row, with her full tank of gas. She was glad to be alive, but even in her dazed state of mind, she knew the real criminals were the police, who were probably bored of writing parking tickets and tired of stopping drivers for seat belt violations, and were swept into this cowboy-and-Indian mentality by a hunger for some real police action. She didn't feel like falling to the ground in thanksgiving for escaping such foolishness.

Lois shakily unlocked the side door to her tract home, poured herself a glass of wine, sat down at the kitchen table, and wondered what to do. Such a moment required some kind of response, something more than a prayer of gratitude or some platitude like, "It wasn't my time to go." She decided to write a letter to the Traffic Division of the Tustin Police, whose chief officer she found on the Tustin city website. She opened her desk, pulled out the yellow legal pad, which she usually used for composing letters she never sent, and began to write:

Dear Sergeant Gray,

I think I may have accidently wandered onto a movie set today. I was caught in a high-speed police chase in downtown Tustin, with police cars flying over the center divider on Red Hill Avenue in pursuit of a tan panel truck. I'd like to know if your officers moonlight as stunt car drivers. If you were shooting a movie, don't you think it would have been smart to give us some warning, or if this was reality TV, don't I get a check? What crime could justify such risk, such recklessness, on a city street? Were they chasing a murderer? I thought the law was written to protect the innocent.

Sincerely,
Lois Smith

She read her letter. It was too confrontational, too smart-ass. Sergeant Gray would throw it in the trash as a personal affront. There would be no response. She would write a letter that he would never expect, something so la-la land that even though he threw it away, the subliminal message might linger. Reading a letter from a kook, he might even drop his defenses long enough to hear her plea.

Dear Sergeant Gray,

Today as I waited for the light to change at Red Hill and Walnut Avenue, my mind left my body and flew into the magnolia trees in a backyard in the Deer Run tract adjacent to Red Hill. I was amazed that a star ninety-four million miles from Earth was helping the trees grow through photosynthesis as the sunlight shimmered on the waxen, shiny leaves. I had the thought that natural law is far superior to civil law. Has it ever occurred to you that catching a petty thief is as simple as taking down his license number and finding his residence through the *DMV*, as simple as the sunlight finding the leaves of a magnolia tree in faraway Tustin, California? The power of sunlight might easily incinerate a magnolia tree, but the sun wisely keeps a far distance and still gets the job done.

Sincerely,
Lois Smith

Before she could change her mind, Lois addressed an envelope to Sergeant Gray, pulled a Liberty Bell stamp off a sheet of stamps and walked her letter to the mailbox.

Raul Alvarez

MAKE ME A HOOT OWL TOO, SWEETHEART

Raul Alvarez was born in Fullerton in 1985 and attended Fullerton High School. He received his BA in English from CSU Fullerton in 2008 and his MFA in creative writing from Columbia College Chicago in 2012. His poetry has been included in several literary journals, including *PANK*, *Court Green*, *Pinwheel*, and *Fanzine*, and he has been nominated for a Pushcart Prize. He works for the Northwest Immigrant Rights Project in Seattle, Washington.

In 2011, Fullerton police fatally beat a mentally ill man named Kelly Thomas, and the ensuing community activism and legal action by Thomas's father helped bring national attention to law enforcement failures and allegations of abuse. Alvarez explores the incident in this essay, taken from his first book, *There Was So Much Beautiful Left*, published by Boost House in 2015.

A FEW YEARS AGO three police officers beat a homeless bipolar schizophrenic man to death with their fists over the course of about 10 minutes. His name was Kelly, he used to hang out by the McDonald's next to my high school, and my mom loved him.

She's bipolar and schizophrenic too. She'd buy Kelly a couple cheeseburgers when she took me and my brother through the drive-thru because she's a saint and has a good heart and knows when someone needs a burger to help the day go down. She also convinced herself without ever asking him if he liked cheeseburgers that he liked cheeseburgers more than anything else, which is nice and is also odd, and explains a lot about my mother.

He'd sometimes smile and he'd sometimes say nothing and he'd sometimes shuffle his feet awkwardly but he'd always accept the burger and hold it in his hands like you'd hold a gentle and important object given to you by someone you respect.

My mother would hold mostly one-way conversations at Kelly during these exchanges. "Oh beautiful this is for you! Can you believe the weather hahahahaha it's just utterly Parisian! You know my sons think you're swell, don't you? They really do even if they don't say it. You're a doll this is for you don't let it ruin your figure." My mother is the sum total of all the characters in a Fitzgerald novel. She is a raw nerve of earnest love.

So when some officers received a report that a man was breaking into cars in a parking lot downtown they went over and saw Kelly, who they knew because everyone knew him because in Fullerton there aren't a lot of homeless people and it's easy to point them out when you're driving to your friend's house or your job or your mom's or your church or wherever like, "hey look there's that guy" and you feel sad or you feel numb or really you feel like people become part of the scenery like your family around the dinner table or the pastor who gives the big deal sermons on holidays.

And Kelly was having a bad night, of course, because when you're schizophrenic things are pretty much a roll of the dice and that night the dice said FUCK YOU and Kelly's victims were business owners who subsist on decorum and the officers' victim was a lonely guy who subsisted on the chance kindness of strangers and a nightmarish, random, crippling fear. An interesting part of this story is that the person that called the cops on him is the owner of a place called the Slidebar and he used to be the lead singer of the band Lit, whose biggest hit was the song "My Own Worst Enemy."

Kelly was acting rashly. He was initially non-cooperative. He was being slightly violent. Yes, obviously. He was a victim of an illness that tears your consciousness into pieces so small you can't remember the sound of your voice. And multiple grown men blessed with rational minds and steady work and a familiar place to sleep decided to eschew a night of difficult grace for a night of difficult violence and Kelly's body finally resembled his beaten mind on the floor of his home, the city streets of Fullerton, California.

In the surveillance video of Kelly's murder, which is awful, which is terribly and unequivocally awful, he spends 1 minute taunting the officers, 2 minutes apologizing, 3 minutes pleading for them to stop, and the small remainder of his life crying Dad, Dad, Dad, Dad, Dad.

I recently called my mom and asked her if she remembered Kelly.

"Who?"

"Kelly Thomas."

"Who's that?"

"He was the young guy who used to hang out by the McDonald's by Fullerton High. You always used to talk to him."

"Oh sweetheart I thought he was a friend of yours!"

"Mom, you didn't think that. He was homeless and at least 10 years older than me."

"Oh I remember him, he was such a cutie! How's he doing?"

After two years of red tape and criminal charges and protests, the three men, Officer Manuel Ramos, Officer Jay Cicinelli, and Officer Joseph Wolfe, who killed Kelly by crushing his chest until his lungs collapsed, who killed Kelly by prying his face open, who killed Kelly by persistent fistfuls, were declared unanimously not guilty of second-degree murder and use of excessive force and involuntary manslaughter by a trial of 12 human beings.

"He was murdered, Mom."

"Oh honey what are you talking about?"

"He was the guy on TV that the police killed. Didn't you see that story?"

"Oh honey.

If you write about him make him a hoot owl. He had wise eyes sweetheart, you need to talk about his wise eyes.

Make me a hoot owl too."

The morning I heard the news I sat staring at nothing in particular and felt ashamed. I felt ashamed for not looking Kelly in the eyes 12 years before as I sat in the passenger seat of my mother's neon green Geo Metro.

I felt ashamed for not stepping out of the car and putting my hands on both sides of his face and mouthing the words I love you and I will remember you when I am older and living in a city you've never been to where the weather is a complete asshole and when I remember you I will remember an article in the Atlantic I read about the systemic torture of mentally ill inmates in South Carolina prisons who did not get away with murder who did not get away with murder who did not get away with murder but who were forced to live in solitary confinement for 8 years without medication or human contact or a toilet who were forced to lay tied down to a table with wet rags and left with their legs and arms splayed outside during winter nights and who were each and every one a hoot owl just like you because you are all dead and when you ate you ate with joy and shuffled your feet or you are still standing with nothing in your hands the second before Officer Ramos says the history of schizophrenia is complex and does not lend itself easily to a linear narrative and you say bring it on and Officer Ramos says you see these fists because they're getting ready to fuck you up and you say bring it on and maybe my mom is there too waiting to be plucked like an eyelash from your wise eyes before they are reborn into a quiet, hungry blue.

IRVINE

*I*rvine: a new Silicon Valley. Electronic
factories with no openings to the outside
world, like integrated circuits....By a terrible
twist of irony it just had to be here, in the hills
of Irvine, that they shot Planet of the Apes.

—JEAN BAUDRILLARD, FROM *AMERICA*, 1989
(TRANSLATED BY CHRIS TURNER)

Joan Didion

---

from *WHERE I WAS FROM*

Joan Didion was born in 1934 in Sacramento and earned a BA in English from UC Berkeley. She has had a long career in literary journalism and as a novelist, screenwriter, memoirist, and playwright. Her early collection *Slouching Towards Bethlehem* (1968) established her career as an essayist, and her melding of political and personal writing—frequently about her own identity as a Californian—is a hallmark of her work, most recently in evidence in her nonfiction collection *We Tell Ourselves Stories in Order to Live*. Her five novels include *Play It As Lays* and *Democracy*.

Her 2003 essay collection, *Where I Was From*, considers the history and culture of California through the experience of her own privileged family—an experience that frequently challenges the pioneer narrative and confronts its contradictions and hypocrisies. In this excerpt from the book, she turns her critical eye to the story of one singular Orange County family.

IN THE MAY 1935 ISSUE of the *American Mercury*, William Faulkner published one of the few pieces of fiction he set in California, a short story he called "Golden Land." "Golden Land" deals with a day in the life of Ira Ewing, Jr., age forty-eight, a man for whom "twenty-five years of industry and desire, of shrewdness and luck and even fortitude," seem recently to have come to ashes. At fourteen, Ira Ewing had fled Nebraska on a westbound freight. By the time he was thirty, he had married the daughter of a Los Angeles carpenter, fathered a son and a daughter, and secured a foothold in the real estate business. By the time we meet him, eighteen years later, he is in a position to spend fifty thousand dollars a year, a sizable amount in 1935. He has been able to bring his widowed mother from Nebraska and install her in a house in

Glendale. He has been able to provide for his children "luxuries and advantages which his own father not only could not have conceived in fact but would have condemned completely in theory."

Yet nothing is working out. Ira's daughter, Samantha, who wants to be in show business and has taken the name "April Lalear," is testifying in a lurid trial reported on page one ("April Lalear Bares Orgy Secrets") of the newspapers placed on the reading table next to Ira's bed. Ira, less bewildered than weary, tries not to look at the accompanying photographs of Samantha, the "hard, blonde, and inscrutable" daughter who "alternately stared back or flaunted long pale shins." Nor is Samantha the exclusive source of the leaden emptiness Ira now feels instead of hunger: there is also his son, Voyd, who continues to live at home but has not spoken unprompted to his father in two years, not since the morning when Voyd, drunk, was delivered home to his father wearing, "in place of underclothes, a woman's brassiere and step-ins."

Since Ira prides himself on being someone who will entertain no suggestion that his life is not the success that his business achievement would seem to him to promise, he discourages discussion of his domestic trials, and has tried to keep the newspapers featuring April Lalear and the orgy secrets away from his mother. Via the gardener, however, Ira's mother has learned about her granddaughter's testimony, and she is reminded of the warning she once gave her son, after she had seen Samantha and Voyd stealing cash from their mother's purse: "You make money too easy," she had told Ira. "This whole country is too easy for us Ewings. It may be all right for them that have been born here for generations, I don't know about that. But not for us."

"But these children were born here," Ira had said.

"Just one generation," his mother had said. "The generation before that they were born in a sod-roofed dugout on the Nebraska wheat frontier. And the one before that in a log house in Missouri. And the one before that in a Kentucky blockhouse with Indians around it. This world has never been easy for Ewings. Maybe the Lord never intended it to be."

"But it is from now on," the son had insisted. "For you and me too. But mostly for them."

"Golden Land" does not entirely hold up, nor, I would guess, will it ever be counted among the best Faulkner stories. Yet it retains, for certain Californians, a nagging resonance, and opens the familiar troubling questions. I grew up in a California family that derived, from the single circumstance of having been what Ira Ewing's mother called "born here for generations," considerable pride, much of it, it seemed to me later, strikingly unearned. "The trouble with these new people," I recall hearing again and again as a child in Sacramento, "is they think it's supposed to be easy." The phrase "these new people" generally signified people who had moved to California after World War Two, but was tacitly extended back to include the migration from the Dust Bowl during the 1930s, and often further. New people, we were given to understand, remained ignorant of our special history, insensible to the hardships endured to make it, blind not only to the dangers the place still presented but to the shared responsibilities its continued habitation demanded.

If my grandfather spotted a rattlesnake while driving, he would stop his car and go into the brush after it. To do less, he advised me more than once, was to endanger whoever later entered the brush, and so violate what he called "the code of the West." New people, I was told, did not understand their responsibility to kill rattlesnakes. Nor did new people understand that the water that came from the tap in, say, San Francisco, was there only because part of Yosemite had been flooded to put it there. New people did not understand the necessary dynamic of the fires, the seven-year cycles of flood and drought, the physical reality of the place. "Why didn't they go back to Truckee?" a young mining engineer from back East asked when my grandfather pointed out the site of the Donner Party's last encampment. I recall hearing this story repeatedly. I also recall the same grandfather, my mother's father, whose family had migrated from the hardscrabble Adirondack frontier in the eighteenth century to the hardscrabble Sierra Nevada foothills in the nineteenth, working himself up into writing an impassioned letter-to-the-editor over a fifth-grade textbook in which one of the illustrations summed up California history as a sunny progression from Spanish Señorita to Gold Miner to Golden Gate Bridge. What the illustration seemed to my grandfather to suggest was that those responsible for the textbook believed the settlement of California to have been "easy," history rewritten, as he saw it, for the new people. There were definite ambiguities in this: Ira Ewing and his children were, of course, new people, but so, less than a century before, had my grandfather's family been. New people could be seen, by people like my grandfather, as indifferent to everything that had made California work, but the ambiguity was this: new people were also who were making California rich.

Californians whose family ties to the state predate World War Two have an equivocal and often uneasy relationship to the postwar expansion. Joan Irvine Smith, whose family's eighty-eight-thousand-acre ranch in Orange County was developed during the 1960s, later created, on the twelfth floor of the McDonnell Douglas Building in Irvine, a city that did not exist before the Irvines developed their ranch, the Irvine Museum, dedicated to the California impressionist or plein air paintings she had begun collecting in 1991. "There is more nostalgia for me in these paintings than in actually going out to look at what used to be the ranch now that it has been developed, because I'm looking at what I looked at as a child," she told *Art in California* about this collection. Her attraction to the genre had begun, she said, when she was a child and would meet her stepfather for lunch at the California Club, where the few public rooms in which women were at that time allowed were decorated with California landscapes lent by the members. "I can look at those paintings and see what the ranch was as I remember it when I was a little girl."

The California Club, which is on Flower Street in downtown Los Angeles, was then and is still the heart of Southern California's old-line business establishment, the Los Angeles version of the Bohemian and

Pacific Union Clubs in San Francisco. On any given day since World War Two, virtually everyone lunching at the California Club, most particularly not excluding Joan Irvine, has had a direct or indirect investment in the development of California, which is to say in the obliteration of the undeveloped California on display at the Irvine Museum. In the seventy-four paintings chosen for inclusion in *Selections from the Irvine Museum,* the catalogue published by the museum to accompany a 1992 traveling exhibition, there are hills and desert and mesas and arroyos. There are mountains, coastline, big sky. There are stands of eucalyptus, sycamore, oak, cottonwood. There are washes of California poppies. As for fauna, there are, in the seventy-four paintings, three sulphur-crested cockatoos, one white peacock, two horses, and nine people, four of whom are dwarfed by the landscape and two of whom are indistinct Indians paddling a canoe.

Some of this is romantic (the indistinct Indians), some washed with a slightly falsified golden light, in the tradition that runs from Bierstadt's "lustrous, pearly mist" to the "Kinkade Glow." Most of these paintings, however, reflect the way the place actually looks, or looked, not only to Joan Irvine but also to me and to anyone else who knew it as recently as 1960. It is this close representation of a familiar yet vanished landscape that gives the Irvine collection its curious effect, that of a short-term memory misfire: these paintings hang in a city, Irvine (population more than one hundred and fifty thousand, with a University of California campus enrolling some nineteen thousand students), that was forty years ago a mirror image of the paintings themselves, bean fields and grazing, the heart but by no means all of the cattle and sheep operation amassed by the great-grandfather of the founder of the Irvine Museum.

The disposition of such a holding can be, for its inheritors, a fraught enterprise. "On the afternoon of his funeral we gathered to honor this man who had held such a legacy intact for the main part of his ninety-one years," Jane Hollister Wheelwright wrote in *The Ranch Papers* about the aftermath of her father's death and the prospect of being forced to sell the Hollister ranch. "All of us were deeply affected. Some were stunned by the prospect of loss; others gloated, contemplating cash and escape.

We were bitterly divided, but none could deny the power of that land. The special, spiritually meaningful (and often destructive) impact of the ranch was obvious. I proved it by my behavior, as did the others."

That was 1961. Joan Irvine Smith had replaced her mother on the board of the Irvine Company four years before, in 1957, the year she was twenty-four. She had seen, a good deal more clearly and realistically than Jane Hollister Wheelwright would see four years later, the solution she wanted for her family's ranch, and she had seen the rest of the Irvine board as part of the problem: by making small deals, selling off bits of the whole, the board was nibbling away at the family's principal asset, the size of its holding. It was she who pressed the architect William Pereira to present a master plan. It was she who saw the potential return in giving the land for a University of California campus. It was she, most importantly, who insisted on maintaining an interest in the ranch's development. And, in the end, which meant after years of internecine battles and a series of litigations extending to 1991, it was she who more or less prevailed. In 1960, before the Irvine ranch was developed, there were 719,500 people in all of Orange County. In 2000 there were close to 3 million, most of whom would not have been there had two families, the Irvines in the central part of the county and the inheritors of Richard O'Neill's Rancho Santa Margarita and Mission Viejo acreage in the southern, not developed their ranches.

This has not been a case in which the rising tide floated all boats. Not all of Orange County's new residents came to realize what would have seemed the middle-class promise of its growth. Not all of those residents even had somewhere to live: some settled into the run-down motels built in the mid-1950s, at the time Disneyland opened, and were referred to locally, because they had nowhere else to live and could not afford the deposits required for apartment rental, as "motel people." In his 1986 *The New California: Facing the 21st Century,* the political columnist Dan Walters quoted *The Orange County Register* on motel people: "Mostly Anglo, they're the county's newest migrant workers: instead of picking grapes, they inspect semiconductors." This kind of week-by-week or even day-by-day living arrangement has taken hold in other parts of the country, but remains particularly entrenched in Southern California, where apartment rents rose to meet the increased demand from people priced out of a housing market in which even the least promising bungalow can sell for several hundred thousand dollars. By the year 2000, according to *The Los Angeles Times,* some hundred Orange County motels were inhabited almost exclusively by the working poor, people who made, say, $280 a week sanding airplane parts, or $7 an hour at Disney's "California Adventure" park. "A land celebrating the richness and diversity of California, its natural resources, and pioneering spirit of its people," the web site for "California Adventure" read. "I can look at these paintings and look back," Joan Irvine Smith told *Art in California* about the collection she bought with the proceeds of looking exclusively, and to a famous degree, forward. "I can see California as it was and as we will never see it again." Hers is an extreme example of the conundrum that to one degree or another confronts any Californian who profited from the boom years: if we could still see California as it was, how many of us could now afford to see it?

Andrew Lakritz

THE BIRTH OF THE SANTA ANAS

Andrew Lakritz was born in Tucson, Arizona, in 1956 and grew up in the
San Joaquin Valley. He received his BA, MFA, and PhD from UC Irvine. He
is the author of a book on American literary modernism called *Modernism
and the Other in Stevens, Frost, and Moore*, and his poems and articles have
been published in numerous journals and literary magazines. He has taught
cultural studies and English and American literature in the United States,
Poland, Brazil, and Kazakhstan. For the last sixteen years he has worked in
financial technologies.

Gleaned from his time living in Orange County while a UC Irvine graduate student, he told us that "The Birth of the Santa Anas," first published in
the Irvine Valley College journal the *Elephant Ear* in 1984, is "a reverie on the
winds that impact Orange County each winter, typically in February, whipping down canyons and dry gulches and having a reputation for putting the
population, especially young people, on edge."

> For every child there is a stone,
> and for every stone a hundred red coals
> burn through the unhealed air
> that catches at the window locks,
> pulls at eucalyptus root, overhauls
> red clay thatch, discovers in moments
> of repose the shadow's empty inertia:
> canyon homes burn into themselves,
> send charred offerings to the sea.

Many children have come into the world of late.
I know this for in a dream I saw the red coals
of Havana cigars burn darkly from a hundred
balconies near my own. When I awoke this morning,
I lit one for myself, unfolded an old lawn chair
nostalgic for a lawn, and listened,
fifteen feet above the winter grass:
"It's a girl" wailed the still morning
against a mother's good nature.

Soon the winds came up, and I knew
that smoking the slow fire down its bolt
there on the hovering deck would clear air
of all its late-drawn poisons,
of all the cries from incommodious corners,
of all the shadows caught unkempt, disheveled,
from underneath unhoused stones,
of all the shadows lying in wait.

About the stones uncovered deep
where the sun has never gone down
and wind is just rumor:
what is left when the only stones we find
have been breeding in fleshy folds
all those wild nights, waiting
for a benediction the last one out
had forgotten? Who was the last one out?
Where had he gone?

We would remember, later,
only that a child had come into the room.
She could hear the wind gust outside
but what it meant for her I could not read.
Only the tumbleweeds knew what they wanted:

their dreamy bones flew on,
and swallows raced a hundred miles an hour
into the blank hot morning,

and with every burst of wing as from a cannon
I heard that child cry down the long future.

Kim Stanley Robinson

---

from *THE GOLD COAST*

Kim Stanley Robinson was born in Illinois in 1952 but grew up in Southern California. He earned a BA in literature from UC San Diego, an MA in English from Boston University, and a PhD from UC San Diego, for which he wrote his doctoral thesis on the novels of Philip K. Dick. The winner of multiple Hugo and Nebula Awards, Robinson has written nineteen books and dozens of short stories. He is noted for exploring ecological and political themes as both a novelist and a thinker.

In these excerpts from his 1988 novel *The Gold Coast*—the second book of his Three Californias trilogy—Robinson juxtaposes the actual story of Orange County's "development" with a nightmarish fictional, and yet perhaps nearly inevitable, anti-history of a profoundly unplanned community built on the destruction of once-wild lands. Out of love for the remaining natural world, tenderly described by the author, the novel's hero reluctantly embraces resistance to the twenty-first-century dystopia that today, thirty years later, may seem indistinguishable from reality.

IN 1940 THE population was 130,000. By 1980 it was 2,000,000. At that point the northwestern half of the county was saturated. La Habra, Brea, Yorba Linda, Placentia, Fullerton, Buena Park, La Mirada, Cerritos, La Palma, Cypress, Stanton, Anaheim, Orange, Villa Park, El Modena, Santa Ana, Garden Grove, Westminster, Fountain Valley, Los Alamitos, Seal Beach, Huntington Beach, Newport Beach, Costa Mesa, Corona del Mar, Irvine, Tustin: all of these cities had grown, merged, melted together, until the idea that twenty-seven cities existed on the land was just a fiction of administration, a collection of unnoticed street signs, announcing borders that only the maps knew. It was one city.

This new megacity, "Orange County North," had as its transport system the freeways. The private car was the only way; the little train system of the early days had been pulled out, like the more extensive electric rail network in Los Angeles, to make more room for cars. In the end there were no trains, no buses, no trams, no subways. People had to drive cars to work, to get food, to do all the chores, to play—to do anything.

So after the completion of the Santa Ana Freeway in the late 1950s, the others quickly followed. The Newport and Riverside Freeways bisected the county into its northwest and southeast halves; the San Diego Freeway followed the coast, extended the Santa Ana Freeway south to San Diego; the Garden Grove, Orange, and San Gabriel Freeways added ribbing to the system, so that one could get to within a few miles of anywhere in Orange County North that one wanted to go, all on the freeways.

Soon the northwestern half was saturated, every acre of land bought, covered with concrete, built on, filled up. Nothing left but the dry bed of the Santa Ana River, and even that was banked and paved.

Then the Irvine Ranch was bought by a development company. For years the county government had taxed the ranch as hard as it could, trying to force it out of agriculture, into more tract housing. Now they got their wish. The new owners made a general plan that was (at first) unusually slow and thoughtful by Orange County standards; the University of California was given ten thousand acres, a town was built around it, a development schedule was worked up for the rest of the land. But the wedge was knocked into the southeast half of the county, and the pressure for growth drove it ever harder.

Meanwhile, in the northwest half the congestion grew with an intensity that the spread to the southeast couldn't help; in fact, given the thousands of new users that the southward expansion gave to the freeway system, it only made things worse. The old Santa Ana Freeway, three lanes in each direction, was clogged every day; the same was true of the Newport Freeway, and to a lesser extent of all the freeways. And yet there was no room left to widen them. What to do?

In the 1980s a plan was put forth to build an elevated second story for the Santa Ana Freeway, between Buena Park and Tustin; and in the 1990s, with the prospect of the county's population doubling again in ten years, the Board of Supervisors acted on it. Eight new lanes were put up on an elevated viaduct, set on massive pylons thirty-seven feet above the old freeway; they were opened to southbound traffic in 1998. Three years later the same was done for the Newport and Garden Grove Freeways, and in the triangle of the elevated freeways, three miles on each side, the elevated lanes were joined by elevated gas stations and convenience stops and restaurants and movie theaters and all the rest. It was the beginning of the "second story" of the city.

The next generation of freeways were the Foothill, Eastern, and San Joaquin, all designed to ease the access to the southern half of the county. When those were in it made sense to connect the ends of the Garden Grove and Foothill Freeways, which were only a few miles from each other; and so they were spliced by a great viaduct above Cowan and Lemon Heights, leaving the homes below devalued but intact. Then the new Santiago and Cleveland Freeways were built in the same way, flying through the sky on great pylons, above the new condos springing up everywhere in the back hills, in what used to be Irvine Ranch, Mission Viejo Ranch, O'Neill Ranch—now the new towns of Santiago, Silverado, Trabuco, Seaview Terrace, San Juan Springs, Los Pinos, O'Neill, Ortega, Saddleback, Alicia, and so on and so on. And as the land was subdivided, platted, developed, covered with concrete, built up, the freeway system grew with it. When the national push for the electromagnetic road track system began, the freeways of Orange County were in place and ready for it; it only took five years to make the change, and work created by this transformation helped head off the recession of the Boring Twenties before it plunged into outright worldwide depression. A new transport system, a new boom; always the case in Orange County, as in all the American West.

So the southeast half of Orange County, when the flood burst over the Irvine Ranch and the development began, grew even faster than the northwest half had, fifty years before. In thirty quick years it became indistinguishable from the rest of the megacity. The only land left was the Cleveland National Forest. The real estate companies hungrily eyed this empty, dry, hilly land; what condos could be put up there, what luxury homes, on the high slopes of old Saddleback Mountain! And it only took a sympathetic administration in Washington to begin the dismemberment of this insignificant little national forest. Not even any forest there! Why worry about it! The county was crowded, they needed that 66,000 acres for more homes, more jobs, more profits, more cars, more money, more weapons, more drugs, more real estate, more freeways! And so that land was sold too.

And none of that ever went away.

Nobody home.

How did it happen?

At first it was a result of the tracts, the freeways, the cars. If you lived in a new suburb, then you had to drive to do your shopping. How much easier to park in one place, and do all your shopping in one location!

So the malls began. At first they were just shopping centers. A big asphalt parking lot, surrounded on two or three sides by stores; there were scores of them, as in most of the rest of America.

Then they became complexes of parking lots mixed with islands of stores, as in Fashion Square, the oldest shopping center in the county. They were popular. They did great at Christmas-time. In effect they became the functional equivalent of villages, places where you could walk to everything you needed—villages tucked like islands into the multilayered texture of autopia. Once you parked at a shopping center, you could return to a life on foot. And at that idea the body, the brain-stem, said Yeah.

South Coast Plaza was one of the first to go beyond this idea, to complete the square of stores and roof it, putting the parking lot on the outside. Call it a mall. An air-conditioned island village—except, of course, that all the villagers were visitors.

When South Coast Plaza opened in 1967 it was a giant success, and the Segerstrom family, heirs to the lima bean king C. J. Segerstrom, kept building on their land until they had the mall of malls, the equivalent of several fifty-story buildings spread out over a thousand acres, all of it enclosed. A sort of spaceship village grounded on the border between Santa Ana and Costa Mesa.

They made a lot of money.

Other malls sprang up, like daughter mushrooms in a ring around SCP. They all grew, enclosing more space, allowing more consumers to spend their time indoors. Westminster Mall, Huntington Center, Fashion Island, the Orange Mall, Buena Park Center, the City, Anaheim Plaza, Brea Mall, Laguna Hills Mall, Orange Fair Center, Cerritos Center, Honer Plaza, La Habra Fashion Square, Tustin Mall, Mission Viejo Fair, Trabuco Marketplace, the Mission Mall, Canyon Center, all were in place and flourishing by the end of the century, growing by accretion, taking up the surrounding neighborhoods, adding stores, restaurants, banks, gyms, boutiques, hairdressers, aps, condos. Yes, you could live in a mall if you wanted to. A lot of people did.

By 2020 their number had doubled again, and many square miles of Orange County were roofed and air-conditioned. When the Cleveland National Forest was developed there was room for a big one; Silverado Mall rivaled SCP for floor space, and in 2027 it became the biggest mall of all—a sign that the back country had arrived at last.

The malls merged perfectly with the new elevated freeway system, and midcounty it was often possible to take an off-ramp directly into a parking garage, from which one could take an escalator through the maze of a mall's outer perimeter, and return to your ap, or go to dinner, or continue your shopping, without ever coming within thirty feet of the buried ground. Everything you needed to do, you could do in a mall.

You could live your life indoors.

And none of that, of course, ever went away.

This is the chapter I have not been able to write.

Through the 1950s and 1960s the groves were torn down at the rate of several acres every day. The orchard keepers and their trees had fought off a variety of blights in previous years—the cottony cushion scale, the black scale, the red scale, the "quick decline"—but they had never faced this sort of blight before, and the decline this time was quicker than ever. In these years they harvested not the fruit, but the trees.

This is how they did it.

Gangs of men came in with trucks and equipment. First they cut the trees down with chain saws. This was the simple part, the work of a minute. Thirty seconds, actually: one quick downward bite, the chain saw pulled out, one quick upward bit.

The trees fall.

Chains and ropes are tossed over the fallen branches, and electric reels haul them over to big dumpsters. Men with smaller chain saws cut the fallen trees into parts, and the parts are fed into an automatic shredder that hums constantly, whines and shrieks when branches are fed into it. Wood chips are all that come out.

Leaves and broken oranges are scattered over the torn ground. There is a tangy, dusty citrus smell in the air; the dust that is part of the bark of these trees has been scattered to the sky.

The stumps are harder. A backhoelike tractor is brought to the stump. The ground around the stump is spaded, churned up, softened. Chains are secured around the trunk, right at ground level, or even beneath it, around the biggest root exposed. Then the tractor backs off, jerks. Gears grind, the diesel engine grunts and hums, black fumes shoot out the exhaust pipe at the sky. In jerks the stump heaves out of the ground. The root systems are not very big, nor do they extend very deeply. Still, when the whole thing is hauled away to the waiting dumpsters, there is a considerable crater left behind.

The eucalyptus trees are harder. Bringing the trees down is still relatively easy; several strokes of a giant chain saw, with ropes tied around the tree to bring it down in the desired direction. But then the trunk has to be sawed into big sections, like loggers' work, and the immense cylinders are lifted by bulldozers and small cranes onto the backs of waiting trucks. And the stumps are more stubborn; roots have to be cut away, some digging done, before the tractors can succeed in yanking them up. The eucalyptus have been planted so close together that the roots have intertwined, and it's safest to bring down only every third tree, then start on the ones left. The pungent dusty smell of the eucalyptus tends to overpower the citrus scent of the orange trees. The sap gums up the chain saws. It's hard work.

Across the grove, where the trees are already gone, and the craters bulldozed away, surveyors have set out stakes with red strips of plastic tied in bows around their tops. These guide the men at the cement mixers, the big trucks whose contents grumble as their barrels spin. They will be pouring foundations for the new tract houses before the last trees are pulled out.

Now it's the end of a short November day. Early 1960s. The sun is low, and the shadows of the remaining eucalyptus in the west wall—one in every three—fall across the remains of the grove. There are nothing but craters left, today; craters, and stacks of wood by the dumpsters. The backhoes and tractors and bulldozers are all in a yellow row, still as dinosaurs. Cars pass by. The men whose work is done for the day have congregated by the canteen truck, open on one side, displaying evening snacks of burritos and triangular sandwiches in clear plastic boxes. Some of the men have gotten bottles of beer out of their pickups, and the *click pop hiss* of bottles opening mingles with their quiet talk. Cars pass by. The distant hum of the Newport Freeway washes over them with the wind. Eucalyptus leaves fall from the trees still standing.

Out in the craters, far from the men at the canteen truck, some children are playing. Young boys, using the craters as foxholes to play some simple war game. The craters are new, they're exciting, they show what orange roots look like, something the boys have always been curious about. Cars pass by. The shadows lengthen. One of the boys wanders off alone. Tire tracks in the torn dirt lead his gaze to one of the cement mixers, still emitting its slushy grumble. He sits down to look at it, openmouthed. Cars pass by. The other boys tire of their game and go home to dinner, each to his own house. The men around the trucks finish their beers and their stories, and they get into their pickup trucks—thunk! thunk!—and drive off. A couple of supervisors walk around the dirt lot planning the next day's work. They stop by a stack of wood next to the shredder. It's quiet, you can hear the freeway in the distance. A single boy sits on a crater's edge, staring off at the distance. Cars pass by. Eucalyptus leaves spinnerdrift to the ground. The sun disappears. The day is done, and shadows are falling

across our empty field.

J. Mark Smith

REFLECTIONS ON THE GNATCATCHER
AND THE TOLL ROAD

J. Mark Smith was born in Eugene, Oregon, in 1965. A hiker and birder, Smith lived in Modjeska Canyon while earning his PhD in English at UC Irvine, and he now teaches English at MacEwan University in Edmonton, Alberta. He has published a poetry collection, *Notes for a Rescue Narrative*, and nonfiction essays and reviews in addition to scholarly papers.

Smith's careful 1995 essay from *The Ear* considers the politics of natural resources management and the poetry of wilderness as observed during the fractious debate surrounding the impact of the so-called Transportation Corridor on the native coastal habitat of the endangered gnatcatcher. Smith's thoughtful prose is rooted in firsthand observation and analysis as well as historical perspective. It is also deeply personal in its expression of affinity for wild Orange County, particularly the author's consideration of "two sorts of belonging" to it.

A MALE GNATCATCHER IS calling when I arrive at the "Tollroad" ravine, but he and his family are not in sight. From the sound, they've moved 20 or 30 m from the spot where I stumbled into them a day before. In this gully of the UCI Ecological Reserve (one lying directly in the path of the planned take for the San Joaquin Hills Tollroad), there are other sounds. An Anna's hummingbird sits motionless atop a shrub before coming to life with a high grinding sound. A flock of tittering house finches rises in the air. I move sideways through the buckwheat and sage, stopping once to tug on a spider's funneled web.

The male and female gnatcatcher are making low flights through the ravine, but there is no sign of the fledglings. Three were counted a few days ago. I hear some calls, soft, answering the male's sometime strident tone. They have moved a little north and west again, right up on the edge of some thick sage interspersed with mustard. Suddenly two fledglings, one after the other, appear out of the scrub to have a look at me. One perches on a dry mustard stalk and fluffs himself. The fledglings are about two-thirds the size of the adult female, their feathers a bluer-grey. The male (with black tail and head) calls to them; they fly back into the scrub. The third does not appear.

After I have sat in the encelia for a time, breathing the wonderful sour odor of these sunflower-family blossoms, the noise of traffic obtrudes, as does the talk of occasional cyclists on Newport Hills Road. Across the bay, planes catapult at a 45-degree angle from the John Wayne airport, then level out with a boom. I look up, and the hillsides to the south have been surveyed and quartered. The lot across the road, which abuts a creek, is being graded.

On a cloudy April morning a few weeks earlier, I sat in the scrub at the same spot while a female gnatcatcher preened herself yards away on a dried mustard stalk. I watched her intently through binoculars, though my eye could not follow. The ruffling movements of her tiny grey head and wings were rapid as an animation done with playing cards. The female gnatcatcher weighs all of five grams. When nesting begins, she will, in the space of one day, lay four 1 g. eggs. I sat and watched, and she showed herself to me as a sort of cartoon.

It troubled me then, and it troubles me now to think the relation will not ever be otherwise. After all, our world and theirs barely touch, unless it is by bulldozer. Although four coastal California gnatcatcher pairs were active on the campus reserve that year, I was never privy to anything more than glimpses of their lives. An ecology student showed me an empty nest one morning, hidden in the encelia—a snug little cup at ankle-level, woven of grass and down and cobweb. Another evening I watched a male and female gnatcatcher flitting about a sage clump with bits of nest material in their beaks. Only days afterwards the eggs had hatched and the chicks were fledged, but I was not witness to these happenings.

They elude us, it seems, and we have no use for them. One can call a gnatcatcher from the scrub with the birder's universal alarm *pshee-pshee-pshee*. Most will respond to this poor facsmile of their own call. But, perversely, the call alerts the birds only to local and specific dangers; to the larger threat, the danger posed by the mimic invader of their very world, they are oblivious. Fledglings will pop out of the scrub to perch on the shoulder of an observer. Still, researchers in the ecology department at Irvine and elsewhere are making do with very basic gnatcatcher observations. Very little known is known about their range, what they eat (they *don't* eat gnats). Little is known, in short, about their world.

There are reasons for the sketchiness of data. Even a very well trained human eye has difficulty telling individual gnatcatchers apart. Some of the birds in Orange County have been banded, to bring them more tangibly and measurably into our realm. Identification is usually the first task undertaken by those who are concerned about the well-being of a particular species. A friend of mine, for example, has done work in the Galapagos on penguins. She used to band her birds' legs with colored markers. The newer technique is to inject a silicon chip into a neck muscle so as to be able to identify each penguin with a scanner. It is better for the birds, my friend tells me, since banded individuals are found to be statistically more susceptible to predation.

I too am interested in how to catch sight of a living creature. If Thoreau jokes about the saunterer in the wood returning to his senses, a walker may slip as easily into the scrub of the San Joaquin hills. And there he will find living things in their places. More strange yet, he will find place, and life in place, to be of an essence—the wrens on their cactuses, the gnatcatchers where they must be. Concealed for all eternity, they have somehow been called out by the right rocks, the right grasses and sages and spiny stuff. And again, on a lesser scale, these entities are called out by an observer, by a walker returning to his senses. They show themselves to the walker, not as expert or as scientist, but as someone ready to meet the creatures halfway, someone called out himself.

The situation of the walker must involve two kinds of belonging. A way to think about the first kind of belonging is to say that an organism's ecological context is its meaning. Things in their place! It is true that ecology no longer teaches harmony or equilibrium; all is instead contingency, subtly patterned randomness. The biological context may last no longer than a dash of foam on rock, or a snowfield in a hollowed cirque. And yet all living things are in some way at home. The gnatcatcher's mewling in the coastal sage scrub; the movement of a male sea-lion on a foamy rock; the stain of red algae in a high altitude snowbank—these things belong to a biotic situation, and the meaning of any aspect of their lives holds only with reference to all the relationships which comprise that situation.

But consider again the walker, and what he sees, and what he shows of himself in seeing. Imagine the utterances of a Huntington Beach surfer-dude, the upright posture of an Irvine Company developer, the ambivalent look of an environmental consultant. These meanings cannot be gathered from the biotic situation; nor are they immanent to it. The context is other than biological. Every human belongs to a temporal and historical situation; and interlocking situations make for complex cultural subdivisions. This second kind of belonging is not exactly like being a sea-lion at home on a rock. It is a belonging that is in itself very difficult to see, perhaps impossible to see beyond. Inevitably, there is distortion or limitation in the relation between the two sorts of belonging.

The gnatcatcher is not the first unusual and elusive animal to face extirpation in Orange County. The other I am thinking of is the grizzly bear, a creature which might seem to have nothing in common with the tiny bird of the sage scrub. The stories of such extinctions are enlightening in their fashion. One such account, Jim Sleeper's *A Grizzly Introduction to the Santa Ana Mountains,* tells a folk-history of contact between the bears and Europeans in 19th century California. The bee-keepers of the canyons and the ranchers of the Saddleback valley waged war against the grizzly whenever it came down out of the chaparral. From the 1850s there are stories of *vaqueros,* at the ranch of cattle baron Don José Sepulveda, who lassoed bears and pitted them in the ring against the fiercest of bulls. And it was common throughout the latter decades of that century for L.A. hunting parties to come out to the Saddleback area for sport. The last grizzly of the Santa Anas was shot and killed at Trabuco Canyon in 1908.

Sleeper's book is a curious document. The author notes in the preface that he has never actually seen a grizzly. The book is full of tall tales, glorifications of butchery (men who boasted of having killed two or three hundred bears in a lifetime), accounts of improbably huge and grotesque bruins. It is peppered with period illustrations of savage beasts by artists who evidently had just as little acquaintance with grizzlies. The tales collected in Sleeper's book tell almost nothing reliable about the bears themselves, except for the remarkable fact that they were here, in Southern California, less than twenty miles from Anaheim. When I walk in the hills above Silverado or Modjeska today, it is with a shock that I think of the great bear digging for roots, gorging on toyon berry perhaps, or searching the canyon sycamores for honeycombs.

Sleeper writes the human history of a place in relation to a creature that does not exist, and that never did exist, properly, for us. Or did it? The grizzly bear of the Santa Anas made a powerful mark on the imagination of its neighbors. The bear called out fear and hatred in the people who lived here. And though it is difficult for me to be entirely sympathetic with my predecessors—ranchers, bee-keepers, prospectors—in the canyons, I can at least acknowledge that the grizzly bear *meant* something different to them than myself. The grizzly called out fear and hatred in those people. It may be that we are now able to pay attention to the grizzly bear (if nowhere in the state of California) in ways that are not only fearful and violent expressions of human possibility. But more than ever the grizzly calls out in us—as scientists, tourists, wilderness enthusiasts, natural resource management experts, or whatever—our own meanings.

I wonder if the plight of the gnatcatcher in Orange County is symptomatic of limitation in the relation between two sorts of belonging. It is certainly not a problem to be solved by refining our knowledge, by learning from past mistakes. We already possess the recorded history of our disastrous relation to one animal, the grizzly bear. The largest and most obvious of North American mammals, extirpated locally, appears now through a tissue of fabrications and gunmen's legends. In a century's time the gnatcatcher will appear through a similar tissue of EIR's and newspaper articles. There is no way that a commuter travelling on the freeways of Orange County—and that includes just about everyone who claims to live here—can even catch sight of a 5 g. bird. Maybe we should not fret about these missed sightings? Surely nothing is more definitive of humanity than oversight, unfortunate as its consequences may be? But it is possible that we are grievously mistaken in the way we understand oversight.

In Orange County the earth is disappearing under a wash of suburbs. Even the builders admit the losses. One face-saving strategy government and developers have come up with is known as "mitigation banking." A developer puts a suburb on several acres of coastal sage scrub, and promises to "rebuild" that habitat elsewhere—at an old landfill site for instance. Marshes are filled in, and bulldozed; and plots of already disturbed land known to be subject to winter flooding are designated "wetlands" instead. I have seen one example of mitigation banking: a forlorn mudhole at Mason Park with sprinkler nozzles planted in the bare spaces between struggling shrubs.

The manipulation of categories is rather interesting in itself, for mitigation banking enacts one possible version of the human relation to the natural world. The business practices of the Irvine Co., the largest developer in Orange County, seem to embody the idea that the human and the natural are one, insomuch as both can be prevailed upon or induced to appear by volition. It is a local joke that the four Southern Californian seasons are fire, flood, earthquake, and drought. In such circumstances, with large human populations in a land area that cannot conceivably support them, there is no getting around a need for "the control of nature." But besides what appear to be pragmatic imperatives, there is much at stake philosophically. Various technologies and masterplans have effectively dissolved the sage scrub and the gnatcatcher into entities that may be constructed or dismantled or reconfigured at will. Prevailing models of biological science have further worked to cover over what I have called the two kinds of belonging. All natural and human phenomena are understood instead as belonging to one very complex system; and limitations on human understanding are simply a matter of not having sufficient knowledge or control of its variables. Oversight means failure of predictive power or technical know-how.

Coming from a very different philosophical position is the concurrent effort by a few environmental groups in O.C. to "restore" degraded coastal sage scrub. The difference between mitigation and restoration is the difference between a public relations campaign and a genuine practice of stewardship. Peter Bowler, a UCI instructor and restorationist, advocates a modern eco-version of the parable of the talents. Bowler says the point of restoration is "to strengthen and extend existing situations," not to compensate for habitat loss elsewhere. The difference depends fundamentally on how one understands oversight. The bureaucrats and developers who promote mitigation banking see in the land only a short-term future, and a future configured entirely by human action in the present moment. The practice of restoration, on the other hand, begins from a human present that moves toward a future necessarily involved with the past. It requires not just the restoration of shrubs and grasses and soils, but also the stewarding of human strengths and weaknesses.

Restorationists have had considerable problems in coming up with "performance criteria" for success. There are many different patterns of ecological "richness"; within a healthy habitat area, numerous associations and sub-associations and succession stages are imaginable.

The relationships get more intricate each time we look. No sage scrub restoration site, for instance, has ever recovered from a burn and developed into a late-successional stage. Some find the mismatch of natural complexity and human measure embarrassing. Restorationists are sensitive to the criticism that their practice is no more than a pretentious form of landscaping or revegetating. Defenders reply that restoration is a young technology, that it needs time to develop methodologies.

The charge may not be best answered by the promise of ever finer evaluation criteria. There are certain phenomena a scientific model will never catch sight of; and the modeller too will always have his blindnesses. Ecological restoration is rooted in richer philosophical soil than most of the sciences because it acknowledges that natural presence has a human history, that certain conditions are involved in what we see. Whatever a creature or a habitat or an ecosystem can mean to us comes out of a history of relation to places and to place. That meaning is of course not an *arbitrary* intellectual creation. A wetland cannot be created by an act of will; a sage scrub habitat is not an artifact. Nor does human meaning exhaust the deeper being of the creature or habitat or ecosystem. And yet these places show an order made comprehensible by the human history of relation to such a place. In chronicles and anecdotes, in measurements and moods, human meanings and non-human orderings bleed together. Both are cause for wonder.

It is humility then that distinguishes the practice of restoration from the technological projects of our day. Humility, in this context, comports itself in two modes: first, toward the mysterious continuity of human history; second, toward those hypothetical periods of evolutionary transformation, huge and alien stretches of time, also past. True restoration will, from a human perspective, take a long time. Today's restorationists say the success of a project cannot be assessed in less than a generation (twenty to thirty years). Several generations would be preferable. Obviously the dimensions of a human life limit that figure. The practice of restoration has a modest but noteworthy spiritual importance exactly because it calls attention to those limits.

Too often, in late twentieth-century America, the living seem to share nothing with the dead. Indeed, Irvine's master-planned suburbs have made no provision for the cemetery.

This local conflict between "mitigation" and "restoration" philosophies, and temporal orientations, may have some bearing on other problems, such as run-away growth. The final Environmental Impact Statement for the San Joaquin Hills Tollroad, for instance, reports: "The County's housing stock is projected to grow at a faster rate than the population. Housing units are expected to increase about 53% between the years 1980–2010 while population is expected to increase by about 27%." Whatever the motive behind publishing it, the statistic defies sense. And one need only look around O.C. to confirm its truth. In prosperous Southern California, houses are being built faster than people can fill them.

During a time of desperate post-war housing shortage, the German philosopher Martin Heidegger wrote a well-known essay on the ties between building and dwelling and thinking. He pointed out that the real problem of settling in a place, of dwelling, is not addressed by building houses. Orange County stands now in exactly the opposite situation economically (though one could look to the homeless of Santa Ana, or the L.A. core, for local housing shortages). We have an excess of houses, and of freeways, and more than ever a "dwelling" problem. Heidegger thought that human beings, who live in time, who must die, are never naturally at home. Humans need to learn to dwell; they must learn to belong to their own meanings. Those meanings, though their origin is elsewhere, can be sought nowhere except the present. In this sense, humans must perpetually rehabilitate, or restore, their own lives. "The real dwelling plight lies in this, that mortals must ever search anew for the essence of dwelling, that they *must ever learn to dwell.*" Dwelling, as Heidegger thought of it, is living at peace in the present. It is a walker's peace. The alternative is, in the developers' idiom, unmitigated homelessness.

Such thought is very far indeed from that which dominates development plans for Orange County. The tollroad builders deny that the freeway will cause growth. It will, they admit, have "growth inducing impacts." It is all too appropriate that deficit-financed empire builders should employ this word "inducement" (from L., *ducere*): to prevail on; to persuade; to give rise to by artificial means. The word makes sense only within the matrix of the immediate future. Something is induced to appear, like a baby, like a housing development. One cannot tear a history from the past. The fullness of the present cannot be prodded so as to become fuller. But a man can be induced, by some inexorable logic, to venture out upon the freeway. And at every moment of his life he will be a commuter.

From the vantage point of our own compulsions, the meaning of the gnatcatcher flips by like a shuffled deck of cards. We cannot persuade the songbirds, cannot prevail upon living things. They will not appear at our will. We must learn to dwell with them. And who in Southern California will be told how to live?

Colette LaBouff Atkinson

ROUTE

Colette LaBouff Atkinson was born in Los Angeles in 1966 and received an MFA in poetry and a PhD in English from UC Irvine. She called Orange County home from 1988 until 2011. Her nonfiction has been published in the *Santa Monica Review*, the *Seneca Review, Orange Coast Magazine*, and the *Los Angeles Times Magazine*. She currently lives in New Mexico.

In reference to this selection from *Mean*, a 2008 book of prose poems, she told us of her "longtime interest in the way nature both thrives and is threatened in suburban Orange County: a setting of commutes, new buildings, and old creatures all together in one place that can, in fact, be loved." The book explores the connotations of "mean"—meanness, meaning, intention, scarcity—through perspective, landscape, cultural references, and personal experience.

The turkey vultures spent nights on the Light of Christ,
a Lutheran Church and preschool where they'd line up for
sleep. They were chased away, probably by the pastor, who
worried about the message they'd send: *death and carnage
here!* How misunderstood. Still, no one wants to think
about how, with blood-red heads, they eat the dead. Ugly
stepsisters of the Condors, the vultures moved up the road.
They come home now the same time I do. Black and circling,
they linger for updrafts, wait for permission. Sometimes I
wait for the green and like the idling exhaust, a dead stop.
At Culver and Michelson, the birds, coming from the south,
circle and circle on thermals and make a hard left. I make a

right; the sun, its light now losing, backs me. We cross each
other; they bow and I stretch up. Flying reminders of the
fifth commandment, they're in sight of three gum trees where
Culver meets Sandburg. Over condos and traffic and golf,
they—black hearts—face the ocean. They never glance back
at their old home. Even if they were able to reflect, what's
to consider? There's nothing savage in them. At home, I pull
my windblown hair into a knot. It's dusk. We tuck our heads
into pillows, wings.

Shirley Geok-Lin Lim

RIDING INTO CALIFORNIA

Shirley Geok-Lin Lim was born in Malacca, Malaysia, in 1944. She has won a Fulbright fellowship and a Wien International scholarship, and she earned her PhD from Brandeis University. She is the winner of a Commonwealth Poetry Prize (the first for both a woman and a person of Asian ancestry) and two American Book Awards, the second of which was for *Among the White Moon Faces*, a memoir that narrates her immigration from a British colonial childhood to the United States. Lim is recognized as a multi-genre writer who plays with a range of poetic forms. Her most recent collections of poetry are *The Irreversible Sun, Ars Poetica for the Day,* and *Do You Live In?*

In "Riding into California," from *What the Fortune Teller Didn't Say* (1998), Lim wryly describes a richly meaningful moment infused with cultural and political implications that go well beyond the everyday circumstances portrayed.

If you come to a land with no ancestors
to bless you, you have to be your own
ancestor. The veterans in the mobile home
park don't want to be there. It isn't easy.
Oil rigs litter the land like giant frozen birds.
Ghosts welcome us to a new life, and
an immigrant without home ghosts
cannot believe the land is real. So you're
grateful for familiarity, and Bruce Lee
becomes your hero. Coming into Fullerton,
everyone waiting at the station is white.

The good thing about being Chinese on Amtrak
is no one sits next to you. The bad thing is
you sit alone all the way to Irvine.

Marie Connors

ASSOCIATION POOL

Marie Connors was born in 1950 in Nashville, Tennessee, and received BA and MA degrees from the University of Memphis. She moved to Orange County in 1986, graduating from UC Irvine with an MFA in poetry. Her work has appeared in literary journals including *Faultline*, *The Ear*, and the *South Coast Poetry Journal*. She has taught writing and film at area colleges and universities and is a lifetime birder.

Her previously unpublished poem "Association Pool" draws inspiration, she told us, from personal experience as well as "the serene geometry of place so characteristic of Southern California." Connors's careful attention to the natural world, and her detailed reordering and coordination of color, makes it hard to see that familiar contrived community facility of the neighborhood swimming pool as anything but beautiful—until she invites us to consider otherwise.

> Here in this suburban place that calls itself
> a city, a private park in a planned
> development where the grass stays
>
> green, where the sprinklers swirl open
> at discrete intervals and fallen branches
> are soon cleared away, the noisy motor, strapped
>
> to the immigrant's back, disperses stray
> particles so we're spared other more subtle
> sounds, like footsteps over brittle bark.

Now a woman in a bathing cap swims
within a single lane, not because she doesn't
feel free, but because a certain steadiness

comes second nature in this orderly world.
The bougainvillea's perfectly red today.
There's fresh paint on the pergola. The position

of the sun is our only obstacle and this
can be repaired by rotating chairs. A picnic
appears on a tablecloth: salmon and crusty

bread. Photos of women we have secretly loved
change hands. To be known as a lesbian
makes one of us tremble, the other

breathes so quietly she could be dead.
The swimmer smiles at us and leaves the gate
unlocked when we show her we have a key.

ANAHEIM

*I wanted flat land that
I could shape.*

—WALT DISNEY, 1954

Paul J. Willis

COMMON GROUND

Paul J. Willis was born in Fullerton in 1955 and received his BA from Wheaton College and his MA and PhD from Washington State University. A former poet laureate of Santa Barbara and now a professor of English at Westmont College, his work has appeared widely, including in the 1996 volume of *Best American Poetry*, edited by Adrienne Rich. His most recent collections are *Rising from the Dead* (2009) and *Say This Prayer into the Past* (2013).

"Common Ground," written about a grandfather Willis mainly knew through family stories, offers a poignant telling of a familiar tale of agricultural pioneers who abandoned their lifestyles and handed over their farmland for development as housing tracts or, in this case, a theme park. Garrison Keillor read the poem on National Public Radio, and the recording can be accessed on his *Writer's Almanac* website. "Common Ground" was written in 1994 and first published in *Visiting Home* (2008).

> Today I dug an orange tree out of the damp, black earth.
> My grandfather bought a grove near Anaheim
> at just my age. Like me, he didn't know much.
> "How'd you learn to grow oranges, Bill?"
> friends said. "Well," he said, "I look at what
>
> my neighbor does, and I just do the opposite."
> Up in Oregon, he and his brother discovered
> the Willamette River. They were both asleep
> on the front of the wagon, the horses stopped,
> his brother woke up. "Will," he said, "am it a river?"

My grandfather, he cooked for the army during the war,
the first one. He flipped the pancakes up the chimney,
they came right back through the window onto the griddle.
In the Depression he worked in a laundry during the night,
struck it rich in pocketknives. My grandfather,

he liked to smoke in his orange grove, as far away on the property
as he could get from my grandmother,
who didn't approve of life in general, him in particular.
Smoking gave him something to feel disapproved for,
set the world back to rights. Like everyone else,

my grandfather sold his grove to make room
for Disneyland. He laughed all the way to the bank,
bought in town, lived to see his grandsons born
and died of cancer before anyone wanted him to, absent
now in the rootless presence of damp, black earth.

Steve Martin

from *BORN STANDING UP*

Steve Martin was born in Texas in 1945 and was raised in California. He graduated from Garden Grove High School and attended Santa Ana College and UCLA. His major works include the screenplays for *L.A. Story* and *Roxanne*, the essay collection *Cruel Shoes*, the novella *Shopgirl* (and its film adaptation), the play *Picasso at the Lapin Agile*, and, most recently, the Tony-nominated musical *Bright Star*, coauthored and composed with Edie Brickell.

The actor, comedian, musician, writer, director, playwright, and magician grew up in Fullerton. He worked in the old magic store on Main Street, USA, in Disneyland, as recalled fondly in these excerpts from his bestselling memoir, *Born Standing Up: A Comic's Life*.

A WIDE SWATH OF our Inglewood neighborhood was scheduled to be flattened by the impending construction of the San Diego freeway. The steamrollers were soon to be barreling down on our little house, so the search was on for a new place to live. My father's decision profoundly affected my life. Orange County, California, forty-five minutes south of Inglewood, was a real estate boomtown created from the sprawl of Los Angeles. It consisted of interlocking rectangles of orange groves and tract homes and was perfectly suited to my father's profession. Housing developments rose out of the ground like spring wells, changing the color of the landscape from desert brown to lawn green, and my parents purchased a brand-new tract home for sixteen thousand dollars. I was ten years old when my family moved from complicated and historic Los Angeles to uncomplicated and nonhistoric Garden Grove, where the sky was blue and vast but without the drama of Wyoming, just a flat dead sky of ease. Everything from our toes to the horizon was the same, except for the occasional massive and regal oak tree that had defied the developer's scythe. This area of Orange County gleamed with newness, and the move enabled me to place my small hand on Opportunity's doorknob.

In the summer of 1955, Disneyland opened in Anaheim, California, on a day so sweltering the asphalt on Main Street was as soft as a yoga mat. Two-inch headlines announced the event as though it were a victory at sea. A few months later, when a school friend told me that kids our age were being hired to sell Disneyland guidebooks on weekends and in the summer, I couldn't wait. I pedaled my bicycle the two miles to Disneyland, parked it in the bike rack—locks were unnecessary—and looked up to see a locomotive from yesteryear, its whistle blowing loudly and its smokestack filling the air with white steam, chugging into the turn-of-the-century depot just above a giant image of Mickey Mouse rendered in vibrantly colored flowers. I went to the exit, told a hand-stamper that I was applying for a job, and was directed toward a souvenir stand a few steps inside the main gate. I spoke with a cigar-chomping vendor named Joe and told him my résumé: no experience at anything. This must have impressed Joe, because I was issued a candy-striped shirt, a garter for my sleeve, a vest with a watch pocket, a straw boater hat, and a stack of guidebooks to be sold for twenty-five cents each, from which I was to receive the enormous sum of two cents per book. The two dollars in cash I earned that day made me feel like a millionaire.

Guidebooks were sold only in the morning, when thousands of people poured through the gates. By noon I was done, but I didn't have to leave. I had free admission to the park. I roamed through the Penny Arcade, watched the Disneyland Band as they marched around the plaza, and even found an "A" ticket in the street, allowing me to choose between the green-and-gold-painted streetcar or the surrey ride up Main Street. Because I wisely kept on my little outfit, signifying that I was an official employee, and maybe because of the look of longing on my face, I was given a free ride on the Tomorrowland rocket to the moon, which blasted me into the cosmos. I passed by Mr. Toad and

Peter Pan rides, toured pirate ships and Western forts. Disneyland, and the idea of it, seemed so glorious that I believed it should be in some faraway, impossible-to-visit Shangri-la, not two miles from the house where I was about to grow up. With its pale blue castle flying pennants emblazoned with a made-up Disney family crest, its precise gardens and horse-drawn carriages maintained to jewel-box perfection, Disneyland was my Versailles.

I became a regular employee, age ten. I blazed short-cuts through Disneyland's maze of pathways, finding the most direct route from the Chicken of the Sea pirate ship to the Autopia, or the back way to Adventureland from Main Street. I learned speed-walking, and I could slip like a water moccasin through dense throngs of people, a technique I still use at airports and on the sidewalks of Manhattan. Though my mother provided fifty cents for lunch (the Carnation lunch counter offered a grilled cheese sandwich for thirty-five cents and a large cherry phosphate with a genuine red-dye-number-two cherry for fifteen cents), the big difference in my life was that I was self-reliant and funded. I was so proud to be employed that some years later—still at Disneyland—I harbored a secret sense of superiority over my teenage peers who had suntans, because I knew it meant they weren't working.

In Frontierland, I was fascinated by a true cowboy named Eddie Adamek, who twirled lariats and pitched his homemade product, a pre-fab lasso that enabled youngsters to make perfect circles just like their cowboy heroes. Eddie, I discerned, was living with a woman not his wife, the 1955 equivalent of devil worship. But I didn't mind, because his patronage enabled me to learn rope tricks, including the Butterfly, Threading the Needle, and the Skip-Step. A few years later, after my tenure as guidebook salesman ended—perhaps at thirteen I was too old—I became Eddie's trick-rope demonstrator, fitting in as much work as I could around my C-average high school studies.

In my mapping of the Disney territory, two places captivated me. One was Merlin's Magic Shop, just inside the Fantasyland castle gate, where a young and funny magician named Jim Barlow sold and demonstrated magic tricks. The other was Pepsi-Cola's Golden Horseshoe

Revue in Frontierland, where Wally Boag, the first comedian I ever saw in person, plied a hilarious trade of gags and offbeat skills such as gun twirling and balloon animals, and brought the house down when he turned his wig around backward. He wowed every audience every time.

The theater, built with Disneyland's dedication to craftsmanship, had a horseshoe-shaped interior adorned with lush gay-nineties decor. Oak tables and chairs crowded the saloon's main floor, and a spectacular mirrored bar with a gleaming foot rail ran along one side. Polished brass lamps with real flames gave off an orangey glow, and on the stage hung a plush golden curtain tied back with a thickly woven cord. A balcony lined with steers' horns looped around the interior, and customers dangled their arms and heads over the railing during the show. Four theater boxes stood on either side of the stage, where VIPs would be seated ceremoniously behind a velvet rope. Young girls in low-cut dance-hall dresses served paper cups brimming with Pepsi that seemed to have an exceptionally stinging carbonated fizz, and the three-piece band made the theater jump with liveliness. In the summer the powerful air-conditioning made it a welcome icebox.

The admission price, always free to everyone, made me a regular. Here I had my first lessons in performing, though I never was on the stage. I absorbed Wally Boag's timing, saying his next line in my head ("When they operated on Father, they opened Mother's male"), and took the audience's response as though it were mine. I studied where the big laughs were, learned how Wally got the small ones, and saw tiny nuances that kept the thing alive between lines. Wally shone in these performances, and in my first shows, I tried to imitate his amiable casualness. My fantasy was that one day Wally would be sick with the flu, and a desperate stage manager would come out and ask the audience if there was an adolescent boy who could possibly fill in.

Merlin's Magic Shop was the next best thing to the cheering audiences at the Golden Horseshoe. Tricks were demonstrated in front of crowds of two or three people, and twenty-year-old Jim Barlow took the concept of a joke shop far beyond what the Disney brass would have officially allowed, except it was clear that the customers enjoyed his kidding. Coiled springs of snakes shot out of fake peanut-brittle cans, attacking the unsuspecting customer who walked through the door. Jim's greeting to browsers was, "Can I take your money—I mean help you?" After a sale, he would say loudly, "This trick is guaranteed!... to break before you get home." Like Wally, Jim was genuinely funny, and his broad smile and innocent blond flattop smoothed the way for his prankster style. I loitered in the shop so often that Jim and I became buddies as I memorized his routines, and I wanted more than ever to be a magician.

The paraphernalia sold in the magic store was exotic, and I was dazzled by the tricks' secret mechanics. The Sucker Die Box, with its tricky false fronts and gimmicked door pulls, thrilled me. At home, I would peruse magic catalogs for hours. I was spellbound by the graphics of another era, unchanged since the thirties, of tubes that produced silks, water bowls that poured endlessly, and magic wands that did nothing. I dreamed of owning color-changing scarves and amazing swords that could spear the selected card when the deck was thrown into the air. I read advertising pamphlets from distant companies in Ohio that offered collapsible opera hats, pre-owned tuxedos, and white-tipped canes. I had fantasies of levitation and awesome power and, with no Harry Potter to be compared to, my store-bought tricks could go a long way toward making me feel special. With any spare money I had, I bought tricks, memorized their accompanying standard patter, and assembled a magic show that I would perform for anyone who would watch, mostly my parents and their tolerant bridge partners.

One afternoon I was in the audience at the Golden Horseshoe, sipping my Pepsi and mouthing along with Wally Boag, when I blacked out and collapsed. I remember my head striking the table. A few seconds later, I was sitting back up but unnerved. Nobody noticed, but I reported this incident to my mother, and she called Dr. Kusnitz, perhaps Orange County's only Jewish doctor, who lived next door. "What was it?" he asked. "It was a thump in my chest," I said. Tests confirmed I had a heart murmur more spookily expressed as a prolapsed mitral valve, a mostly benign malady that was predicted to go away as I aged.

It did, but it planted in me a seed of hypochondria that poisonously bloomed years later.

After poor sales ended my trick-roping days, I spent a year working away from the action, in the sheet-metal-gray storage room of Tiki's Tropical Imports in Adventureland, where I pinned finger-piercing price tags onto straw hats (I'm sure my bloody screams alarmed the nearby dock loaders). On my infrequent trips to the actual store, I was entertained by a vibrant Biloxi-born store manager named Irene, who, I now realize, was probably the first neurotic I ever met. Her favorite saying—"Well, excuse me for livin'!"—stuck in my head. I had heard rumors of a job opening up at the magic shop, and longing to be free of the sunless warehouse, I went over and successfully applied, making that day the happiest of my life so far. I began my show business career a few days later, at age fifteen, in August 1960. I stood behind a counter eight hours a day, shuffling Svengali decks, manipulating Wizard decks and Mental Photography cards, and performing the Cups and Balls trick on a rectangle of padded green felt. A few customers would gather, usually a young couple on a date, or a mom and dad with kids. I tried my first jokes—all lifted from Jim's funny patter—and had my first audience that wasn't friends or family. My weekends and holidays were now spent in long hours at Disneyland, made possible by lax child labor laws and my high school, which assigned no homework. At closing time, I would stock the shelves, sweep the floor, count out the register, and then bicycle home in the dark.

The magic shop purveyed such goodies as the arrow-through-the-head and nose glasses, props I turned into professional assets later on. Posted behind the scenes, too risqué for Disneyland's tourists, was a little gag postcard that had been printed in Japan. It said "Happy Feet," and featured the outline of the bottoms of four feet, two pointed up, two pointed down. After I studied it for about an hour, Jim Barlow explained that it was the long-end view of a couple making love.

There were two magic shops—the other was on Main Street—and I ran between them as necessary. In the Main Street store, there was a booth, really an alcove, where you could get your name printed in a headline, WANTED, HORSE THIEF, YOUR NAME HERE, and I mastered the soon-to-be-useless art of hand typesetting. The proprietor, Jim—a different Jim—laughed at me because I insisted on wearing gardening gloves while I worked with the printing press. I couldn't let the ink stain my hands; it would look unsightly when I was demonstrating cards. At the print shop I learned my first life lesson. One day I was particularly gloomy, and Jim asked me what the matter was. I told him my high school girlfriend (for all of two weeks) had broken up with me. He said, "Oh, that'll happen a lot." The knowledge that this horrid grief was simply a part of life's routine cheered me up almost instantly.

My time at the magic shop gave me a taste of performing and convinced me that I never wanted to wait on customers again. I didn't have the patience; my smile was becoming plastered on. I then crossed all kinds of jobs off my list of potentials, such as waiting tables or working in stores or driving trucks: How could my delicate fingertips, now dedicated to the swift execution of the Two-handed Pass, clutch the heavy, callus-inducing steering wheel of a ten-ton semi?

But there was a problem. At age eighteen, I had absolutely no gifts. I could not sing or dance, and the only acting I did was really just shouting. Thankfully, perseverance is a great substitute for talent. Having been motivated by Earl Scruggs's rendition of "Foggy Mountain Breakdown," I had learned, barely, to play the banjo. I had taught myself by slowing down banjo records on my turntable and picking out the songs note by note, with a helpful assist from my high school friend John McEuen, already an accomplished player. The only place to practice without agonizing everyone in the house was in my car, parked on the street with the windows rolled up, even in the middle of August. Also, I could juggle passably, a feat I had learned from the talented Fantasyland court jester Christopher Fair (who could juggle five balls while riding a high unicycle) and which I practiced in my backyard using heavy wooden croquet balls that would clack against each other, pinching my swollen fingers in between. Despite a lack of natural ability, I did have the one element necessary to all early creativity: naïveté, that fabulous quality that keeps you from knowing just how unsuited you are for what you are about to do.

After high school graduation, I halfheartedly applied to and was accepted at Santa Ana Junior College, where I took drama classes and pursued an unexpected interest in English poetry from Donne to Eliot. I had heard about a theater at Disneyland's friendly, striving rival, Knott's Berry Farm, that needed entertainers with short acts. One afternoon I successfully auditioned with my thin magic act at a small theater on the grounds, making this the second happiest day of my life so far.

My final day at the magic shop, I stood behind the counter where I had pitched Svengali decks and the Incredible Shrinking Die, and I felt an emotional contradiction: nostalgia for the present. Somehow, even though I had stopped working only minutes earlier, my future fondness for the store was clear, and I experienced a sadness like that of looking at a photo of an old, favorite pooch. It was dusk by the time I left the shop, and I was redirected by a security guard who explained that a photographer was taking a picture and would I please use the side exit. I did, and saw a small, thin woman with hacked brown hair aim her large-format camera directly at the dramatically lit castle, where white swans floated in the moat underneath the functioning drawbridge. Almost forty years later, when I was in my early fifties, I purchased that photo as a collectible, and it still hangs in my house. The photographer, it turned out, was Diane Arbus. I try to square the photo's breathtakingly romantic image with the rest of her extreme subject matter, and I assume she saw this facsimile of a castle as though it were a kitsch roadside statue of Paul Bunyan. Or perhaps she saw it as I did: beautiful.

E. L. Doctorow

---

from *THE BOOK OF DANIEL*

E. L. Doctorow was born in 1931 and raised in the Bronx. He earned a BA
in philosophy at Kenyon College and completed a year of graduate school
in drama at Columbia before being drafted. He worked in publishing before
becoming a successful writer. The author of several classic American novels,
including *Ragtime* and *Billy Bathgate*, Doctorow lived in Corona del Mar
during his time as a visiting writer at UC Irvine.

This excerpt from *The Book of Daniel* (1971) is a tart sociological consideration of a visit to Disneyland by the novel's main character, the grown
son of convicted "atom spies" in the 1950s. The narrator, a political radical, spares no criticism of what he sees in the harmful fantasies contrived to
manipulate, placate, and distract Americans at a time of revolutionary grassroots political movements. It offers a sharp, mean, and funny critique from a
dissident young man on his way to a reunion with a family friend associated
with the government's prosecution of his parents.

THIS FAMOUS AMUSEMENT park is shaped like a womb. It is situated
in a flatland of servicing motels, restaurants, gas stations, bowling
alleys and other places of fun, and abuts on its own giant parking
lot. A monorail darts along its periphery, in a loop that carries to the
Disneyland Hotel. A replica 19th-century railroad line, the Sante Fe
and Disneyland, complete with stations, conductors, steam engine and
surrey type cars, delineates its circumference. Within the park itself five
major amusement areas are laid out on different themes: the American
West, called Frontierland; current technology, which is called Tomorrowland; nursery literature, called Fantasyland; and Adventureland,
which proposes colonialist exploration of wild jungles of big game

and native villages. Customers are invited to explore each area and its delights according to their whim. In the center of the park, where all the areas converge, there is a plaza; and the fifth thematic area, an avenue called Main Street USA, a romantic rendering of small-town living at the turn of the century, leads like the birth canal from the plaza to the entrance to the park.

As in all amusement parks the featured experience is the ride, or trip. The notability of Disneyland is its elaboration of this simple pleasure. You will not find the ordinary roller coaster or Ferris wheel except disguised as a bobsled ride down a plastic Matterhorn, or a "people mover." In toy submarines with real hatches, the customer experiences a simulated dive underwater, as bubbles rise past the portholes and rubber fish wag their tails. The submarines are said to be nuclear and bear the names of ships of the American nuclear fleet. Disneyland invites the customer not merely to experience the controlled thrills of a carny ride, but to participate in mythic rituals of the culture. Your boat ride is a Mississippi sternwheeler. Your pony ride is a string of pack mules going over the mountains to where the gold is. The value of the experience is not the ride itself but its vicariousness.

Two problems arise in the customer's efforts to fulfill Disneyland's expectations of him. The first is that for some reason while the machinery of the rides is impressively real—that is to say, technologically perfect and historically accurate—the simulated plant and animal and geological surroundings are unreal. When you take the jungle river cruise the plants and animals on the banks betray their plastic being and electronic motivation. The rocks of the painted desert or grand canyon cannot sustain the illusion of even the least sophisticated. The second difficulty is that Disneyland is usually swarming with people. People are all over the place in Disneyland. Thus the customers on the Mark Twain Mississippi steamboat look into the hills and see the customers on the mule pack train looking down at them. There is a constant feedback of human multiplicity, one's own efforts of vicarious participation constantly thwarted by the mirror of others' eyes.

Within the thematic unities of Disneyland, there are numbers of references, usually in the form of rides, exhibits or stores, to figures or works of our literary heritage. Some of these are Alice in Wonderland (Mad Hatter's Teacup Ride), Peter Pan (Peter Pan Flight), Life on the Mississippi (Mark Twain Riverboat), Wind in the Willows (Mr. Toad's Wild Ride), Swiss Family Robinson (Swiss Family Tree House), and Tom Sawyer (Tom Sawyer's Island Rafts). In addition there are implications of proprietary relationships with various figures of history, myth and legend such as King Arthur, Sleeping Beauty, Snow White, Casey Jones, Mike Fink, Jean Lafitte, and Abraham Lincoln. It is hard to find a pattern in the selection of these particular figures. Most of them have passed through a previous process of film or film animation and are made to recall the preemptive powers of the Disney organization with regard to Western culture. But beyond that no principle of selection is obvious. It is interesting to note, however, that Walt Disney's early achievements in his original medium, the animated cartoon, employed animal characters of his own devising. The animated cartoon itself, except for Disney's subsequent climb into the respectability of public domain literature, came to express the collective unconsciousness of the community of the American Naïve. A study today of the products of the animated cartoon industry of the twenties, thirties and forties would yield the following theology: 1. People are animals. 2. The body is mortal and subject to incredible pain. 3. Life is antagonistic to the living. 4. The flesh can be sawed, crushed, frozen, stretched, burned, bombed, and plucked for music. 5. The dumb are abused by the smart and the smart destroyed by their own cunning. 6. The small are tortured by the large and the large destroyed by their own momentum. 7. We are able to walk on air, but only as long as our illusion supports us. It is possible to interpret the Disney organization's relentless program of adaptation of literature, myth and legend, as an attempt to escape these dark and rowdy conclusions of the genre—in the same way a tenement kid from the Lower East Side might have grown up with the ambition of building himself a mansion on Fifth Avenue. Yet, ironically, many of the stories and characters chosen by Disney for their cultural respectability are just as dark and just as rowdy. The original *Alice in Wonderland* is a symbolic and surreal work by a benign deviate genius. Mark Twain was an atheist and a pornographer, and his great work, *Huckleberry Finn,* is a nightmare of childhood in confrontation with American social reality. In this light it is possible to understand the aesthetics of cartoon adaptation as totalitarian in nature.

It is clear that few of the children who ride in the Mad Hatter's Teacup have read or even will read *Alice*, let alone the works of Mark Twain. Most of them will only know Alice's story through the Disney film, if at all. And that suggests a separation of two ontological degrees between the Disneyland customer and the cultural artifacts he is presumed upon to treasure in his visit. The Mad Hatter's Teacup Ride is emblematic of the Disney animated film, which is itself a drastic revision in form and content of a subtle dreamwork created out of the English language. And even to an adult who dimly remembers reading the original *Alice*, and whose complicated response to this powerfully symbolic work has long since been incorporated into the psychic constructs of his life, what is being offered does not suggest the resonance of the original work, but is only a sentimental compression of something that is itself already a lie.

We find this radical process of reduction occurring too with regard to the nature of historical reality. The life and life-style of slave-trading America on the Mississippi River in the 19th century is compressed into a technologically faithful steamboat ride of five or ten minutes on an HO-scale river. The intermediary between us and this actual historical experience, the writer Mark Twain, author of *Life on the Mississippi*, is now no more than the name of the boat. Piracy on the high seas, a hundred and fifty years of harassment of European mercantile exploration and trade, becomes a moving diorama of all the scenes and situations of the pirate movies made by Hollywood in the thirties and forties. When the customer is invited then to buy, say, a pirate hat in one of the many junk shops on the premises, the Pavlovian process of symbolic transference to the final consumer moment may be said to be complete.

The ideal Disneyland patron may be said to be one who responds to a process of symbolic manipulation that offers him his culminating and quintessential sentiment at the moment of a purchase.

The following corporations offer shows and exhibits at Disneyland: Monsanto Chemical Co., Bell Telephone, General Electric, and Coca-Cola. Other visible corporate representation includes McDonnell Aircraft, Goodyear, Carnation Milk, Sunkist, Eastman Kodak, Upjohn Pharmaceuticals, Insurance Company of North America, United Air Lines, and Bank of America.

Obviously there are political implications. What Disneyland proposes is a technique of abbreviated shorthand culture for the masses, a mindless thrill, like an electric shock, that insists at the same time on the recipient's rich psychic relation to his country's history and language and literature. In a forthcoming time of highly governed masses in an overpopulated world, this technique may be extremely useful both as a substitute for education and, eventually, as a substitute for experience. One cannot tour Disneyland today without noticing its real achievement, which is the handling of crowds. Coupled open vans, pulled by tractors, collect customers at various points of the parking areas and pour them out at the entrance to the park. The park seems built to absorb infinite numbers of customers in its finite space by virtue of the simultaneous appeal of numbers of attractions at the same time, including not only the fixed rides and exhibits and restaurants and shops but special parades and flag raising and lowering ceremonies, band concerts, and the like. (At Christmas time Main Street residents in period dress sing Christmas carols at the foot of a large odorless evergreen whose rubberized needles spring to the touch.) In front of the larger attractions are mazes of pens, designed to hold great numbers of people waiting to board, or to mount or to enter. Guards, attendants, guides, and other personnel, including macrocephalic Disney costume characters, are present in abundance. Plainclothes security personnel appear in any large gathering with walkie-talkies. The problems of mass ingress and egress seem to have been solved here to a degree that would light admiration in the eyes of an SS transport officer.

One is struck by the number of adult customers at Disneyland unaccompanied by small children. One notices too the disproportionately small numbers of black people, of Mexicans, possibly because a day at Disneyland is expensive. There is an absence altogether of long-haired youth, heads, hippies, girls in miniskirts, gypsies, motorcyclists, to the point that one gives credence to the view that Disneyland turns away people it doesn't like the looks of. This particular intelligence occurred to Linda Mindish as Dale rolled into the parking acreage. The day was hazy and smog indicated the outlines of the sun. When we parked and boarded one of the tractor trains, the clean-cut girl conductor looked at me in what I thought was a regretful manner, her knowledge of my fate conflicting with the natural attraction she felt for my shoulder locks and fuck-everyone persona. Linda obviously did not know whether she was happy or distressed that I might not get in. I don't think she thought I would quietly go away.

I decided that if I was hassled I would break the line and jump over the turnstile. Dale bought the tickets and I noticed significant looks between a guard and a ticket-taker. A man approached me. Dale headed him off and talked to him for a moment. The thing was I was a freak, yes, but he would take the responsibility. Our tickets were presented and like a foreigner going through customs I was accepted into Disneyland.

Linda and I and Dale walked briskly down Main Street USA. We passed a horse-drawn trolley, an old-time double-decker bus. We passed a penny arcade with Charlie Chaplin flipcard Movieolas. Giant music boxes that make the sound of the whole band. We passed an apothecary. A red and white striped ice cream parlor. People sat smiling in beerless beer gardens. People filled the sidewalks and the street. People strolled past the bay-windowed shops. People stared at me.

"How do we find him?" I asked Linda.

"They'll be in Tomorrowland," she said. "That's what he likes best." In the Plaza at the end of Main Street we go through the gates of Tomorrowland. The whole world turns colorfully modern. Linda leads us to the Richfield Autopia.

People wait to board the little gas cars of the Richfield Autopia, a tracked ride that offers the illusion of steering to the person behind the wheel. Little snarling Autopia convertibles pile up at the freeway stop, drivers jump out, and drivers waiting their turns at assigned and numbered places jump in. Cars stream by, the air is filled with the droning of kicky toy engines. Linda points over the fence. There he is. With Sadie next to him, sitting straight and proud. In the toy car. She has a whole book of tickets. She hands another ticket up to the attendant and they don't get out. Selig grips the wheel waiting for the new run to begin. His arms are bare, he wears an Hawaiian shirt. He is incredibly old. His chin moves up and down, his lips flap against each other, his mouth opens and closes and there flashes across his face a moment of astonishment, a moment of pugnacity, astonishment, pugnacity, in alternating palsies of the nerve. He is white-haired. His hands shake as they grip the wheel. A car bumps them from the back, a child laughs, their grey heads look up to heaven, and they lurch forward on the journey into Autopia.

My heart was beating wildly. I found myself needing more air than I had. I was aware that Dale and Linda were on either side of me and were watching me closely.

"I want to talk to him, Linda."

"You still do?"

"Yes."

She was very grim. In a few minutes Selig and Sadie came into view and pulled up again. Sadie prepared another ticket for the attendant and for a moment did not hear her daughter calling to her.

"Mama! Mama!"

But the car shot off again, Sadie looking back over her shoulder to see who had called her.

It was decided that Dale and I would retire to the shade of the Coca-Cola Tomorrowland Terrace while Linda waited for her parents and prepared them for meeting me. I felt as if we were making arrangements for a burial. At the Coca-Cola Terrace a rock band was just finishing a set. The rock musicians had short hair. They waved and their stage sank out of sight to the applause of the matrons.

"He's senile," Dale said to me as we sat waiting. "She tried to tell you that. There's nothing left up here," he said tapping his temple.

People stood on line for hamburgers and Coca-Cola. Embossed on the edges of my vision were all the errant tracks of the overhead rides and rocket spins, the sinking submarines and the swiveling cars; the starting and stopping of strollers, the ruthless paths of careening infants. I sat with my arms folded at the formica café table. In the middle of my eye, out in the sun the Mindish family was about to deploy itself. Linda beckoned and Dale went out to join them.

Sadie Mindish was being stubborn. She believed if she came any closer some terrible contamination, or sudden death, would befall her. She kept peering in my direction and then giving Linda hell. Linda spoke to Dale and Dale held the old lady's hand and talked to her. Sadie pulled her hand away and waved her arm in my direction. The lawyer stood in front of her to block me from her vision.

Linda came toward the terrace leading her father by the elbow.

I sat across the orange formica café table from Dr. Selig Mindish. His daughter kneeled beside him asking him if he'd like a chocolate milk shake. Her knees were blanched in her sheer stockings.

"Chocolate milk shakes are his favorite," she explained to me. Then in a louder voice she asked her father again if he wanted a milk shake.

I leaned forward with my hands on my knees so that he had to see me. The whites of his eyes were discolored. He needed a shave. Brown spots and moles had attacked his skin. His white hair was thinned out. His eyes were sunken in age sockets of fat and skin. His jaw moved up and down, his lips made the sound of a faucet dripping as they met and fell apart. But there was still in him the remnant of rude strength I remembered.

I said, "Hello, Mr. Mindish. I'm Daniel Isaacson. I'm Paul and Rochelle's son. Danny?"

Linda was kneeling beside him holding his hand. He struggled to understand me. His head stirred like a turtle's head coming out of its shell. He smiled and nodded. Then as he looked in my eyes he became gradually still, and even his facial palsy ceased, and he no longer smiled. I was sickened to see water well from the congested yellow corners of his eyes. Tears tracked down his face.

"Denny?"

"It's all right, Papa," Linda was saying. She patted his hand. She had begun to cry. "It's all right, Papa."

"It's Denny?"

For one moment of recognition he was restored to life. In wonder he raised his large, clumsy hand and touched the side of my face. He found the back of my neck and pulled me forward and leaned toward me and touched the top of my head with his palsied lips.

Philip K. Dick

---

from *A SCANNER DARKLY*

Born in Chicago in 1928, Philip K. Dick grew up in California, attending Berkeley High School and UC Berkeley. His major works include *Do Androids Dream of Electric Sheep?*, *Martian Time Slip*, and *The Man in the High Castle*, and many of his books have been adapted into wildly popular films, including *Blade Runner* (1982) and, more recently, *A Scanner Darkly* (2006). At the time of his death in Santa Ana, he had published forty novels and more than a hundred short stories.

The legendary writer's impact—on speculative and literary fiction, culture, film, and how we think of science and technology—is almost inestimable. In this passage from one of his most famous novels, Dick anticipates artificial intelligence, biotechnology, and the total surveillance state in a joyfully sardonic sendup of both law enforcement and business culture. Although first published in 1977, this book aims at targets no less available for critique today than they were forty years ago.

"GENTLEMEN OF THE Anaheim Lions Club," the man at the microphone said, "we have a wonderful opportunity this afternoon, for, you see, the County of Orange has provided us with the chance to hear from—and then put questions to and of—an undercover narcotics agent from the Orange County Sheriff's Department." He beamed, this man wearing his pink waffle-fiber suit and wide plastic yellow tie and blue shirt and fake leather shoes; he was an overweight man, overaged as well, overhappy even when there was little or nothing to be happy about.

Watching him, the undercover narcotics agent felt nausea.

"Now, you will notice," the Lions Club host said, "that you can barely see this individual, who is seated directly to my right, because he is wearing what is called a scramble suit, which is the exact same suit he wears—and in fact must wear—during certain parts, in fact most, of his daily activities of law enforcement. Later he will explain why."

The audience, which mirrored the qualities of the host in every possible way, regarded the individual in his scramble suit.

"This man," the host declared, "whom we will call Fred, because this is the code name under which he reports the information he gathers, once within the scramble suit, cannot be identified by voice, or by even technological voiceprint, or by appearance. He looks, does he not, like a vague blur and nothing more? Am I right?" He let loose a great smile. His audience, appreciating that this was indeed funny, did a little smiling on their own.

The scramble suit was an invention of the Bell Laboratories, conjured up by accident by an employee named S. A. Powers. He had, a few years ago, been experimenting with disinhibiting substances affecting neural tissue, and one night, having administered to himself an IV injection considered safe and mildly euphoric, had experienced a disastrous drop in the GABA fluid of his brain. Subjectively, he had then witnessed lurid phosphene activity projected on the far wall of his bedroom, a frantically progressing montage of what, at the time, he imagined to be modern-day abstract paintings.

For about six hours, entranced, S. A. Powers had watched thousands of Picasso paintings replace one another at flash-cut speed, and then he had been treated to Paul Klees, more than the painter had painted during his entire lifetime. S. A. Powers, now viewing Modigliani paintings replace themselves at furious velocity, had conjectured (one needs a theory for everything) that the Rosicrucians were telepathically beaming pictures at him, probably boosted by microrelay systems of an advanced order; but then, when Kandinsky paintings began to harass him, he recalled that the main art museum at Leningrad specialized in just such nonobjective moderns, and he decided that the Soviets were attempting telepathically to contact him.

In the morning he remembered that a drastic drop in the GABA fluid of the brain normally produced such phosphene activity; nobody was trying telepathically, with or without microwave boosting, to contact him. But it did give him the idea for the scramble suit. Basically, his design consisted of a multifaced quartz lens hooked to a miniaturized computer whose memory banks held up to a million and a half physiognomic fraction-representations of various people: men and women, children, with every variant encoded and then projected outward in all directions equally onto a superthin shroudlike membrane large enough to fit around an average human.

As the computer looped through its banks, it projected every conceivable eye color, hair color, shape and type of nose, formation of teeth, configuration of facial bone structure—the entire shroudlike membrane took on whatever physical characteristics were projected at any nanosecond, and then switched to the next. Just to make his scramble suit more effective, S. A. Powers programmed the computer to randomize the sequence of characteristics within each set. And to bring the cost down (the federal people always liked that), he found the source for the material of the membrane in a byproduct of a large industrial firm already doing business with Washington.

In any case, the wearer of a scramble suit was Everyman and in every combination (up to combinations of a million and a half subbits) during the course of each hour. Hence, any description of him—or her—was meaningless. Needless to say, S. A. Powers had fed his own personal physiognomic characteristics into the computer units, so that, buried in the frantic permutation of qualities, his own surfaced and combined...on an average, he had calculated, of once each fifty years per suit, served up and reassembled, given enough time per suit. It was his closest claim to immortality.

"Let's hear it for the vague blur!" the host said loudly, and there was mass clapping.

In his scramble suit, Fred, who was also Robert Arctor, groaned and thought: This is terrible.

Once a month an undercover narcotics agent of the county was assigned at random to speak before bubblehead gatherings such as this. Today was his turn. Looking at his audience, he realized how much he detested straights. They thought this was all great. They were smiling. They were being entertained.

Maybe at this moment the virtually countless component of his scramble suit had served up S. A. Powers.

"But to be serious for just a moment," the host said, "the man here..." He paused, trying to remember.

"Fred," Bob Arctor said. S. A. Fred.

"Fred, yes." The host, invigorated, resumed, booming in the direction of his audience, "You see, Fred's voice is like one of those robot computer voices down in San Diego at the bank when you drive in, perfectly toneless and artificial. It leaves in our minds no characteristics, exactly as when he reports to his superiors in the Orange County Drug Abuse, ah, Program." He paused meaningfully. "You see, there is a dire risk for these police officers because the forces of dope, as we know, have penetrated with amazing skill into the various law enforcement apparatuses throughout our nation, or may well have, according to most informed experts. So for the protection of these dedicated men, this scramble suit is necessary."

Slight applause for the scramble suit. And then expectant gazes at Fred, lurking within its membrane.

"But in his line of work in the field," the host added finally, as he moved away from the microphone to make room for Fred, "he, of course, does not wear this. He dresses like you or I, although, of course, in the hippie garb of those of the various subculture groups within which he bores in tireless fashion."

He motioned to Fred to rise and approach the microphone. Fred, Robert Arctor, had done this six times before, and he knew what to say and what was in store for him: the assorted degrees and kinds of asshole questions and opaque stupidity. The waste of time for him out of this, plus anger on his part, and a sense of futility each time, and always more so.

"If you saw me on the street," he said into the microphone, after the applause had died out, "you'd say, 'There goes a weirdo freak doper.' And you'd feel aversion and walk away."

Silence.

"I don't look like you," he said. "I can't afford to. My life depends on it." Actually, he did not look that different from them. And anyhow, he would have worn what he wore daily anyhow, job or not, life or not. He liked what he wore. But what he was saying had, by and large, been written by others and put before him to memorize. He could depart some, but they all had a standard format they used. Introduced a couple of years ago by a gung-ho division chief, it had by now become writ.

He waited while that sank in.

"I am not going to tell you first," he said, "what I am attempting to do as an undercover officer engaged in tracking down dealers and most of all the source of their illegal drugs in the streets of our cities and corridors of our schools, here in Orange County. I am going to tell you"—he paused, as they had trained him to do in PR class at the academy—"what I am afraid of," he finished.

That gaffed them; they had become all eyes.

"What I fear," he said, "night and day, is that our children, your children and my children..." Again he paused. "I have two," he said. Then, extra quietly, "Little ones, very little." And then he raised his voice emphatically. "But not too little to be addicted, calculatedly addicted, for profit, by those who would destroy this society." Another pause. "We do not know as yet," he continued presently, more calmly, "specifically who these men—or rather animals—are who prey on our young, as if in a wild jungle abroad, as in some foreign country, not ours. The identity of the purveyors of the poisons concocted of brain-destructive filth shot daily, orally taken daily, smoked daily by several million men and women—or rather, that were once men and women—is gradually being unraveled. But finally we will, before God, know for sure."

A voice from the audience: "Sock it to 'em!"

Another voice, equally enthusiastic: "Get the commies!"

Applause and reprise severally.

Robert Arctor halted. Stared at them, at the straights in their fat suits, their fat ties, their fat shoes, and he thought, Substance D can't destroy their brains; they have none.

"Tell it like it is," a slightly less emphatic voice called up, a woman's voice. Searching, Arctor made out a middle-aged lady, not so fat, her hands clasped anxiously.

"Each day," Fred, Robert Arctor, whatever, said, "this disease takes its toll of us. By the end of each passing day the flow of profits—and where they go we—" He broke off. For the life of him he could not dredge up the rest of the sentence, even though he had repeated it a million times, both in class and at previous lectures.

All in the large room had fallen silent.

"Well," he said, "it isn't the profits anyhow. It's something else. What you see happen."

They didn't notice any difference, he noticed, even though he had dropped the prepared speech and was wandering on, by himself, without help from the PR boys back at the Orange County Civic Center. What difference anyhow? he thought. So what? What, really, do they know or care? The straights, he thought, live in their fortified huge apartment complexes guarded by their guards, ready to open fire on any and every doper who scales the wall with an empty pillowcase to rip off their piano and electric clock and razor and stereo that they haven't paid for anyhow, so he can get his fix, get the shit that if he doesn't he maybe dies, outright flat-out dies, of the pain and shock of withdrawal. But, he thought, when you're living inside looking safely out, and your wall is electrified and your guard is armed, why think about that?

"If you were a diabetic," he said, "and you didn't have money for a hit of insulin, would you steal to get the money? Or just die?"

Silence.

In the headphone of his scramble suit a tinny voice said, "I think you'd better go back to the prepared text, Fred. I really do advise it."

Into his throat mike, Fred, Robert Arctor, whatever, said, "I forget it." Only his superior at Orange County GHQ, which was not Mr. F., that is to say, Hank, could hear this. This was an anonymous superior, assigned to him only for this occasion.

"Riiiight," the official tinny prompter said in his earphone. "I'll read it to you. Repeat it after me, but try to get it to sound casual."

Slight hesitation, riffling of pages. "Let's see...'Each day the profits flow—where they go we—' That's about where you stopped."

"I've got a block against this stuff," Arctor said.

"'—will soon determine,'" his official prompter said, unheeding, "'and then retribution will swiftly follow. And at that moment I would not for the life of me be in their shoes.'"

"Do you know why I've got a block against this stuff?" Arctor said. "Because this is what gets people on dope." He thought, this is why you lurch off and become a doper, this sort of stuff. This is why you give up and leave. In disgust.

But then he looked once more out at his audience and realized that for them this was not so. This was the only way they could be reached. He was talking to nitwits. Mental simps. It had to be put in the same way it had been put in first grade: *A* is for Apple and the Apple is Round.

"*D*," he said aloud to his audience, "is for Substance D. Which is for Dumbness and Despair and Desertion, the desertion of your friends from you, you from them, everyone from everyone, isolation and loneliness and hating and suspecting each other. *D*," he said then, "is finally Death. Slow Death, we—" He halted. "We, the dopers," he said, "call it." His voice rasped and faltered. "As you probably know. Slow Death. From the head on down. Well, that's it." He walked back to his chair and reseated himself. In silence.

"You blew it," his superior the prompter said. "See me in my office when you get back. Room 430."

"Yes," Arctor said. "I blew it."

They were looking at him as if he had pissed on the stage before their eyes. Although he was not sure just why.

Striding to the mike, the Lions Club host said, "Fred asked me in advance of this lecture to make it primarily a question-and-answer forum, with only a short introductory statement by him. I forgot to mention that. All right"—he raised his right hand—"who first, people?"

Arctor suddenly got to his feet again, clumsily.

"It would appear that Fred has something more to add," the host said, beckoning to him.

Going slowly back over to the microphone, Arctor said, his head down, speaking with precision, "Just this. Don't kick their asses after they're on it. The users, the addicts. Half of them, most of them, especially the girls, didn't know what they were getting on or even that they were getting on anything at all. Just try to keep them, the people, any of us, from getting on it." He looked up briefly. "See, they dissolve some reds in a glass of wine, the pushers, I mean—they give the booze to a chick, an underage little chick, with eight to ten reds in it, and she passes out, and then they inject her with a mex hit, which is half heroin and half Substance D—" He broke off. "Thank you," he said.

A man called up, "How do we stop them, sir?"

"Kill the pushers," Arctor said, and walked back to his chair.

He did not feel like returning right away to the Orange County Civic Center and Room 430, so he wandered down one of the commercial streets of Anaheim, inspecting the McDonaldburger stands and car washes and gas stations and Pizza Huts and other marvels.

Roaming aimlessly along like this on the public street with all kinds of people, he always had a strange feeling as to who he was. As he had said to the Lions types there in the hall, he looked like a doper when out of his scramble suit; he conversed like a doper; those around him now no doubt took him to be a doper and reacted accordingly. Other dopers—See there, he thought; "other," for instance—gave him a "peace, brother" look, and the straights didn't.

You put on a bishop's robe and miter, he pondered, and walk around in that, and people bow and genuflect and like that, and try to kiss your ring, if not your ass, and pretty soon you're a bishop. So to speak. What is identity? he asked himself. Where does the act end? Nobody knows.

What really fouled up his sense of who and what he was came when the Man hassled him. When harness bulls, beat cops, or cops in general, any and all, for example, came cruising up slowly to the curb near him in an intimidating manner as he walked, scrutinized him at length with an intense, keen, metallic, blank stare, and then, often as not, evidently on whim, parked and beckoned him over.

"Okay, let's see your I.D.," the cop would say, reaching out; and then, as Arctor-Fred-Whatever-Godknew fumbled in his wallet pocket, the cop would yell at him, "Ever been ARRESTED?" Or, as a variant on that, adding, "BEFORE?" As if he were about to go into the bucket right then.

"What's the beef?" he usually said, if he said anything at all. A crowd naturally gathered. Most of them assumed he'd been nailed dealing on the corner. They grinned uneasily and waited to see what happened, although some of them, usually Chicanos or blacks or obvious heads, looked angry. And those that looked angry began after a short interval to be aware that they looked angry, and they changed that swiftly to impassive. Because everybody knew that anyone looking angry or uneasy—it didn't matter which—around cops must have something to hide. The cops especially knew that, legend had it, and they hassled such persons automatically.

This time, however, no one bothered him. Many heads were in evidence; he was only one of many.

What am I actually? he asked himself. He wished, momentarily, for his scramble suit. Then, he thought, I could go on being a vague blur and passers-by, street people in general, would applaud. Let's hear it for the vague blur, he thought, doing a short rerun. What a way to get recognition. How, for instance, could they be sure it wasn't some other vague blur and not the right one? It could be somebody other than Fred inside, or another Fred, and they'd never know, not even when Fred opened his mouth and talked. They wouldn't really know then. They'd never know. It could be Al pretending to be Fred, for example. It could be anyone in there, it could even be empty. Down at Orange County GHQ they could be piping a voice to the scramble suit, animating it from the sheriff's office. Fred could in that case be anybody who happened to be at his desk that day and happened to pick up the script and the mike, or a composite of all sorts of guys at their desks.

But I guess what I said at the end, he thought, finishes off that. That wasn't anybody back in the office. The guys back in the office want to talk to me about that, as a matter of fact.

He didn't look forward to that, so he continued to loiter and delay, going nowhere, going everywhere. In Southern California it didn't make any difference anyhow where you went, there was always the same McDonaldburger place over and over, like a circular strip that turned past you as you pretended to go somewhere. And when finally you got hungry and went to the McDonaldburger place and bought a McDonald's hamburger, it was the one they sold you last time and the time before that and so forth, back to before you were born, and in addition bad people—liars—said it was made out of turkey gizzards anyhow.

They had by now, according to their sign, sold the same original burger fifty billion times. He wondered if it was to the same person. Life in Anaheim, California, was a commercial for itself, endlessly replayed. Nothing changed; it just spread out farther and farther in the form of neon ooze. What there was always more of had been congealed into permanence long ago, as if the automatic factory that cranked out these objects had jammed in the *on* position. How the land became plastic, he thought, remembering the fairy tale "How the Sea Became Salt." Someday, he thought, it'll be mandatory that we all sell the McDonald's hamburger as well as buy it; we'll sell it back and forth to each other forever from our living rooms. That way we won't even have to go outside.

Harryette Mullen

VARIATION ON A THEME PARK

Harryette Mullen was born in 1953 in Florence, Alabama, and grew up in Fort Worth, Texas. She graduated from UT Austin and went on to study at UC Santa Cruz. Currently a professor of English at UCLA, she is a poet, short story writer, and most recently the author of the collection *Urban Tumbleweed: Notes from a Tanka Diary*.

"Variation on a Theme Park" is from the collection *Sleeping with the Dictionary*, a finalist for a National Book Award, a National Book Critics Circle Award, and a *Los Angeles Times* Book Prize. It was also included in 2008's *Great American Prose Poems: From Poe to the Present*. An esteemed language poet, Mullen employs a punny title and playful word games to trigger conscious and subconscious associations by way of a familiar attraction.

My Mickey Mouse ears are nothing like sonar. Colorado
is far less rusty than Walt's lyric riddles. If sorrow is
wintergreen, well then Walt's breakdancers are dunderheads.
If hoecakes are Wonder Bras, blond Wonder Bras grow on
Walt's hornytoad. I have seen roadkill damaged, riddled and
wintergreen, but no such roadkill see I in Walt's checkbook.
And in some purchases there is more deliberation than in
the bargains that my Mickey Mouse redeems. I love to herd
Walt's sheep, yet well I know that muskrats have a far more
platonic sonogram. I grant I never saw a googolplex groan.
My Mickey Mouse, when Walt waddles, trips on garbanzos.
And yet, by halogen-light, I think my loneliness as reckless as
any souvenir bought with free coupons.

Susan Straight

from *I BEEN IN SORROW'S KITCHEN AND LICKED OUT ALL THE POTS*

Susan Straight was born in 1960 in Riverside, where she has lived and worked most of her life. Her engagement with history, family, and place is abundantly shown in her journalism, essays, short stories, and nine novels, including *Aquaboogie, Between Heaven and Here*, and *Highwire Moon*, a finalist for the National Book Award. She teaches in the writing program at UC Riverside.

In this chapter from her second book, published in 1992, Straight explores place and perspective through the eyes of Marietta, an African American Gullah-speaking native of South Carolina, whose early morning walks in a suburban neighborhood dramatize her perspective on an unfamiliar, sometimes hostile landscape. Yet, her discoveries at sidewalk-level seem, finally, to challenge the prejudices and assumptions of the tract housing construction of daily life.

ALONG THIS WALL, she saw patches of green. The brown cinder blocks must have had narrow gaps somewhere because, when she came closer, every ten feet or so there was a springy vine, a wild ivy or maybe a grape, tumbling out of a crack. But they were so regularly spaced—how had someone planted seeds in the cement?

The bending plants, pouring down the wall like little waterfalls, were the only green Marietta had seen since she left the gate of the condominium complex. She looked away from the shady side of the wall to the hills all around her. This was the farthest she'd ever walked, and she was at the edge of the developed land. Red tile roofs, white stucco walls like all the other houses and condos, covered the hills in wide crescents.

"Tracks," she said to herself. That was what she had heard Carolanne call them, the curve on curve of houses laid out behind walls. Covering the hills like big smiles, she thought, red lips and white, white teeth. Mouths laughing forever. Baby Poppa saying, "Look at those girls when your sons come home to visit—every mouth for miles gets to grinning."

The land was gold where it had been left bare, the grass burned pale or gone in the vacant lots where she walked and the dirt had been leveled for new houses. And the sky was white here in California, already no-color from the heat and it was only the end of May. Sky so bright from the first minute of day, before 6 A.M., not like Pine Gardens, where even on the longest, hottest days the oaks and their long moss curls kept the light spotted and deep. She reached out and ran her hand along this rough wall, touching the vines. This must be an older track, because the street was slightly grayed, like the sun had been working it for a while. Not like the deep black asphalt of the brand-new complex where they lived. Tendrils brushed her fingers; where did the vines find water in the walls?

There surely wasn't water anywhere else, only from sprinklers. She knew by the way the gentle slope went before her that the depression ahead wasn't a river, the way it would be at home, but the freeway again. The same place she had ended up last week, walking down a different road next to another track. She could hear the traffic-wind, and quickly she came to the end of the wall and the hard-packed dirt that was everywhere past the sidewalk. At the chainlink fence lining the banks of the freeway, she watched the cars swim slowly past her. Six-thirty—morning rush hour, Carolanne said. The tips of dried weeds tangled in the wire near her feet, rustling like autumn cornstalks when she nudged them.

"Don't think you can go out this early and nobody'll see you," Carolanne had told her pointedly when she'd seen Marietta come back from a walk one morning. She'd looked at Marietta's dusty black shoes, her shirt. "Rush-hour people are out before six."

Along the curve of fence, she kept on until she saw one of the green freeway signs, huge because it was so close. BEACHES—an arrow pointed down toward the left lanes. LOS ANGELES—another pointed to the right lanes.

Nate and Calvin had taken her to Los Angeles one day and the beach the next. L.A. was a too-fast jumble of buildings to her, because she was still tired and dazed from the long drive across the country, but they wanted to show her the university and the dorms where they'd lived.

But Newport Beach—the blue and sand of this ocean, the huge waves—was a surprise. Nate wore his practice jersey, LOS ANGELES RAMS across the front, and he smiled big as a banana when a blond kid walking close to the water shouted, "Daddy, that's Nate and Calvin Cook! They got drafted by the Rams and I saw them on TV!"

Marietta had tried to imagine fishing there, but the broad expanse of sand was covered with towels and people and umbrellas; no reeds or grasses where fish could hide, no point jutting out into the water, no place to see green until they drove to Balboa, a word Nate liked to roll around his tongue. "It's private, see all the houses, Mama? I'm a have to get you one, oh, next year, most def," he had said.

"You best worry bout this year, fool," Calvin had said.

"Don't let your mouth write a check your behind can't cash," Carolanne had said sharply behind them. Little Freeman slept, his head lolling on her shoulder.

Following the line of traffic, the car roofs stacked together tight as Freeman's toy trains, only gave her a headache. All the exhaust made dancing wavers in the air. At the street that led back up the hill, she turned.

Hadn't been here but a month and already she was out of walks. She'd been walking in the space of time after the boys left for the field and before Carolanne and Freeman woke up. The boys had to run and work out early, before the heat and smog filled the air. Every morning, Calvin dressed in his sweats at five-thirty, and when she heard his feet thud on the carpet, she got up to make him biscuits and grits. "Mama, I ain't eatin till we get back," he said. "Come on, now."

"You best get use to good food again, not that McDonald food. How you muscle gon work on air and grease?" She handed him a plate wrapped in foil, for Nate. "Take this and I see you when you back."

He would walk next door, pound for a minute, and when she looked outside in the gray dark, she could see Nate put the food in his mouth as he leaned into the dashboard light.

Jump around like crickets in these new condominium rooms, run and lift weight in the morning, then don't know what for do rest a the day. Talking bout rookie mini-camp over but official training camp start in July—that almost two month away.

A scratch of tires, quick as a burp, came again and again ahead of her. The line of cars waited to get out of the walls. Only one street led into the square of houses, and each car rushed through the stop sign, slowing just a second so the drivers could stare at her and then look past her; then they swerved out to join the line snaking up the hill to the main road and the freeway.

They turned away from her quickly. She tensed, made herself breathe. She'd forgotten about them for a while. Her clothes, her back. Damn, that woman big. Damn, that woman black. Is that a *woman*? The knock on the condo door—Uh, excuse me, I'm looking for the lady of the house. Uh, the owner? She held her shoulders tight, breathed, until she crossed between two cars. The first time she'd walked—Uh, need a lift, buddy? someone had said behind her. When she turned, a security guard leaned out his car window, growing a sunset across his cheeks. "Sorry, uh, sorry. Are you lost, ma'am?"

Her clothes were wrong. Already, through the open glass doors of their adjoining balconies, she'd heard Carolanne say on the phone, "We look black enough, okay? It ain't like there's a whole lot of us in the complex—try none. And what's she gonna wear? She ain't fitting into no Spiegel's. I *gave* her the catalog, okay?"

That first week she'd lived here—when Carolanne had tried to smile and not study her, when she didn't know if she could just open their door or if she had to knock—she'd stood outside, hearing Freeman's cries after the boys had left, and pushed the door open. She had seen the way Carolanne looked at her clothes, her scarf, but she didn't know what Carolanne was trying to tell her.

"Where you going, anyway?"

"Just walk, what wrong with the baby?"

"He has diarrhea."

"I stop at the store when I walk for some more rice—you can give he rice water."

"There's no store around here you can walk to—this is Anaheim Hills." Carolanne squinted at her. "You can't drive, really? You're exercise walking?"

Marietta felt the air on her palms. She carried nothing in her hands, she had finally realized, no weights to swing or tiny radio with headphones or little white towel. By nine or ten each morning, when she watched out her window, she could see the other women from the condos walking, usually in pairs, wearing pink or yellow or lavender sweatsuits, white shoes, white headbands or visors. They swung their arms and weights, their feet round and hard on the pavement. They were dressed right; she looked like she was headed to a store or cemetery or house that needed cleaning. "Great workout, huh!" one had called to her, and she thought, Carry you some grocery, two baby, and a basket of peach fe exercise. Walk to the store—two mile.

But there was no store here. Squares and circles of streets inside the walls, and she'd gotten lost in one that first week, a maze of white stucco fronts and square-closed garages all the same, staring like boxes on the game shows Carolanne watched sometimes. Tiny trees like feather dusters in planters along the walls. She was almost home now, back to the huge sign that said EDGEWILD OAKS—LUXURY CONDOMINIUMS IN THE ANAHEIM HILLS.

She had forgotten about these two trees. The huge gnarled oaks and branches that reached out past their giant fenced-in planter—one on each side of the guard gate where she had to nod each time to the eyes. A woman came out of the section of cobblestone road between the two trees. "Aren't they beautiful?" she said when she saw Marietta and smiled. She wore a purple sweatsuit and purple hoop earrings. "I'm always so happy to see they left them here."

"I never knew oak trees live in California," Marietta murmured.

"California live oaks," the woman said. "Do you work in the neighborhood?" She smiled again and stretched her arms behind her.

"No. I live here with my son."

"Oh! Where are you from?" The woman's voice was southern-soft.

"South Carolina."

"I'm from Georgia!" she said. "I didn't expect oaks, either." She smiled once more and began to walk quickly, her arms pumping like she was boxing with the air.

Peggy Hesketh

---

from *TELLING THE BEES*

Born in Monroeville, Pennsylvania, in 1954, journalist Peggy Hesketh currently teaches writing at UC Irvine. A longtime Anaheim resident, she has lived most of her life in the same home, across the street from poet Grant Hier, with whom she has been friends for decades.

Her debut novel, *Telling the Bees*, inspired by the 1983 Bee Lady murders of Anaheim, has been widely translated. In it, Hesketh tells the story of old Orange County through a combination of sad reminiscence and a joyful recounting of youth, with a mystery story, too—all portrayed via the lonely discipline and devotion of a "bee man." The novel's locale is a big backyard lot behind a prefab house, complete with fruit trees, apiary, and neighborly first-generation suburban pioneers—often Midwesterners—enduring against ferocious change. In this chapter, our hero considers his neighborhood, presaging a personal story that Hesketh described to us as one of "dreams, regrets, and the passing of time and place."

T HE BEES TRAVEL along the high-tension wires, just as surely as one true sentence follows the next. I am not sure why bees took to this peculiar mode of travel, but I suspect they have their reasons, and their reasons have everything to do with the Bee Ladies' murder.

There is a family living not far from my home that mistakenly holds the electricity that hums and buzzes over their heads responsible for all the people in our neighborhood who have chanced to die in recent years. It is a complicated theory based on the deleterious effects of electromagnetic fields. I hardly know this family beyond what I have been able to discern from the slogans on the handmade signs they display in their front yard. I know they believe the overhead wires that run above our homes cause all manner of human ailments, and for this reason they have planted a growing field of carefully tended crosses in their lawn, one for each neighbor who has died since they began keeping track of such things shortly after moving into one of the newer housing tracts not far from my home nearly eight years ago.

I only spoke to them once, not long after they'd begun planting crosses in their lawn. It was one of those impossibly warm Southern California days that almost always occurs in early February, the sort of day that sings to those who wish to leave behind the bone-chilling heartbreak of winter and make a new life for themselves in the promise of eternal sunshine.

I probably would not have stopped to talk to this particular family, except that I was driving slowly past their home so that I might get a better look at the crosses and the curious signs on their lawn. Because of the heat, my car windows were open.

"Hey, Grandpa!" I heard a man shout. My initial instinct was to press my acceleration pedal down. But then I heard another voice. A woman's voice. It sounded determined yet vulnerable at the same time.

"You will help us?"

I know it seems foolish. They were strangers. But they were my neighbors as well. I pulled to the curb. The woman smiled and rushed to the edge of her lawn. She was thin and agitated, with dark, lanky hair and an oily copper complexion. She held a clipboard in her hand.

"Can you sign this?" she said, running around to the driver's side of my car. She handed me the clipboard and a pen through my open window.

"¿Por favor?"

"May I read it first?"

She glanced back at the man who stood thirty feet away in the gape of the open garage, a beer in one hand and some sort of power tool in the other. She nodded quickly at me.

As I read through the xeroxed copy of the petition which would ban all manner of overhead electrical wires in residential neighborhoods, it seemed prudent to ask the woman who stood so desperately by my car door why she was doing what she was doing, but that wouldn't have been polite.

Instead, I inquired where she was from. That is what new neighbors do. At least, that is what they used to do. This is how I learned she was originally from Texas, somewhere south of Dallas, that she'd moved to California with her father, who was in the military. It is also how I learned that she loved sunshine and open spaces, and that she feared the overhead power lines, which she said reminded her of barbed-wire fences.

When I was finished reading her petition, I told her I was very sorry but I did not wish to sign it. I told her it made no sense to me. She squeezed her eyes shut, and she thanked me just the same, scurrying back to the garage and handing the clipboard to the man I can only assume was her husband. I heard shouting as I pulled away from the curb. It was only later that I realized I'd forgotten to ask her name.

The following December my neighbors took to stringing their crosses with winking colored lights to mark the Christmas season. The spring after that they tied pastel pink and blue and yellow ribbons on the crosses at Eastertide. Independence Day is now demarcated by tiny American flags, and every October they drape their crosses in orange and black crepe paper and set a lighted jack-o'-lantern in their midst. And all the while, their field of crosses continues to grow. I found their agitated theories rather ludicrous, disturbing even. But what disturbed me for far too long is that I did not recognize a single name on any of their crosses.

My neighbors are no longer my neighbors. There is no longer any visceral connection between us other than that they are the strangers who live nearest to me. Day after day all I hear are leaf blowers and cars with pounding speakers that cruise slowly down my street, and night after night sirens wail and helicopters beat the air over my home with a roar that makes my head hurt.

So much noise.

I suspect this is why my bees no longer produce as much honey as they used to, nor does it taste quite as sweet as it once did.

Though I am an old man and my memory has begun to fade, I still recall a quiet time when the road in front of my home was made of dirt and gravel, and my dear mother could rock on our front porch swing and greet each and every one of our neighbors by their given names. But that time is long gone, and with it a definition of home and family that inextricably linked bricks and mortar and genes and bloodlines.

I have tried to adjust as best I can to this modern era, and I have found that thankfully my bees continue to wax and wane with the seasons. They remind me that the hundreds and thousands of births and deaths that occur each honey season are the natural life cycle of the hive, and this in turn has helped to ease my pain at the passing of all of the people I have held dear. Death is a constant in life. I thought I had long since made my peace.

But then, last August, I saw a new cross on my neighbors' front yard. I noticed it because it was different from the rest. Not the cross itself, which was fashioned from the same t-shaped slats of wood, nailed together, scrawled with a name and date of death, and planted in the ground. What *was* different were the flowers and candles and stuffed animals and balloons crowded around its spindly stake. In all the times I had driven past this house on my way to my honey consignments, or the library, the grocery store, the gas station, and whatever other random errand drew me less and less frequently from my home, I had never seen such a singular display on their lawn. Summer was just ending. There was no holiday to commemorate.

Had my neighbors been gathered in their garage workshop with what had become over the years a progressively more menacing group of friends, shouting, listening to loud music, and imbibing liquor, I surely would not have stopped to examine this curious memorial. But on this particular evening their garage door was down, as were my automobile windows, and I thought I caught the faint scent of eucalyptus and orange blossoms in the air. Despite all my better instincts, I pulled to the curb with a firm twist on my unpadded steering wheel, climbed out of my old Ford Fairlane, and approached what was from my rough count the twenty-first cross on the lawn.

There was a flickering phalanx of tall glass candleholders painted with pictures of saints that made the cross appear more like an altar than my neighbors' usual generic protest. Scattered around the candles were prayer cards and hand-scrawled notes. Many were written in Spanish and attached to sprays of carnations and baby's breath wrapped in grocery store cellophane. There were also bunches of roses, geraniums, calla lilies, and hydrangeas that clearly were snipped from backyard gardens, and two or three plush bears and a cheap felt pirate's hat piled among the flowers. Though the memorial was crude, there was no mistaking that the grief expressed was both real and personal.

I bent down to read the hand-painted lettering on the cross: *Christina Perez: 1974–2011.*

That I did not recognize the name when I first read it saddened me as none of the other names on the crosses before it had. When the name finally struck a chord, some months later, it shattered what little faith I had left in all I still held dear. And yet, it brought me some small measure of comfort at the same time. The first I'd felt in far too many years.

My neighbors continue to blame the electricity for all that has gone wrong around them because they need something to blame for what they have found lacking in their own lives. They never knew the Bee Ladies, or a time not so long ago when the wires did not whine and sputter over their heads like an angry swarm. They do not recall quiet summer evenings thick with the sweet scent of eucalyptus, jasmine, and orange blossoms as I do. They believe malevolence needs a scientific explanation that can be measured in voltages and magnetic fields.

I do not subscribe to my neighbors' strange theories, or their garish memorial displays, but I am no longer as inclined to judge their scientific folly as harshly as I once did. Perhaps our need to make sense of profound loss is what makes us not so different after all.

Grant Hier

---

from *UNTENDED GARDEN*

Born in 1957, Grant Hier is a graduate of Sunny Hills High in Anaheim. He earned an MA from CSU Long Beach and is currently a professor of English and the chair of liberal arts and art history at the Laguna College of Art and Design. He has been awarded the Nancy Dew Taylor Prize for Literary Excellence in Poetry and the Kick Prize. He lives in southwestern Anaheim, across the street from his lifelong friend, novelist Peggy Hesketh.

Hier has lived in the same modest tract house for most of his life, and it is the setting of his book-length meditation on its physical and metaphorical place in memory, history, and imagination. *Untended Garden* looks back at the history of the area's native peoples and includes more than seventy Tongva words. "This poem began," Hier told us, "as a way to research questions I had as a child, digging in the dirt of the new tract home, wondering what I would find beneath me." In these selected passages he recounts the real and imagined journey of a teenage alter ego through time and geography via a storm drain connecting the lives of both human and creature ancestors.

> when I was thirteen
> I chained my bedroom door from the inside
> left a note on my pillow that I was "out for a walk"
>
> slipped the screen from the casement window
> and climbed quietly out of my family's new home
> into the still August night

I trotted down the hill
walked through the tract streets
named for places far away that I had never seen

and wandered down to the concrete ravine
three miles away to seek the course of the river
approaching from the other side

        where coyote howl
        once curved the night
        like the waters themselves

I followed its flat bed
between concrete banks
rising on either side like wings

to the place where the walls
steepened and narrowed
and a feeder conduit five feet across

pierced through the sloping wall
the source behind its black circle opening
unknown

I lowered my head as if in respect
and stepped inside the concrete pipe's
dark circumference

each breath and step echoed
with water trickles
the darkness dank and thick

no room to stand
I remained bent forward
as if falling into each new step

leaning into the future
with no expectation
other than to risk and step out

and see where it led me
a rite of passage I can see now
a test to prove myself

[...]

unknowingly following
   a young woman's footprints
   once made in deep mud

   following creek beds
   carrying her child
   to the Council Tree

our footfalls lacing now
odd dance partners in perfect step but for
centuries between

but for the Portland cement
binding sand aggregate and granite
into this fallopian drainpipe cocoon

   imaginal buds transforming

unsure if my eyes were open
or closed in the carbon blackness
losing track of all time

   to the point of no time

convergence of place
across an unlighted Noh play stage
simultaneity and singularity

   beyond differentiation

I thought   (or dreamt in my waking state)
that I was seeing sparks
      as the blind see "phantom light"

      or an amputee
      feels an itch in the limb
      no longer attached

      synapses to the missed past

      a downed power line flailing

      internal chaos snapping
      orange and blue sparks
      glint of copper through black

      the snake sliced clean in two
      by a *schlunk* of shovel blade
      whips its cursive memory of wholeness

      to curl
      back upon
      itself

I stopped and touched my fingertips
to the bridge of my nose
my eyes burning

I pressed my lids
until checkerboard black-and-white
patterns danced and fluttered

      like the palimpsest
      erased from a lifescript of skin twitches
         faint echoes of double helix
         muscle memory from forefathers
         and foremothers stored dormant
         for centuries in a chain of DNA

inherited then released in common
gestures:

a sidelong glance at news of sorrow
echoed sklent
in the great-great-grandson
the akimbo pose
with a cracking of thumb joint
on hip bone
done the same
by the fourteenth mother back

the idle roaming of tip of tongue
to explore the narrow ridges
on the back of the teeth
and the palatine raphe
on the roof of the mouth
just as the common mother
rocking with eyes closed
thirty-six million sunsets ago
taught us all

and we stumble ahead
unaware of the sources of our grace
from whence or from whom
what similar shapes once displaced the sky
as the sheets slept on night after night
inherit folds
ironed sharp by the dead weight
of those asleep

plane after plane
consonantal remnants furrowed
creases that lace this history
ghosts of lines once stained

erasure yielding the clear impression
    of what was written here before
subtle as the web of wrinkles
netting each knuckle

    dried river and delta fan
flux of hand repeating
palm whorl manuscripts
in crows-feet meters
rerouted trails
still extant
in relief

not better

necessarily

    abandoned

    epidermal white
        of shed conception

    scraped parchment cicatrix
smooth skin of rubbed vellum
and veins fading
under rubbery cover
etched relief
whispering traces of the stories
behind us and under us

once the repetition of my footfalls
became a meaningless ring
like a familiar word repeated to nonsense

a blade of light appeared
plunging diagonally
across the nothingness ahead

I quickened my staggering gait toward it
my thoughts re-gaining shape
surfacing as if from deep underwater

my chest flooded warm
with the thought of miasma mist
exhaled into the open night

darkness expunged
and the re-filling of lungs
with morning

when I got to the wedge of light
slanting in as if from a Vermeer window
I saw it was a steep conduit jutting forty-five degrees

a hollow arm reaching in
from the other side
as if to save me

I extended my arms up
and into the narrow chute
wedged my shoulders against its sides

kicked myself up off of the floor
my ribs supporting my entire weight
wet shoes suspended midair

halfway in

halfway out

I wriggled
my heavy form
up toward freedom

and emerged finally
into a shallow sloping chamber
with a thick steel plate as lid

flush with the street
at the seam of the curb

I rolled onto my back
and pushed with bunched legs
until the heavy plate
squawked its submission and swung aside
revealing a cobalt blue sky

I rocked to my feet
and slowly uncurled
clicking my spine
straight again
an exhausted sob choking free

pant legs soaked
from the storm-drain soup
of lawn sprinkler runoff
and the piss and excrement
of rats, birds, and homeless

in the diffused light of pre-dawn
my wet shirt clinging to my spine
tail lights streaked past
as nauseating wakes of diesel fuel clouds
gusted into my face

from *whoosh* after *whoosh* of passing travelers

when I saw the radio transmission tower
I realized my bearings:

I was facing Los Angeles
unseen in the distance
my home was behind me

I was standing on the arterial road
paralleling the Santa Ana freeway

only a few hundred yards
from Coyote Creek

on the other side of the sooty chain-link

just a few yards from my face
cars and trucks roared past

each unaware of my journey
each rumbling their unknown loads

toward Ursa Minor

ACKNOWLEDGMENTS

WE TWO are fairly recent immigrants to, and now also enthusiastic boosters and recommenders of, the County of Orange. Thanks to the beloved teachers who first brought us here and who helped us to understand, engage critically with, persevere against, write about, and even celebrate the region: Peter Carr of CSU Long Beach and Oakley Hall and MacDonald Harris of UC Irvine. We are indebted to the South Orange County Community College District for the sabbatical time that seeded this book, and to Lewis Long and the faculty union, who faithfully defend sabbaticals each time contract negotiations come around. Thanks also to our collegial friends and friendly colleagues who over many years have shared their good ideas and good books with us: Roy Bauer, Dawn Bonker, Norm Johnson, Michelle Latiolais, Jim Mamer, OC Parks historic parks manager Sue McIntire, Virginia Shank, Jeff Solomon, Linda Thomas, Angelo and Marilyn Vassos, CSU Fullerton professor Steve Westbrook, and David Womack.

Sometimes you are lucky to meet the best people at exactly the best time. For their examples of scholarship, activism, and solidarity at CSU Long Beach, we acknowledge professors Betty Brooks, Robert Brophy, Roland Bush, David Fine, Sherna Gluck, Sondra Hale, David Peck, and Ray Zepeda.

Special thanks to Dean of Humanities Georges Van Den Abbeele, Beryl Schlossman, Julia Lupton, and Jonathan Alexander, all of UC Irvine (where else?), and to Dean Patrick Fuery of Chapman University and Dean Karima Feldhus of Irvine Valley College.

Thanks also to Gustavo Arellano, to editorial mentor Martin J. Smith, to stalwart booster Kedric Francis, and to writer and teacher Tom Zoellner, whose encouragement and advocacy kept us on track.

We have been fortunate to rely on the direction of dedicated staff members of Orange County Public Libraries, including regional branch manager Stephanie Brown and Lucille Cruz and Ruth Loc of our own terrific local Library of the Canyons branch. Thanks also to librarians Steve McLeod and Audra Eagle Yun of UC Irvine's Special Collections and Archives.

To Janet Tonkovich and her mother, Eunice Harris of La Habra, we are grateful for the serendipitous discovery of our family's relationship to the poet Ann Stanford, whose presence in this volume is crucial.

For their camaraderie, inspiration, and example we thank the Community of Writers at Squaw Valley.

We are especially grateful for the abiding direction and commitment of Heyday's founding publisher, Malcolm Margolin, who saw in our project an endeavor worthy enough to include in the proud catalog of our favorite people's publishing house, with its commitment to a community of shared empathy, ecological wisdom, and mutual aid.

Finally, we thank Gayle Wattawa, Lisa K. Marietta, and the Heyday family and, most especially, our patient, wise editor in chief, Eve Bachrach, who taught us how to do it, and so helped make this a better book.

This book is for our son, Louis (Orange County School of the Arts '20), and in fond memory of Jeanie Bernstein and Peter Carr, defenders of people and place.

PERMISSIONS

LISA ALVAREZ. "At the Last Bookstore" by Lisa Alvarez, © 2015 by Lisa Alvarez. Reprinted by permission of the author.

RAUL ALVAREZ. "Make Me a Hoot Owl Too, Sweetheart" from *There Was So Much Beautiful Left* by Raul Alvarez, © 2015 by Raul Alvarez. Reprinted by permission of the author.

GUSTAVO ARELLANO. "'Our Climate Is Faultless': Constructing America's Perpetual Eden" from *Orange County: A Personal History* by Gustavo Arellano, © 2008 by Gustavo Arellano. Reprinted with the permission of Scribner, a Division of Simon & Schuster, Inc. All rights reserved.

COLETTE LABOUFF ATKINSON. "Route" from *Mean* by Colette LaBouff Atkinson, © 2008 by Colette LaBouff Atkinson. Reprinted by permission of the University of Chicago Press.

GREG BILLS. Excerpt from *Fearful Symmetry* by Greg Bills, © 1996 by Greg Bills. Used by permission of Dutton, an imprint of Penguin Publishing Group, a division of Penguin Random House LLC.

JAMES P. BLAYLOCK. Excerpt from *The Last Coin* by James P. Blaylock, © 1988 by James P. Blaylock. Reprinted by permission of the author.

STEPHANIE BROWN. "The Lost Coast, California" from *Allegory of the Supermarket* by Stephanie Brown, © 1998 by Stephanie Brown. Reprinted by permission of the University of Georgia Press.

PETER CARR. "Anthem: Aliso Creek" from *Anthem: Aliso Creek* by Peter Carr, © 1971 by Peter Carr. Reprinted by permission of Jean Bernstein.

MICHAEL CHABON. "Ocean Avenue" from *A Model World* by Michael Chabon, © 1991 by Michael Chabon. Reprinted by permission of HarperCollins Publishers.

ABOUT THE EDITORS

LISA ALVAREZ grew up in and around Los Angeles and remembers driving with her family to visit Orange County as a child, reveling in the novelty of the then new freeways, seeing in the agricultural fields of beans and berries what her family called "the country," and waiting to catch the first snowy glimpse of Disneyland's Matterhorn from Interstate 5. She has since made the county home, first as a graduate student in UC Irvine's MFA fiction program during the late 1980s and then as a professor of English at Irvine Valley College since the early '90s. Her poetry and prose has appeared in local publications including *Faultine*, the *Los Angeles Times*, *OC Family*, the *OC Register*, and the *OC Weekly*, as well as other journals, magazines, and anthologies. For a number of years, she edited Irvine Valley College's community literary journal *The Ear*. After living for over a decade in Laguna Beach's El Morro Canyon, now a state park, she currently resides in Modjeska Canyon with her husband, Andrew Tonkovich, and their son, Louis. Their home, which overlooks Madame Modjeska's house, Arden, is shaded by native oaks as well as by olive trees planted by Modjeska more than a century ago.

ANDREW TONKOVICH'S forays into Orange County reach back thirty years and include joining Alliance for Survival protests against the San Onofre Nuclear Generating Station (now closed due in part to grassroots citizen activism) and participating, with his wife, Lisa Alvarez, in Catholic Worker–sponsored civil disobedience demonstrations against an international arms convention held in Santa Ana. After working as a community peace and justice activist in Santa Monica, he received an MFA in writing from UC Irvine, where he now teaches undergraduate research writing and is president of the union representing librarians and lecturers. He has lived in the county for twenty-five years and written essays for *Orange Coast Magazine*, contributed reviews and calendar items to the *OC Weekly* since its founding, and produced a column for the *OC Register* magazine profiling singular county residents—from a school crossing guard to the Garden Grove mayor. He currently pens the "Canyon Beat" column for the *Foothills Sentry* and finds himself the curator of a collection of paintings, drawings, and notebooks of the poet and activist Peter Carr, a mentor and enduring inspiration.

HEYDAY

ABOUT HEYDAY

HEYDAY IS an independent, nonprofit publisher and unique cultural institution. We promote widespread awareness and celebration of California's many cultures, landscapes, and boundary-breaking ideas. Through our well-crafted books, public events, and innovative outreach programs we are building a vibrant community of readers, writers, and thinkers.

THANK YOU

It takes the collective effort of many to create a thriving literary culture. We are thankful to all the thoughtful people we have the privilege to engage with. Cheers to our writers, artists, editors, storytellers, designers, printers, bookstores, critics, cultural organizations, readers, and book lovers everywhere!

We are especially grateful for the generous funding we've received for our publications and programs during the past year from foundations and hundreds of individual donors. Major supporters include:

Anonymous; Arkay Foundation; Richard and Rickie Ann Baum; Randy Bayard; Jean and Fred Berensmeier; Edwin Blue; Jamie and Philip Bowles; John Briscoe; California Humanities; John and Nancy Cassidy; Graham Chisholm; The Christensen Fund; Jon Christensen; Steve Costa and Kate Levinson; Lawrence Crooks; Nik Dehejia; Topher Delaney; Chris Desser and Kirk Marckwald; Frances Dinkelspiel and Gary Wayne; The Roy and Patricia Disney Family Foundation; Tim Disney; Marilee Enge and George Frost; Richard and Gretchen Evans; The Stoddard Charitable Trust; John Gage and Linda Schacht;

GETTING INVOLVED

To learn more about our publications, events and other ways you can participate, please visit www.heydaybooks.com.